有机化学实验

英汉双语版

（第三版）

Experimental Organic Chemistry

(Third Edition)

主 编 薛思佳 季 萍 Larry Olson

副主编 赵三虎 任新峰 朱 晔

科 学 出 版 社

北 京

内 容 简 介

本书是“有机化学(第二版)立体化教材”的《有机化学实验(英汉双语版，第三版)》部分，与《有机化学(第二版)》和《有机化学学习指导(第二版)》配套出版，方便教学选用。

本书采用英汉两种语言，英文为主，中文相应对照，结合国内外有机化学实验教学的实际编写而成。全书分为6章：有机化学实验的一般知识、有机化学实验的基本操作、有机化合物的制备、综合性实验、文献实验和附录。附录编写了常用实验数据、与化学和有机化学有关的Internet网址及有机化学实验操作考试复习题。

本书可使学生在掌握有机化学实验技能的同时，提高专业英语的阅读能力和水平。可作为高等学校化学、化学(师范)、应用化学和化学工程与工艺专业，以及材料化学、生物技术、制药工程、食品、医药卫生、环境科学和园艺等相关专业的有机化学实验教材；也可以作为有机化学及相关专业硕士研究生的实验参考书；对备考硕士研究生的读者也是一本好的参考书。

图书在版编目(CIP)数据

有机化学实验=Experimental Organic Chemistry: 英汉双语版 / 薛思佳等主编. —3版. —北京：科学出版社，2016.9

ISBN 978-7-03-049693-5

I. ①有… II. ①薛… III. ①有机化学-化学实验-高等学校-教材-英、汉 IV. ①O62-33

中国版本图书馆CIP数据核字(2016)第199924号

责任编辑：郭慧玲 / 责任校对：何艳萍
责任印制：张 伟 / 封面设计：迷底书装

科 学 出 版 社 出版
北京东黄城根北街16号
邮政编码：100717
http://www.sciencep.com

北京虎彩文化传播有限公司 印刷

科学出版社发行 各地新华书店经销
*

2005年2月第 一 版 开本：787×1092 1/16
2007年8月第 二 版 印张：15 3/4
2016年8月第 三 版 2023年6月第十二次印刷
字数：380 000

定价：48.00元

(如有印装质量问题，我社负责调换)

第三版前言

本书是“有机化学(第二版)立体化教材”的《有机化学实验(英汉双语版，第三版)》部分，与《有机化学(第二版)》和《有机化学学习指导(第二版)》配套出版，方便教学选用。

《有机化学实验（英汉双语版，第二版）》自2007年8月出版以来，满足了普通高校实施双语教学的需要，受到高校教师和学生的欢迎和肯定。为贯彻落实“全面提高人才自主培养质量，着力造就拔尖创新人才”，编者在调研的基础上，根据多年来在使用过程中发现的不足和目前高校有机化学实验教学改革的需要，对第二版教材进行了修订。

为适应部分院校有机化学实验教学的实际需要，本书第 3 章增加了 4-硝基苯胺的制备，乙酰二茂铁的制备和生物法合成乙醇 3 个实验;第 4 章增加了从菠菜叶中提取和分离叶色素，从红辣椒中提取、分离和鉴定辣椒红素和 β-胡萝卜素 2 个实验；重新编写了附录中有机化学实验操作考试复习题。为适应网络教学的需要，更新和补充了英文部分 Chapter 1 的 Chemical Literature 以及中文部分附录中与化学有关的 Internet 网址。

本书由薛思佳、季萍、Larry Olson(Arizona State University，USA)担任主编，赵三虎、任新峰、朱晔担任副主编。参加本书编写与修订工作的有：上海师范大学薛思佳，上海工程技术大学任新锋，石家庄学院朱晔、冯海燕、贾会珍、朱云云，忻州师范学院赵三虎、翟保评、孙金鱼等教学一线教师。

由于编者水平有限，书中疏漏和不妥之处在所难免，敬请读者批评指正。欢迎使用，更期盼读者能够喜欢本立体化教材。

编　者

2023 年 6 月于上海

第二版前言

Experimental Organic Chemistry(《有机化学实验》,英汉双语版)自 2005 年 2 月出版以来，因为适应了当前普通高校实施双语教学的需要，受到了高校教师和学生们的欢迎与肯定。在广泛调研的基础上，根据两年多来使用中存在的不足和目前高校有机化学实验教学改革的需要,编者代表于 2007 年 3 月在上海针对本书的第一版内容进行了研讨,拟定了如下修改意见：

1）更正了第一版中出现的错误。

2）增加连续性和综合性实验内容，精选文献实验内容，适当增加基本操作部分和有机化合物光谱鉴定部分的内容。

3）删除了一些内容较为陈旧，实验药品或产品毒性较大，环境污染较严重的实验。增加了一些新的或有一定操作难度的实验。对同一类型的实验增加了可供选择的内容，使教材更具普适性。

4）对每个实验的中、英文进行适当的调整，力求做到既有利于本书第二版内容的编排，又有利于有机化学实验的教学与实践，又尽量使内容不重复。

5）为增加教学的信息量，附录中增加部分与有机化学有关的 INTERNET 网址。

本书由薛思佳、季萍、Larry Olson (Arizona State University, USA) 主编。参加第二版修订工作的单位和教师为：上海师范大学：薛思佳，林静容，刘国华，肖海波；上海工程技术大学：宋小平，任新锋；石家庄学院：朱云云，贾会珍；忻州师范学院：赵明根，赵三虎；浙江台州师院：蒋华江；盐城师院：王庆东等同志。

第二版教材得到“上海市高校本科教育高地建设项目”的资助。赛默飞世尔科技(上海)有限公司分子光谱部(原美国热电尼高力仪器公司)为本书提供了红外光谱图。在此一并致谢。

限于编者水平，书中错误和不妥之处难以避免，敬请指正。

编　者

2007 年 6 月于上海

第一版前言

近年来，有机化学实验课程在教学内容、教学方法、教学手段上有了很大的变化。实验技术的更新、双语教学的实施不断地为这门传统的基础实验课程注入了新的活力。我们在“上海市教委重点教材建设”专项基金的支持下，在总结多年来有机化学实验的教学经验及近年来实施双语教学实践的基础上，参考了许多国内外出版的同类教材，并向国内外同行请教，注重有机实验的小量化、绿色化，以英文为主，中文相对应，编写完成了这本《有机化学实验》中英文双语教材。

本书对基本操作和实验方法用英文作了较为详细而精炼的描述。为了加强基本实验技能的训练，使学生加深对实验原理和实验操作的理解，本书在有关章节中均附有详细的注释、思考题、参考文献，以便于教学或学习。除了对薄层色谱、柱色谱、纸色谱、气相色谱、液相色谱、红外光谱、核磁共振谱等进行介绍外，绝大多数的有机合成实验中都附有红外光谱图。本书中涉及的合成实验是我们多年来教学研究与实践所形成的较成熟的实验，其中有些实验对以往毒性较大的实验进行了改革，有些更新了实验内容，还有些则完全创新，如微波萃取等。为拓宽教学内容、激发学习兴趣，本书还引入了具有微型化、特色化的文献实验。

本书在写作过程中得到了美国 Arizona State University 的 Larry Olson 教授的大力帮助。他以多年的教学经验，为本书提出了许多很好的建议，并主审了本书的英文部分，在此向他致以深深的谢意。

第一版由季萍，薛思佳，Larry Olson（Arizona State University, USA）主编。编委会成员：季萍（上海工程技术大学），薛思佳（上海师范大学），张爱东（华中师范大学），宋小平（上海工程技术大学），邹建平（苏州大学），张凤琴（东华大学），潘健民（上海工程技术大学），徐永芬（东华大学）。

本书得到“上海市教委重点教材建设基金”的资助，美国热电尼高力仪器公司为本书提供了所有的红外谱图，部分高校的实验教师对本书的完成给予了大力支持，对此一并表示真诚的感谢。

由于作者水平有限，不当之处在所难免，敬请读者批评赐教。

编　者

2004 年 12 月

Contents

目　录

Chapter 1 Introduction

Experimental organic chemistry is an integral and basic part of organic chemistry course. With the coming of new techniques, this course is being directed towards the development of small-scale experiment, high-efficient operation and the use of environment-friendly chemicals. The purpose of this course is to provide an opportunity to observe the reality of compounds and reactions, learn something of the operations and techniques that are used in experimental organic chemistry and in other areas, data-processing with computer, and further understand the basic principles of organic chemistry. Students should get into the habit of "preparation (pre-lab)—experiment and record (in-lab) —summary (post-lab)".

1.1 General Rules for the Organic Chemistry Lab

In order to ensure all experiments go smoothly and laboratory safety is observed, all students must abide by the following rules when entering into an organic lab:

(1) Familiarize yourself with the safety rules for lab work and learn about how to correctly use water, power, gas, hood, fire extinguisher and so on. Get to know what to do in the event of experimental accidents. Everyone, before doing the experiment, should be well prepared, understand the hazardous nature and safe usage of chemicals and promote safety consciousness. The experimental instruments and equipment must be used with care, adhering to their operating procedures. Report all abnormal conditions to your instructor to minimize the operational hazards.

(2) Before doing an experiment, check all glass equipment. During experiment, use it carefully and skillfully; after experiment, clean it up and keep it in order.

(3) In the experiment, keep your experimental area and whole lab tidy, operate with care, and adhere to the experimental procedures as well as reagent specifications and dosage required in every experiment. If you want to make any change, ask your instructor to get authorization. Never leave an ongoing experiment unattended.

(4) Before using chemicals, read their labels carefully. Use them only as required in the experiment. Cover the stopper of the container immediately after use, and avoid the stoppers being confused as well as chemicals being contaminated. Don't leave a mess for someone else to clean up. Don't change the position at random of normal reagents and common instruments in the lab such as balance, desiccator, refractometer and so on.

(5) Your full attention must be given to what you are doing during the experimental period. Don't be careless or clown around in lab. You can hurt yourself or other people. Don't speak loudly and eat or drink in the lab.

(6) In-lab or post-lab, all kinds of solid or liquid waste should be placed in various authorized containers.

(7) Before leaving lab, check carefully whether water, power and the gas are switched off safely, and wash your hands thoroughly with soap and water.

1.2 General Lab Safety

Generally speaking, organic experiment utilize mainly glassware, chemicals and electrical appliances, all of which can do harm for the human body and environment if used improperly. Chemicals are hazardous because of their flammable, explosive, volatile, corrosive and toxic properties. Also, there is the possibility of experimental accidents to glass equipment and electrical appliances if operated incorrectly. Therefore, organic lab is potentially one of the most dangerous locations for students.

1.2.1 Fire-proof

The experimental operation must be normalized and the apparatus is assembled correctly. Flammable, explosive and volatile chemicals mustn't be discarded randomly and must be recovered specifically after the experiment. They should be kept away from an open flame. In case of a fire, first of all, cut power and the gas off, move the flammable and explosive reagents away, and then put the fire out in a proper way using a fire extinguisher, asbestos cloth, covering with sand, or rushing water and so on.

1.2.2 Explosion-proof

The apparatus should be assembled correctly. The whole system should not be made tight in the process of normal distillation and reflux. Distillation to dryness is also a dangerous practice because of the possible presence of peroxides or other explosive materials in the dry residue in the flask. The glassware and apparatus should be checked first to determine whether it can withstand the system pressure before vacuum distillation. If you don't add any boiling chips when starting distillation, stop heating immediately and re-add them after cooling. Keep the cooling water moving smooth during distillation.

A fierce explosion or combustion can be produced when some organic compounds come into contact with oxidizers. Beware of their handling and storage.

1.2.3 Poisoning-proof

There are different ratings of toxicity among most organic reagents. The experiment with an irritative or toxic gas discharged must be always carried out in a hood or in a well-ventilated circumstance, or using a gas trap.

The manipulation of toxic or corrosive chemicals should follow the designated procedures strictly. Don't touch or come into contact directly with them. Keep them away from your mouth or cuts or abrasions of the skin, and never pour them into the sewer.

If you have some poisoning symptoms such as dizziness, headache, or other symptoms during the experiment you should leave the laboratory area and move to an area where you can breath fresh air and rest. In case of the poisoning is severe or symptoms persist, you should receive medical treatment.

1.2.4 Prevent Chemical Burns

Chemicals such as strong acid, strong base, bromine, etc, should be used with great care in order to avoid contact with your skin which could cause chemical burns. In case of such an accident, wash the affected area immediately with copious amounts of running water, and then further treatments as follows:

Acid-injury: use 1% $NaHCO_3$ solution for the eye-wash and 5% $NaHCO_3$ solution for skin-wash.

Base-injury: use 1% boric acid for the eye-wash and 1%～2% acetic acid for the skin-wash.

Bromine-injury: wash immediately with alcohol, and smear with glycerol or coat with a scald ointment.

If the situation is severe, go to hospital after first aid.

1.2.5 Cuts and Scalds

An accident involving cut or scald occurs in the use of glassware or manipulation of glassware if operated improperly. In case of such an accident, deal with it by the following methods.

Cuts: Cuts from broken glass are a constant potential hazard during experiments. The cut should be rinsed thoroughly with running water or hydrogen peroxide for a while to ensure that all tiny pieces of glass are removed. After this, wipe the cut with merbromin, bind up with gauze; if the cut is severe, first bind up with gauze, and then send the patient to the hospital.

Scalds: Smear some scald ointment on the affected area if the situation is just a bit superficial; coat scald ointment and go to the hospital for further treatment if the situation is severe.

1.3 Disposal of Lab Waste

Experimental operations always generate different kinds of solid or liquid waste. Waste disposal has been one of the major environmental problems of modern society. Special measures should be taken to observe national regulations and local organic lab rules of waste disposal. The handling of such wastes in the lab can be done in the following way:

(1) All waste generated in the lab can be classified into solid or liquid waste, and hazardous or nonhazardous waste, and disposed of properly. Some hard-to-handle hazardous waste should be delivered to environmental department for special treatment.

(2) Small amounts of acids, such as hydrochloric, sulfuric, and nitric, or base such as sodium or potassium hydroxide, should be neutralized first and diluted with large amounts of water before flushing down the drain.

(3) Organic solvents should be poured into properly labeled waste containers and stored in a well-ventilated place.

(4) Nonhazardous solid waste such as paper, broken glass, corks, alumina, silica gel, magnesium sulfate, calcium chloride, and so on, should not be blended with other hazardous waste, and can probably go into the ordinary dustbin. Hazardous solid waste should be disposed of in a labeled container. The exact name of the contents should be written on the label.

(5) Chemicals that can react violently with water should be decomposed in a suitable way in a hood before disposal.

(6) Some carcinogens and substances suspected of causing cancer must be handled with great care, avoiding contact with your body.

1.4 Common Lab Equipment and Apparatus

1.4.1 Lab Equipment

A typical set of lab equipment including glassware with standard-taper ground glass joints and non-glass equipment is shown in Fig. 1.1.

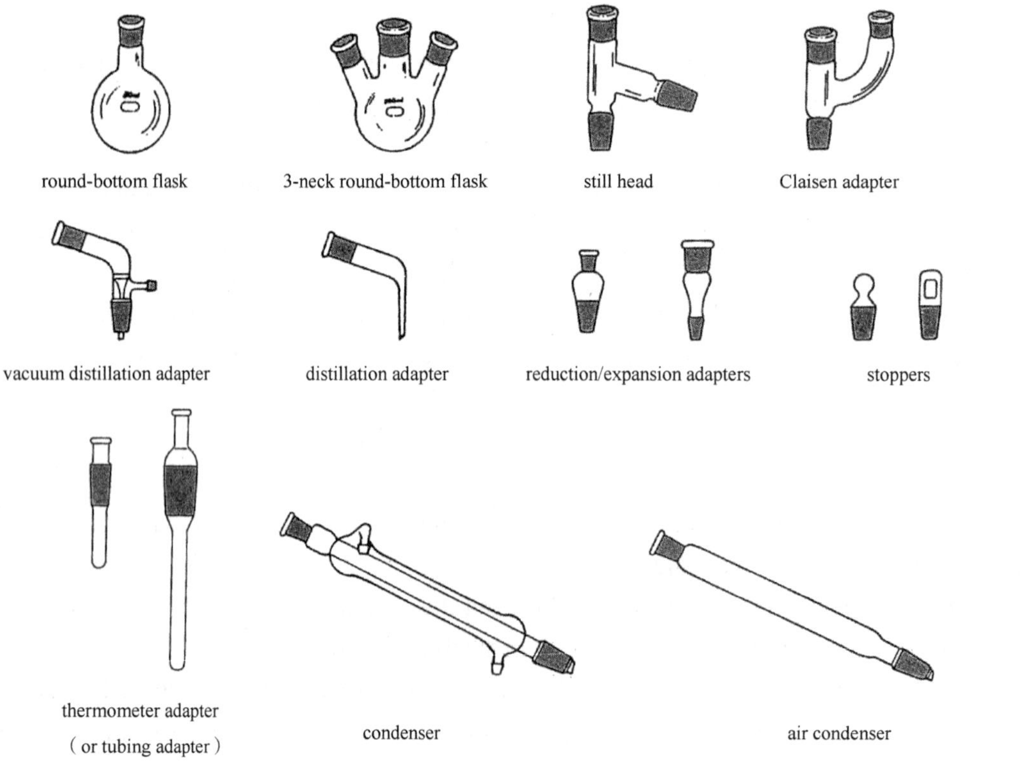

Fig. 1.1 Common Organic Apparatus

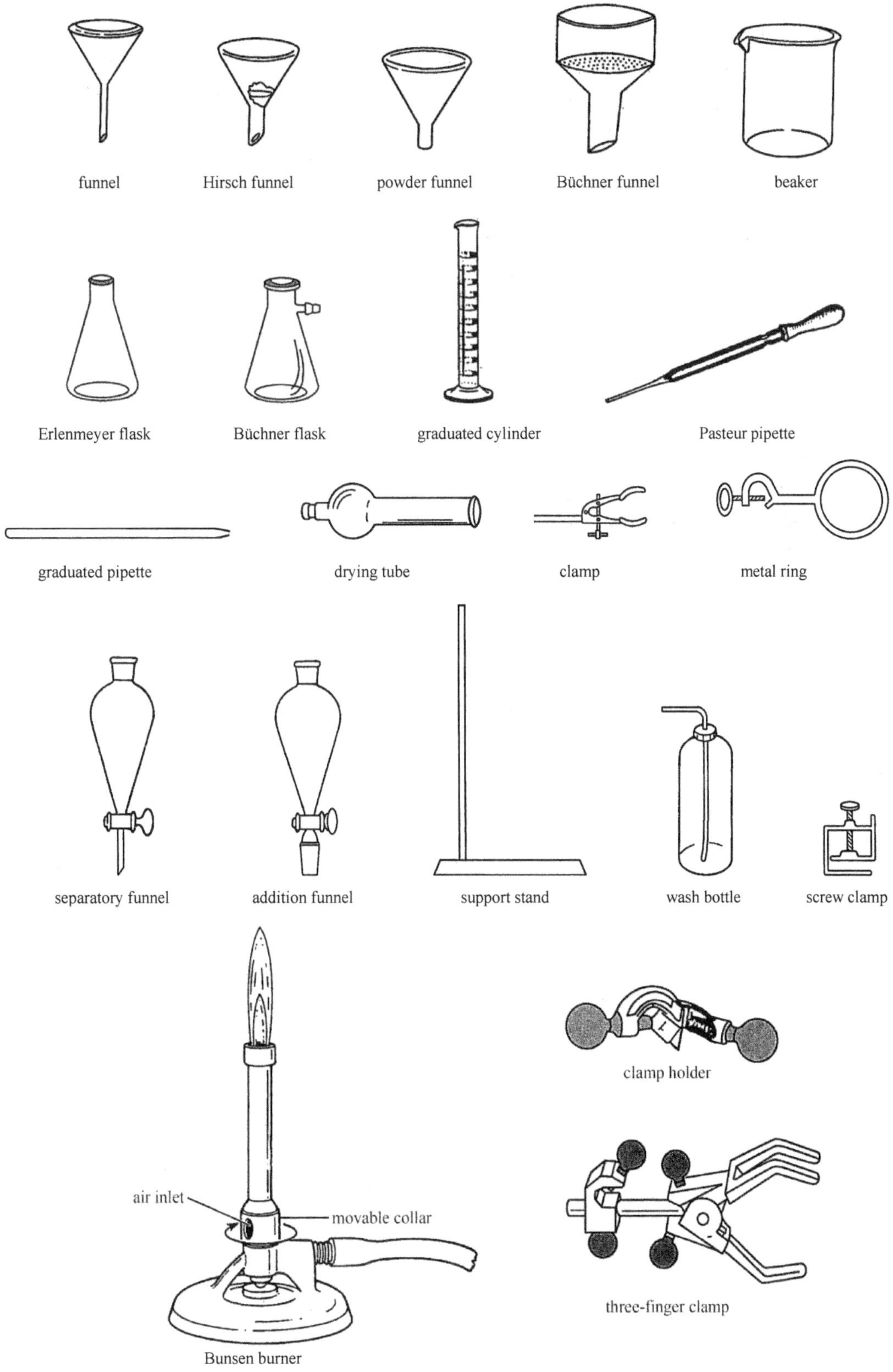

Fig. 1.1 (Continued)

Note 1

Round-bottom flask for distillation, reflux;

Three-neck flask for more complicated reaction set-ups (two-neck flasks are also available);

Erlenmeyer flasks for titration, crystallization, preparation;

Beakers for heating, mixing;

Addition funnel for adding liquids;

Separatory funnel for extraction and reaction work-up;

Condenser for distillation;

Air condenser for distillation with high boiling liquids;

Drying tube for drying gases;

Still head for distillation;

Various adapters for distillation, vacuum distillation;

Suction flask (filter flask) for collecting the filtrate.

Note 2

(1) All should be used carefully, avoiding impact or breakage.

(2) Don't heat directly except the beaker, flask and tube.

(3) Erlenmeyer flask and flat-bottom flask cannot withstand reduced pressure and should not be used in such systems.

(4) After cleaning up glassware containing a stopper, a small piece of paper must be put between the stopper and ground joint to avoid adhesion.

(5) The glass of a mercury bulb is thin and ease-to-break, thus should be used with care. Never use it as a stirring rod. After use, cool it down, and rinse it afterwards to keep away from cracking. The measurement of thermometer doesn't go beyond its graduated range.

1.4.2 Common Apparatus

Common apparatus are shown in Fig.1.2 to Fig. 1.7.

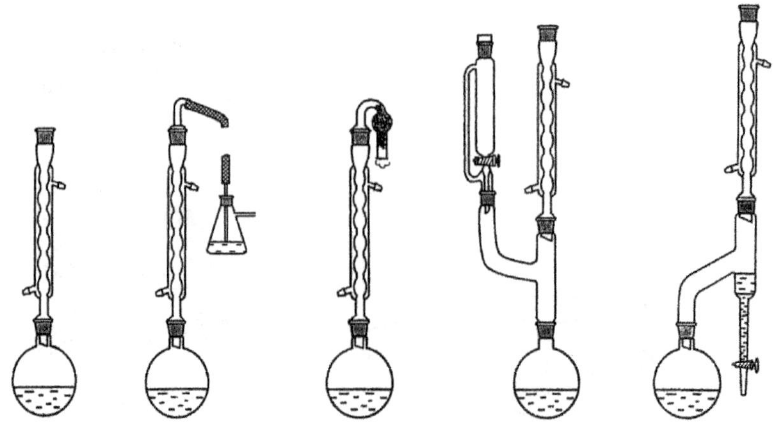

(a) (b) (c) (d) (e)

Fig. 1.2 Reflux Apparatus

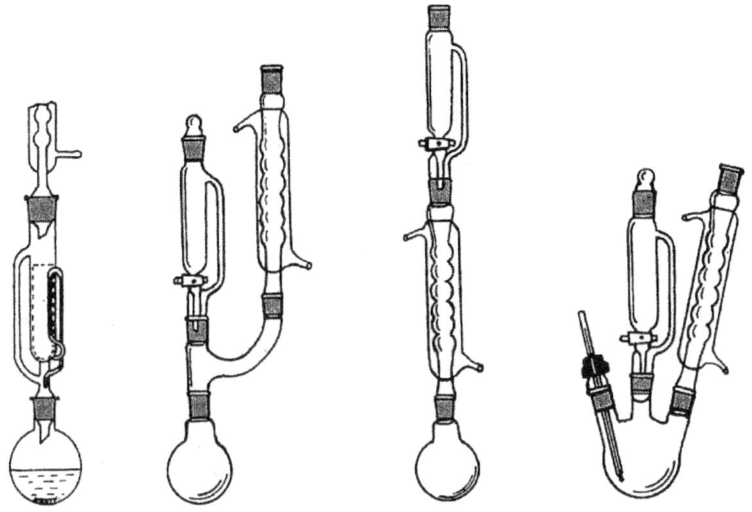

(f) (g) (h) (i)

Fig. 1.2 (Continued)

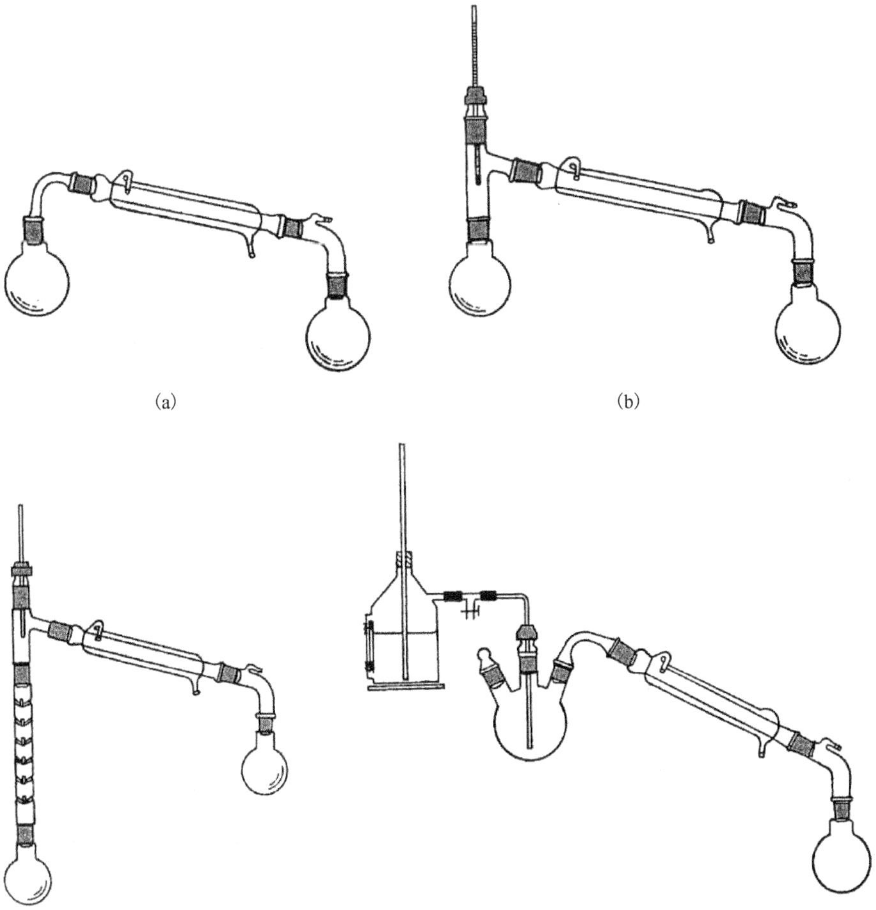

(a) (b)

(c) (d)

Fig. 1.3 Distillation Apparatus

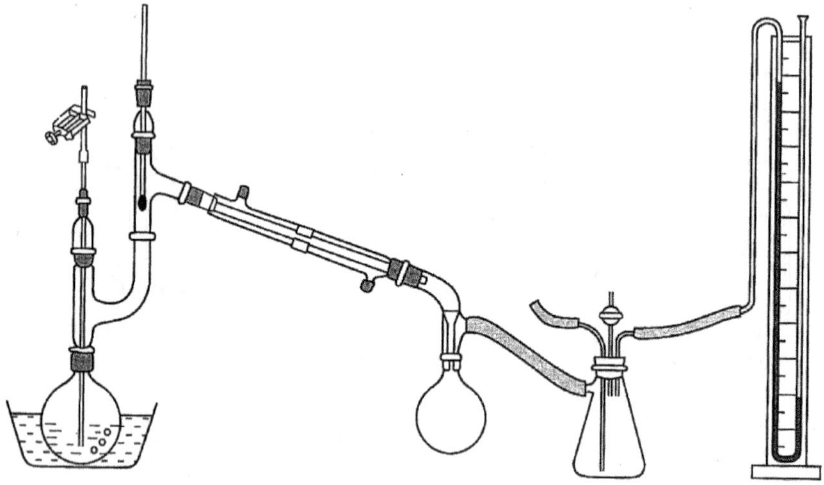

(e) vacuum distillation

Fig. 1.3 (Continued)

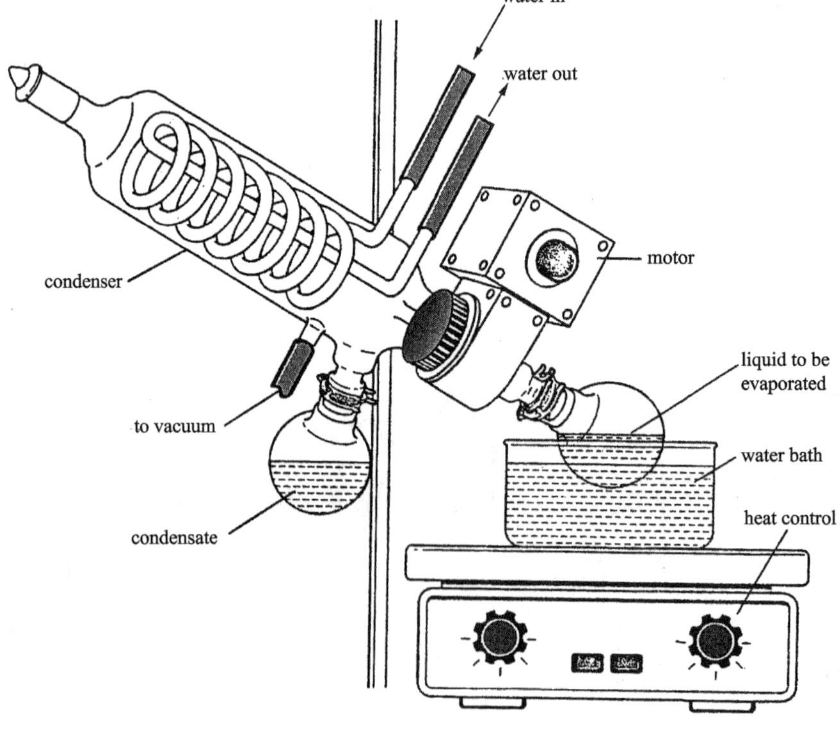

Fig. 1.4 A Rotatory Evaporator with Condenser and Receiving Flask

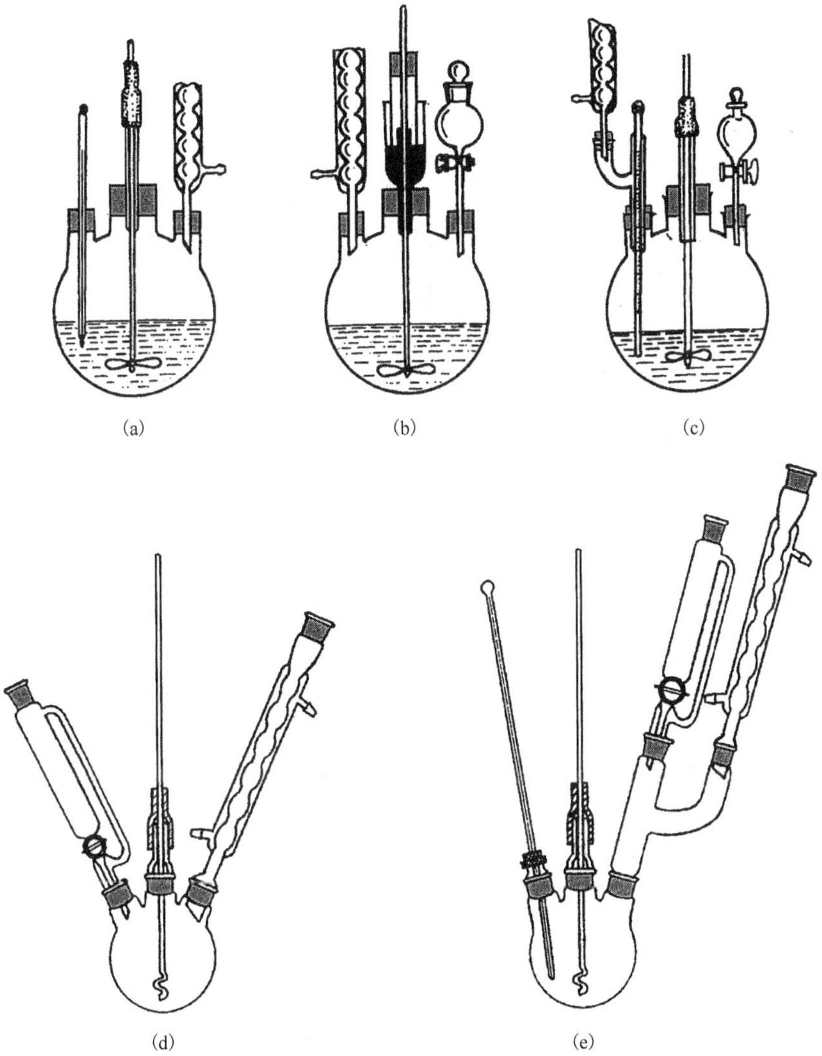

Fig. 1.5 Stirring Apparatus

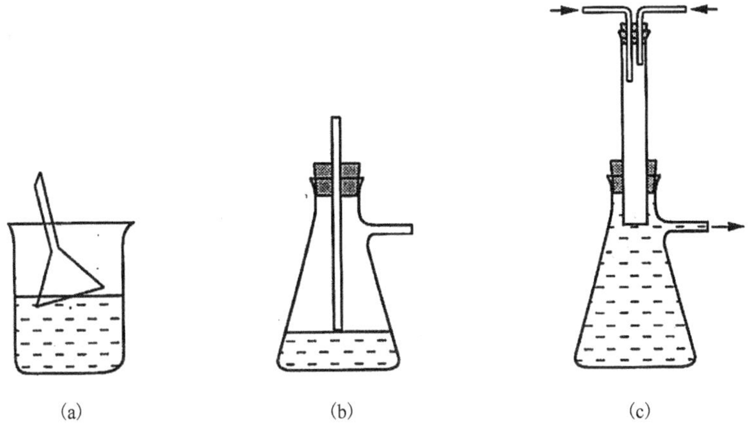

Fig. 1.6 Gas Trap Apparatus

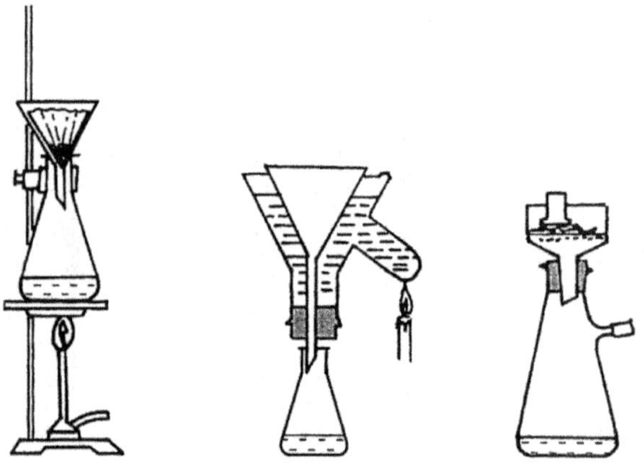

(a) (b) (c)

Fig. 1.7 Heat Filtration and Vacuum Filtration

Notes

(1) All glassware and accessories must be clean and fitted properly.

(2) When assembling the apparatus follow the principle "bottom-to-top, left-to-right", step by step.

(3) When disassembling, observe the rule of "right-to-left, up-to-down", one by one.

(4) A reaction apparatus under the ordinary pressure must have an opening to the atmosphere to avoid development of a dangerously high pressure within the system when heat is applied.

(5) All experimental apparatus must be tight, right, tidy and safe. All ground-glass joints should be made connected snugly.

The rotary evaporator is used for the removal of volatile solvent from solution, leaving behind the non-volatile component (see Fig. 1.4).

1.4.3 Cleaning Glassware

Always wash your glassware at the end of the experiment with water and either detergent or a mild scouring powder using an appropriate brush to remove most organic chemicals adhered to the glass walls. The inside and outside of all pieces of apparatus should be scrubbed, and rinsed thoroughly with water afterwards. The final resin can also be done with distilled or deionized water as required. Sometimes an ultrasonic oscillator might be useful for cleaning.

Never use chemical reagent or organic solvent thoughtlessly to rinse glassware. This may produce waste, and create a hazardous situation, resulting in additional pollution to our environment.

1.4.4 Drying Glassware

The common methods of drying glassware are as follows:

Air dry: In order to let water stream down, the glassware can be left upside down on a drying rack to dry.

Oven dry: The glassware can be dried quickly by placing it in an oven. For complete drying, glass should be left in an oven at 110~120℃ for several hours. Besides this, an airflow drier or hair drier also can be used.

Organic solvent dry: When wet glassware must be dried quickly for immediate use, it may be rinsed with small amounts of organic solvent such as 95% ethanol or acetone, which must be drained into an assigned bottle after use. Use hair drier to evaporate solvent afterwards.

Experiment: Practice on Simple Glass Working

Cutting and bending a glass tube and rod as well as preparing a capillary are all the primary operations in organic exiperiment.

1. Cutting a Glass Tube and Rod

(1) Place the glass tube (or rod) flat on the table. Hold the tube firmly and create a scratch on the glass wall surface by drawing a tiny sand wheel or three corner file perpendicularly across it a couple of times (Do not saw back and forth. A short, single sharp scratch is more likely to produce a clean even edge. At the same time, keep the tube dry).

(2) Hold the tube in both hands, one on each side of the scratch. Keep your thumbs as close as possible to the scratch away from your body. Apply gentle pressure with your thumbs behind the scratch and push with the fingers in the direction of its length. The glass tube should break cleanly at the scratch (Keep them away from your eyes when broken).

(3) Light the burner and get a hot blue flame. Pass one end of tube or rod through the flame a few times, rotating the tube until the rough edges become smooth [1].

2. Bending Glass Tube

(1) Light the burner and open the air hole. This gives a hot blue flame. Using both hands, rotate the dry tube in a declining position back and forth through the top of the flame.

(2) Keep rotating the tube until it glows red and has become soft. Then take the tube out of the flame and bend to the desired angle.

(3) Don't twist the tube while heating and bending in order to ensure that the two ends of the bent tube remain in the same plane.

(4) It is necessary to get a smooth bend without any kinks or constrictions. Check whether the bend is at the required angle (e.g. 90°) and whether the whole tube is in one plane[2] after the tube is bent. Then put it on the asbestos mat to cool (Don't put it on the table directly).

3. Procedure

(1) Take several used tubes to practice the basic operation of cutting, heating, rotating and bending, to improve your glassworking skills.

(2) Preparation of a stirring rod: take a glass rod of 5mm diameter and 20cm length. Heat the two ends of the tube respectively in a hot blue flame until each end of it becomes round-shaped.

(3) Bending the tube: take two tubes of 5mm diameter, and bend them into 90° and 70° tubes respectively[3].

4. Notes

[1]Do not heat too much and do not stop rotating. Place the hot glass on an asbestos pad to cool. When the tube is cool, fire polish the other cut end. Again allow to cool. Be careful of the rough edges of the tube which sometimes may cut your hands.

[2]After bending the tube, anneal it in a small flame and then put it on an asbestos pad directly.

[3]The length of the glass tube is changeable as required.

1.5 Drying and Drying Agent

Drying is a very useful technique in organic experiments. The common drying method can be primarily divided into physical and chemical ones. The physical drying method includes absorption, dehydration of molecular sieve, etc. The chemical drying method is to use drying agent to remove water. The latter is based on the chemical reaction with water or with water to form hydrated compounds.

1.5.1 Drying a Liquid Organic Compound

1. Selection of Drying Agent

Usually a small portion of the desired drying agent is added directly to an organic solution. Four points must be followed when selecting a drying agent: ①there should be no reaction with organic compound to be dried; ②it should be insoluble in the organic compound to be dried; ③it should have a large capacity of water uptake; ④it should absorb water quickly and be low cost.

The properties of common drying agents are shown in Table 1.1.

Table 1.1 The Properties of Some Drying Agents

Drying agent	Capacity	Intensity	Speed
$CaCl_2$	0.97 ($CaCl_2 \cdot 6H_2O$)	Medium	Very fast, but stand longer
$MgSO_4$	1.05 ($MgSO_4 \cdot 7H_2O$)	Weak	Very fast
Na_2SO_4	1.25	Weak	Slow
$CaSO_4$	0.06	Strong	Fast
K_2CO_3	0.2	Quite weak	Slow
CaO	—	Strong	Very fast
P_2O_5	—	Strong	Fast
Molecular sieves	About 0.25	Strong	Fast

Some common drying agents for organic compounds are shown in Table 1.2.

Table 1.2 Some Common Drying Agents for Organic Compounds

Organic Compound	Drying agent
Hydrocarbon	$CaCl_2$, Na, P_2O_5
Halohydrocarbon	$CaCl_2$, $MgSO_4$, Na_2SO_4, P_2O_5
Alcohol	K_2CO_3, $MgSO_4$, CaO, Na_2SO_4
Ether	$CaCl_2$, P_2O_5, Na
Aldehyde	$MgSO_4$, Na_2SO_4
Ketone	K_2CO_3, $CaCl_2$, $MgSO_4$, Na_2SO_4
Acid, Phenol	$MgSO_4$, Na_2SO_4
Ester	$MgSO_4$, Na_2SO_4, K_2CO_3
Amine	KOH, NaOH, K_2CO_3, CaO
Nitrocompound	$CaCl_2$, $MgSO_4$, Na_2SO_4

2. Dosage of Drying Agent

The proper dosage of a drying agent, usually more than its theoretical value, can be figured out, based on its capacity to take up water and water solubility in the target organic compound. In view of molecular structure, slightly move drying agent can be used for those compounds containing the water-philic group. But the drying agent must be used appropriately. The drying of compound is incomplete if there is insufficient drying agent, but loss of the organic compound results from too much drying agent due to surface adsorption. So the general dosage is 0.5～1g drying agent per 10mL liquid.

3. Procedure

Before drying, remove water from organic compounds as much as possible, using a separatory funnel if necessary. Then add a small amount of drying agent directly to the organic solution. Swirl the solution and let it stand while you observe the drying agent. If it is all clumped together, add more[1] and observe how a solution with drying agent looks when it is clumped and when it is free-flowing. Continue swirling and observing the solution for several minutes, adding more drying agent [2] only until a fresh addition no longer forms clumps[3]. In most cases, the particle size of drying agent should be handpicked suitably. The larger the particle size, the slower the speed of drying; the smaller the particle size, the more organic substances can be absorbed onto the surface.

4. Notes

[1] There is no set "rule" as to how much drying agent needs to be added. The amount required depends on the amount of water in the solution which you are drying, and this amount varies from experiment to experiment.

[2] You must cap bottles of drying agents between uses!

[3] Common drying agents are anhydrous inorganic salts which readily take up water to become hydrated. At the end of the drying process, the hydrated salt is removed from the organic solution.

1.5.2 Drying Solid Organic Substances

Air dry: Spread solid samples out on a watch glass or filter paper and allow them to air dry.

Oven dry: You can dry solid samples more quickly by putting them on a hot-water-bath or in a large beaker in an oven at a temperature below their melting point in order to avoid their decomposition.

Other drying method: Infrared desiccator, vacuum desiccator, etc.

1.6 Heating and Cooling

Heating and cooling is one of the basic techniques in the organic chemistry laboratory.

1.6.1 Heating

There are several common heat sources such as the gas, alcohol and electric power in the organic chemistry laboratory. Heating method can be divided into direct and indirect ones. To avoid possible problems from straightforward heating, use the following alternate heating method when necessary:

Air-bath: With the principle of indirect heating by hot-air, the liquid can be heated above 80℃. The most common air bath in the experiment is heating with a wire gauze and a Bunsen burner or with an electric heating mantle, which is designed only for heating round-bottom flask.

Water bath: Usually a heated water bath is a convenient way of heating a liquid below 80℃. During this operation, the vessel must be immersed into a water bath so that the surface of water bath is kept higher than inside surface of solution.

Oil bath: The usable range of oil bath is 100～250℃. The highest temperature that oil bath can reach is dependent upon what material is used. The plant oil used in the lab can reach 200～220℃, and liquid wax can reach 220℃. Pay attention to the safety when heating an oil-bath to prevent from accidental fires or splattering from water introduced into the hot oil.

Sand bath: When a heating temperature is required to get higher than those listed above, one can often use a sand bath. Its highest operating temperature is 350℃.

1.6.2 Cooling

Cooling is also needed when the organic experiment has to be run at low temperature. Use the following cooling method, based on different requirements.

For ordinary cooling, the container with reactant must be put into cold water. Choose ice or ice-water mixture for cooling below room temperature. For cooling below 0℃, use broken ice and some inorganic salts mixed with certain ratio as a cooling agent (Table 1.3). Solid CO_2 mixed respectively with acetone, chloroform or other solvents can reach −78℃. Liquid nitrogen can be as cold as −196℃.

When temperature is below –38℃, don't use a mercury thermometer but an ethanol-based low temperature thermometer.

Table 1.3 Ice-salt Mixtures

Salt	Ratio (Salt : ice)	Lowest temperature Approx. (℃)
NH_4Cl	1 : 4	–15
$NaNO_3$	1 : 2	–18
NaCl	1 : 3.3	–21
$CaCl_2 \cdot 6H_2O$	1 : 1	–29
$CaCl_2 \cdot 6H_2O$	1 : 0.7	–55

1.7 Experimental Record and Laboratory Report

1.7.1 Experimental Record

It is essential to keep a notebook to record the observations directly made during experiments, in a concise, precise and thorough way. Make good preparation before you come to lab by reviewing the theory and seeking information about the chemicals involved. If you prepare well, you will save time and effort. In general, the experimental record include the following parts:

A. Write a title and general statement of the experimental apparatus and process to be done.

B. Note any special observation or precautions required.

C. Jot down any chemical or biological hazards it presents.

1.7.2 Experimental Report

Usually, the experimental report should cover the following parts:

A. Experimental title.

B. Purpose of the experiment: main techniques introduced by the experiment.

C. Theoretical background: chemical reaction; balanced chemical equations or reaction mechanism.

D. Experimental apparatus.

E. Experimental procedure.

F. Experimental observations: color change, precipitation, solubility, etc.

G. Results and discussion: Analysis of your data and brief comment on sources of error in your experiment.

H. Conclusions.

I. Reference.

1.8 Chemical Literature

The abundance of organic chemistry literature can be overwhelming. With the widespread use of computer, the search for organic chemistry literature is getting easier and faster. In this part, selected examples from different literature sources are given, along with the brief remarks.

1.8.1 Laboratory Handbooks

(1) *CRC Handbook of Chemistry and Physics* (annual editions), published by the CRC Press, Boca Raton, FL. It contains about 15 000 organic compounds with physical properties. Organic compounds are alphabetically ordered. This handbook is cross-referenced to *Beilstein Handbook* and contains a molecular formula index.

(2) *Merck Index of Chemicals and Drugs* (12th), an Encyclopedia of chemicals, drugs and biologicals, published by the Merck Company, Rahway, NJ. It gives a concise summary of the physical and biological properties as well as uses, toxicity and hazards of more than 10 000 compounds, with some literature references. All compounds including synonyms and trade names are alphabetically ordered. This handbook has a formula index and a subject index.

(3) *Beilstein Handbook of Organic Chemistry*: This handbook is a chemical information system for organic compounds consisting of structure, property, reaction and bibliographic databases covering over 7 millions substances and 5 millions reactions. It was originally published in German, but it is now published in English. Records in the database include structures, data on chemical and physical properties such as melting point, boiling point and spectral identification, as well as reference to the chemical literature. The search can also be done online.

1.8.2 Journals

Main research journals include:

(1) *Journal of the Chemical Society* (*Perkin Transactions*). Published by the Royal Society of Chemistry (UK). Mainly devoted to organic synthesis.

(2) *Journal of American Chemical Society*. It is the most important and prestigious journal in chemistry.

(3) *Angewandte Chemie International Edition*. Published by Wiley Online Library (Germany). It is maintaining its leading position among the general chemistry journals.

(4) *Journal of Organic Chemistry*. Published by American Chemical Society. Includes all areas of organic chemistry.

(5) *Chemical Reviews*.Also published by American Chemical Society. Comprehensive reviews on chemistry.

(6) *Tetrahedron* and *Tetrahedron Letters*. The first is full articles about organic chemistry, and the second is for timely publication of short communication, most of them relate to organic synthesis.

(7) *Journal of Chemical Education*. Published by the Division of Chemical Education of the

American Chemical Society. Mainly devoted to chemical education.

1.8.3 Chemical Abstracts

Chemical Abstracts, published by the American Chemical Society, is the most complete chemical information resource. It began in 1907 and annually publishes abstracts coming from about 9000 journals as well as books, conference proceedings, dissertations and patents. *Chemical Abstracts* have several indexes including chemical substance, general subject, author, formula, patent number, all of which are accumulated at five-year intervals. It provides concise summaries of original research articles in journals and listings of reviews and books. Also, it is possible to search *Chemical Abstracts* online.

1.8.4 Online Resources

Searching for information online is more and more convenient, with the fast growth of internet. There are many ways to get chemical resources from the internet.

(1) Online Libraries

http://www.nlc.gov.cn/

http://www.lib.tsinghua.edu.cn/

http://www.lib.pku.edu.cn/html

(2) Online Periodical Resources

http://www.chinajournal.net.cn/

http://www.cqvip.com/

(3) Online Patent Resources

http://www.patents.ibm.com/

http://patent.com.cn/

http://cnpatent.com/

(4) Database Resources

http://www.colby.edu/chemistry/cmp/cmp.html

http://www.chemfinder.camsoft.com/ (basic property of compounds)

http://www.sioc.ac.cn/lccdeb/sjk.htm (IR spectrum database)

(5) Other Website

http://www.acs.org/

http://www.ccs.ac.cn/

http://www.chemsoc.org/

http://www.csir.org/ (Chemistry Software and Information Resources)

http://www.organicchem.com/

http://chemnet.com.cn/

http://www.reagent.com.cn/

http://www.chemonline.net/

Chapter 2　Basic Experimental Techniques

2.1　Melting Point Determination

2.1.1　Principle

The melting point of a substance is defined as the temperature at which the liquid and solid phases exist in equilibrium with one another. If heat is added to a mixture of the solid and liquid phases of a pure substance at the melting point, ideally no rise in temperature will occur until all the solid has melted and been converted to liquid. If heat is removed from such a mixture, the temperature will not drop until all the liquid solidifies. Thus, the melting point and freezing point of a pure substance are identical.

The relationship among phase compositions, total supplied heat, and temperature for a pure compound is shown in Fig. 2.1. It is assumed that heat is being supplied to the compound at a slow and constant rate, and the elapsed time of heating is a cumulative measure of the supplied heat. At temperatures below the melting point, the compound exists in the solid phase, and the addition of heat causes the temperature of the solid to rise. As the melting point is reached, the first small amount of liquid appears, and equilibrium is established between the solid and liquid phases. As more heat is added, the temperature does not change. Since the additional heat causes the solid to be converted to liquid, with both phases remaining in equilibrium. When the last of the solid melts, the heat subsequently supplied causes the temperature to rise linearly at a rate that depends on the rate of heating.

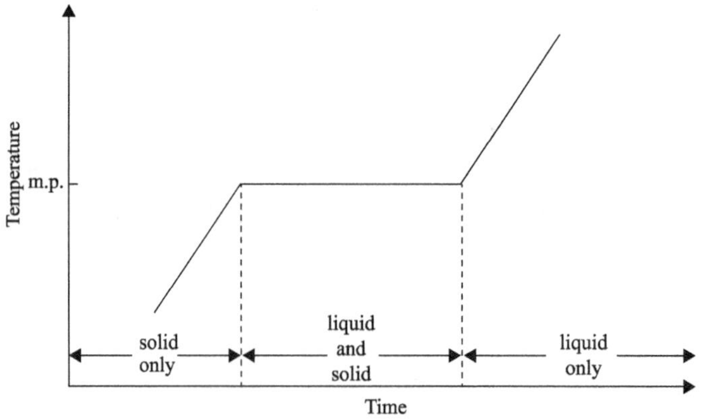

Fig. 2.1　Phase Change with Time and Temperature

2.1.2　Methods and Apparatus

1. Capillary Tubes and Sample Preparation

Commercially available capillary tubes have one end already sealed and the other opened end to permit introduction of the sample. The sample is put into the tube as follows (also see Fig. 2.2). Place a small amount of the solid whose melting point you wish to determine on a clean watch glass and tap the open end of the capillary tube into the solid on the glass so that a tiny amount is forced about 2~3mm into the tube. To get the solid to the closed end of the tube, take a piece of 6~8mm glass tubing about 45cm long, place this tube vertically on a hard surface (bench top or floor), and drop the capillary tube (sealed end down) through the large tube several times. Surprising as it might seem, the capillary tube does not break, and the solid ends up packed at the sealed end of the capillary tube!

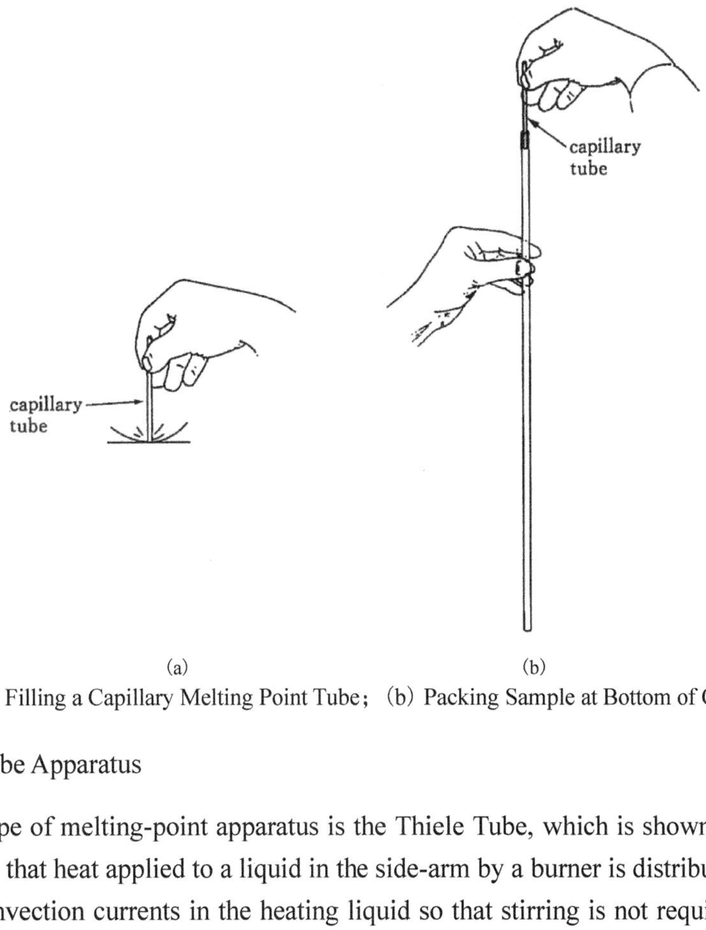

Fig. 2.2 (a) Filling a Capillary Melting Point Tube; (b) Packing Sample at Bottom of Capillary Tube

2. Thiele Tube Apparatus

A simple type of melting-point apparatus is the Thiele Tube, which is shown in Fig. 2.3. This tube is shaped so that heat applied to a liquid in the side-arm by a burner is distributed to all parts of the vessel by convection currents in the heating liquid so that stirring is not required. Temperature control is accomplished by adjusting the flame produced by the burner, which may seem difficult at first but can be mastered with practice.

Proper use of the Thiele tube is required to obtain reliable melting points. Secure the capillary tube to the thermometer at the position indicated in Fig. 2.3; use either a rubber band or a small segment of rubber tubing for this purpose. Be sure that the band used to hold the capillary tube on the thermometer is as close to the top of the tube as possible. Support the thermometer, with the capillary tube containing the sample already attached, with a cork in the apparatus, as shown in Fig. 2.3, or by carefully clamping the thermometer so that it is immersed in the oil. The thermometer and capillary tube must not contact the glass of the Thiele tube in any way. Make sure that the height of the heating fluid is approximately at the level indicated in Fig. 2.3. The oil will expand on heating. For this reason, the rubber band should be in the position indicated. Otherwise, the hot oil will come in contact with the rubber and melt it, and the sample tube will fall into the oil.

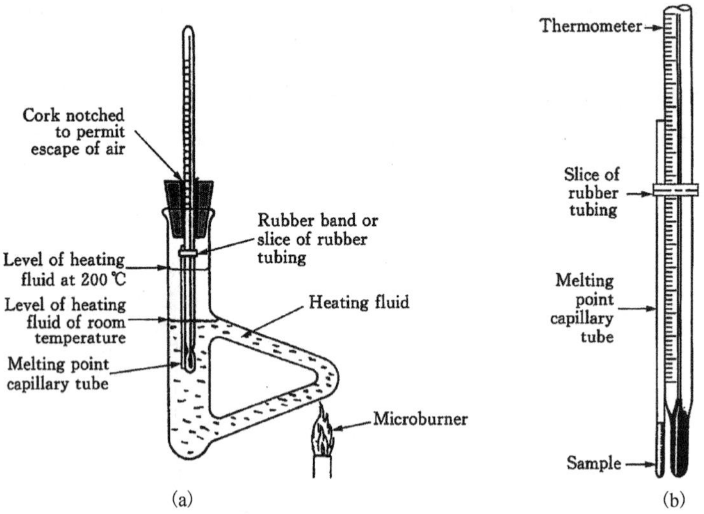

Fig. 2.3 (a) Thiele Melting-Point Apparatus;
(b) Arrangement of Sample and Thermometer for Determination of Melting Point

Heat the Thiele tube at the rate of one to two degrees per minute in order to determine the melting point. The maximum temperature to which the apparatus can be heated is dictated by the nature of the heating fluid.

3. Melting Point Determination

The determination of the melting point involves taking the capillary tube containing the sample and heating it in an appropriate apparatus until the solid melts. Best results are obtained by heating the sample at the rate of about two degrees per minute. Many organic compounds undergo a change in crystalline structure just before melting, usually as a consequence of the release of solvent of crystallization. The solid takes on a softer, perhaps "wet", appearance, which may also be accompanied by the shrinkage of the sample in the capillary tube. These changes of the sample should not be interpreted as the beginning of the melting process. Wait for the first tiny drop of liquid to appear. Melting invariably occurs over a temperature range, and the melting-point range is defined as the temperature at which the first tiny drop of liquid appears up to and including the temperature at which the solid has melted completely.

4. Digital Melting Point Apparatus

To measure the melting point, the digital melting-point apparatus is convenient, exact and easy to operate. For example, the WRS-1 digital melting-point apparatus adopts the technique such as photoelectric checking and digital temperature display, and is equipped with automatic show of early and full melt. The above apparatus can be connected to a recorder and can record melting curves automatically. With the integrated circuit, this apparatus can reach the initiative temperature rapidly and has a 6-shift optional automatic controller of the linear rate for rising or falling temperatures. The early and full melting readings can be automatically recorded without the need for personal intervention.

Procedure

(1) Turn the on-off switch to on. Let it stabilize for 20min.

(2) Set the initial temperature by dialing the switch board. Press the initial temperature button and input this temperature. Then the preset light is on.

(3) Select the rate of temperature for rising and turn the wave band to required place.

(4) Plug in the capillary containing a sample when the preset light goes out. Now the melt light showing early goes out.

(5) Set the ammeter to zero, press the temperature button of rising. The early melt light will remain on for several minutes, and then the full melt reading will show.

(6) Press the early melt button, then record the early and full melt temperature until the early melt reading is displayed.

Press the temperature button of falling and lower the temperature to room temperature. Turn the on-off switch to off.

2.1.3 Experiment

Determination of capillary-tube melting point

1. Known compounds: acetanilide or benzoic acid or urea

Determine the melting-point ranges for each of these substances, using the capillary-tube melting-point procedure. Repeat as necessary until you obtain accurate results and are confident with the procedure. Since the melting points of these compounds are known, it is not necessary to first determine their approximate melting points.

2. Unknown compound

Accurately determine the melting range of an unknown pure compound supplied by your instructor. It is advisable to determine the approximate melting point by rapid heating before obtaining an accurate melting range.

2.1.4 Questions

(1) Describe errors in procedure that may cause an observed capillary melting-point of a pure compound.

(a) to be lower than the correct melting point

(b) to be higher than the correct melting point

(c) to be broad in range (over several degrees)

(2) Criticize the following statements by indicating whether each is true or false, and if false, by explaining why.

(a) An impurity always lowers the melting point of an organic compound.

(b) A sharp melting point for a crystalline organic substance always indicates a pure single compound.

(c) If the addition of a sample of compound A to compound X does not lower the melting point of X, X must be identical to A.

(d) If the addition of a sample of compound A lowers the melting point of compound X, X and A cannot be identical.

2.2 Recrystallization

2.2.1 Principle

Recrystallization is the most frequently used operation for purifying organic solids. This technique is based on the fact that the solubility of an organic compound in a given solvent will often increase greatly as the solvent is heated to its boiling point. When it is first heated in such a solvent until it dissolves, then cooled to room temperature or below, an impure organic solid will usually recrystallize from solution in a much purer form than its original form. Most of the impurities will either not dissolve in the hot solution (from which they can be filtered) or remain in dissolved form in the cooled solution (from which the pure crystals are filtered).

2.2.2 Procedure

1. The General Procedures for Recrystallization

(1) Select a suitable solvent.

(2) Dissolve the crude product in the hot solvent and make it saturated.

(3) Filtrate off undissolved impurities. If the solution shade is deep, decolorize and then do filtration.

(4) Cool down the solution or evaporate the solvent to make the crystals precipitate. The impurities are left in the solution or are crystallized out and the desired product is left in the solution.

(5) Collect the crystals by filtration, rinse the crystals and remove the last traces of solvent.

(6) Dry the crystals.

2. The Choice of Solvent System

In the operation of recrystallization, the choice of used solvent is critical to achieve high purity and recovery. As a suitable solvent, the following requirements should be met:

(1) Does not react with the substance to be purified.

(2) Possesses high solubility if the solute at elevated temperature and low solubility at low temperature.

(3) If the impurities are insoluble in the hot solvent, filter them out at the high temperature; if the impurities are soluble in the cold solvent, leave them in the solution and separate them from the solution after crystallization.

(4) Form trim crystals of the purified material.

(5) The boiling point of the solvent is neither too low nor too high. It is difficult to separate and operate when it is too low because of the small change of solubility. It is not easy to remove the traces of the solvent when its boiling point is too high.

(6) Low price and available easily.

The common solvents used in the purification of most organic solids are: water, ethanol, acetone, petroleum ether, carbon tetrachloride, benzene and ethyl acetate, etc.

In choosing the solvent the chemist is guided by the principle "similar chemical structures will dissolve one another" or "likes dissolve likes". That is the solute tends to be dissolved in a certain solvent with the analogous structure or polarity. The solubility of some common compounds can be found in reference handbooks, such as "solubility of Inorganic and Organic Compounds" (Ed. Stephen, et. al., 1963). However, in practice, the suitable solvent can only be chosen from the solubility test, as shown in the following procedure:

Weigh about 0.1g of the finely divided solid into a test tube, add 1mL of the solvent, shake and stir the mixture to see if the solid will dissolve. If not, the mixture should be warmed very gently with stirring and shaking. If the solid dissolves in the cold solvent or with gentle warming, the solvent will be unsuitable. Now carefully heat the mixture to boiling with stirring. If the solid does not dissolve readily, add more solvent in 0.5mL portions (gently boiling and stirring after each addition) until it dissolves or until the total volume of the added solvent is about 3mL. If the solid does not dissolve (or nearly so) by this time, probably, the solvent is not suitable; if it does dissolve (except for insoluble impurities), cool the solution down by scratching it to see if crystallization occurs. If crystals appear, examine them visually for apparent yield and evidence of purity (absence of extraneous color, good crystal structure). If necessary, repeat the process with other solvent until a suitable one is identified. If no single solvent is satisfactory, it is possible to employ a mixture of two solvents, termed a solvent pair. Choose one solvent in which the compound is quite soluble and the other in which it is comparatively insoluble (make sure that the two are miscible). These are solvent pairs that are often employed: the mixture of ethanol and water, or the mixture of ethanol and ethyl ether, or the mixture of ethanol and acetone, or the mixture of ethyl ether and petroleum ether, or the mixture of benzene and petroleum ether, etc.

3. The dissolution of the solid

Be cautious of flammable solvents, stick to the procedure described by your supervisor.

The organic solvents are either flammable or poisonous. Maybe they are both flammable and poisonous. Remember to extinguish any flames nearby. The reaction should be carried out in the hood. A three-neck flask or a round-bottom flask is often employed as a container because its flask mouth is comparatively narrow, decreasing volatility and helping the material dissolve quickly with stirring. If the solvent has a low boiling point and is flammable, heating it directly on the asbestos gauge should be prohibited. Fit a reflux condenser on the boiling flask and select proper heat sources on the basis of the boiling point. The reflux condenser should be fitted on too if the material does not dissolve very well and its heating time is too long to protect the loss of the solvent.

Put the crude product into a container with a narrow flask mouth, add some solvent less than the calculated value and then add dropwise until the product exactly dissolves while it is heated. 20%～100% of solvent is allowed to be added to dilute the solution otherwise the crystals will separate very quickly when the hot solution is filtered. If the applied amount of the solvent is unknown, a small amount of solvent is added and the solvent is heated to the boiling point. If the solid still does not dissolve completely, add the solvent bit by bit until the solid exactly dissolves at the boiling point. This is the process of dissolving.

The product may appear in an oleaginous state in the process of dissolving. It is very disadvantageous for recrystallization because it can bear both impurities and a small amount of solvent at the same time. This phenomenon should be avoided, therefore, and it can be done in the following ways:

(1) The boiling point of the chosen solvent should be lower than the melting point of the solute.

(2) If a solvent of a lower boiling point can not be found, dissolve the material at a temperature below its melting point.

When a solvent pair is employed, the material can be dissolved in the quite soluble solvent at an elevated temperature first, and if the solution is colorized, powdered charcoal is employed to remove the colored impurities. Filter out the insoluble impurities-absorbed charcoal while the solution is hot. Heat the filtrate near to the boiling point, and add the less soluble solvent until it just reaches turbidity. If the turbidity does not vanish when it is heated, the quite soluble solvent should be added carefully until the solution becomes clear. Lay the solution in a proper place for crystallization. If the proper proportion for the recrystallization is known, prepare the solvent pair first and do the recrystallization according to the method of a single solvent.

4. The Removal of the Impurities

Filter the hot solution to remove the insoluble impurities. When the solution is a few degrees below the boiling point, add some activated carbon to remove the colored impurities if the crude sample of a compound known to be white yields a colored recrystallization solution.

5. The Separation of Crystals

Set aside the hot filtrate in place and cool it down slowly. It will need a few hours. Maybe it will need a longer time in some circumstances. Neither cool the filtrate down quickly because it will make the crystals very small nor make the crystals too large because it will intermix with the original liquor and make it very difficult to dry. When the large crystals are formed, stir the solution strongly and have it form small crystals.

Dropping a few seed crystals into the solution will benefit the formation of crystals or scratch the wall of the container with a glass rod if the crystals do not separate in the cold solution.

If crystals cannot be separated from some oily material, the solution should be heated until it is clear. Cool down the solution naturally and stir up acutely to disperse the oily material until the oily material disappears.

If the material can not be purified successfully by crystallization, the other methods (such as chromatography and ion exchange resin, etc) should be used to purify the material.

6. The Collection and Washing of the Crystals

The crystals are collected by swirling and pouring the magma into a porcelain Büchner funnel or Hirsch funnel (small and conical shape). The funnel is fitted with a rubber stopper or conical sleeve which is seated in the neck of a heavy-wall side-arm filter flask or side-arm test tube connected to an aspirator. The apparatus for vacuum filtration of solids are showed as Fig. 2.4. These porcelain funnels are fitted with a circle of filter paper; the perforations permit liquid to drain rapidly into the evacuated flask. Be sure that the filter paper is flat. If necessary, trim the filter paper so that it covers the perforations completely but is creased into a channel at the side wall of the funnel. Wet the paper with solvent and turn on the aspirator to seat the paper firmly. After transferring the mixture to the funnel, scrape loose any liquid clinging to the wall of the flask and rinse it in with a small portion of the filtrate or a little more solvent.

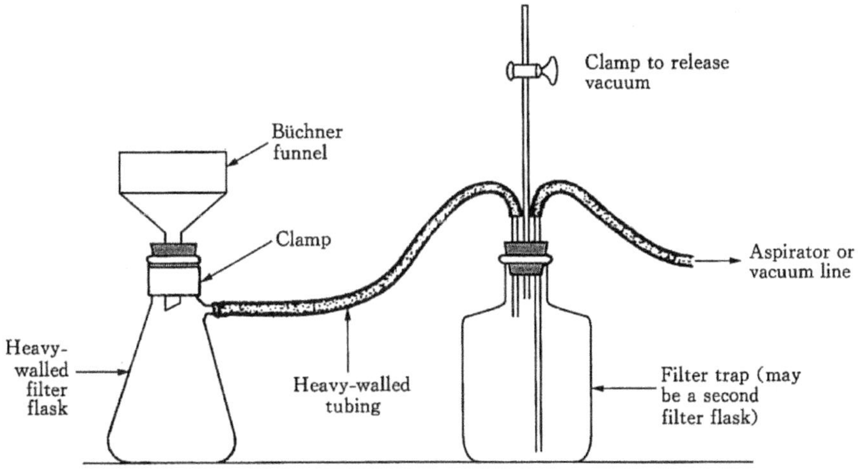

Fig. 2.4 Apparatus for Vacuum Filtration of Solids

The crystals should be compacted with a spatula to express as much solvent as possible. If the crystals mass is not too dense, it may be possible to remove most of the residual solvent by allowing the aspirator to pull air through the funnel for a few minutes.

The Hirsch funnel and side-arm test tube can be used in small-scale crystallizations.

2.2.3 Experiment

Recrystallization of impure acetanilide

Procedure

(1) Place 4g of impure acetanilide in a 250mL Erlenmeryer flask, add 50mL of pure water and heat to boiling with the aid of a burner or hot plate.

(2) If it does not dissolve, add some water properly until no more solid appears to dissolve in the boiling solution.

(3) Cool the solution slightly, add about 0.1g of activated carbon, and reheat it to boiling for a few minutes.

(4) Filter the hot solution with a fluted filter paper (shown as Fig. 2.5) or a Büchner funnel which has been soaked with hot water. Collect the filtrate with an Erlenmeyer flask while keeping the solution and the Büchner funnel warm.

(5) Set the hot filtrate in place and cool it down. Then separate the crystals of acetanilide and do the filtration in terms of the rules which are mentioned in the above paragraphs.

(6) Extrude the crystals with a glass nail or stopcock. Keep on filtering and remove the original liquor as much as possible.

(7) Disconnect the rubber tube from the aspirator and turn off the aspirator. Add some distilled water (as solvent) to cover and mix them intimately with a glass rod and turn on aspirator to drain the solvent.

(8) Repeat the process if necessary. Spread the crystals onto a piece of filter paper and allow them to air-dry completely.

(9) Determine the weight and melting point of the purified product. Calculate the percent recovery. The solubility of acetanilide in water: 5.5g/100mL (100℃); 0.53g/100mL (0℃).

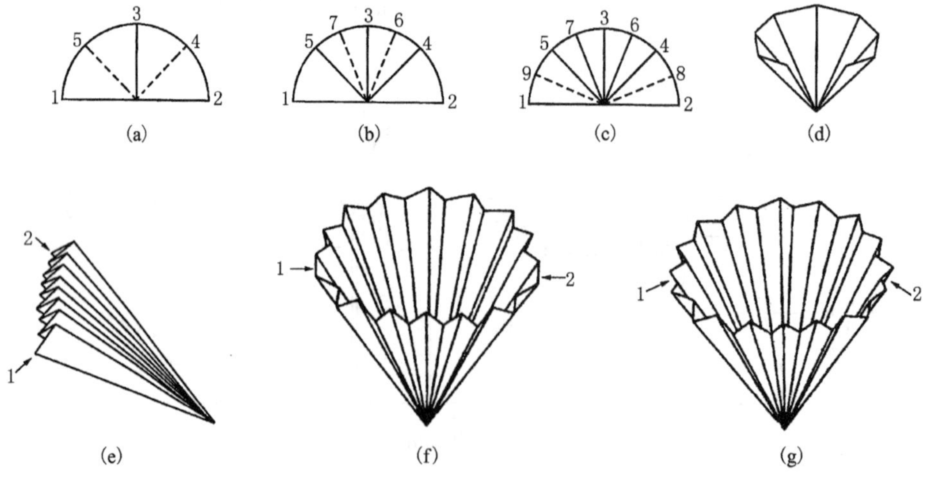

Fig. 2.5　Folding Filter Paper to Produce Fluted Filter Paper

2.2.4　Notes

When you are using a water pump, it is very important to have a safety trap mounted in the vacuum line leading from the filter flask.

2.2.5 Questions

(1) How many steps does the process of recrystallization involve? What is the purpose of each step?

(2) Why should the amount of the solvent consumed in recrystallization be neither too much nor too little? How should you do it exactly?

(3) Why should the amount of the solvent added in dissolving the rude product be less than that by calculations? What is the purpose of adding the solvent bit by bit until the solid exactly dissolves at the boiling point?

2.3 Simple Distillation and Fractional Distillation

2.3.1 Simple Distillation

1. Principle

Distillation has been used for centuries in the purification and separation of liquid organic substances. When the vapor pressure of the liquid being heated equals the atmospheric pressure on the surface of the liquid, it boils. The temperature, at that moment, is called boiling point. Simple distillation is a process that consists of boiling a liquid and condensing the vapor to the liquid state.

Every pure organic compound has a fixed boiling point at a certain pressure. Whenever possible, simple distillation is always used to separate liquid mixtures which have boiling points more than about 30℃ apart. But sometimes an organic compound together with other components can form a binary or ternary azeotrope mixture which also has a definite boiling point. So it is difficult to say whether a liquid is a pure organic compound, based on its definite boiling point.

The boiling range of a pure compound is about 0.5～1℃, but that of mixture is larger. Usually you can determine the boiling point of a liquid compound by distillation.

2. Procedure

(1) Assemble a simple distillation apparatus shown in Fig. 2.6 according to the "bottom-to-top" and "left-to-right" principle. Make sure all taper joints are connected securely. Select a round-bottom flask of such a size that it should be no more than one-half full. Insert a thermometer into the distillation head through a thermometer adapter with the top of the mercury bulb lined up with the bottom of the side-arm of head so that the bulb will be bathed in distillate vapors just before they enter the condenser.

(2) Put the liquid into flask through a separatory funnel, add a couple of boiling chips[1], and introduce the cooling water into a condenser[2].

(3) First heat slowly with a heating mantle, and then gradually increase the power, make the liquid boil, and start distilling[3].

(4) Adjust the heating source, maintain distillation at a rate of 1～2d/s, and record the

temperature of first distillate (maybe forerun, if any).

(5) Keep heating speed constant, continue to distill, and collect all distillates over the range of the desired temperature. Discontinue distilling any liquid[4] when no distillates come out and the temperature decreases suddenly.

(6) Remove the heating source, stop the cooling water, and disassemble the apparatus following the right-to-left and top-to-bottom principle.

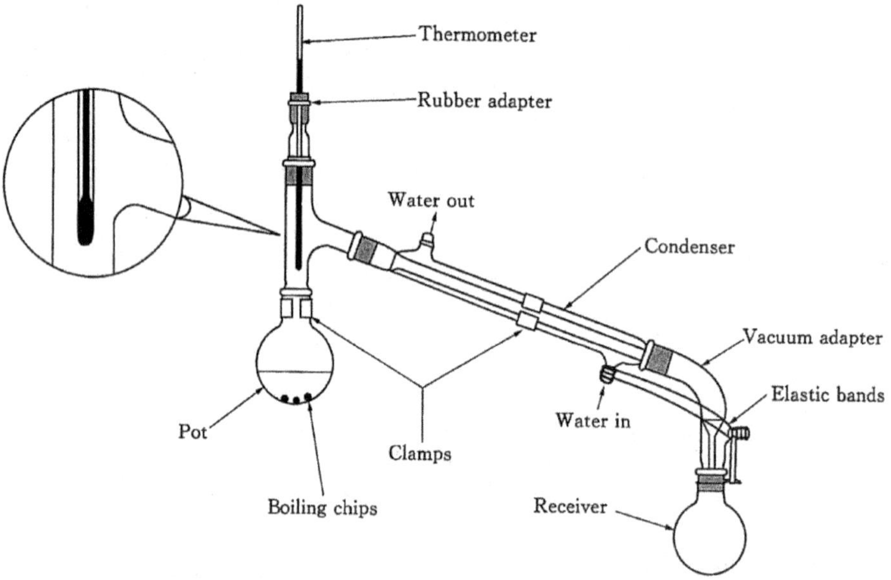

Fig. 2.6 Typical Apparatus for Simple Distillation

3. Experiment

Simple distillation of ethanol

Take a certain amount of ethanol as a sample, assemble an apparatus of simple distillation, heat with a water bath, and carry out the operation of simple distillation.

4. Notes

[1] Adding boiling chips can produce smooth bubbling and prevent boil-over or bumping of the liquid. Avoid adding them to a heated liquid. If distilling is started after heating is stopped, fresh boiling chips should be added to the cool solution and then heat can be reapplied.

[2] Introduce tap water from a hose into the lower condenser nipple and have it exit out of the upper nipple.

[3] The temperature at this moment is the boiling point of the distillate.

[4] Don't distill to dryness to prevent any experimental accidents.

5. Questions

(1) Why are boiling chips not added into a heated liquid?

(2) Why should the distillation apparatus have an opening to the atmosphere at the end?

2.3.2 Fractional Distillation

1. Principle

Fractional distillation, more effective than simple distillation, is also a commonly used technique of the separation and purification of liquid organic compounds with a smaller boiling point difference.

Fractional distillation is a distillation operation with a fractionating column which is equivalent to several successive simple distillations. As the vapor from the distillation flask rises up through the fractionating column, it condenses on the column packing and revaporizes continuously. Every revaporization of the condensate is just a separate distillation. In fact, vapor and condensate are passing in opposite directions through the column; more volatile component ascends through the column, while less volatile components descend. The counter-flow is essential for effective separation in a fractionating column. The vapors pass up through the column and condense upon heat exchange with the cooler surface of the column. There exists heat exchange between vapor and condensate. This results in the more volatile components rising faster in the fractionating column. If repeated, that means the process goes through many vaporization-condensation cycles and has the effect of many distillations. So there is a high ratio of the more volatile components near the top of fractionating column, and on the other hand, the high boiling-point components are moving downward to the distillation flask. When the column efficiency is high enough, the vapor out of the top of the fractionating column is close to the pure low-boiling component, meanwhile, the high boiling-point components are in the flask. Thus, components with small differences in boiling point can be separated.

2. Procedure

(1) Select a fractionating column, assemble an apparatus of fractional distillation shown in Fig. 2.7[also see Fig. 1.3 (c)]. Make sure all joints are connected well.

(2) Put the liquid to be distilled into a flask, add a couple of boiling chips, and introduce tap water into the condenser.

(3) Control heating speed, maintain a takeoff of no more than 1～2d/s[1].

(4) Collect distillates at different temperature ranges[2], record the temperature of the different distillates respectively.

3. Experiment

Separation of ethanol-water mixture with fractional distillation

(1) Place 60mL of 70% ethanol solution into a 100mL round-bottom flask, add one or two tiny boiling chips, and assemble an apparatus of fractional distillation with a proper fractionating column.

(2) Introduce tap water into a condenser, heat with a water bath, control the heating rate[3], and collect a forerun.

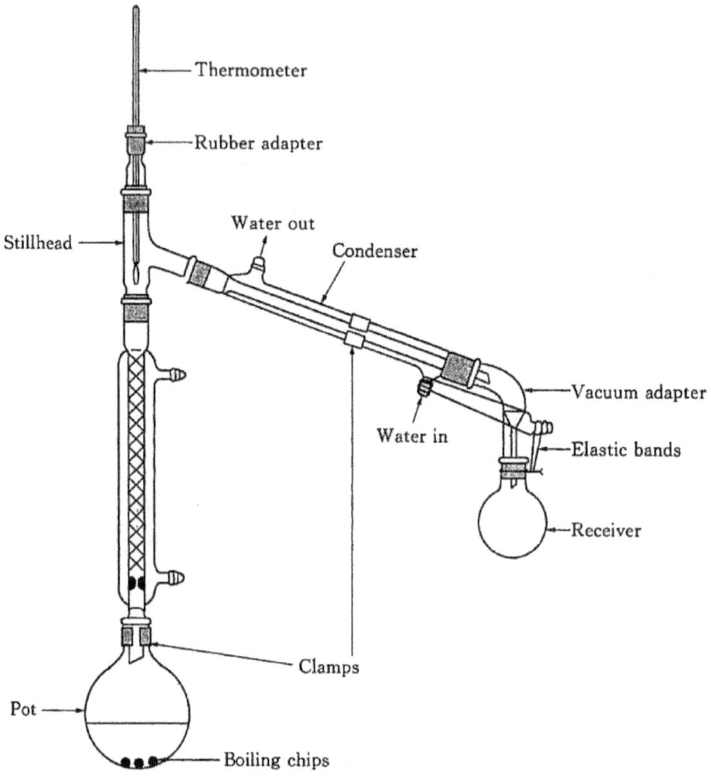

Fig. 2.7 Typical Apparatus for Fractional Distillation

(3) Change the receiver when the temperature rises to 78℃, collect distillate, maintain a takeoff of no more than 1～2d/s, and record the temperature[4].

(4) When the temperature decreases continuously[5], stop heating immediately. Record the volume of forerun, distillate and residue, respectively. Determine the distillate concentration by weight percent[6].

4. Notes

[1] If the distillation rate is too quick, the purity of products will decrease. If the distillation rate is too slow, the distillation temperature fluctuates up and down. To reduce the heat loss in a fractionating column, usually use asbestos rope to wrap it.

[2] Don't distill to dryness.

[3] Make the vapor rise slowly to the top of fractionating column.

[4] Due to variations in accuracy of thermometers, the temperature may differ slightly from the true value.

[5] When the distillation is close to completion, the mercury bulb cannot be embraced by the vapor of ethanol because of the shortage of ethanol vapor, resulting in the decrease of temperature.

[6] The weight percent concentration of ethanol, determined by an alcohol densimeter, reaches 89%～94%.

5. Questions

(1) What is an azeotropic mixture? Why cannot its components be separated by fractional distillation?

(2) Describe the characteristics of simple distillation and fractional distillation respectively.

2.4 Steam Distillation

2.4.1 Principle

Steam distillation, one of the immiscible phases being water, is one of the most commonly used methods of separating and purifying liquids. In this method steam is passed into the immiscible and volatile liquid in the distillation flask, and then the water and organic compound co-distill, condense in the condenser, and are collected in the normal way.

According to the law of partial pressure, the total vapor pressure above the mixture is the sum of the partial pressures of the pure individual components. Therefore, when the sum of the individual vapor pressures is equal to the atmospheric pressure, the mixture will start boiling at a lower temperature (boiling point) than either of the individual components. That means that the organic compound will distill out below its normal boiling point.

In the distillate, the weight ratio of organic compound (W_A) and water (W_{H_2O}) can be expressed as in equation (1).

$$\frac{W_A}{W_{H_2O}}=\frac{p_A M_A}{p_{H_2O} M_{H_2O}} \tag{1}$$

Steam distillation is applicable to the following situations: ①a high boiling-point organic compound which decomposes at its boiling point; ②a mixture containing inorganic salts or other organic solids, not suitable for distillation, filtration and extraction; ③a mixture containing large amounts of resin-like, nearly intractable substances or non-volatile impurities which is hard to isolate or purify in any other way.

In order for steam distillation to be feasible, the substances to be purified should have these characteristics: ①insoluble or immiscible in water; ②no reaction with water when co-boiling; ③having a certain vapor pressure at 100℃.

2.4.2 Procedure

(1) Assemble an apparatus shown in Fig. 2.8 and Fig. 2.9[also see Fig. 1.3 (d)]. Make sure to fasten securely and smoothly steam lines at all points and keep the lines from the steam generator to three-neck flask as short as possible.

(2) Pour the distillate into the round-bottom flask. Be certain that the flask is filled to no more than one-third of its capacity. Make sure that all connections are tight.

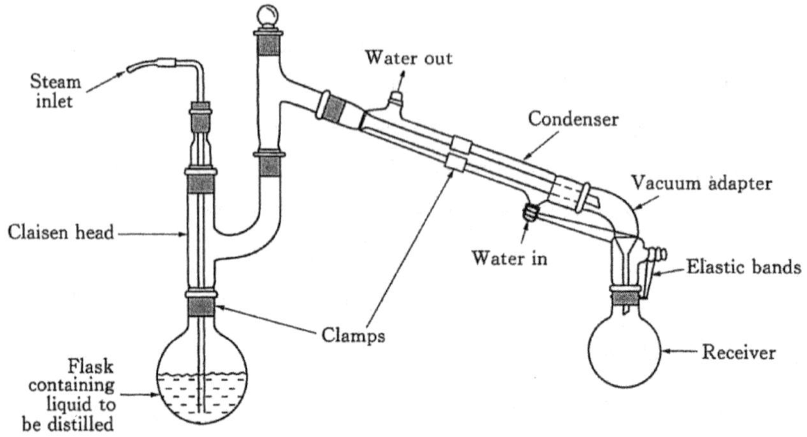

Fig. 2.8 Apparatus for Steam Distillation

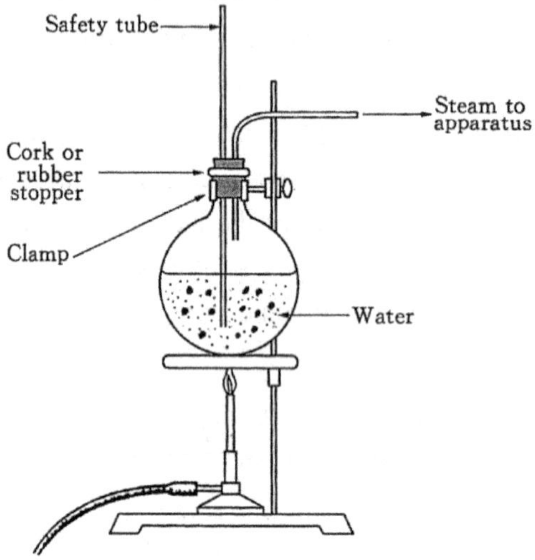

Fig. 2.9 Steam generator

(3) Open the screw clamp on the T-tube connecting the three-neck flask and the vapor generator before distillation. Introduce tap water to the condenser. Heat the steam generator. When steam goes out of vapor generator and begins to enter the flask[1], close the clamp up.

(4) Adjust a heating source and make sure that the rate of distillate entering the receiver is at 1～2d/s[2].

(5) When oily droplets are no longer observable or the distillate turns transparent or clear, stop heating immediately.

(6) Open the clamp, remove the heat source[3], disassemble the apparatus, in turn.

2.4.3 Experiment

Extraction of paeonolum[4] from Chinese Herb——Xu Chang Qing

(1) Place 5g of Xu Chang Qing into 250mL flask, add 20mL of water. Set up a steam-distillation apparatus, open the screw clamp on the T-tube, and introduce cooling water.

(2) Heat the steam source[5]. When steam flow out of T-tube, close the screw up and let steam enter into a three-neck flask.

(3) Adjust the heat source and steam flow rate, keep a takeoff of no more than 1～2d/s. When the distillate turns from a milky emulsion into clear and transparent drops of water, the distillation is complete.

(4) Open the clamp, remove the burner from the vapor generator.

(5) Smell the distillate, take a droplet of distillate on a small piece of filter paper. After evaporation, observe whether there is any oil stain on the filter paper.

(6) Take 1～2mL of distillate, stir it evenly, add 2～4d of 1% $FeCl_3$/ethanol solution, observe what happens.

2.4.4 Notes

[1]At this moment the solution in the flask bubbles furiously, the mixture of organic compound and water co-distills off soon.

[2]In order to avoid filling with condensed water in the three-neck flask during distillation, heat the flask with a small flame to make the on-going distillation proceed more quickly. Watch the water level height in the safety column at all times. If abnormal, open the clamp immediately, remove heat source, get rid of any troubles, and then go ahead.

[3]Avoid letting the liquid from the flask back up into the steam line.

[4]Extracting volatile oil from Xu Chang Qing, the main substance is paeonolum. Its chemical structure is shown as follows:

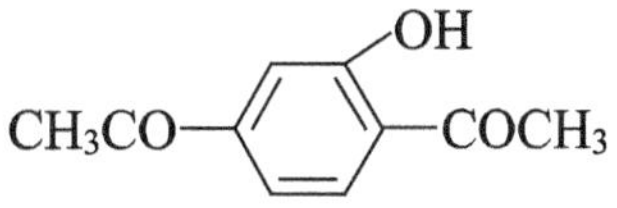

[5]Water in the vessel from steam generator should be no more than two-thirds full or else boiling water will probably rush out of the steam generator, causing thermal burns.

2.4.5 Questions

(1) Please describe the basic principle of steam distillation?

(2) What are the functions of the T-tube and safety column?

(3) How do you judge that steam distillation is complete?

2.5 Vacuum Distillation

2.5.1 Principle

When the pressure over a liquid is reduced, the liquid boils at a lowered temperature. As its name implies vacuum distillation is distillation under reduced pressure. As a rule, most liquids that boil around 200℃ or above at normal atmospheric pressure can be purified by vacuum distillation, since above that temperature, chemical transformations are more likely.

At pressures near atmospheric pressures, a drop in pressure of 10mmHg (1.33kPa) generally lowers the boiling point of a substance by about 0.5℃. At lower pressures, a 10℃ drop in boiling point is observed for each halving of pressure. For example, a compound with a boiling point of 100℃ at 20mmHg (2.67kPa) would boil at about 90℃ at 10mmHg (1.33kPa).

A more accurate estimate of the change in boiling point with a change of pressure can be made by using a nomograph (Fig. 2.10). How to use the nomograph: Assume a reported boiling point of 234℃ at 100kPa (760mmHg). To determine the boiling point at 2.0kPa (15mmHg) Connect 234℃ (column B) to 2.0kPa (15mmHg) (column C) with a transparent ruler and observe where this intersects column A (113℃). The approximate boiling point will be 113℃ at 2.0kPa (15mmHg).

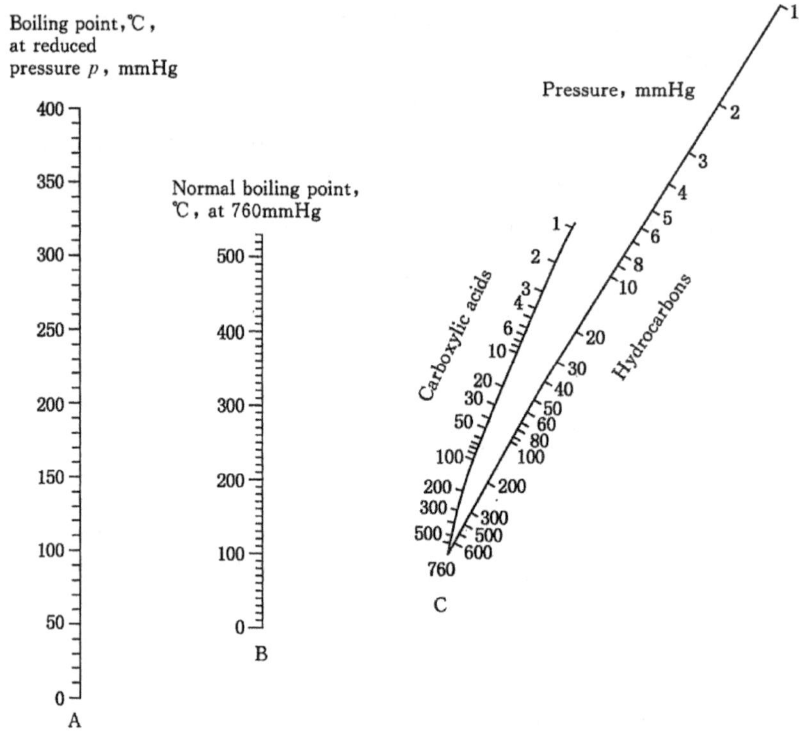

Fig. 2.10 A Nomograph for Estimating Boiling Points at Different Pressures

2.5.2 Apparatus

The Fig. 2.11 and Fig. 2.12 show the standard scale apparatus for vacuum distillation. The main equipment and supplies include the heat source, round-bottom flask, Claisen head, capillary bubbler, thermometer, condenser, vacuum adapter, receiving flask, trap, manometer and vacuum sources (a water aspirator or a vacuum pump).

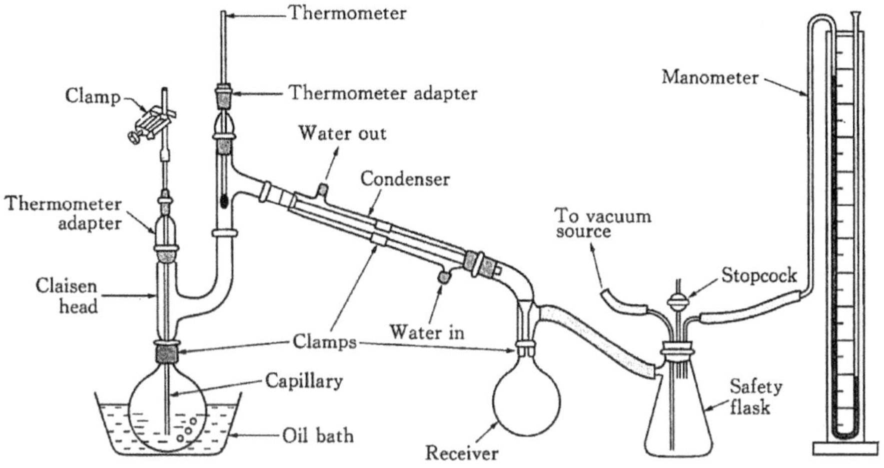

Fig. 2.11 Apparatus for Vacuum Distillation

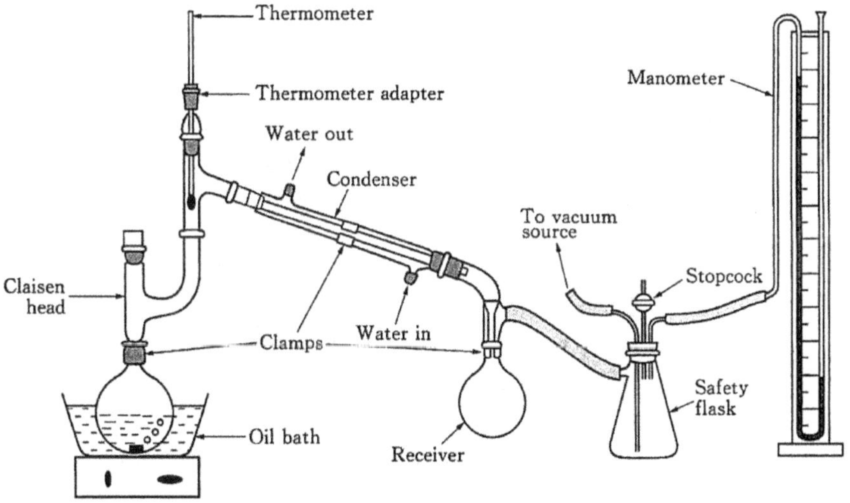

Fig. 2.12 Apparatus for Vacuum Distillation with a Magnetic Stirrer

The principal difference between a vacuum and an atmosphere distillation set-up is that in vacuum distillation, the system must be airtight and able to hold a vacuum. The glassware used to assemble them must be able to withstand the vacuum; for example, large, thin-walled Erlenmeyer flasks cannot be used. Use vacuum grease to seal all glass-to-glass connections. Stopcock grease flows too easily under heat to hold a vacuum. Use only heavy-walled vacuum tubing to prevent collapsing under vacuum. Connections between rubber and glass, as well as ground-joint connections, must be secure and airtight.

Under vacuum, most solvents boil well below room temperature, therefore, any solvent in the material to be distilled must be removed prior to distillation.

Heat Sources: The heat source should be capable of providing constant, uniform heating to prevent from bumping and superheating and to maintain a constant distillation rate. An oil bath provides the most uniform heating. A microscale vacuum distillation can be carried out using a sand bath.

Smooth-Boiling Devices: You can reduce bumping and foaming during a vacuum distillation by using a magnetic stirring device, or micro-porous boiling chips. Otherwise, you can construct a flexible capillary bubble, about as fine as a cat's whisker, by heating a section of glass tubing and drawing it out, then the glass is scored in the center of this drawn-out section and broken. A short rubber tube with a screw clamp should be placed at the top of the bubble to control the rate of bubbling. The bubble is inserted into the boiling flask through a thermometer adapter (or a rubber stopper if necessary) so that its tip extends to within a millimeter or two of the bottom (see Fig. 2.11). Under vacuum, this device should deliver a very fine stream of air bubbles preventing development of the large bubbles that cause bumping.

Vacuum Fraction Collectors: A vacuum adapter rather than a bent adapter must be used, since this adapter has a standard-taper joint connection for a round-bottom flask and a tubing connection for the vacuum source. If more than one fraction is to be collected, a vacuum fraction collector should be used. A multiple-flasked receiver for vacuum distillation is shown in Fig. 2.13.

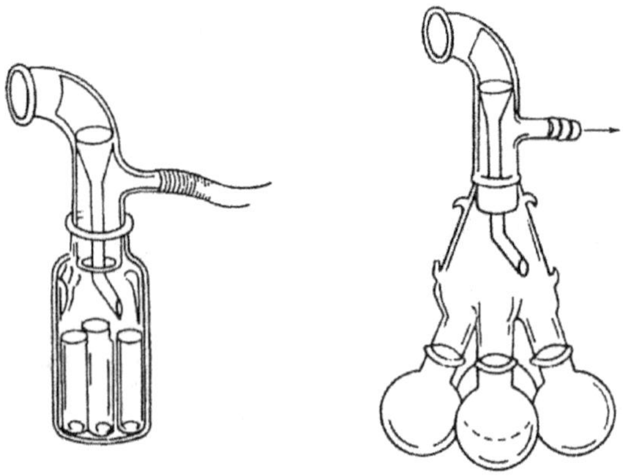

Fig. 2.13 Multiple-Flasked Receiver for Vacuum Distillation

Vacuum Sources: A vacuum can be obtained by using either a mechanical pump or a water aspirator. A mechanical pump must be used for distillation at pressure lower than 20mmHg (2.67kPa). If a mechanical pump is used, it must be protected by traps and several absorption columns to prevent vapors of distillate from passing into it. For pressures of 20mmHg (2.67kPa) and above, a water aspirator is usually satisfactory.

An aspirator must be provided with a solvent trap to prevent backup of water into the receiving flask due to changes of water pressure to reduce pressure fluctuations throughout the system. A thick-walled filter flask makes a suitable trap if it is provided with a pressure release valve and hooked up to the aspirator.

Pressure Measurement: Place a manometer (pressure-measuring device) between the vacuum source and the vacuum adapter. Two kinds of closed-end manometers are suitable for measuring pressure. In either of these manometers, the unit difference in the levels of mercury in mm, is equal to the pressure in the system. The mercury in a manometer can present a hazard if the vacuum is broken suddenly——air rushing in can push the mercury column forcefully to the closed end of the tube, breaking it and releasing toxic mercury into the laboratory. For many reasons, the vacuum must always be released slowly. It is advisable to open the manometer to the system only when a pressure reading is being made.

2.5.3 Steps in Vacuum Distillation

(1) Assemble the apparatus illustrated in Fig. 2.11 or Fig. 2.12, applying vacuum grease at all joints. With an empty distillation flask, test the seals by applying vacuum after closing the screw clamp at the top of the capillary tube and closing the stopcock of the safety flask. You should be able to obtain a pressure of approximately 20mmHg (2.67kPa) using an aspirator or a much lower pressure with a mechanical pump. If you cannot obtain this low pressure, you should use the pinch clamp to isolate various parts of the system to find the leak (s).

After checking the empty system, break the vacuum by opening the stopcock of the safety flask slowly while watching the mercury in the manometer rise.

(2) Using a funnel with a stem, pour the liquid to be distilled (cool and solvent-free) into the distillation flask until the flask is no more than half-full. Add a few micro-porous boiling chips if you are not using a capillary tube. After closing the stopcock of the safety flask, apply a full vacuum with the aspirator or the mechanical pump. Adjust the screw clamp until a fine stream of bubbles appears from the bottom of the capillary tube. You should be able to attain nearly the same low pressure as when the distillation flask was empty.

If a new leak has developed, seal it before proceeding.

(3) Adjust the pressure and let the system stand for a few minutes until the pressure is no longer changing. Watching the manometer, adjust the clamp if you want to conduct the distillation at a specific pressure, other than maximum attainable vacuum. Turn on the condenser cooling water, heat the liquid, with an oil bath and distill it. Record the temperature and pressure, then check them occasionally. If the pressure changes, adjust the heat input according ly. The distillate should be collected at a rate of about 1～2d/s.

(4) At the end of the distillation, remove the heat source, and slowly open the screw clamp and the stopcock of the safety flask to release the vacuum. Then turn off the aspirator or the mechanical pump.

(5) If a forerun must be removed, or if you are collecting fractions, you should break the vacuum and change the receivers. A more convenient way to collect fractions is to use a multiple-flasked receiver (Fig. 2.13). With a multiple-flasked receiver you can collect several fractions before breaking vacuum. You must cool the flask when sudden violent boiling or forthing might occur after you reestablish the vacuum.

(6) Remove the receiving flask and clean all glassware as soon as possible after disassembly to keep the ground-glass joints from sticking.

2.5.4 Experiment

Purification of crude furaldehyde by vacuum distillation.

Put 20mL of crude furaldehyde into a 50mL of dry distillation flask, assemble the apparatus for vacuum distillation and distill it.

Pure furaldehyde is a colorless liquid. The boiling point is: 161.8℃/101.33kPa, 103℃/13.33kPa, 67.8℃/2.67kPa, 18.5℃/0.133kPa.

2.5.5 Questions

(1) Using the nomograph in Fig. 2.10, approximate the boiling points of the following substance at atmospheric pressure (760mmHg).

1, 6-hexanediol, b.p.132℃ (10mmHg, 1.33kPa)

(2) Explain why a vacuum distillation apparatus should be checked for leaks before the material to be distilled is placed in the flask.

2.6 Solvent Extraction and Solution Washing

2.6.1 Principle

Solvent Extraction is a technique frequently used in the organic chemistry laboratory to separate or isolate a desired species from a mixture of compounds or from impurities. Substances for extraction usually are solid or liquid. The apparatus for extraction from liquid is called separatory funnel, and its use is one of the essential operations for organic chemistry experiments. For a solid mixture, liquid-solid extraction can be performed with a Soxhlet extractor (Fig. 2.14)[1]. Solution washing is the reverse process of solvent extraction. Usually it is performed in the case of impurities in a solution that can be extracted by another immiscible solvent, which has a small solubility to the desired substance. Separatory funnels are also the essential apparatus for solution washing, and the principle is similar to that of solvent extraction. Here we will focus our discussion on solvent extraction.

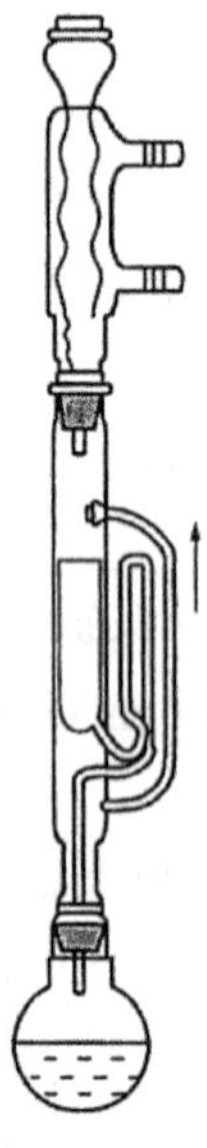

Fig. 2.14 Soxhlet Extractor

The extraction principle can be illustrated by the following calculation. It is assumed that the solution is comprised of an organic compound *X* dissolved in a solvent *A*. If we will extract *X* from *A*, we can choose a solvent *B*, which has a higher solubility to *X* than *A*, and it is immiscible and does not react with *B*. Place the solution into a separatory funnel, then add *B*, shake or swirl the funnel and stand the funnel upright until a sharp demarcation line appears between the two layers because of the immiscibility of *B* with *A*. The concentration ratio of *X* in solvent *B* and *A* is a constant at a given temperature, and the ratio is also called the distribution coefficient, expressed as *K*. This relationship is known as *the distribution principle,* which can be expressed by the following equation:

$$\frac{\text{Concentration of } X \text{ in the solvent } A}{\text{Concentration of } X \text{ in the solvent } B}=K$$

According to the distribution principle, in order to economize solvent and improve extraction efficiency, multiple extractions with small volumes of extracts are more efficient than a single extraction with a large volume, and it can be explain by calculation.

The First Extraction

Assume:

V = the volume of the solution to be extracted (mL) (The volume of the solution can be regarded as the volume of the solvent A, because of the small amount of the solute X);

W_0 = the total weight of the solute (X) in the solution to be extracted (g);

S = the volume of the solvent B employed for the first extraction (mL);

W_1 = the weight of the solute (X) remained in the solvent A after the first extraction (g);

Then:

$W_0 - W_1$ = the weight of the solute (X) extracted in the solvent B after the first extraction (g);

$\frac{W_1}{V}$ = the concentration of the solute (X) in the solvent A after the first extraction (g/mL);

$\frac{W_0 - W_1}{S}$ = the concentration of the solute (X) in the solvent B after the first extraction (g/mL);

From $\dfrac{\frac{W_1}{V}}{\frac{(W_0 - W_1)}{S}} = K$, we can obtain the result: $W_1 = W_0\left(\dfrac{KV}{KV+S}\right)$.

The Second Extraction

Assume:

V = the volume of the solution to be extracted (mL);

W_2 = the weight of the solute (X) remained in the solvent A after the second extraction (g);

S = the volume of the solvent B used in the second extraction (mL);

Then:

$W_1 - W_2$ = the weight of the solute (X) in the solvent B after the second extraction (g);

$\frac{W_2}{V}$ = the concentration of the solute (X) in the solvent A after the second extraction (g/mL);

$\frac{W_1 - W_2}{S}$ = the concentration of the solute (X) in the solvent B after the second extraction (g/mL);

So:

$\dfrac{\frac{W_2}{V}}{\frac{(W_1 - W_2)}{S}} = K$, we will get the result $W_2 = W_1\left(\dfrac{KV}{KV+S}\right)$

Replace W_1 with $W_0\left(\frac{KV}{KV+S}\right)$ (obtained from the first extraction), the above relationship can be rewritten as:

$$W_2 = W_0\left(\frac{KV}{KV+S}\right)^2$$

For more times of extractions, they can be done in the similar way. If we assume the employed volume of the solvent B is S each time, and W_n equals the weight of the solute (X) remained in the solvent A, after multiple (n) extractions (g), we can obtain W_n, from the following equation:

$$W_n = W_0\left(\frac{KV}{KV+S}\right)^n$$

Example

An aqueous solution containing 4g of butanoic acid in 100mL of water is extracted at 15℃ with 100mL benzene. The K value (participation coefficient of butanoic acid between benzene and water) is 1/3. After once extraction with 100mL of benzene, the remained amount of butanoic acid in water is:

$$W_1 = 4\times\frac{\frac{1}{3}\times 100}{\frac{1}{3}\times 100+100} = 1.0\,(\text{g})$$

The extraction efficiency is $\left(\frac{4-1}{4}\right)\times 100\% = 75\%$.

If the 100mL of benzene is divided into three portions, that is the solution extracted three times at each time with the benzene volume 33.33mL, the remained amount of butanoic acid in water after the third extraction is:

$$W_3 = 4\times\left(\frac{\frac{1}{3}\times 100}{\frac{1}{3}\times 100+33.33}\right)^3 = 0.5\,(\text{g})$$

The extraction efficiency should be $\left(\frac{4-0.5}{4}\right)\times 100\% = \frac{3.5}{4}\times 100\% = 87.5\%$

Based on the above calculations, it is known that the multiple extractions are more efficient than a single extraction with the same volume of extraction solvent.

2.6.2 Procedure

The extraction experiment of acetic acid from an aqueous solution by diethyl ether is exemplified the operational procedure.

1. Single Extraction

Support a separatory funnel on a ring of suitable diameter, measure 10mL of the acetic acid aqueous solution ($V_{HAC}:V_{H_2O}=1:19$) with a graduated cylinder and put it into the separatory funnel[2-4]. 30mL of diethyl ether is added into the funnel (Be far away from the flame otherwise it may cause a fire hazard)[5]. Insert the stopper, then pick up the funnel in both hands and invert it with the one hand holding the stopcock and the first two fingers of another hand holding the stopper in place [Fig. 2.15 (a)]. Shake or swirl the funnel gently for a few seconds, vent the funnel slowly by opening the stopcock to release any pressure buildup [Fig. 2.15 (b)]. Close the stopcock and shake the funnel more vigorously, with occasional venting, for 2~3min, so that the two immiscible solvents can contact with each other to increase efficiency.

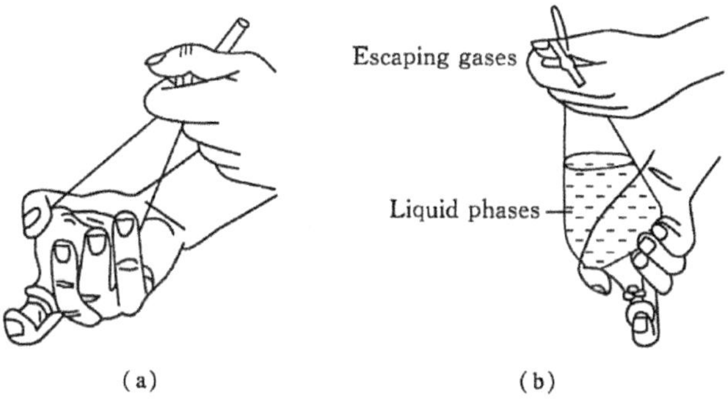

Fig. 2.15 Venting Separatory Funnel

Replace the funnel on the ring, remove the stopper, and allow the funnel to stand until there is a sharp demarcation line between the two layers. Drain the bottom layer into an Erlenmeyer flask by opening the stopcock fully; turn it to slow the drainage rate as the interface approaches the bottom of the funnel. When the interface just reaches the outlet, quickly close the stopcock to separate the layers cleanly.

Add a little (3~4 drops) phenolphthalein solution as the indicator to the drained layer, titrate the solution with the standard aqueous solution of sodium hydroxide (0.2mol/L). Record the consumed volume of the sodium hydroxide solution, and then do the following calculations:

(1) The weight and the percent of the acetic acid in the aqueous layer.

(2) The weight and the percent of the acetic acid in the ether layer.

2. Triple Extractions

Measure 10mL of the acetic acid aqueous solution ($V_{HAC}:V_{H_2O}=1:19$) with a graduated cylinder and put it into a separatory funnel, then repeat the extraction procedure mentioned above with three 10mL portions of ether instead of one 30mL portion as previously done.

Combine the three drained lower layers into an Erlenmeyer flask (50mL) through the outlet of the funnel, and add a little (3～4 drops) of phenolphthalein solution as the indicator. Titrate the solution with the standard aqueous solution of sodium hydroxide (0.2mol/L). Record the consumed volume of the sodium hydroxide solution, and then do the following calculations:

(1) The weight and the percent of the acetic acid in the aqueous layer.

(2) The weight and the percent of the acetic acid in the ether layer.

According to the data from the single extraction and the triple extractions, compare their efficiencies.

2.6.3 Experiment

See the section of Chinese part 2.6.4.

2.6.4 Notes

[1]The solid sample is placed in a porous thimble. The extraction-solvent vapor, generated by refluxing the extraction solvent contained in the distilling pot, passes up through the vertical side tube into the condenser. The liquid condensate then drips onto the solid, which is extracted. The extraction solution passes through the pores of the thimble, eventually filling the center section of the Soxhlet. The siphon tube also fills with this extraction solution and when the liquid level reaches the top of the tube, the siphoning action commences and the extract is returned to the distillation pot. The cycle is automatically repeated numerous times. In this manner the desired species is concentrated in the distillation pot. Equilibrium is not generally established in the system, and usually the extraction effect is very high. After the liquid-solid extraction, the solution can be treated as usual to obtain the desired product.

[2]There are three kinds of separatory funnel-spherical, subulate and pear forms. In organic experiments, a separatory funnel is mainly applied to:

(a) Separate two kinds of liquid which are immiscible and do not react with each other.

(b) Extract a certain component from a solution.

(c) Wash a liquid product or the solution of a solid product with water, aqueous alkaline or acidic solution.

(d) Add dropwise a certain reagent (used as a dripping funnel).

[3]Separatory funnels are very expensive and broken easily. Never prop the funnel on its stem, but support it on a ring, a funnel support, or some other stable support.

[4]The size of the funnel should be such that the total volume of solution is less than three fourths the total volume of the funnel. If the funnel is constructed with a ground-glass stopcock and / or stopper, the ground-glass surface must be lightly greased to prevent sticking, leaking or freezing. If Teflon stoppers and stopcocks are used, greasing is not necessary since they are self-lubricating.

[5]Frequently the volume of extraction solvent and the number of extraction steps are specified in an experimental procedure. If not, it is usually sufficient to use a volume of extraction solvent about equal to the volume of liquid being extracted, divided into at least two portions.

2.6.5 Questions

(1) What will influence the efficiency of extraction and how should the proper solvent be selected?

(2) What is the purpose of using the separatory funnel and what precautions do we need to use?

(3) When two kinds of immiscible liquids are in the separatory funnel, which layer does the material of larger specific gravity lie in? Where does the lower layer release from? How do you prevent the liquid from flowing too quickly when draining it? How do you deliver the liquid of the higher layer into another container?

2.7 Sublimation

2.7.1 Principle

Sublimation is a technique that is especially suitable for the purification of solid substances at the microscale level.

It is particularly advantageous when the impurities present in the sample are nonvolatile under the conditions employed. Sublimation is a relatively straightforward method in that the impure solid need only be heated and mechanical losses are easily kept to a minimum.

The technique has additional advantages: ①it can be the technique of choice for purifying sensitive materials, as it can be carried out under very high vacuum and thus it is effective at low temperature; ②solvents are not involved and indeed, final traces of solvents are effectively removed; ③impurities most likely to be separated are those having lower vapor pressures then the desired substance and, often therefore, lower solubilities, exactly those materials that are very likely to be contaminants in attempts at recrystallization; ④solvated materials tend to dissolve during the process; ⑤in the specific case of water as a solvate, it is very effective even with those substances that are deliquescent. The main disadvantage of the technique is that it may not be as selective as recrystallization. This lack of selectivity occurs when the vapor pressure of the materials being sublimed are similar.

Sublimation can be performed under ambient pressure or reduced pressure. Most materials sublime when heated below their melting points under reduced pressure. Substances that are candidates for purification by sublimation are those that do not have strong intermolecular attractive forces. Naphthalene, ferrocene and *p*-dichlorobenzene are examples of compounds that meet these requirements.

The processes of sublimation and distillation are closely related. Crystals of a solid substance that sublimes, when placed in a heated or evacuated container, will gradually generate molecules in the vapor state by the process of evaporation, (i.e., the solid exhibits a vapor pressure). Occasionally, one of the vaporized molecules will strike the crystal surface or the walls of the container and be held by attractive forces. This latter process is the reverse of evaporation and is termed condensation.

Sublimation is the complete process of evaporation from the solid phase to condensation from the gas phase to form crystals directly without passing through the liquid state.

A typical single-component phase diagram is shown in Fig. 2.16, which relates the solid, liquid and vapor phases of a substance to temperature and pressure. Where two of the areas (solid, liquid, or vapor) touch, there is a line and along each line, the two phases exist in equilibrium. Line *BO* is the sublimation-vapor pressure curve of the substance in question, and only along line *BO* can solid and vapor exist together in equilibrium, At temperatures and pressures along the *BO* curve, the liquid state is thermodynamically unstable. Where the three phases intersect, all three phases exist together in equilibrium. This point is called the triple phase point.

Many solid substances have a sufficiently high vapor pressure near their melting point and they thus can be sublimed easily under reduced pressure in the laboratory. Sublimation occurs when the vapor pressure of the solid equals the applied pressure.

Heating the sample just below the melting point of the solid causes sublimation to occur. The vapors condense on the cold-finger surface, whereas any less volatile residue will remain at the bottom of the flask. Apparatus suitable for sublimation of small quantities are now commercially available.

A sublimation apparatus based on the entrainment principle is illustrated in Fig. 2.17. Air drawn in through the lip of the evaporating dish flows over the material to be sublimed, sweeping the vapors up through the asbestos sheet so that they condense on the funnel or glass wool. The air flow must be gentle enough that the sublimate will not pass through the glass wool and condense inside the funnel stem or rubber tubing.

An example of the purification of a natural product is the alkaloid caffeine. This substance also can be isolated by extraction from tea.

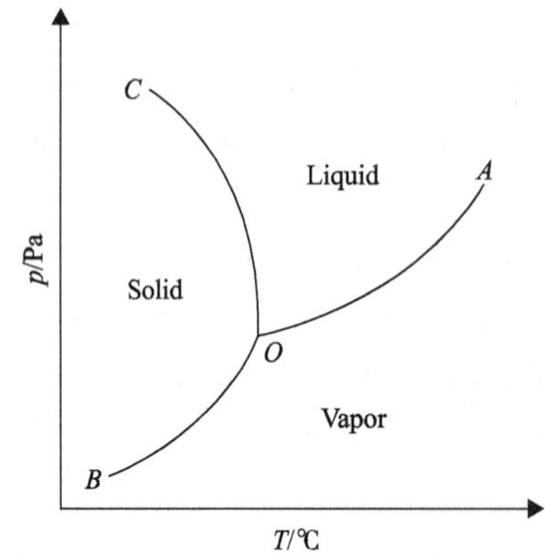

Fig. 2.16　Single-component Phase Diagram

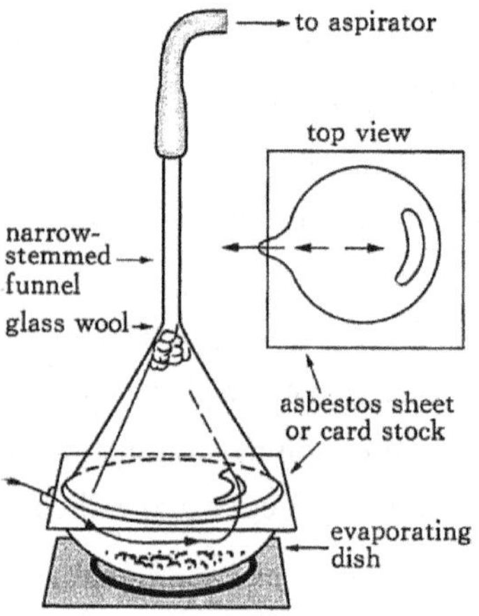

Fig. 2.17　Apparatus for Entrainer Sublimation

2.7.2　Procedure

(1) Construct one of the sublimation setups described above.

(2) Powder the dry material to be sublimed finely (if necessary) and spread it in a thin, even layer over the bottom of the sublimation container (outer beaker, evaporating dish, etc.). Assemble the apparatus and turn on the aspirator or cooling water (or fill the condenser with ice water).

(3) Heat with an appropriate heat source until sublimate begin to collect on the condenser, then adjust the temperature to attain a suitable rate of sublimation without melting or charring the sublimand. If the condenser becomes overloaded with sublimate, cool and disassemble the apparatus to remove the sublimate, then reassemble it and resume heating.

(4) When all of the compound has sublimed or only a nonvolatile residue remains, remove the apparatus from the heat source and let it cool.

(5) Carefully remove the condenser (avoid dislodging any sublimate) and scrape the crystals into a suitable container using a flat-bladed spatula.

2.7.3 Experiment

See the section of 3.14: Isolation of Caffeine From Tea Leaves.

2.8 Refractive Index Determination of Liquid Organic Compound

2.8.1 Principle

Refractive index, or index of refraction is a physical property useful for identifying liquids or indicating their purity. Refraction index is very accurate and can be determined to four decimal places.

Refractive index is the ratio of the velocity of light in vacuum to its velocity in a given substance:

$$n = \frac{V\ \text{vacuum}}{V\ \text{liquid}} = \frac{\sin\alpha}{\sin\beta}$$

wherein:

n = the refractive index at a specified centigrade temperature and wavelength of light

α = the angle of incidence of the beam of light striking the surface of the liquid

β = the angle of refraction of the beam of light in the medium (see Fig. 2.18)

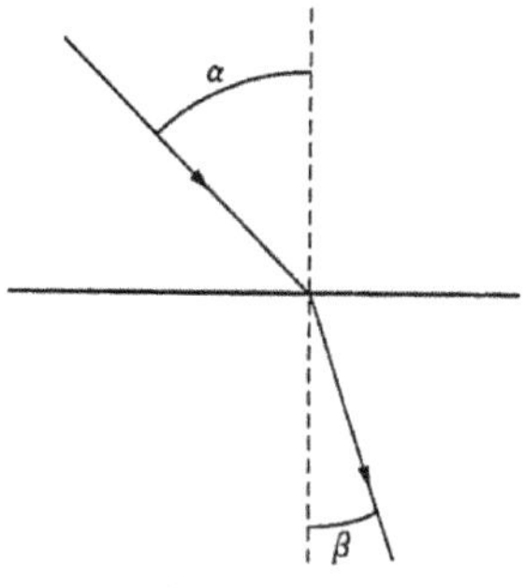

Fig. 2.18 Refraction and Refractive Index

The refractive index for a given medium depends on two variable factors. They are temperature and wavelength. It is usual to report refractive index indicate-measured at 20℃, with a sodium discharge lamp as the source of illumination. The sodium lamp gives off yellow light of 589nm wavelength, the so-called sodium D line. Under these conditions, the refractive index is reported in the following form:

$$n_{\mathrm{D}}^{20} = 1.4892$$

Refractive index decreases as temperature increases. We customarily report refractive index indicated at 20℃. If the measurement is made at other than 20℃ as indicated on the thermometer of the instrument, correct the measurement by using a correction factor.

Variations due to change in temperature are somewhat dependent on the class of compound observed, but are usually somewhere between 3.5×10^{-4} and 5.5×10^{-4} per ℃. Taking the average value of 4.5×10^{-4} serves as a fair approximation for most liquids. The corrected refractive index is given by

$$n_{\text{correct}} = n_{\text{observed}} + 4.5\times10^{-4}\times(t - 20.0)$$

in which t is the thermometer temperature.

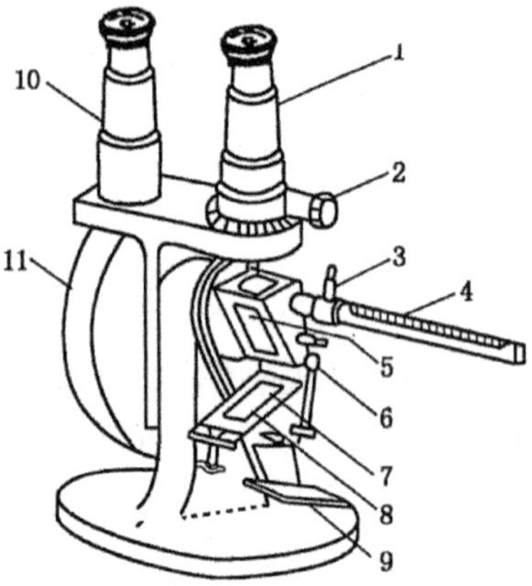

Fig. 2.19　ABBE Refractometer
1. Eyepiece with lens　2. Chromatic adjustment collar　3. Water exit　4. Thermometer
5, 6, 7. Hinged prism　8. Groove for sample
9. Reflector　10. Lens to view index of refraction scale　11. Index of refraction scale

2.8.2　The ABBE Refractometer

The instrument used to measure the refractive index is called a refractometer. The most common instrument is the Abbe refractometer. A common type of Abbe refractometer is shown in Fig. 2.19. Its popularity is due to several factors: ①the refractive index can be directly read in the same place as the adjustment image; ②only a few drops of sample are needed; ③temperature control of sample is possible; ④accuracy is very high. Fig. 2.19 illustrates two views of an Abbe refractometer.

2.8.3　Steps in Determining a Refractive Index

(1) Begin circulation of water from the constant-temperature bath well in advance of using the instrument.

(2) Check the surface of the prisms for residue from the previous determination. If the prisms need cleaning, place a few drops of methanol on the surfaces and blot the surfaces with lens paper.

(3) Squeeze gently the prism handles and swing open the upper prism. Drop two or three drops of the liquid onto the lower prism without touching its surface[1]. Lower the upper prism and lock it into position. For volatile liquids introduce the sample from an eyedropper into the channel alongside the closed prisms.

(4) Turn on the light and look into the eyepiece. Move the lamp arm up and rotate the light so it shines through the window into the sample area.

(5) Now adjust the light and the coarse adjustment knob until the field seen in the eyepieces is illuminated so that the light and dark regions are separated by as sharp a boundary as possible.

Fig. 2.20 illustrates a field with dark and light portions[2].

(6) Press the refractive index scale button and read the value that appears on the field. Now move the boundary out from the cross hairs and recenter it to get a second reading. Take several replicate readings and report the average value. Record the temperature and the make and the model of the instrument.

(7) Taking care not to scratch the surfaces, clean the refractometer prism faces with a soft tissue paper moistened with methanol, ethanol or ligroine immediately after use[3].

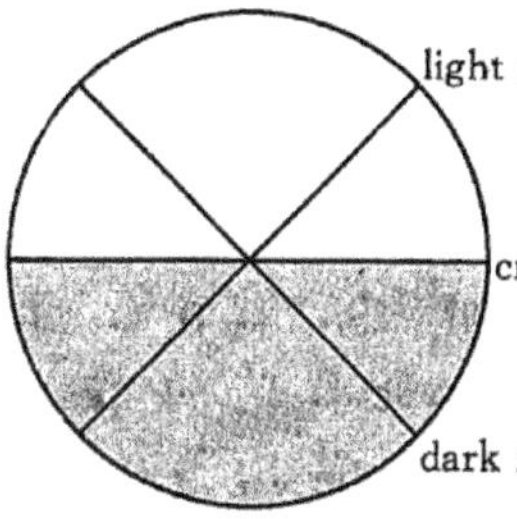

Fig. 2.20 View Through the Eyepiece When the Refractometer Adjusted Correctly

2.8.4 Experiment

You will be given an unknown about 0.5mL of *n*-butyl acetate (n_D^{20} 1.3940) or methyl benzoate (n_D^{20} 1.5454). Your task is to identify the substance by refractometry.

2.8.5 Notes

[1] Extra special care must be taken not to scratch the surfaces of the prisms.

[2] If the boundary has colors associated with it and/or appears somewhat diffuse, rotate the compensator drum on the face of the instrument until the boundary becomes uncolored and sharp.

[3] When you determine refractive index on toxic substances, work in a hood.

2.8.6 Questions

(1) A compound has a refractive index of 1.3968 at 17.5℃, calculate its refractive at 20.0℃.

(2) It is usually recommended that the glass surfaces of a refractometer be cleaned with ethanol or methanol, and not with acetone, what is the reason for this?

(3) Write a stepwise summary of using an Abbe refractometer.

2.9 Optical Rotation Determination

2.9.1 Principle

Certain chiral compounds have the peculiar property of rotating the plane of plane polarized light when it passed through their solutions. This change in the direction of vibration of plane polarized light by a certain angle is called optical rotation. Plane polarized light is produced by passing a beam of ordinary light through a Nicol prism.

The magnitude of the optical rotation depends upon: ①the concentration of the solution; ②the nature of the solvent; ③the temperature; ④the length of the column of the liquid through which the light passes; ⑤the wavelength of the light used. All these factors should always be taken into account while measuring the optical rotation of any compound.

Specific rotatory power is purely a constitutive property. It is used in the identification of certain compounds, in studying the configuration of molecules and deciding the mechanism of certain reactions.

The specific rotatory power is calculated by the formula (1).

$$[\alpha]_{\lambda}^{t} = \frac{\alpha \times 100}{l \times c}(\text{solvent}) \tag{1}$$

where α = observed rotation (in degrees); c = concentration of the sample (g/100mL); l = length of the pole tube (in decimetres); λ = the wavelength of the sodium light used and t = temperature (℃). The solvent used for making the solution should also be mentioned.

If the sample is a liquid, its specific rotatory power is calculated by the formula (2)

$$[\alpha]_{\lambda}^{t} = \frac{\alpha}{l \times d} \tag{2}$$

where d = the density of the liquid.

2.9.2 Apparatus

The apparatus used for the quantitative measurement of optical rotation is known as a polarimeter. A line diagram of a simple polarimeter is shown in Fig. 2.21. It consists of a light source (sodium vapour lamp), a polarizer and an analyzer.

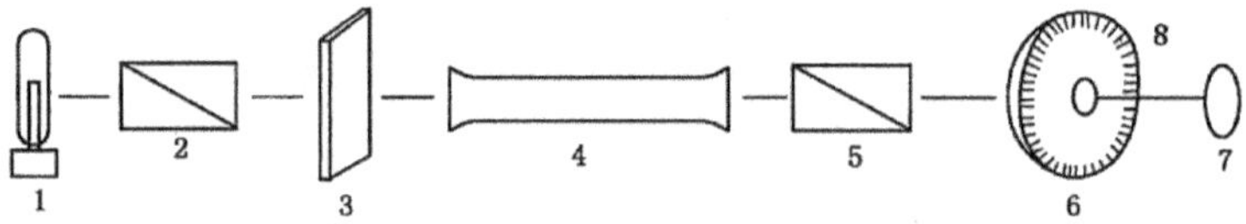

Fig. 2.21 Schematic Diagram of a Simple Polarimeter
1. Light source 2. Polarizer 3. Plane polarized light 4. Polarimeter tube
5. Analyzer 6. Circular scale 7. Ocular 8. Vernier

The polarimeter tube is placed between the polarizer and the analyzer. The polarimeter tube consists of a tube of thick glass having an opening in the middle with accurately ground ends. The open ends of the tube are closed by means of circular plates of glass with parallel sides which are pressed together against the ends of the tube by means of screw caps.

There are three kinds of vision in Fig. 2.22. If the analyzer's plane of polarization is parallel with the polarized light, you can see Image 2. If analyzer's plane of polarization is parallel with polarizer's, you can see the Image 1. If analyzer's plane of polarization equals to 1/2, you can see Image 3. This is the zero point.

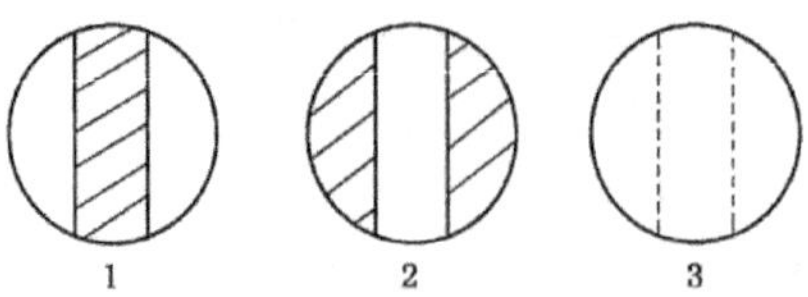

Fig. 2.22 Observation of Optical Rotation in Horizon Thirds Formula Polarimeter

2.9.3 Procedure

(1) Turn the switch on. Let it stabilize for 5min[1].

(2) Fill the tube with distilled water or sample liquid in the sample tube and adjust the zero point. If there is any difference value from the zero point, you should add or subtract the difference value from the reading data.

(3) Choose the proper long sample tube and full fill it with sample liquid[2,3]. Put it in the polarimeter. Turn the coarse adjustment and reset. If Image 3 appears, this data is the optical rotation of the sample. Repeat the determination for three times and take the average.

(4) Calculate the specific rotatory power according to the formula (1) or formula (2).

2.9.4 Experiment

Weigh 2.5g sample (e.g. glucose) accurately by an electronic balance, make up the solution in a 10mL volumetric flask. According to the above method, measure the angle of optical rotation of the sample. The difference between the reading and the zero point is the angle of optical rotation. Write down the length of the polarimeter tube and the temperature. Then calculate the specific rotatory power by the formula (1) or formula (2).

2.9.5 Notes

[1] The polarimeter should be warm up and stabilized.

[2] The sample tube should be full of liquid and not have air bubble.

[3] The cap of sample tube should be twisted suitably to avoid leaking the liquid. If the cap is twisted too tightly, the data is not accurate.

2.10 Chromatographic Techniques

2.10.1 Introduction

A number of natural compounds are co-existent in plants, animals, mines and so on. In industrial production or our laboratory preparation, the reaction products are produced as mixtures and therefore must be separated to obtain the pure compound. Chromatographic techniques are very useful to do this work, not only to separate the mixtures for preparative purposes, but also for qualitative and quantitative analyses of the mixtures. The principle of chromatography is based on the passage of the constituents to be separated between two immiscible phases. For this, the sample is dissolved in the mobile phase, which can be either a gas or a liquid phase, and moved across a stationary phase, which can either be in a column or on a solid surface. The components of the mixture are separated after sufficient running time due to the interactions of constituents with the stationary phase.

Classification of chromatographic methods according to the mobile and stationary phase are: ①gas-solid chromatography; ②liquid-solid chromatography; ③gas-liquid chromatography; ④liquid-liquid chromatography. The solid phases used can be made of a number of materials such as silica gel, alumina, or ion exchange resin. The liquid phases are made by coating immobilized liquid on support materials such as silica gel, porous glass beads and polymer. In the cases of ① and ②, the principle is absorption. Absorption chromatography is based on the direct interaction of the analyte with the solid. In the cases of ③ and ④, the principle is distribution.

Liquid-solid and liquid-liquid chromatography can be undertaken either on a column or on a plane. The former is also called column chromatography and the latter consists of two common types. One is paper chromatography and the other is thin-layer plate chromatography, which is widely used for monitoring the reaction and for preparative purposes. Gas-solid chromatography and gas-liquid chromatography are limited to column chromatography, which is called GC commonly.

2.10.2 Column Chromatography

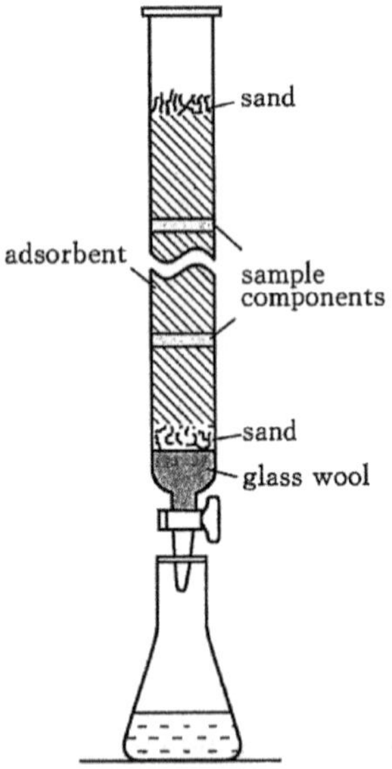

Fig. 2.23 Column Chromatography

1. Introduction

In column chromatography the stationary phase is a solid, which separates the components of a liquid passing through it by selective adsorption on its surface. The types of interactions that cause adsorption are the same as those that cause attraction between molecules, that is, electrostatic attraction, complexation, hydrogen bonding, and van der Waals forces.

A column such as shown in Fig. 2.23 is used to separate a mixture by column chromatography. The column is packed with a finely divided solid such as alumina or silica gel, which serves as the stationary phase, and a sample of the mixture to be separated is applied at the top. If the mixture is a solid, it must be dissolved in a solvent and then applied. The sample will initially be absorbed at the top of the column, but when an eluting solvent, the mobile phase, is allowed to flow through the column, it will carry with the components of the mixture. Owing to the selective adsorption power of the solid phase, the components ideally will move down the column at different rates. A more weakly adsorbed compound will be eluted more rapidly than a more strongly adsorbed compound, because the former will have a higher percentage of molecules in the mobile phase. The progressive separation of the components will appear as in Fig. 2.24.

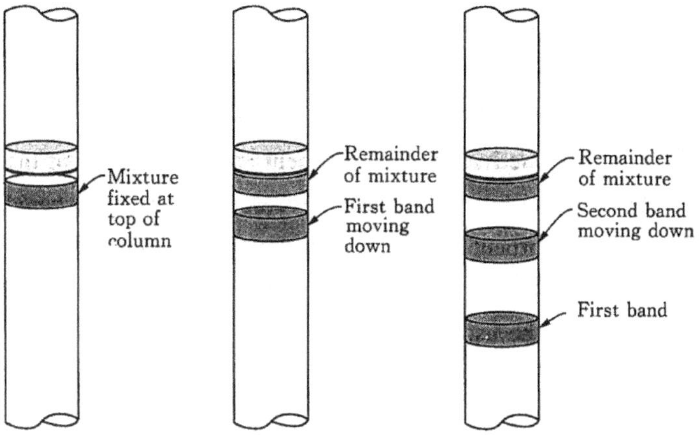

Fig. 2.24 Separation of Component by Column Chromatography

2. Adsorbents

Silica gel ($SiO_2 \cdot xH_2O$) and aluminum oxide (Al_2O_3) are commonly used for the stationary phase in column chromatography. Both adsorbents are generally used with non-polar to moderately polar elution solvents as the mobile phase. Today most chromatographic separations use silica gel, because it allows the separation of compounds with a wide range of polarities. Silica gel also has an advantage over aluminum oxide. It causes few chemical reactions with the substances being separated. Aluminum oxide is more polar, hence polar organic compounds, such as carboxylic acids, amines, phenols, and carbohydrates, adsorb so tightly on an alumina surface that highly polar solvents are needed to dislodge them.

Chromatographic silica gel has 10%~20% adsorbed water by weight and acts as the solid support for water under the conditions of partition chromatography. Compounds separate by partitioning themselves between the elution solvent and the water that is strongly adsorbed on the silica surface.

Activated alumina is available commercially as a finely ground powder in acidic (pH 4), neutral (pH 7), basic (pH 10) formulations and grades. Different brands and grades vary enormously in adsorptive properties.

The separation of very polar compounds may require an adsorbent of less polarity than either silica gel or alumina. For this situation, reverse-phase chromatography may be useful in separating the compounds. Reverse-phase chromatography uses a stationary phase that is less polar than the mobile phase. These conditions cause elution of the more polar compounds first, whereas the less polar compounds adsorb more tightly to the stationary phase.

3. Elution Solvents

In column chromatography, non-polar compounds bind less tightly on the solid adsorbent and dislodge easily with non-polar solvents. Polar compounds adsorb more tightly to the surfaces of metal oxides. Therefore, polar compounds must be eluted, or washed out of the column with polar solvents.

Let's compare the action of a non-polar elution solvent, such as hexane, with that of diethyl ether, a solvent of medium polarity. The primary forces between alumina and hexane molecules are weak van der Waals interactions. Hexane is not bound strongly to the column. Diethyl ether, however, binds more strongly with alumina by dipole-dipole and coordination interactions.

The balance between the activity of the adsorbent and the polarity of the solvent controls the rate at which materials elute from a column. If compounds elute too rapidly and poor separation occurs, either the adsorbent should be stronger or the solvent should be less polar. Conversely, if elution is so slow that only polar solvents are effective, a milder adsorbent is needed. The following gives the usual order of elution, from the least potent (non-polar) to the most powerful (polar) elution solvent.

Alkanes (petroleum ether, hexane, cyclohexane) < Carbon tetrachloride < Toluene < Dichloromethane, diethyl ether < Chloroform < Acetone < Ethyl acetate < Ethanol < Methanol

4. Choosing a Column and Making a Macroscale Column

Once a choice about which adsorbent to use for a separation has been made, you need to decide how much adsorbent to use. This depends on the amount of material that you wish to separate, and the diameter of the column that you use (Table 2.1). A long and thin adsorbent column will retain compounds more tenaciously than will a short, fat one. In general, one should use 20~30 times as much adsorbent as the material to be separated. A 10 : 1 or 15 : 1 ratio of the height of the adsorbent to the column diameter is normal.

Table 2.1 Representative columns

Sample (g)	Silica gel (g)	Column dimensions (diameter × height, in cm)
5	150	3.5×40
2	60	2.0×30

Alumina has a bulk density of about 1g/cm^3, but silica gel has a bulk density of about 0.3g/cm^3. For example, 20g of alumina would fill a column having a 1.5cm diameter to a height of about 11cm. You would need to use a fatter column for the same amount of silica gel.

After you have chosen a column and weighed out the adsorbent that you need, you can prepare the column for use. The construction of such a column is just as crucial to the success of the chromatography as is the choice of adsorbent and elution solvents. If the adsorbent has cracks or channels or if it has a non-horizontal or irregular surface, you will get poor separation.

Clamp the glass chromatography tube in a vertical position onto a ring stand and fill approximately one-half of it either with the first developing solvent that you plan to use or with a less polar solvent. Cover the plug with approximately 6 mm of white sand. The plug and sand serve as a support base to keep the adsorbent in the column and prevent it from clogging the tip.

Pour the adsorbent powder slowly into the solvent-filled column. The stopcock should be closed. Take care that the adsorbent falls uniformly to the bottom. The adsorbent column should be firm, but if it is packed too tightly, the flow of elution solvents will become too slow.

Gentle tapping on the side of the column as the adsorbent falls through the solvent prevents the appearance of bubbles in the adsorbent. The top of the adsorbent must always be horizontal. After all of the adsorbent has been added, carefully pour approximately 4 mm of white sand on top. This layer protects the adsorbent from mechanical disturbances when new solvents are poured into the column later.

The column must never be allowed to dry out once it is made; and the solvent level should never be allowed to go below the upper level of the adsorbent.

5. Elution Techniques

1) Dissolve the Sample

The mixture of compounds being separated is always poured into the column in a solution. The solvent is the preferred solvent for the sample solution. The solution should be as concentrated as possible, preferably no more than 5mL in volume. If the sample is not soluble in the first elution solvent, a very small amount of a more polar solvent can be used to dissolve them.

2) Pour the Solution of the Sample into the Column

Before the solution of the organic mixture is applied to the column, the solvent used in making the column should be allowed to drip out until the liquid level is just at the top of the upper sand layer. Then close the stopcock and pour the mixture to be separated into the column. After reopening the stopcock and allowing the upper level of the solution to reach the top of the sand, stop the flow, fill the column with elution solvent, and proceed to develop the chromatogram. Follow the same procedure when changing elution solvents.

3) Elute the Compounds

The less polar compounds elute first along with the less polar solvents. Polar compounds usually come out of a column only after a switch to a more polar solvent. As the development of the chromatography proceeds under the proper conditions, the compounds in the mixture put onto the top of the column will separate into distinct bands, or zones.

A mixture of two solvents is also commonly used for elution. For example, the development of the column can begin with hexane and, if nothing is eluted from the end of the column with this solvent, a 10% or 20% solution of ether in hexane can be used next. The ether/hexane solution can be followed by pure diethyl ether.

Thin-layer chromatography is one method that allows you to estimate how good a certain solvent will be as an eluent for a chromatographic separation. You should use the same adsorbent material as you expect to use on the column. The highest R_f value for any of the compounds in the mixture should be about 0.3 for a useful elution solvent.

A greater height of developing solvent above the adsorbent layer will provide a faster flow through the column. An optimum flow rate is about 2mL/min. Faster rates do not allow enough time for the adsorption equilibria to take place, and incomplete separation may occur. But if the flow is too slow, poor separation may result from the natural diffusion of the bands. A reservoir at the top of a column can be used to maintain a proper height of elution solvent above the adsorbent.

The size of the eluent fraction collected at the bottom of the column depends on the particular experiment. Common fraction sizes range from 25 to 150mL. If the separated compounds are colored, it is a simple matter to tell when the different fractions should be collected. However, column chromatography is not limited to colored materials. With an efficient adsorbent column, each compound in the mixture being separated will be eluted separately.

4) Collect the Eluted Compounds

Pure components of the mixture are recovered by the evaporation of the solvent in the collected fractions. A rotary vacuum evaporator is commonly used to remove the solvents.

6. Summary of Column Chromatography Techniques

(1) Prepare a properly packed column of adsorbent.
(2) Add the sample mixture to column in a small volume of solution.
(3) Elute the adsorbed compounds with progressively more polar elution solvents.
(4) Collect the eluted compounds in fractions from the bottom of the column.
(5) Evaporate the solvents to recover the separated compounds.

7. Experiment

(1) Use column chromatography to separate the geometric isomers of azobenzene, colored compounds whose separation can be followed visually.

Commercial azobenzene is mainly in the form of the *anti*-isomer, 1, which is orange, but it contains a smaller amount of the *syn*-isomer, 2, which is yellow. The different colors of the two isomers allow one easily to follow the progress of a chromatographic separation on a column.

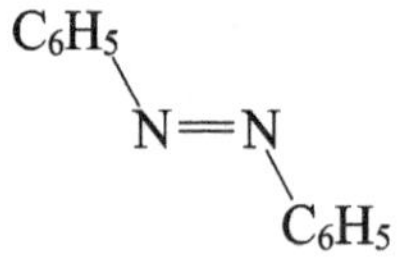

1

anti-Azobenzene

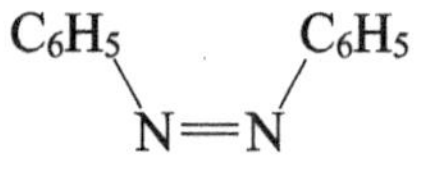

2

syn-Azobenzene

Procedure

Ⅰ. Preparation of Column

Clamp in a vertical position a 50mL buret with its stopcock closed but ungreased. Fill the buret to approximately the 40mL mark with petroleum ether (b.p. 30～60℃) and insert a small plug of glasswool into the bottom of the buret by means of a long piece of glass tubing. Introduce into the buret enough clean sand to form a 1cm layer on top of the glasswool plug. Slowly add 15g of alumina to the buret while continually tapping the column with a “tapper” made from a pencil and a one-holed rubber stopper. The agitation of the column while the alumina is being sifted in assures an evenly packed column. With a little additional petroleum ether, wash down the inner walls of the buret to loosen any adhered alumina. Introduce a 1cm layer of sand at the top of the column. Open the stopcock and allow the solvent to drain just to the top of the upper layer of sand. The column should now be ready to receive the sample.

Ⅱ. Separation and Purification of *anti*-Azobenzene

Obtain 1～2mL of a half-saturated solution of commercial azobenzene in petroleum ether (b. p. 30～60℃). Also obtain a small amount of the solid commercial azobenzene and accurately determine its melting range. To a column prepared as described in part 2.10.2, using 16g of alumina, apply 1.0mL of the azobenzene solution. The solution may be transferred to the column with a pipet, allowing the solution to run evenly down the inside surface of the buret. Open the stopcock and allow the liquid to drain to the top of the sand, in a like manner introduce 1～2mL of fresh petroleum ether to wash down the inner surface of the buret. Again allow the liquid to drain to the top of the sand, fill the buret with fresh petroleum ether. Open the stopcock; as the solvent runs through the column. A broad orange band of the *anti*-isomer of azobenzene should be observed to move slowly down the column. A narrow yellow band of the *syn*-isomer should remain very near the top of the column. Allow petroleum ether to run through the column until the orange band is eluted and collected at the bottom of the column in a small Erlenmeyer flask. Remove most of the solvent by simple distillation and then transfer the final 1～2mL of the concentrated eluent to small round-bottomed flask. Attach the flask to an aspirator or house vacuum line in order to remove the last small amount of solvent under evacuation. When the crystals of the purified *anti*-azobenzene are completely dry, accurately determine their melting point. The reported melting point of *anti*-azobenzene is 68℃.

If desired, after the *anti*-isomer has been eluted from the column, the buret may be refilled with methanol and the *syn*-isomer eluted from the column. Typically, however, an insufficient amount of the *syn*-isomer is obtained for adequate characterization.

(2) Experiment 4.4: Extraction, Separation and Identification Capsanthin and β-Carotene.

8. Questions

(1) Why does the *syn*-azobenzene move down the column faster when methanol is used?

(2) Why does the proper technique for column chromatography involve changing from a less polar to a more polar solvent rather than the reverse procedure?

2.10.3 Thin Layer Chromatography

1. Principle

Thin-layer chromatography (TLC) is one of the most widely used analytical techniques, at the same time it can be used for separating compounds at a scale between mg to g in the laboratory. TLC is a simple, inexpensive, fast, sensitive, and efficient method for determining the number of components in a mixture, for possibly establishing whether or not two compounds are identical, and for following the course of reaction.

Thin-layer chromatography involves the same principles as column chromatography, and it also is a form of solid-liquid adsorption chromatography. In this case, however, the solid adsorbent is spread as a thin layer (approximately 0.25～1mm) on a plate of glass or rigid plastic. A drop of the solution to be separated is placed near one edge of the plate, and the plate is placed in a container, called a developing chamber, with enough of the eluting solvent to come to a level just below the "spot." The solvent migrates up the plate, carrying with the components of the mixture at different rates. The result may then be seen as a series of spots on the plate, falling on a line perpendicular to the solvent level in the container. The retention factor (R_f) of a component can then be measured as indicated in Fig. 2.25.

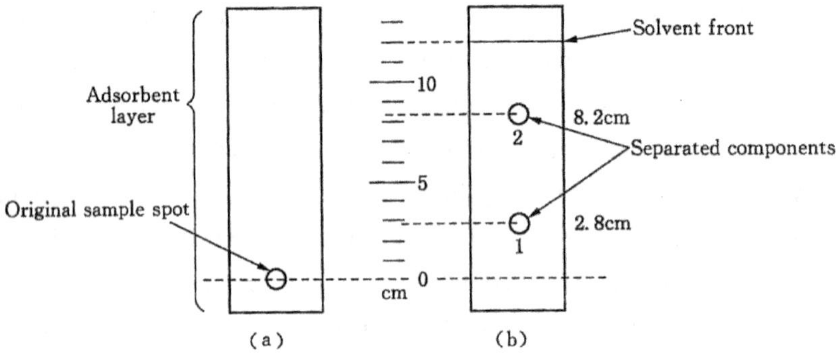

$$R_f = \frac{\text{distance traveled by substance}}{\text{distance traveled by solvent}}$$

$$R_f(\text{compound 1}) = \frac{2.8\text{cm}}{12\text{cm}} = 0.23$$

$$R_f(\text{compound 2}) = \frac{8.2\text{cm}}{12\text{cm}} = 0.68$$

Fig. 2.25 Thin-layer Chromatogram: (a) original plate; (b) developed chromatogram

This chromatographic technique is very easy and rapid to perform. It lends itself well to the routine analysis of mixture composition and may also be used to advantage in determining the best eluting solvent for subsequent column chromatography. However, it should be borne in mind that volatile compounds (b.p.<100℃) cannot be analyzed by TLC.

2. Material of Plates

Thin-layer chromatography uses glass, metal, or plastic plates coated with a thin layer of absorbent as the stationary phase.

3. Developing and Visualization of Thin-layer Chromatography

A small amount of the mixture being separated is spotted on the absorbent near one end of the plate. Then the thin-layer plate is placed in a closed chamber, with the applied spot edge immersed in a shallow layer of developing solvent. The solvent rises through the stationary phase by capillary action. Finally the thin-layer plate is picked up from the developing chamber when the solvent front is about 1cm from the top of the plate. The position of the solvent front is marked immediately with a pencil, before the solvent evaporates. Two methods are available to visualize the spots: ①the plate can be illuminated by exposure to ultraviolet radiation when it is impregnated with a fluorescent indicator; ②The other is placing the plate in a jar containing a few iodine crystals. The spots will color with the brown of iodine.

4. Determination of the R_f

The term R_f stands for "ratio to the front" and is expressed as a decimal fraction: R_f = Distance traveled by compound / Distance traveled by developing solvent front.

The R_f value for a compound depends on its structure and is a physical characteristic of the compound. Whenever a chromatogram is done, the R_f value is calculated for each substance and the experimental conditions recorded. The important data include: ①absorbent on the thin-layer plate; ②developing solvent; ③method used to visualize the compounds and; ④R_f value for each substance.

The measurement is made from the center of a spot to calculate the R_f value for a given compound and measure the distance that the compound has traveled from where it was originally spotted and the distance that the solvent front has traveled.

When two samples have identical R_f values, you should not conclude that they are the same compound without doing further analysis. Carrying out additional TLC analyses on the two samples, using different solvents or solvent mixtures, would be a way to check on their identities.

5. Common Solid Absorbents on the Plates for Thin-layer Chromatography

Two solid absorbents, silica gel ($SiO_2 \cdot xH_2O$) and aluminum oxide (Al_2O_3 also called alumina), are commonly used for thin-layer chromatography. The more polar the compound, the more strongly it will bind to silica gel or aluminum oxide. All solid absorbents used for TLC are prepared from activated, finely ground powder. Activation usually involves heating the powder to remove adsorbed water. Silica gel is acidic, and it separates acidic and neutral compounds. Acidic, basic, or neutral aluminum oxide is adapted to separate non-polar and polar organic compounds.

The plates pre-coated with a layer of adsorbent can be brought commercially. These plates are available in plastic or glass. The longer the distance that the developing solvent moves up the plate, the better will be the separation of the compounds being analyzed. Wider plates can also accommodate many more samples. Large plates with an adsorbent layer 1～2mm thick are used for preparative TLC in which samples of 50～1000mg are separated.

6. Sample Application

The sample must be dissolved in a volatile organic solvent. The best concentration is 1%～2%. The solvent needs a high volatility so that it evaporates almost immediately. Acetone, dichloromethane and chloroform are commonly used.

To analyze a solid, one can dissolve 20～40mg of it in 2mL of the solvent.

Tiny spots of the sample are carefully applied with a micropipet near one end of the plate. Keeping the spots small makes for the cleanest separation. Don't overload the plate with too much sample, as this leads to large tailing spots and poor separation. The micropipet is filled by dipping the constricted end into the solution to be analyzed. Hold the micropipet vertically to the plate and apply the sample by touching the micropipet gently and briefly to the plate about 1cm from the bottom edge. Mark the edge of the plate with a pencil at the same height as the center of the spot; this mark indicates the starting point of compound for your R_f calculation.

7. Choices of Developing Solvent

When the spots of the thin-layer plate is dry, put the thin-layer plate in a developing chamber. To ensure good chromatographic resolution, the chamber must be saturated with solvent vapors to prevent the evaporation of solvent as it rises up the thin-layer plate. Use enough developing solvent to allow a shallow layer (3～4mm) to remain on the bottom. But if the solvent level is too high, the spots may be below the solvent level. Hence the spots dissolve away into the solvent. The chromatogram will be fail.

Uncap the developing chamber and place the thin-layer plate inside with a pair of tweezers. Recap the chamber, and let the solvent move up the plate. The adsorbent will become visibly moist. When the solvent front is within 0.5～1cm of the top of the adsorbent layer, remove the plate from the developing chamber with a pair of tweezers and immediately mark the adsorbent at the solvent front with a pencil. To get accurate R_f values, the final position of the front must be marked before any evaporation occurs.

8. Visualization Techniques

The TLC separations of colored compounds can be seen directly. However, many organic compounds are colorless, so an indirect visualization technique is needed. Commercial thin-layer plates or adsorbents that contain a fluorescent indicator are widely used. A common fluorescent indicator is calcium silicate, activated with lead and manganese. The insoluble inorganic indicator rarely interferes in any way with the chromatographic results and makes visualization straightforward. When the output from a short-wavelength ultraviolet lamp (254nm) shines on the plate in a darkened room or dark box, the plate fluoresces visible light.

Another way to visualize colorless organic compounds is by using their absorption of iodine (I_2) vapor. The thin-layer plate is put in a bath of iodine vapor prepared by placing 0.5g of iodine crystals in a capped bottle. Colored spots are gradually produced from the reaction of the separated substances with gaseous iodine. The spots are dark brown on a white to tan background. After 10～15min, the plate is removed from the bottle.

Visualizing solutions containing reagents that react with the separated substances to form colored compounds can be sprayed on thin-layer plates; alternatively, the thin-layer plates can be dipped in the visualizing solution. Visualization occurs by heating the dipped or sprayed thin-layer plates with a heat gun or on a hot plate. Many of these solutions are specific for certain functional group. Two common visualizing solutions are *p*-anisaldehyde and phosphomolybdic acid.

9. Summary of TLC Procedure

(1) Obtain a pre-coated thin-layer plate of the proper size for the developing chamber.

(2) Spot the plate with a small amount of a 1%~2% solution containing the materials to be separated.

(3) Develop the chromatogram with a suitable solvent.

(4) Mark the solvent front.

(5) Visualize the chromatogram and outline the separated spots.

(6) Calculate the R_f value for each compound.

10. Experiment

1) Identification of *ortho*-nitroaniline and *meta*-nitroaniline by TLC

This experiment is a simple demonstration of TLC to provide practice in the basic techniques of the method.

Safety Note

Nitroanilines are toxic; avoid contact with the skin.

Procedure

(1) Prepare 2~4 TLC capillaries. Obtain very small samples of *ortho*-, *meta*-nitroaniline (about 5mg) Dissolve the samples in about 0.5mL of acetone. Place a spot of *ortho*- nitroaniline solution on the TLC plate about 0.8cm from one edge and about 1cm from the bottom, using a capillary tube to apply the spot. The spot should be 1 or 2mm in diameter. Allow the spot to dry. After this time, apply another spot of *meta*-nitroaniline solution on the plate at the same distance from the bottom as the first and leave about 1cm between the spots. Again, allow the plate to dry.

(2) A wide-mouth bottle with a tightly fitting screw-top cap may be used as a developing chamber. Alternatively, a beaker covered with a watch glass may be used. Place a 0.8cm layer of methylene chloride in the bottom of the developing chamber. Fold a piece of filter paper, as shown in Fig. 2.26 (a), and place it into the developing chamber, as shown in Fig. 2.26 (b). Saturate the chamber with vapors of the solvent by shaking. This inhibits the evaporation of solvent from the plate during the development of the chromatogram. The piece of filter paper helps maintain this saturated state.

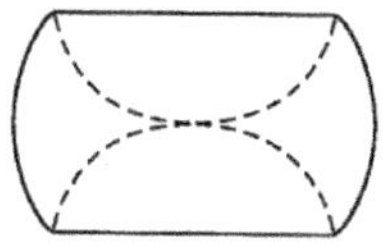

(a)

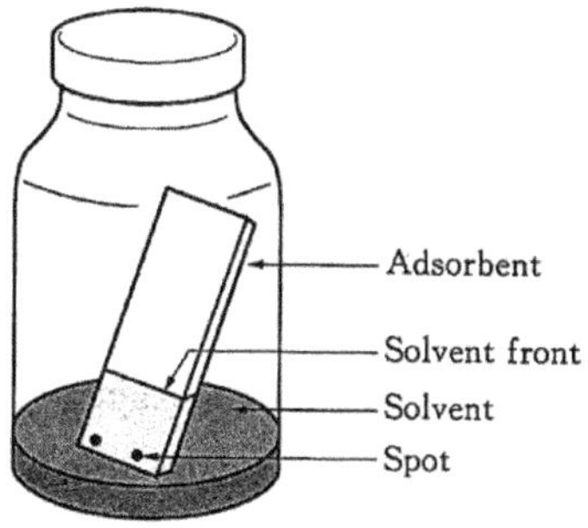

(b)

Fig. 2.26 TLC Chamber

(a) Fold a piece of filter paper; (b) Develop in a developing chamber

(3) Place the chromatogram plate in the chamber, being careful not to splash the solvent onto the plate. The spots must be above the solvent level. Allow solvent to climb to within about 1.5cm

of the top of the plate and then remove the plate and allow it to air-dry. The spots should be visible on the dry plate, but placing them in an iodine vapor jar or viewing them under UV light may bring them out more distinctly.

(4) Determination of the R_f of *ortho*-nitroaniline and the R_f of *meta*-nitroaniline.

2) Experiment 4.3: Extraction and Separation Spinach Leaf Pigments

11. Questions

(1) In a TLC experiment, why must the spot not be immersed in the solvent in the developing chamber?

(2) Arrange the nitroanilines in order of decreasing polarity by TLC?

2.10.4 Gas Chromatography (GC)

1. Principle

In gas chromatography the compounds to be analyzed are vaporized and eluted with the aid of a gas as the mobile phase through the column. The mobile phase is used alone as a carrier gas, so that interactions of the mobile phase with the analyte are of no significance. A solid substance can serve as a stationary phase on which the constituents to be separated can be absorbed. It is termed gas-solid chromatography (GSC) or simply gas chromatography. The use of a liquid as a stationary phase is preponderant for the analysis of organic compounds. It is termed as gas-liquid chromatography (GLC). The predominant separation principle is the partition of substances between the liquid stationary phase and the gaseous mobile phase. Both GSC and GLC are called GC in common terminology.

2. Instrumentation

A schematic gas chromatograph is illustrated in Fig. 2.27. The differences in gas chromatographic systems lie in the type of carrier gas used, in the sample injection system, as well as in the columns and detectors used.

3. Carrier Gases

Nitrogen is commonly used as a carrier gas, and the other inert gases, such as helium, argon and carbon dioxide are too. The choice of carrier gas is, in part, determined by the detector. The gas can be fed through a molecular sieve to remove traces of water. The flow of gas is ensured by the excess pressure of the gas cylinder, so that one can manage without a pump. The carrier flow must be kept constant for reproducible measurements. As long as one is working with a column isotherm, it is sufficient to set the supply pressure of the column using a two-stage reduction value. In the case of a method programmed by temperature, or in column switching, a flow regulator must be used in addition, on account of the changing liquid resistance with temperature.

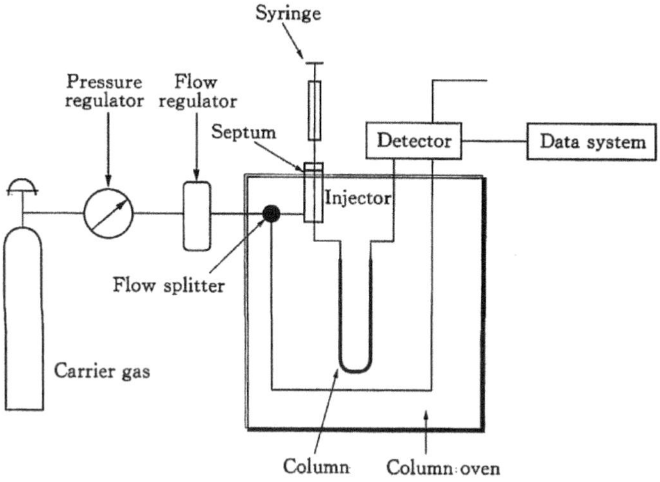

Fig. 2.27 Schematic Diagram of Gas Chromatograph

4. Sample Injection System

The sample can be injected straight into the carrier gas flow when analyzing gaseous samples. Liquid and solid samples must first be vaporized in a flash vaporizer port. The evaporator temperature is typically approximately 50℃ above the boiling point of the least volatile constituent of the sample mixture. The injection system can be heated and connects the flow of the carrier gas with the column. It is sealed from the outside with a silicone rubber diaphragm called the septum. The sample is injected into the system by puncturing the septum. The injection must be carried out in such a way that a plug of vapor is created. A slow injection causes broad pcaks and chromatograms difficult to evaluate.

5. Column Packings and Column Ovens

Separation columns may be manufactured from stainless steel, glass, or fused silica tubes. Fused silica is gaining increasing acceptance as a column material. The strength of columns is ensured by use of polyimide. The columns are stored in an oven for preliminary heating. A distinction is drawn between packed columns and capillary columns. In packed columns the stationary phase is set up on a granular support material. This is fed by a funnel into the column which has an internal diameter of between 3～8mm and is 1～3m long. Capillary columns contain no support material. Here the liquid stationary phase is discharged onto the wall of the capillaries. For example, the liquid coats the column via a plug of concentrated solution of the stationary phase which is pressed through the column at an even speed. Another way consists of evaporating the solvent using a vacuum pump from a column completely filled with a very well diluted solution. Capillaries can be up to 100m long. They have an internal diameter of between 0.15～1mm. Short packed columns can be stored straight or u-shaped in the column oven. Longer packed columns and capillaries are arranged as helices with a diameter of between 10～30cm. The column must be well-heated in the carrier gas flow before removing solvent residues or activating silica gel or molecular sieves.

6. Detectors

The thermal conductivity detector (TCD) and the flame ionization detector (FID) have gained acceptance as universal detectors in gas chromatography. Special detectors are also used for the detection of particular compounds.

2.10.5 High-performance Liquid Chromatogaphy (HPLC)

1. Introduction

The difference between classical LC and HPLC will be explored. For classical LC, large porous particles with d_p (average diameter of the particles) = 100～250μm are packed into columns with internal diameters of 1～5cm. Little pressure is required to permit slow solvent flow between these large particles. Pressure drops are of the order of 0.1 to 1 atmosphere. Flow rates are very slow (approximately 0.1mL/min or less), and separation times very long. If attempts are made to speed up the solvent velocity, say by pumping, column efficiency (already low) and resolution will decrease because of mass-transfer limitations in the deep pores and large interparticle channels. Because of their large surface areas or high ion-exchange capacities, though, the large porous packings exhibit large sample capacities, important in preparative chromatography. Large porous packings are available at a nominal price and can be packed into columns by simple procedures.

A decrease in d_p leads to an increase in column efficiency. These packing materials (in the range $30 \leqslant d_p \leqslant 75$μm), when packed into narrow columns, gave rise to larger back pressures than the classical LC columns. Thus, to assist in mobile-phase flow through the column, high-pressure pumps were required. This was the advent of HPLC. For analytical HPLC, flow rates of 0.5～5mL/min became typical, and pressure drops up to 300 atmospheres were obtained. On the other hand, column efficiency was increased 10 to 100 fold compared to classical LC, and separation times were decreased.

2. Instrumentation

The instruments of HPLC are composed solvent, pump, injector, column, detector and data system, as shown as Fig. 2.28. In normal phase chromatography, *n*-heptane is commonly used, while in the case of reversed-phase chromatography, methanol, acetonitrile, water and their mixed solvents in varied ratio can be used. Short pre-columns are often employed to protect the separation column or for pre-separation. The most important part of HPLC is the columns, which primarily determine the separation efficiency. One can use a column based on the property of compounds to be analyzed. There are many types of the detectors, but the one most widely used is the ultraviolet-visible light detector. It has very high sensitivity, however, it is not able to detect compounds that do not absorb UV light wave length≥200nm.

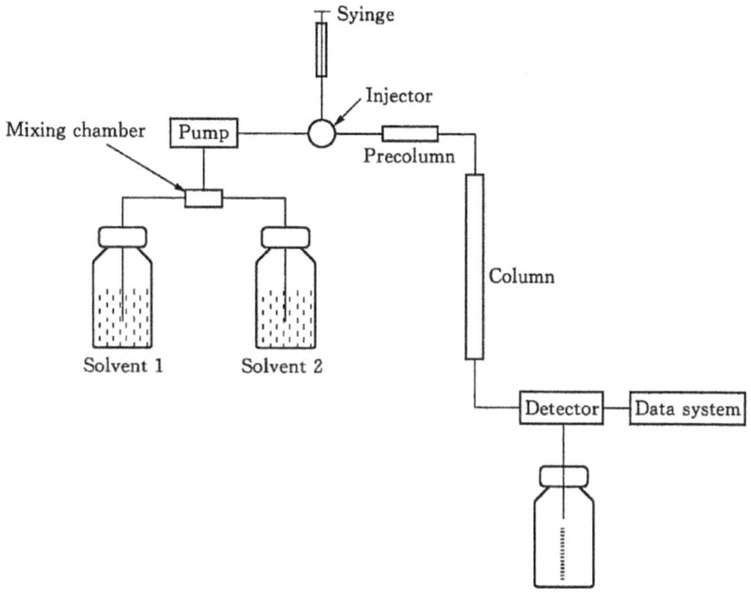

Fig. 2.28 Schematic Diagram of High Performance Liquid Chromatograph

2.11 Spectroscopic Identification of Organic Compound

Pure compounds can be obtained by the recrystallization, distillation and chromatographic techniques etc. The following problem demonstrates how to characterize their structures. This chapter will introduce three common spectroscopic methods for identifying organic compounds: namely, ultraviolet absorption spectrometry (UV), infrared absorption spectrometry (IR) and nuclear magnetic resonance spectrometry (NMR).

The different regions of the electromagnetic spectrum are shown in Fig. 2.29. Nearly every portion of the electromagnetic spectrum from the region of X-rays to those of microwaves and radio waves has been used in elucidating structures of atoms and molecules. A detailed description of the use of the various regions of the electromagnetic spectrum is provided in this section.

10^{19}Hz 10^{15}Hz 10^{13}Hz

Cosmic and γ-rays	X-rays	(UV) Vacuum ultraviolet	(UV) Near ultraviolet	Visible	(IR) Near infrared	(IR) Infrared	Microwave radio

0.1nm 200nm 400nm 800nm 2μm 50μm

Fig. 2.29 The Electromagnetic Spectrum

Line and band spectra are evidences of quantized energy states in matter and of quantized energy transfer between radiation and matter. The amount of energy transferred per photon is given by the expression.

$$E = hc/\lambda$$

where h (Planck's constant) $= 6.63 \times 10^{-34}$ joule seconds (J · s); c (the velocity of light) =

3×10^8 metre per seconds ($m \cdot s^{-1}$) and λ is the wavelength (in metres).

2.11.1 Ultraviolet and Visible Spectroscopy (UV)

1. Principle

When electromagnetic radiation in the UV and visible regions passes through a compound containing multiple bonds, a portion of the radiation is usually absorbed by the compound. Just how much of the radiation is absorbed depends on the wavelength of the radiation and the structure of the compound. The absorption of radiation is caused by the subtraction of energy from the radiation beam when electrons in orbitals of lower energy are excited into orbitals of higher energy.

Of the possible transitions in molecules, those that result in absorption of ultraviolet or visible radiation are the n to π^*, π to π^*, n to σ^*, and σ to σ^* transitions. The σ to σ^* transitions require the greatest energy, and generally occur in the vacuum-ultraviolet at wavelengths below about 150nm. Because the vacuum-ultraviolet region is not accessible in most ultraviolet-visible spectrophotometers, the transitions generally are not of use for routine analysis. Typically n to σ^* transitions occur in the long-wavelength end of the vacuum-ultraviolet region and the short-wavelength end of the near-ultraviolet region (150~250nm). Often an n to σ^* transition occurs when an organic molecule contains a heteroatom (N, O, S, F, Cl, Br, or I). An electron that is in a p orbital of the heteroatom is excited to a σ^* orbital of the molecule. The π to π^* and the n to π^* transitions occur in the near-ultraviolet and visible regions (180~700nm). They are most useful for analysis because those transitions occur in an easily observable spectral region.

Although an electronic transition may be energetically favourable the associated band is sometimes not observed, or if present in the spectrum it is of very low intensity. The n to π^* transition of carbonyl compounds represents a good example. Since the lone pair orbital is orientated orthogonally to the excited state orbital, the overlap between them is minimal. Good orbital overlap is needed if an electron is to move from one orbital to another, so it is not surprising that the intensity of the n to π^* bands of carbonyl compounds are very weak. Generally peaks that are associated with π to π^* transitions are highly absorptive (large absorptivities), thereby making possible quantitative assays at low concentrations.

Ultraviolet and visible spectra are easily measured on solutions, and the Beer-Lambert law is then used to relate the amount of electromagnetic radiation absorbed to the concentration of the sample in a suitable solvent and contained in a cell of known dimensions. This law is expressed in the form

$$A = \lg I_0/I = \varepsilon\, c\, l$$

where I_0 is the intensity of the incident beam, I is the intensity of the transmitted beam, after passage through a cell of length l cm, and c is the concentration of the sample in moles per litre (M), ε[mol/(L · cm)] is the molar absorptivity.

A typical UV absoption spectrum, that of 4-methylacetophenone, is shown in Fig. 2.30. It shows a broad absorption band in the region between 225~275nm. The absorption is at a maximum at 250nm. It is this wavelength that is usually reported in the chemical literature. In addition to reporting the wavelength of maximum absorption (λ_{max}), chemists often report another quantity that indicates the strength of the absorption, ε.

A group which 'gives rise' to an electronic absorption band is described as a *chromophore,* but in practice chemists restrict this description to structural units which are unsaturated or aromatic in nature. The wavelength of the absorptive maximum for a compound depends upon both the chromophore in the molecule and upon the environment of the chromophore. An *auxochrome* is a functional group on an absorbing molecule or ion that does not itself absorb radiation in the ultraviolet-visible region but can cause the absorptive maxium of the molecule to change wavelengths. Generally auxochromes are functional groups, such as NH, OH, SH, and halogens that contain unshared electrons. The presence of an auxochrome in a molecule that contains a chromophore usually causes the absorptive maximum to shift to a longer wavelength (lower energy). That is a *bathochromic* or *red shift.* A *hypsochromic shift* is to a shorter wavelength. If the absorptivity of a chromophore increases with the addition of a substituent to the molecule, the increased absorbance is a *hyperchromic shift.* Hyperchromism is often caused by increased conjugation of single and double bonds within the molecule. A decrease in absorbance owing to the addition of a substituent to a molecule is a *hypochromic shift.*

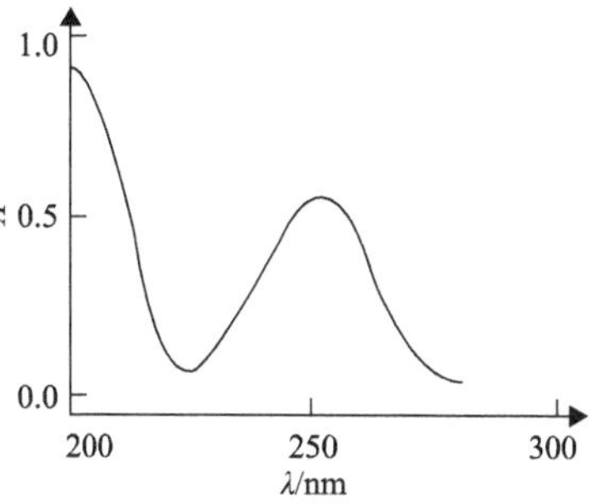

Fig. 2.30 The UV Absorption Spectrum of 4-Methylacetophenone

Because different chromophores have uv-visible absorptive maxima at different wavelengths, it sometimes is possible to identify the absorbing molecule by comparing the wavelength of the absorptive maximum from the spectrum of a sample with the wavelengths of the absorptive maxima of known substances. It usually is not safe to conclude, from the uv-visible spectrum alone, that an unknown substance even contains a particular chromophore. If the unknown substance is known to be one of a limited number of compounds, however, and if all of those compounds have absorptive maxima that differ from each other by at least 10nm, then the spectrum of the sample can be used for qualitative analysis.

2. Instrumentation and Cell Design

The working range for most spectrometers is from 190~750nm. The light from 190~450nm is provided by a deuterium discharge lamp and the remaining wavelengths by a tungsten source. The light is split into two beams, one of which passes through the cell containing the sample in solution, and the other through a matched cell containing the solvent only. Transmitted light from both beams is then compared automatically and the date are plotted. Quartz cells, transparent across the whole range, are employed. The normal operational lower limit of 190nm is set, since below this wavelength air and solvents increasingly absorb ultraviolet radiation.

When making absorbance measurements, the usual procedure is the following:

(1) Adjust the wavelength.

(2) With the shutter closed (no radiation striking the detector), use the dark current control to set the instrument to read 0% T.

(3) With the blank solution in the path of the EMR, open the shutter and adjust the slit width or amplification from the detector to give a 100% T reading. Close the shutter.

(4) With the sample in the path of the EMR, open the shutter and read the percent transmittance, absorbance, or computer-calculated concentration of the sample.

2.11.2 Infrared Spectroscopy (IR)

1. Principle

As implied by the name, infrared absorption spectroscopy is the measurement of the amount of radiation absorbed by compounds within the infrared region (between the visible and microwave regions) of the electromagnetic spectrum. The infrared region consists of radiation with wavelengths between 2.5～15μm correspond to frequencies between 4000～650cm^{-1}. The positions of infrared bands are designated in frequency (cm^{-1}) units in most books, and the illustrative spectra have a horizontal axis that is linear in frequency. The wavelength and frequency scales have a reciprocal relationship, and conversion from one to the other is very simple: $\bar{\nu} = 1/\lambda\,(\text{cm}^{-1})$. Infrared spectrometry provides information on functional groups for example, NH_2, COOH, OH, amide groups (C=O)NH_2, triple bonds (C≡C, C≡N), aryl rings, carbonyl groups (C=O) and double bonds (C=C, C=N, N=N) present in a compound.

Two types of molecular vibrations, stretching and bending, are responsible for most of the peaks of importance in identification of organic compounds. A stretching vibration is a rhythmical movement along the bond axis such that the inter-atomic distance is increasing or decreasing. A bending vibration may consist of a change in bond angle between bonds with a common atom or the movement of a group of atom with respect to the remainder of the molecule without movement of atoms in the group with respect to one another.

The vibrational spectra appear as bands rather than lines because a single energy change is accompanied by a number of rotational energy changes. Therefore, IR spectrometry is also called vibration-rotation spectroscopy. The wave number of absorption depends on the relative masses of the atoms, the force constants of the bonds, and the geometry of the atoms. Clearly shorter and stronger bonds have their stretching vibrations at the higher energy end of the IR spectrum than the longer and weaker bonds. For example, the adsorption wave number of C≡C, C≡N triple bonds and C=O, C=N, C=C, double bonds are the region of 2300～2000cm^{-1} and 1900～1500cm^{-1} respectively. Similarly, bonds to light atoms (e.g. hydrogen), vibrate at higher energy than bonds to heavier atoms. The intensity of the absorption band can be reported in terms of either transmittance (T) or absorbance (A). The former is more useful. Transmittance is the ratio of the intensity of the absorbed beam (I) divided by the intensity of the incident beam (I_0):

$$T = I/I_0$$

Peak intensity can also be reported as absorbance (A), where A is the lg of the inverse of transmittance.

$$A = \lg(1/T)$$

In practice, peak intensities are reported in a less quantitative fashion, the peaks are described simply in terms of strong (s) peaks, medium (m) peaks, weak (w) peaks.

Theoretically, a very simple molecule can give an extremely complex spectrum. However, it is true that certain groups of atoms give rise to bands at or near the same wave number regardless of the structure of the rest of the molecule. For example, C═O absorbs at 1900～1600cm^{-1} and these characteristic bands permit the chemist to obtain useful functional group information by simple inspection and reference to generalized charts of characteristic group wave numbers. In conclusion, it is important that the functional group information can be obtained from IR spectrum.

2. Instrumentation

The basic layout of an IR spectrometer is the same as for an UV spectrometer, except that all components must now match the different energy range of electromagnetic radiation. Very few substances are transparent over the whole of the IR range, but sodium and potassium chloride, and sodium and potassium bromide are most common. The cells used for obtaining IR spectra in solution typically have NaCl windows and liquids can be examined as films on NaCl plates. Solution spectra are generally obtained in chloroform or carbon tetrachloride but this leads to loss of information at longer wavelengths where there is considerable absorption of energy by the solvent. Alternatively, organic solids may be examined as a mull (fine suspensions) in heavy oils. The oils absorb infrared radiation but only in well defined regions of the IR spectrum. Solids may also be examined as dispersions in compressed KBr or KCl discs. To a first approximation, the absorption frequencies due to the important IR chromophores are the same in solid and liquid states.

3. Characteristic Band For Various Organic Compounds

The IR spectrum of a molecule is composed of a lot of bands, the position, shape and intensity of which are influenced strongly by small changes in molecular structures. Fortunately, the characteristic bands of functional groups appearing in the regions 4000～1500cm^{-1}, can be simply identified, although these bands are also influenced by the changes of the molecular structure. The useful wave number of important functional group is summarized as follows.

1) The Region of 4000～3000cm^{-1}

The OH groups, including R—OH (alcohol, strong), Ar—OH (phenol, strong) and RC(═O)—OH (carboxylic acid, strong); the NH groups, including RC(═O)—NHR^1 (Amide, strong), Ar—NH—R^2 (Arylamine, medium), R—NH—R^1 (Alkylamine, weak); and the C—H connected to triple bond (C≡C—H, medium) and C—H connected to double bond (C═C—H, weak) appear in this region.

2) The Region of 3000～2800cm^{-1}

The saturated C—H bonds vibrate in this area.

3) The Region of 2800～2700cm^{-1}

The Fermi resonance of the aldehyde group [R—C(=O)H] appears at 2720cm^{-1} as a weak band.

4) The Region of 2700～2500cm^{-1}

A weak band representing the thiol group (SH) appeared at this area.

5) The Region of 2400～1900cm^{-1}

The triple bonds such as C≡C (weak), C≡N (weak), N≡N (weak) and the C=C=C (weak), N=C=O (strong), N=C=S (strong) bonds appeared in area.

6) The Region of 1900～1600cm^{-1}

The compounds bearing C=O groups such as acyl, chloride, anhydride, ester, ketone, aldehyde, carboxylic acid, amide have strong absorption at this area. Double bonds such as C=C, C=N and N=N also appeared in this area with a weak absorption. Furthermore, the bending vibration of N—H also absorbs the frequency of this area.

7) The Region of 1600～1500cm^{-1}

The aryl ring and NO_2 groups have characteristic bands at this area.

The data mentioned above can simply be summarized in Fig. 2.31.

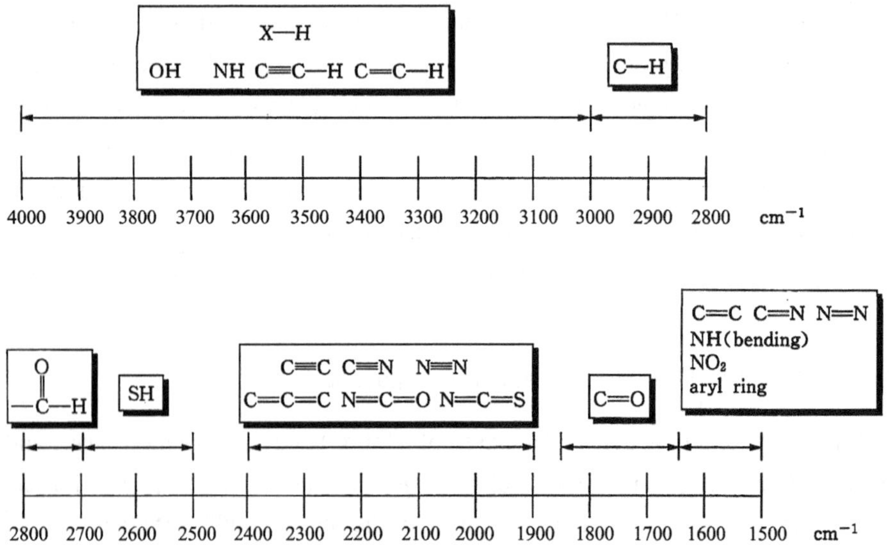

Fig. 2.31　Characteristic functional group absorption

2.11.3 Nuclear Magnetic Resonance Spectroscopy (NMR)

1. Principle

Many atomic nuclei have the property of nuclear spin. When placed between the poles of a magnet, the axis of rotation of the spinning nuclei precess around the axis of the field. This precession can be detected by irradiation with energy in the radiofrequency region of the spectrum. Nuclear Magnetic Resonance (NMR) spectrometry reveals many details of the structure of an organic compound, particularly the interrelated connectivity of its hydrogen and carbon atoms.

All nuclei with an odd mass number are magnetic, as are even mass numbered nuclei with odd numbers of protons and neutrons. It follows that ^{1}H, ^{13}C, ^{19}F, ^{31}P and ^{17}O are magnetic and may generate NMR spectra, whereas nuclei such as ^{12}C, ^{16}O, ^{34}S cannot. If a magnetic nucleus is placed in a magnetic field, it can take up any one of $2I + 1$ orientations (I is the nuclear quantum number). For nuclei with $I = 1/2$, there are just 2 permissible orientations. If the spin is aligned (parallel) to the applied magnetic field, the nucleus is regarded as having a lower energy, $m = 1/2$. The $m = -1/2$ level is then said to be spin opposed or antiparalled to the applied field. The difference in energy between the two spin states is given by

$$\Delta E = h\gamma/2\pi \cdot H_0 \tag{1}$$

where γ is the gyromagnetic ratio having a characteristic value for each nucleus, H_0 is the applied field strength and h is Planck's constant. This equation simply states that ΔE is proportional to magnetic field intensity H_0.

Once two energy levers for the proton have been established, it is possible to introduce energy in the form of radio-frequency radiation (v_0) to effect a transition between these energy levels in a stationary magnetic field of given strength H_0. The energy of radio-frequency radiation can be expressed by

$$\Delta E = hv_0 \tag{2}$$

When the energy of the electromagnetic wave is equal to the energy gap of two levels, energy will be absorbed by the proton. This phenomenon of excitation from the lower level to high level is called nuclear magnetic resonance. Therefore from equation (1) and (2) the resonance frequency of proton is given by

$$v = \gamma/2\pi \cdot H_0$$

In reporting the results of an NMR spectrum, several features of the spectrum are reported: the area under each peak or the integral, the positions of each peak or the chemical shift (δ), and the fine structure of each peak, the multiplicity and coupling constant (J).

One of the most useful features of NMR is that the area under each peak is directly proportional to the number of nuclei in the particular chemical environment. The area under peak is referred to as the integral and is used to determine the numbers of nuclei at chemically different sites in a molecule. Consequently, in the ^{1}H NMR spectrum of ethanol, CH_3CH_2OH, three peaks would be detected for the three chemical different hydrogens, the area under each peak would integrate for a ratio of 3 : 2 : 1. The integral is generally shown as a stepped line above each peak or in numerical form near to the peak.

Nuclei in different chemical environment will experience slightly different magnetic fields and their signals will therefore be at slightly different frequencies. To avoid working with small numbers and to overcome the fact that the resonance frequency is dependent on the external magnetic field, a dimensionless parameter is utilized, the chemical shift (δ). The chemical shift is given as follows and quoted in parts per million (ppm).

$$\delta = (V_{\text{sample}} - V_{\text{reference}}) \times 10^6 / \text{carrier frequency}$$

V_{sample}: resonance frequency of nucleus in sample (Hz)

$V_{\text{reference}}$: resonance frequency of nucleus in a reference compound (Hz)

Carrier frequency: operating frequency of spectrometer for particular isotope (MHz)

In many instances, NMR peaks have fine structure. This is due to the interaction between nuclei spins (which are nuclear magnets) within the molecule. The number of lines, or multiplicity, can be interpreted to determine the number of interacting spins within the molecule. The $n + 1$ rule and Pascal's triangle may be used to predict the number of lines and the relative intensities of lines in a multiplet. The $n + 1$ rule simply states that when a nucleus is coupled to n other nuclei (which must all be equivalent to each other), then the peak for the observed nucleus will be split in to $n + 1$ lines, with intensities given by Pascal's triangle. The size of the separation within the multiplet, the coupling constant, relates to the energy of interaction which can in turn be related to the number of intervening bonds and angles between these.

2. Instrumentation

The first commercial NMR spectrometer, operated at 30MHz frequency with permanent magnets, appeared in 1953. Now, 500~750MHz instruments are common. All of the instruments above 100MHz are based on helium-cooled super-conducting magnets operated in the pulsed FT mode. The other basic requirements besides high field are frequency-field stability, field homogeneity, and a computer interface. The simplied diagram of contemporary NMR spectrometer is shown in Fig. 2.32.

In the NMR experiment, the sample is dissolved in deuterated solvent containing 0.1% TMS (tetramethylsilane) and placed into a 5mm tube. The tube is then placed into the probe, which contains the transmitter and receiver coils and a spinner to spin the tube about its vertical axis in order to average out field inhomogeneities. The most used common deuterated solvent is $CDCl_3$. If the compound detected is difficult to dissolve in $CDCl_3$, then DMSO-d_6 will be a candidate. The spectrum obtained either by continuous-wave (CW) scan or pulse FT at constant magnetic field is shown as a series of peaks whose areas are proportional to the number of protons they represent. Peak areas are measured by an electronic integrator. A proton count from the integration is useful to determine or confirm molecular formula, detect hidden peaks, determine sample purity, and do quantitative analysis. Peak positions (chemical shift) are measured in frequency units from a reference peak.

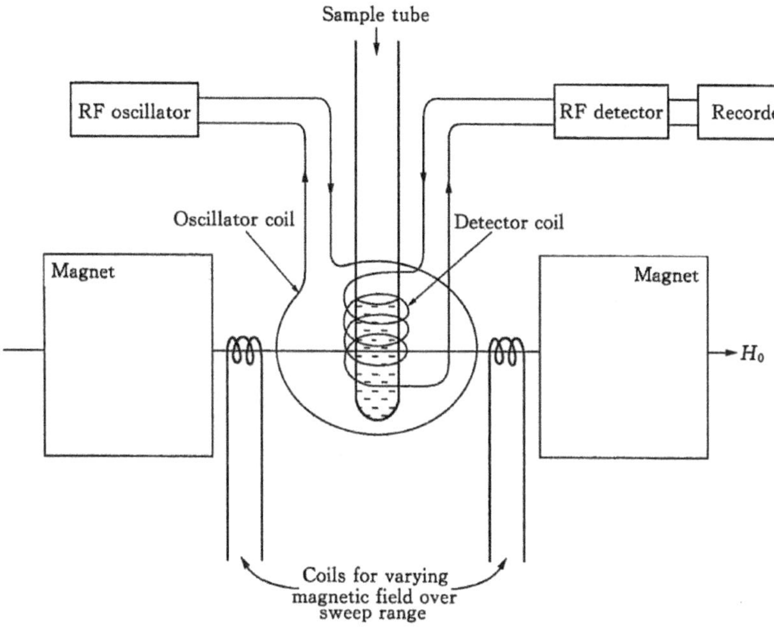

Fig. 2.32 Simplied Diagram of Contemporary NMR Spectrometer

3. ^{1}H NMR Data For Various Organic Compounds

Any effect which alters the density or spatial distribution of electrons around a ^{1}H nucleus will alter its chemical shift. The chemical shift reflects the molecular structure and it can therefore be used to obtain structural information. Table 2.2 and 2.3 give the characteristic shifts for ^{1}H nuclci in organic compounds.

Table 2.2 Typical chemical shift values

Compounds	δ(ppm)	Compounds	δ(ppm)
CH_4	0.23	$CH_2{=}CH_2$	5.25
CH_3CH_3	0.86	Benzene	7.26
CH_3Cl	3.05	CH_3CHO	2.20(CH_3), 9.80(CHO)
CH_2Cl_2	5.33		
$CHCl_3$	7.27		

Table 2.3 Typical ^{1}H chemical shift ranges

Group	δ(ppm)
Tetramethylsilane (TMS)	0
CH_3 groups attached to sp^3 hybridized carbon atoms	0.8~1.2
CH_3O	3.5~4.3
CH_3N	2.0~3.0
$CH_3(C{=}O)$	2.0~2.3

Continued

Group	δ (ppm)
CH_2 groups attached to sp^3 hybridized carbon atoms	1.0~1.5
CH groups attached to sp^3 hybridized carbon atoms	1.2~1.8
C≡CH	2~3
Olefinic protons	5~8
Aromatic protons	6~9
Aldehyde protons	9~10

Note that the protons of OH, NH_2, (C═O) NH_2 have no characteristic chemical shift ranges. Their values vary from the experimental conditions such as temperature, concentration and so on. Fortunately, they can be identified by *in-situ* exchange with D_2O, which causes the peaks to disappear from the spectrum.

Basic ^1H acquisition and processing see section 2.11.3 in Chinese.

Chapter 3 Experiments

3.1 Preparation of Cyclohexene

Principle

Cyclohexene is usually prepared by cyclohexanol dehydration in an acid catalyzed reaction using strong, concentrated mineral acid, such as sulfuric acid or phosphoric acid. Since sulfuric acid often causes extensive charring in this reaction, phosphoric acid, which is comparatively free of this problem, will be used.

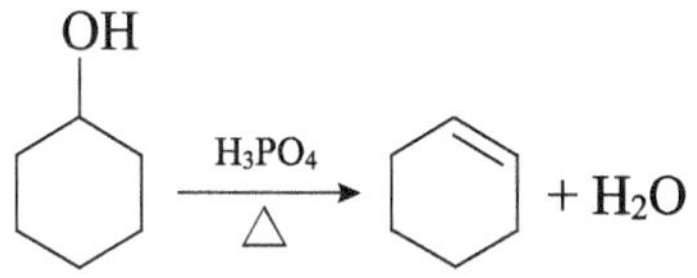

Apparatus and Materials

Apparatus fractional distillation			
Materials			
cyclohexanol	10.4mL (10g, 0.1mol)	b.p.116℃	$d = 0.9642^{20/4}$ g/mL
85% phosphoric acid	4mL		
sodium chloride	1g		
5% aqueous sodium carbonate solution			
anhydrous calcium chloride			

Time 4h

Procedure

(1) Pour 10.4mL (10g, 0.10mol) of cyclohexanol and 4mL of 85% phosphoric acid into a 50mL round-bottom flask. Mix the solution thoroughly by swirling the flask and add several boiling stones.

(2) Assemble a fractional distillation apparatus[1] as illustrated in Fig. 2.7, then use a short fractional column and a 50mL Erlenmeyer flask as the receiving flask. Immerse the receiving flask up to its neck in an ice-water bath to minimize the escape of cyclohexene vapors into the laboratory.

(3) Heat the reaction mixture with an asbestos pad until the products begin to boil. The temperature of the distilling vapor must not exceed 90℃[2]. The collected liquid in the receiving

flask is a mixture of cyclohexene and water.

(4) When only a few milliliters of residue remain in the flask, stop the distillation.

(5) Add 1g solid sodium chloride to the distillate in the receiving flask to saturate the water layer, and shake the flask gently[3].

(6) Decant the distillate into a separatory funnel, add 3~4mL of 5% aqueous sodium carbonate solution (or 0.5mL of 20% aqueous sodium hydroxide solution[4]) and shake the separatory funnel gently until no more gas is evolved when the funnel is vented.

(7) Draw off the lower aqueous layer and then pour the upper layer (crude cyclohexene) through the neck of the separatory funnel into a dry small Erlenmeyer flask. Add about 1~2g of anhydrous calcium chloride to the flask and swirl the mixture occasionally until the solution becomes clear[5].

(8) Decant the dry cyclohexene solution into a dry 50mL of round-bottom flask. Add several boiling stones and distill it with a water bath[6]. Use a weighted 50mL round-bottom flask submerged up to its neck in an ice-water bath as the receiver.

(9) Collect the fraction that boils between 80~85℃ in the weighted flask, then calculate the percentage yield.

Pure cyclohexene is a colorless liquid, b.p.82.98℃, n_D^{20} 1.4465, d_4^{20} 0.808.

Brief Summary

1. Objectives

(1) Study the principle and method of preparing cyclohexene by acid-catalyzed dehydration of cyclohexanol.

(2) Master the techniques of fractional distillation and simple distillation with a water bath.

2. Notes

[1] The equilibrium will be shifted in favor of the product, cyclohexene, by distilling it from the reaction mixture while it is being formed.

[2] The cyclohexene (b.p.83℃) will co-distill with the water that is formed (b.p.70.8℃), and the starting material, cyclohexanol, also co-distills with the water (b.p.97.8℃), so the distillation must be done carefully, not allowing the temperature to rise above 90℃.

[3] The salt minimizes the solubility of the organic product in the aqueous layer.

[4] As a small amount of phosphoric acid co-distills with the products, it must be removed by washing with aqueous sodium carbonate solution.

[5] The solution should become clear, and if it is still cloudy, add an additional 0.5g of drying agent, swirl and last for an additional 10min.

[6] Make sure that all the glassware you will use for distilling is clean and dry. Dry all the glassware in an oven (110℃) for 10min.

IR Spectrum

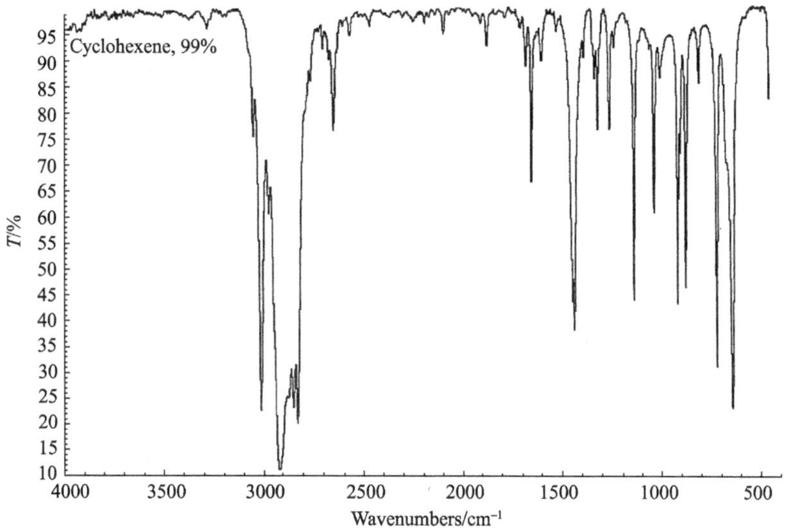

Questions

(1) Why must the temperature on the top of the fractional column during the reaction period be controlled?

(2) What is the purpose of adding salt before the layers are neutralized and separated?

(3) Why must any acid be neutralized with sodium carbonate before the final distillation of cyclohexene?

3.2 Preparation of 1-Bromobutane

Principle

1-Bromobutane can be easily prepared by allowing 1-butanol to react with sodium bromide and concentrated sulfuric acid.

Main reactions

$$NaBr + H_2SO_4 \longrightarrow HBr + NaHSO_4$$

$$n\text{-}C_4H_9OH + HBr \xrightleftharpoons{\triangle} n\text{-}C_4H_9Br + H_2O$$

Secondary reactions

$$CH_3CH_2CH_2CH_2OH \xrightarrow[\triangle]{H_2SO_4} CH_3CH_2CH{=}CH_2 + CH_3CH{=}CHCH_3$$

$$2CH_3CH_2CH_2CH_2OH \xrightarrow[\triangle]{H_2SO_4} CH_3CH_2CH_2CH_2OCH_2CH_2CH_2CH_3$$

Apparatus and Materials

Apparatus reflux with a gas trap			
Meterials			
1-butanol	9.3mL (7.4g, 0.12mol)	b.p.117.2℃	$d = 0.8098^{20/4}$ g/mL
sodium bromide	12.5g (0.12mol)		
concentrated sulfuric acid	14.5mL (0.27mol)		$d = 1.841^{20/4}$ g/mL
10% aqueous sodium hydroxide			
anhydrous calcium chloride			

Time 5h

Procedure

(1) Place 12.5g (0.12mol) of sodium bromide in a 100mL round-bottom flask, add 12mL of water and 9.3mL (7.4g, 0.1mol) of 1-butanol, shake the flask frequently[1].

(2) Cool down the mixture in the ice-water bath and slowly add 14.5mL of concentrated sulfuric acid with continuous swirling. Add several boiling stones to the mixture.

(3) With the help of a rubber stopper, connect the condenser to a gas trap made with an inverted funnel in the beaker, set up a reflux apparatus, then place some water and sodium hydroxide pellets in the beaker.

(4) Heat the mixture with an asbestos pad until the mixture begins to reflux gently. Reflux the solution for 30min. During the reaction period, the flask should be shaken frequently[1].

(5) Turn off the heating source and cool the mixture down. Remove the condenser with the gas trap. Assemble a simple distillation apparatus.

(6) Distill the mixture until the distillate appears to be clear[2].

(7) Transfer the distillate to a separatory funnel, add 15mL of water to it and wash the mixture. Allow the layers to separate.

(8) Remove the organic layer and save it in another dry separatory funnel. (Which layer contains the 1-bromobutane?)[3]

(9) Wash the organic layer with 6mL of cold concentrated sulfuric acid[4]. Let the mixture stand for a few minutes until the two layers are completely separated.

(10) Save the organic layer. Wash the organic layer with 15mL of water again, then with 15mL of 10% NaOH (to remove traces of acid) and finally with 15mL of water (to remove salts and sodium hydroxide). Check the pH of the water layer with pH paper. It should be close to 7, if not, repeat the water wash[5].

(11) Dry the crude 1-bromobutane using a small amount of anhydrous calcium chloride in a small Erlenmeyer flask until the liquid is clear.

(12) Decant the clear liquid into a dry distilling flask. distill and collect the fraction that boils between 99～103℃. Weigh the product and calculate the percentage yield[6].

Pure 1-bromobutane is a colorless liquid, b.p.101.6℃, d_4^{20} 1.2758, n_D^{20} 1.4401.

Brief Summary

1. Objectives

(1) Study the principle and method of preparing 1-bromobutane from 1-butanol by treatment with sodium bromide and concentrated sulfuric acid.

(2) Learn the technique of reflux with a gas trap apparatus and washing.

2. Notes

[1] It is important to shake the flask frequently during the feed and the reaction, if not, the yield of the reaction will decrease.

[2] Check the miscibility in water by adding one drop of distillate to 0.5mL of water in a test tube.

[3] Be careful to save the organic layer.

[4] Sulfuric acid is used to get rid of unreacted 1-butanol and the by-products 1-butene, 2-butene and dibutyl ether from crude 1-bromobutane.

[5] It is important to keep all the layers from different washes clearly labeled until the end of the experiment.

[6] Estimated yield is about 52%.

IR Spectrum

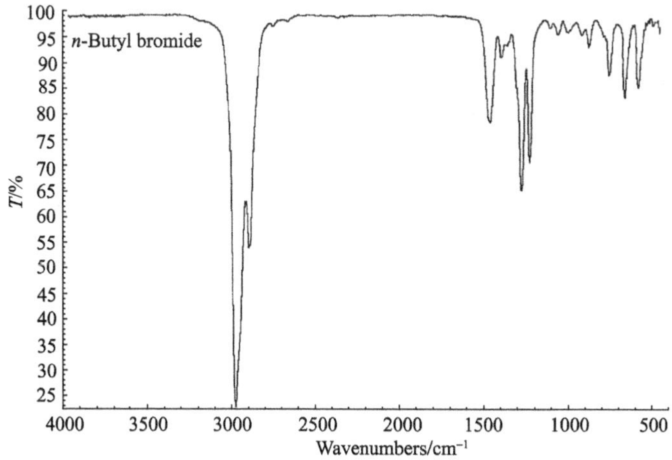

Questions

(1) Sulfuric acid plays several roles in the reactions, can you describe them?

(2) Dibutyl ether, 1-butene and 2-butene can be obtained as by-products in the reactions, explain how to remove them by sulfuric acid in the form of equations.

(3) Why must the crude 1-bromobutane be dried carefully with anhydrous calcium chloride prior to the final distillation?

(4) Why must the organic layer be washed with water before washing with 10% NaOH (to remove trace acid) in the work-up procedure for 1-bromobutane?

3.3 Preparation of Triphenylmethanol

Principle

Triphenylmethanol will be prepared by the following Grignard reaction.

Method 1

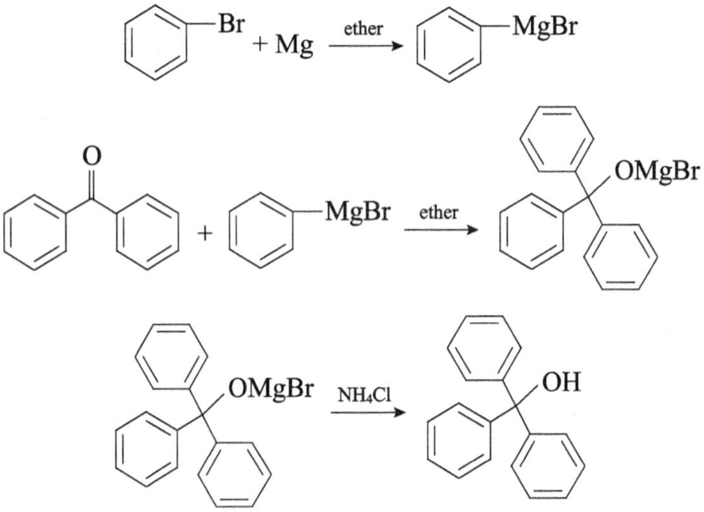

Method 2

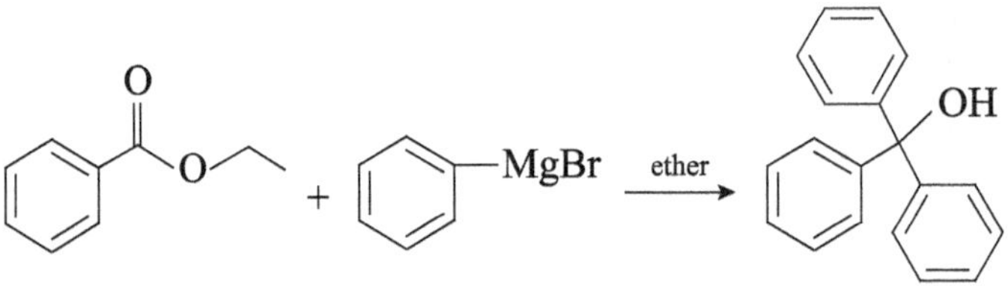

Secondary reaction

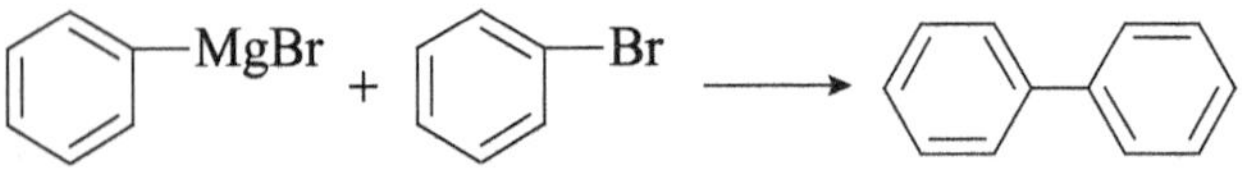

Apparatus and Materials

Apparatus　mechanical stirrer with a reflux condenser and a dropping funnel

Materials

bromobenzene	5.3mL (7.85g, 0.05mol)	b.p.156℃
	$d = 1.495^{20/4}$ g/mL	
anhydrous diethyl ether	20mL	b.p.34.5℃
	$d = 0.7138^{20/4}$ g/mL	
Magnesium turning or ribbon	1.4g (0.055mol)	

diphenyl methanone	9g (0.05mol) $d = 1.0975^{20/4}$ g/mL	m.p.49℃
ethyl benzoate	1.4mL (1.5g, 0.01mol) $d = 1.0458^{20/4}$ g/mL	b.p.213℃
iodine crystal	a small piece	
saturated ammonium chloride solution	40mL	
petroleum ether (b.p.60～90℃)	20mL	

Time 7～8h

Procedure

Method 1

(1) Fit a clean, dry 250mL of three neck round-bottom flask equipped with a stirring machine, a dry reflux condenser and a dropping funnel[1].

(2) Prepare two dry tubes containing anhydrous calcium chloride. Fit these to the top of the condenser and dropping funnel. Attach the water hoses to the condenser and turn on the cooling water.

(3) Add 1.4g (0.055mol) of magnesium turnings[2] and a small iodine crystal to the flask[3].

(4) Prepare a solution of bromobenzene in diethyl ether by dissolving 5.3mL (0.05mol) of bromobenzene in 20mL of anhydrous diethyl ether, and pour it into the dropping funnel (with the stopcock closed). Add 4～5mL of this solution, dropwise, to the reaction flask.

(5) Place the flask in a warm-water bath (45～50℃) and the diethyl ether will begin to boil. The brownish solution should soon turn colorless[4]. Then remove it from the warm-water bath.

(6) Begin stirring the reaction mixture and add the rest bromobenzene/ether solution from the dropping funnel at a speed that maintains a moderate reflux[5].

(7) When all the bromobenzene has been added and the reaction stops refluxing spontaneously, heat the reaction in the warm-water bath (45～50℃) for 30min.

(8) Cool the flask containing the phenylmagnesium bromide with an ice-water bath. Place a solution made from 9g (0.05mol) of diphenyl methanone and 25mL of anhydrous diethyl ether in the dropping funnel, and slowly add it dropwise, while stirring the solution, to the phenylmagnesium bromide solution.

(9) After the addition is complete, reflux the mixture for 30min, using a warm-water bath at 45～50℃.

(10) Place the reaction flask in an ice-water bath. With the aid of the dropping funnel, 40mL of saturated ammonium chloride solution is added while stirring[6].

(11) Set up a simple distillation apparatus using a water bath as the heat source and slowly distill the diethyl ether.

(12) Add 20mL of low-boiling petroleum ether (b.p.60~90℃) to the reaction flask and stir the crude product for several minutes[7].

(13) Cool the flask in an ice-water bath and collect the crude product by vacuum filtration.

(14) Recrystallize the crude triphenylmethanol using a mixed solvent of two parts of petroleum ether (60~90℃) and one part of ethanol (95%).

(15) Dry the solid, determine the melting point and calculate the percentage yield[8].

Pure triphenylmethanol is a white crystal, m.p.164.2℃.

Method 2

(1) Fit a dry 100mL three neck round-bottom flask equipped with a dry reflux condenser and a dropping funnel. Place drying tubes on both the dropping funnel and the condenser[1].

(2) Add 0.5g (0.02mol) of magnesium turnings[2] and a small iodine crystal[3] into the flask.

(3) Dissolve 2.1mL (0.02mol) of bromobenzene in 10mL of anhydrous diethyl ether, stir the solution and pour it into the dropping funnel (with the stopcock closed). Add dropwise 2~3mL of this solution to the reaction flask[9].

(4) Once the reaction has begun, as evidenced by the brownish solution soon turning colorless and the bubbling action in the absence of heat, add the remaining bromobenzene solution dropwise from the dropping funnel at a speed that maintains a moderate reflux[5].

(5) After the addition is complete, heat the mixture under reflux gently for 30min on a warm-water bath (45~50℃).

(6) Cool down the reaction mixture to room temperature, place a solution made from 1.4mL (1.5g 0.01mol) ethyl benzoate and 5mL of anhydrous diethyl ether in the dropping funnel and begin dropwise addition of the solution to the phenylmagnesium bromide solution.

(7) After the addition is complete, reflux the mixture with a warm-water bath for 30min.

(8) Cool the flask with a cool-water bath, slowly add the solution containing 2.5g of ammonium chloride and 20mL of water from the dropping funnel while stirring[6].

(9) Distill the diethyl ether on a water bath until crystals of triphenylmethanol begin to occur. Add 15mL of petroleum ether (b.p.60~90℃)[7] to the reaction flask and stir the crude product for a few minutes.

(10) Complete the crystallization process in an ice-water bath, filter, and collect the product by vacuum filtration.

(11) Recrystallize the crude triphenylmethanol using the same method as described in method 1.

(12) Dry the solid, determine the melting point and calculate the percentage yield[10].

Pure triphenylmethanol is a white crystal, m.p.164.2℃.

Brief Summary

1. Objectives

(1) Study the principle and method of preparing of triphenylmethanol by the Grignard reaction.

(2) Learn the techniques of stirring, reflux, extraction, distillation and recrystallization.

2. Notes

[1] Make sure that all your glassware and reagents are thoroughly dry before conducting the experiment. It is critical to maintain completely dry conditions throughout the formation and reaction of the Grignard reagent.

[2] Bright magnesium ribbon can be used instead of magnesium turning. Scrape both side of the ribbon with an abrasive to remove any oxide, cut the ribbon into small pieces (approx. 5mm).

[3] Add a small crystal of iodine and promote the heterogeneous reaction at the surface of the magnesium sometimes.

[4] It indicates that the reaction has begun.

[5] The rate of addition should be adjusted so that the reflux ring in the water cooled condenser is no more than half-way up the inner tube. If the reaction becomes too vigorous, the more biphenyl by-product will form.

[6] The role of the saturated ammonium chloride solution is to decompose the additional product, forming the crude triphenylmethanol.

[7] The crude product contains the desired triphenylmethanol and also the biphenyl by-product. Most of the biphenyl can be removed by dissolving in the petroleum.

[8] You will obtain 4～5g of products, the estimated yield is 35%.

[9] It may be necessary to warm the flask in a beaker of warm water (45～50℃) for a few minutes to initiate the reaction.

[10] The estimated yield is 48% in this experiment.

IR Spectrum

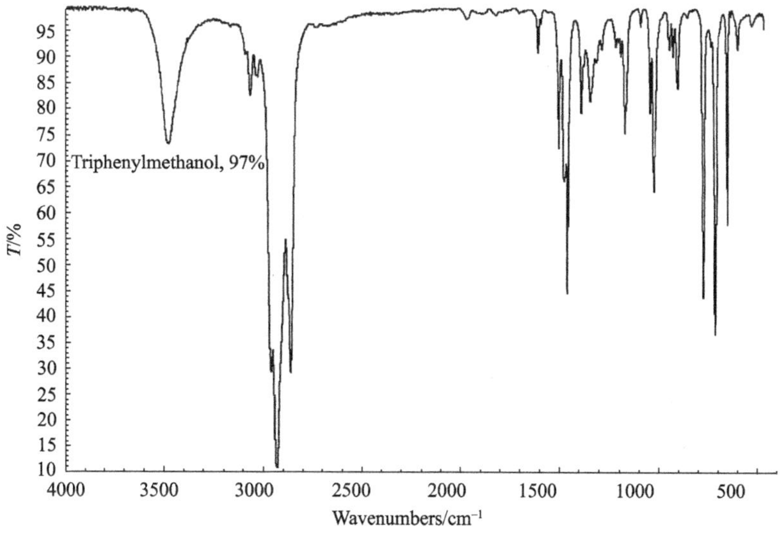

Questions

(1) In the preparation of the Grignard reagent, anhydrous conditions must be remained during the reaction. What will happen if water gets into the system?

(2) Provide methods for preparing the following compounds by the Grignard method.

(a) $CH_3CH_2CH(OH)CH_3$　　(b) $CH_3CH_2CH_2C(=O)OH$

(c) 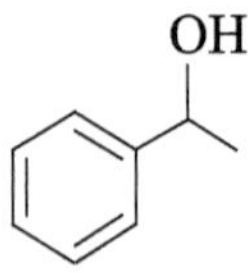　　(d) 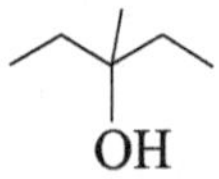

3.4 Preparation of Dibutyl Ether

Principle

Ethers are usually important organic solvents in organic synthesis as they can dissolve most organic chemicals. Normally there are two methods to prepare an ether: intermolecular dehydration of an alcohol catalyzed by concentrated acids and the Williamson synthesis from the reaction of an alkali metal salt of alkanolate with a primary alkyl halide. There are two facts that should be keep in mind: ①the dehydration method is usually performed for the preparation of a symmetric ether with a low boiling point; ②the dehydration catalyzed by concentrated acid is an equilibrium and some measures should be taken to shift the equilibrium reaction to right, such as increasing the amount of one of the reactants or removal of one of the products from the reaction mixture. In the present experiment, concentrated sulfuric acid is employed to achieve the intermolecular dehydration of 1-butanol and formation of dibutyl ether while water, one of the products, is removed from the reaction mixture with a water separator. The reaction is shown below:

$$2CH_3CH_2CH_2CH_2OH \xrightleftharpoons{H_2SO_4,\ 134\sim135℃} CH_3CH_2CH_2CH_2OCH_2CH_2CH_2CH_3 + H_2O$$

The reaction temperature should be carefully controlled, as a side reaction, an elimination reaction to produce 1-butene, will take place in case the reaction temperature is higher than 135℃.

$$CH_3CH_2CH_2CH_2OH \xrightleftharpoons[>135℃]{H_2SO_4} C_4H_8 + H_2O$$

Apparatus and Materials

Apparatus	reflux with a water segregator
Materials	

1-butanol	25g (31mL, 0.34mol)	b.p.117.2℃	$d = 0.8098^{20/4}$ g/mL
conc.sulfuric acid	8g (4.5mL)		$d = 1.841^{20/4}$ g/mL
anhydrous calcium chloride			

Time 5h

Procedure

(1) Place 25g (31mL, 0.34mol) of 1-butanol and about 8g (4.5mL) concentrated sulfuric acid into a 100mL two-neck flask. Shake or swirl and mix them fully, and add a boiling stone into the flask.

(2) Set up the apparatus according to Fig. 3.1. A thermometer is placed in one neck while a water separator in another neck. On the top, a condenser is fitted.

(3) Add water into the separator until the level is 3.5cm lower than the side neck. Heat the flask on an asbestos pad to make the solution boil slightly, and make sure the reflux starts[1].

(4) Continue to heat the flask until the temperature of the content increases to 134～135℃ (this process needs about 20min). When the water separator is filled with water, it shows that the reaction is nearly completed[2].

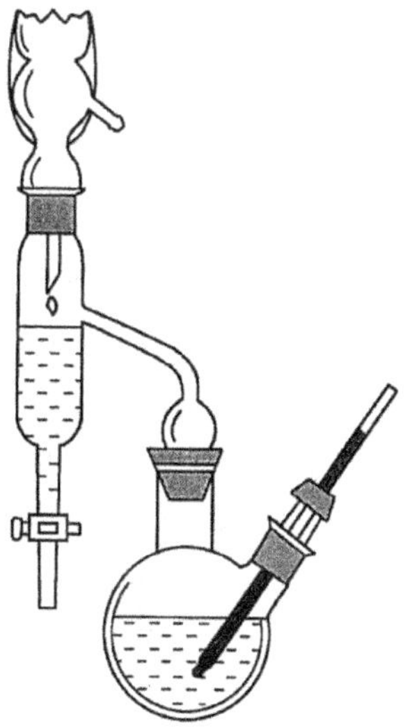

Fig. 3.1 The Apparatus for the Preparation of Dibutyl Ether

(5) Move the heating source away and let the reaction mixture cool down, pour out the mixture and water from the water separator into a 100mL separatory funnel, in which 50mL of water is contained. Shake and swirl the funnel well, then let it stand for a moment to make sure two layers are well separated. Separate the upper layer as the crude product, dibutyl ether.

(6) Wash and extract it twice with 25mL 50% H_2SO_4[3] each time, and then with 25mL of water once. Dry it with anhydrous calcium chloride.

(7) Filter the product into a distilling flask, distill and collect the fraction of 139～142℃. 7～8g of the product can be obtained in this experiment.

The boiling point of pure dibutyl ether is 142℃, d_4^{20} 0.769, $n_D^{20} = 1.3992$.

Brief Summary

1. Objective

(1) Learn the principle and method of preparation of ethers by intermolecular dehydration.

(2) Learn the experimental operation of the water separator.

2. Notes

[1] The surface of the liquid in the water separator increases gradually because of evaporation of the water from the reaction and the 1-butanol evaporated. They are gathered in the water separator through the condenser. Water is in the lower; 1-butanol, its density is lower than that of water, forms the upper layer. It overflows into the reaction flask when the separator is full of liquid.

[2] If heating is continued, the solution will become black and the byproduct butene will be produced.

[3] 1-Butanol can dissolve in 50% H_2SO_4 solution, but dibutyl ether rarely have such a solubility. So 1-butanol can be removed from the crude dibutyl ether, based on the above principle.

IR Spectrum

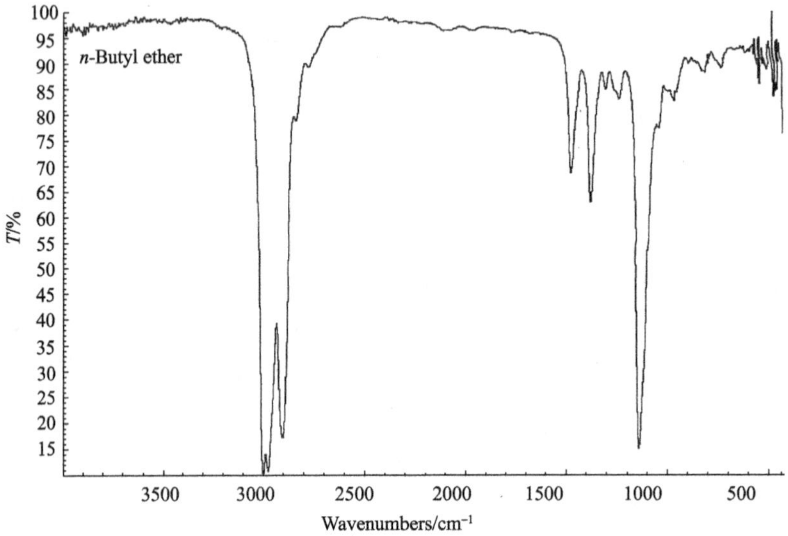

Questions

(1) Why the water separator should be used in the preparation of dibutyl ether?

(2) How do you know the reaction is nearly completed?

3.5 Preparation of Benzoic Acid and Phenylmethanol

Principle

When an aldehyde with no α-hydrogen reacts with concentrated alkali solution, there occurs self oxidation-reduction reaction between molecules, in which one molecule of aldehyde is reduced to an alcohol and another is oxidized to an acid. This kind of reaction is called the Cannizzaro reaction. Therefore, benzoic acid and phenylmethanol are prepared through a Cannizzaro reaction.

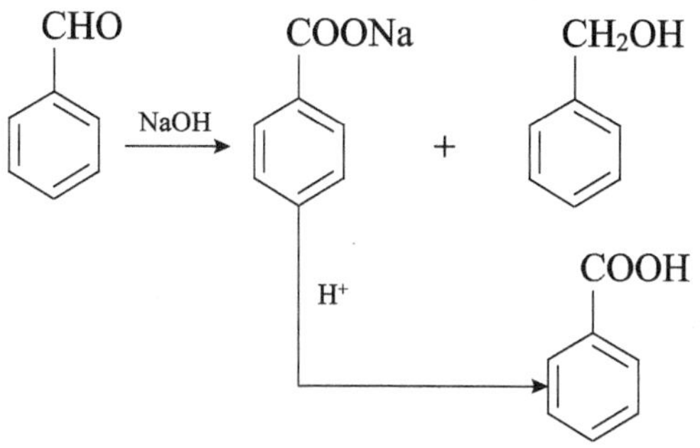

Apparatus and Materials

Apparatus distillation			
Materials			
benzaldehyde	20.5mL (21.3g, 0.20mol),	b.p.179.2℃,	d=1.0415$^{20/4}$ g/mL
sodium hydroxide	17.5g (0.44mol)		
diethyl ether		b.p.34.5℃,	d=0.7138$^{20/4}$ g/mL
hydrochloric acid	d = 1.18g/mL		
saturated aqueous sodium bisulfite solution			
anhydrous magnesium sulfate			
10% sodium carbonate solution			

Time 5h

Procedure

(1) Dissolve 17.5g (0.44mol) of solid sodium hydroxide[1] in 17.5mL of water by swirling it in a 250mL of Erlenmeyer flask or round-bottom flask. Cool the mixture down to room temperature.

(2) Place 20.5mL (21.3g, 0.20mol) of fresh-distillated benzaldehyde into the NaOH solution batchwise[2]. Cork the flask securely and shake the flask vigorously until a wax-like solution is formed.

(3) Allow the stoppered flask to stand overnight or until the next laboratory period[3].

(4) Add about 60～70mL of water to the mixture, stopper the flask, and shake it.

(5) If some crystals originally present do not dissolve, add a little more water, and break up the solid with a glass rod, then shake the mixture. Repeat the procedure until all solids are in the solution.

(6) Pour the solution into a separatory funnel, and extract the solution three times with 16mL of diethyl ether each[4]. Combine the ether solutions, wash it with 8mL of saturated aqueous sodium bisulfite[5], 16mL of 10% aqueous sodium carbonate and 16mL of water, respectively.

(7) Dry the organic solution over anhydrous magnesium sulfate.

(8) Heat the crude product in a water bath, distill the ether fraction out. Then drain the water out of the condenser of the apparatus, continue to distill phenylmethanol and collect the fraction that boils between 198～204℃.

(9) Weigh the product and calculate the yield. Pure phenylmethanol is a colorless liquid,

b.p.205.3℃, d_4^{20} 1.0419, n_D^{20} 1.5396.

(10) Pour the alkaline aqueous solution from the separatory funnel into a mixture of 65mL of concentrated hydrochloric acid, 65mL of water, and about 40g of crushed ice. Stir vigorously during the addition.

(11) Cool the resultant mixture in an ice bath, and collect the solid benzoic acid by vacuum filtration.

(12) Recrystallize the crude benzoic acid from water, dry the product, and determine its melting point.

(13) Weigh the product and calculate the yield. Pure benzoic acid is a white needle-shaped crystal, m.p.122.13℃.

Brief Summary

1. Objectives

(1) Study the principle and method of preparing benzoic acid and phenylmethanol from benzaldehyde through the Cannizzaro reaction.

(2) Master the techniques of distillation and recrystallization.

2. Notes

[1] Sodium hydroxide solution is corrosive. Avoid splashing it on your skin. If you do so, wash it immediately with cold water.

[2] Benzaldehyde must be freshly distilled and added in batches.

[3] Crystallization should occur in the meantime.

[4] Ether is flammable, It should be far from the fire.

[5] Remove the benzaldehyde by formation of its sodium bisulfite addition product.

IR Spectrum

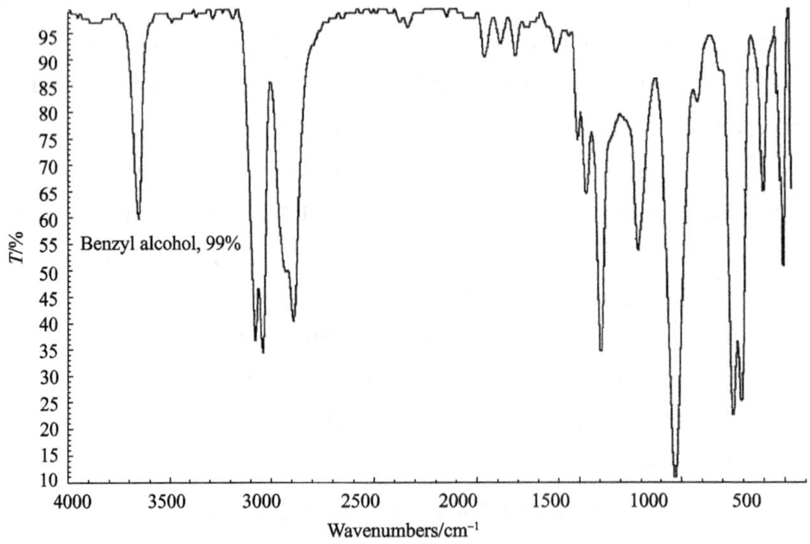

Questions

(1) The Cannizzaro reaction occurs much more slowly in dilute sodium hydroxide solution than in concentrated solution. Why?

(2) By what means would saturated aqueous sodium bisulfite remove unchanged benzaldehyde from the reaction mixture?

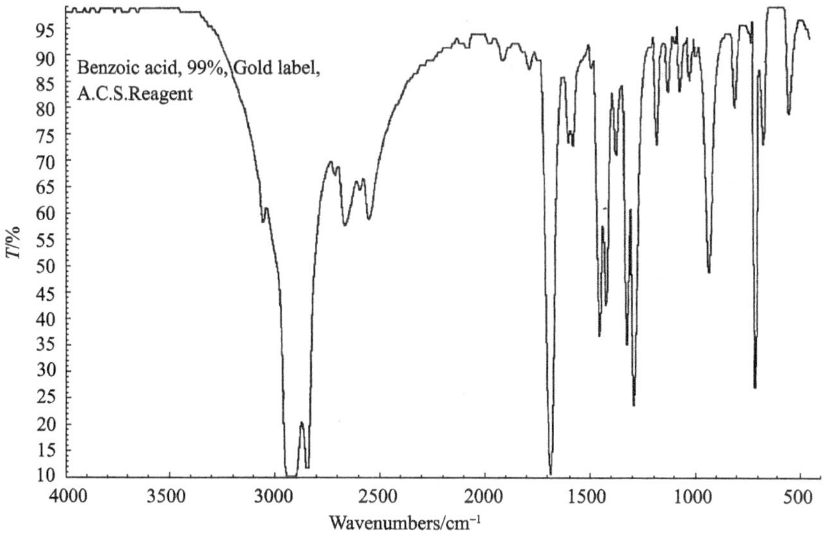

3.6 Preparation of Cyclohexanone

Principle

Cyclohexanone is usually prepared by the oxidation of cyclohexanol using sodium hypochlorite or chromic acid as an oxidizing agent.

Method 1

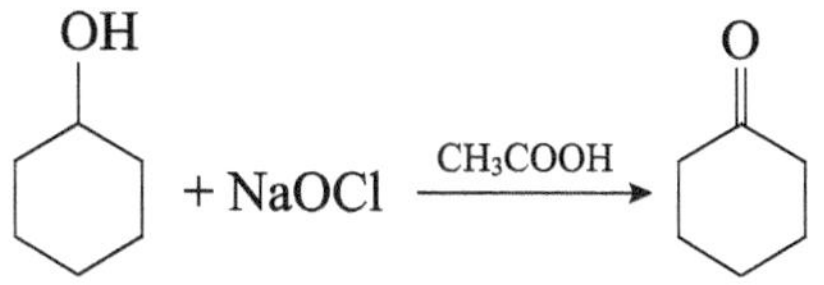

Method 2

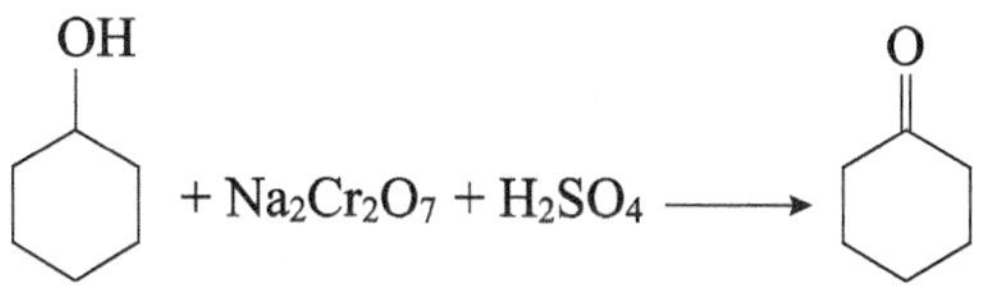

Apparatus and Materials

Apparatus　mechanical stirrer with a reflux condenser and a dropping funnel

Materials

cyclohexanol	5.2mL (5g, 0.05mol)	b.p.161.5℃	$d = 0.9642^{20/4}$ g/mL
glacial acetic acid	25mL	b.p.118℃	$d = 1.049^{20/4}$ g/mL
sodium hypochlorite solution	38mL (0.07mol, 1.8mol/L)		
sodium bichromate	20g (0.268mol)		
diethyl ether	25mL		
KI-starch paper			
saturated sodium bisulfite solution			
aluminum chloride	3g		
anhydrous sodium carbonate			
anhydrous magnesium sulfate			
sodium chloride			
concentrated sulfuric acid (98%)	14.8mL		

Time　4h

Procedure

Method 1

(1) Set up a 250mL three-neck flask with a mechanical stirrer, a dropping funnel and a thermometer. Add 5.2mL (5g, 0.05mol) of cyclohexanol and 25mL of glacial acetic acid and cool the resulting solution in an ice bath.

(2) Begin stirring the reaction mixture and add 38mL (0.07mol) of sodium hypochlorite solution (1.8mol/L) from the dropping funnel at the a speed that maintains the temperature between 30～35℃. Then keep on stirring for 5min.

(3) The aqueous layer is monitored periodically using KI-starch paper. If a positive test is not obtained, 5mL of sodium hypochlorite solution should be added[1].

(4) The resulting solution is stirred at room temperature for 30min, and saturated, aqueous sodium bisulfite solution is added dropwise to the reaction mixture until the solution gives a negative KI-starch test[2].

(5) To the reaction mixture, 30mL of water and 3g of aluminum chloride[3] were added and the crude product is distilled using an absestos pad until the distillate becomes clear.

(6) Anhydrous sodium carbonate is added, with stirring, to the distillate in small portions[4], until the evolution of CO_2 gas ceases. Then add 2.5g of NaCl to the mixture[5].

(7) Pour the mixture into a separatory funnel and save the organic layer. Dry the crude cyclohexanone using a small amount of anhydrous magnesium sulfate.

(8) Decant the clear liquid into a dry distilling flask and distill the crude product. Collect the fraction that boils between 150～155℃. Weigh the product and calculate the percentage yield.

Pure cyclohexanone is a colorless liquid, b.p.155℃, n_D^{20} 1.4507.

Method 2

(1) Place 5.2mL (5.0g, 0.05mol) of cyclohexanol and 25mL of diethyl ether into a three-neck flask equipped with a mechanical stirrer, a reflux condenser and a dropping funnel. Shake the mixture to a uniform consistency and put the flask in an ice water bath to cool it down to about 0℃.

(2) Dissolve 20g (0.066mol) of $Na_2Cr_2O_7 \cdot 2H_2O$ in 60mL of water by swirling it in a 250mL beaker. With stirring, 26.8g (14.8mL, 0.268mol) of concentrated sulfuric acid (98%) is added slowly, and then 40mL of water is added to dilute the solution. Cool the mixture down to about 0℃.

(3) With vigorous stirring, 50mL of chromic acid solution which were prepared in step 2 is added slowly through the dropping funnel. The chromic acid solution should be added within 10min with a well controlled rate. When accomplished, keep on stirring for 20min.

(4) Pour the solution into a separatory funnel, remove the organic layer, and extract the water layer two times with two 15mL aliquots of ether. Combine the ether solutions, wash them with 15mL of 5% sodium carbonate solution and four times with 15mL of water. Dry the organic solution with anhydrous magnesium sulfate.

(5) Heat the crude product in a water bath and distill the ether fraction out. Then drain the water out of the condenser of the apparatus. Continue to distill cyclohexanone and collect the fraction that boils between 150～155℃.

(6) Weigh the product and calculate the yield. Pure cyclohexanone is a colorless liquid. b.p.155℃, n_D^{20} 1.4507.

Brief Summary

1. Objectives

(1) Learn the principles and methods of preparing cyclohexanone by the oxidation of cyclohexanol using sodium hypochlorite or chromic acid as an oxidizing agent.

(2) Master the techniques of stirring, extraction and distillation.

2. Notes

[1] An excess of hypochlorite oxidizing agent should be maintained through the reaction period.

[2] In order to remove the excess sodium hypochlorite, saturated sodium bisulfite solution should be added.

[3] Aluminum chloride can prevent the foaming during the distillation.

[4] Anhydrous sodium carbonate is added to neutralize the acetic acid present in the product mixture.

[5] The solubility of cyclohexanone in water is 2.4g/100mL at 31℃, in order to aid in layer separation, 2.5g of sodium chloride is added.

IR Spectrum

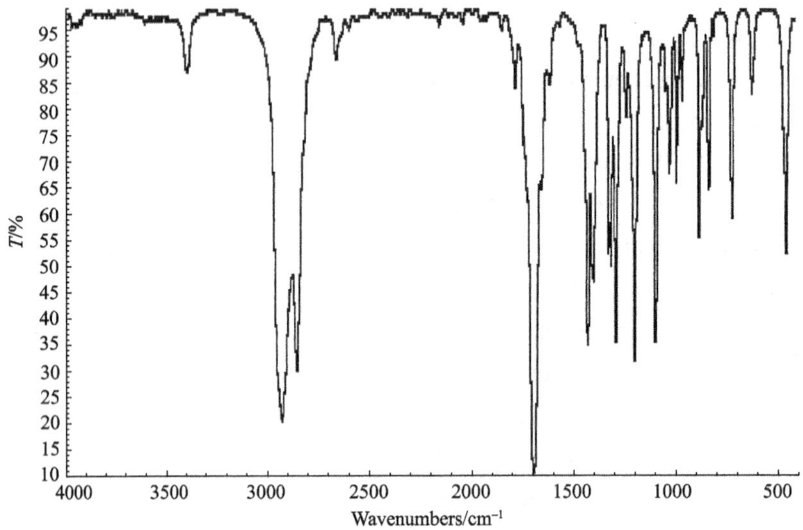

Questions

(1) Why a saturated solution of sodium bisulfite should be added to the reaction mixture in method 1.

(2) In method 1, anhydrous sodium carbonate should be added into the distillate, why?

3.7 Preparation of Hexanedioic Acid

Principle

Hexanedioic acid is one of the raw materials for the manufacture of 6, 6-nylon. It can be easily prepared from cyclohexanol oxidation using 50% nitric acid as an oxidizer.

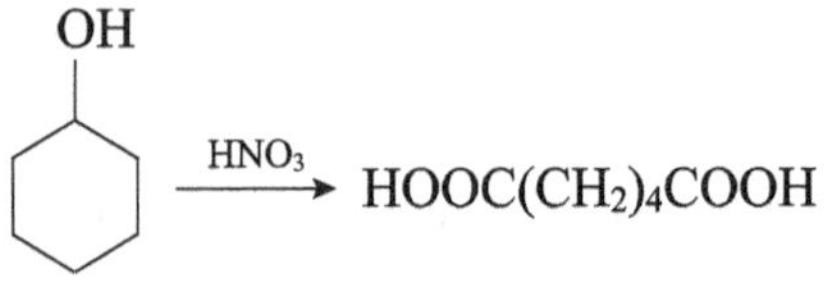

Apparatus and Materials

Apparatus reflux with a dropping funnel and a thermometer.

Materials

cyclohexanol	5.2mL (5g, 0.05mol),	b.p.161.5℃,	$d = 0.9642^{20/4}$ g/mL
50% nitric acid	16mL (0.17mol)		
10% sodium hydroxide solution			

Time 5h

Procedure

(1) Set up a 125mL three-neck flask with a dropping funnel, a thermometer and a reflux condenser connected to a gas absorption apparatus, in which sodium hydroxide solution (10%) is used to absorb the NO_2 gas produced during the reaction[1].

(2) Fill the three-neck flask with 16mL of 50% nitric acid[2, 3].

(3) Preheat the nitric acid solution up to 80℃ with the water bath. Add a drop of cyclohexanol while shaking the solution and monitor the temperature increase. Wait to add the second drop when the temperature goes back to 85℃, then add dropwise the cyclohexanol slowly for a total amount of 5.2mL (5g, 0.05mol)[4]. Keep on shaking the reactor while adding dropwise, trying to maintain the temperature between 85～90℃[5] by controlling the speed of addition.

(4) When the addition is finished, keep on shaking and heat the flask with a water bath at 80～90℃, incubate the reaction for 15min, until there is no umber gas coming up.

(5) Cool the reactor to separate the solid out.

(6) Filter the solid, wash it with 3mL of water and press the water out[6].

(7) Desiccate, weigh and calculate the yield.

The pure hexanedioic acid is a white ridge-like crystal, m.p.153℃.

Brief Summary

1. Objectives

(1) Study the principle and method of preparing hexanedioic acid from cyclohexanol oxidation.

(2) Master the experimental techniques of reflux and recrystallization.

2. Notes

[1] The gas outlet of the NO_2 trap apparatus should not be underwater, or water could be sucked back into the flask.

[2] Attention! Cyclohexanol and dense nitric acid should not be measured and mixed with the same graduated cylinder, or an acute, sudden reaction will take place if they encounter each other.

[3] The NO_2 gas is toxic, so the apparatus should be gas-tight and placed in the hood preferably.

[4] This is an exothermic reaction, so just add the reagent slowly to avoid explosion caused by too fierce a reaction.

[5] Too high a temperature can be controlled by a cool water bath; too low a temperature raised with a heated water bath.

[6] If needed, purification by recrystallization can be carried out from hot water.

IR Spectrum

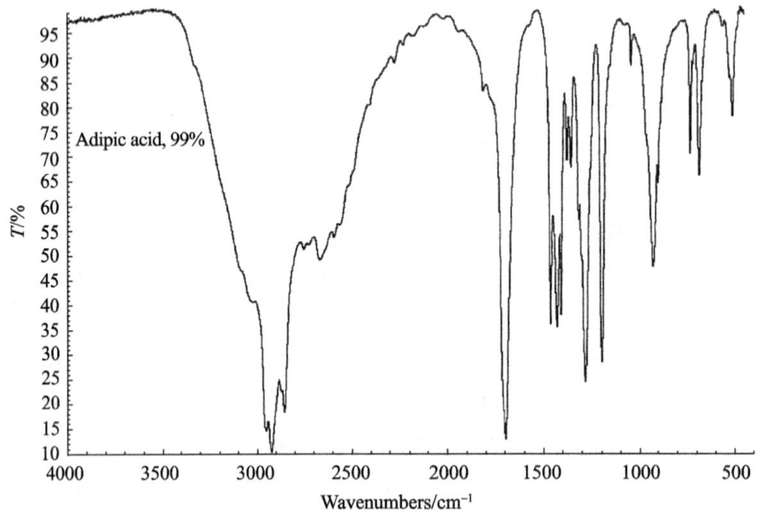

Question

Why is it strongly required to control the temperature of oxidation reaction?

3.8 Preparation and Characterization of Cinnamic Acid

Principle

When benzaldehyde is mixed with an anhydride and heated in the existence of the corresponding carboxylate, an *α*, *β*-unsaturated acid can be prepared through the Perkin reaction.

During the course of this experiment, potassium carbonate can be used to substitute for potassium acetate in the Perkin reaction, because it will shorten the reaction time and improve the product yield.

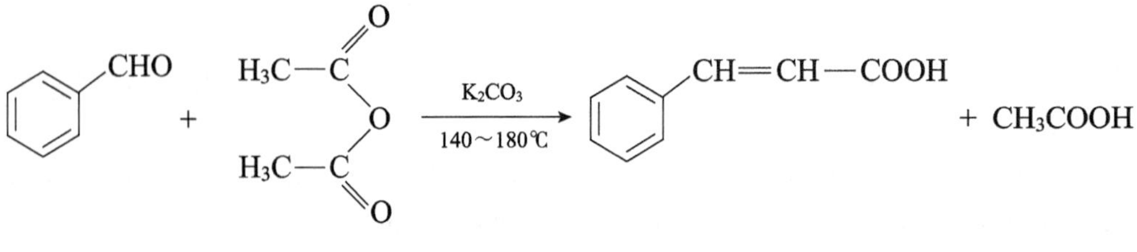

Apparatus and Materials

Apparatus reflux, steam distillation

Materials

benzaldehyde	3mL (3.15g, 0.03mol)	b.p.179.2℃	$d = 1.0415^{20/4}$ g/mL
acetic anhydride	8mL (8.64g, 0.085mol)	b.p.139.6℃	$d = 1.0820^{20/4}$ g/mL
anhydrous potassium carbonate	4.2g (0.03mol)		
concentrated hydrochloric acid			$d = 1.18$g/mL
10% sodium hydroxide solution	20mL		

Time 6h

Procedure

(1) Place 3mL (3.15g, 0.03mol) of benzaldehyde, 8mL (8.64g, 0.085mol) of acetic anhydride, 4.2g (0.03mol) grinded anhydrous potassium carbonate and a boiling stone into a 250mL round-bottom flask. Among these materials, benzaldehyde[1] and acetic anhydride[2] are both redistilled before use. Heat the mixture to reflux on the asbestos pad for about 45min. Because carbon dioxide will be released in the process, bubbles will be produced at an early stage of the reaction.

(2) Cool down the reaction mixture, and add 20mL of water into the flask with shaking or stirring by a glass rod to avoid bulk masses formation. Distill excessive benzaldehyde from the flask by means of steam distillation.

(3) Then cool the flask down and add 20mL 10% sodium hydroxide solution as well. Make sure all the cinnamic acid is converted into the sodium salt and dissolves completely.

(4) Filter the solution into a 250mL beaker and cool down to room temperature, stir and acidify it with concentrated hydrochloric acid and check it with Congo-red test paper until it becomes blue.

(5) Filter the solution and wash the solid with an appropriate amount of cold water. Keep the aspirator running until the filter residue becomes dry. Air-dry the crude product. About 3g product can be obtained (65%～75%).

(6) The crude product can be recrystallized with hot water or the mixture of water and ethanol (the ratio is 3 : 1, by volume). The melting point of pure cinnamic acid is 135.6℃[3].

(7) Identify the product by IR spectrum.

Brief Summary

1. Objectives

(1) Learn the theory and method of the preparation of cinnamic acid through the Perkin reaction.

(2) Learn the experimental operation of reflux and steam distillation.

2. Notes

[1] Benzoic acid may be produced by the automatic oxidation of benzaldehyde if it is stored for a long time. Benzaldehyde should be redistilled before use otherwise the existence of trace benzoic acid not only influences the progress of reaction, but also is difficult to be removed, hence the quality of the product can be ensured. The fraction of 170～180℃ is collected and employed as the starting material.

[2] Acetic anhydride may convert into acetic acid when it is exposed to moisture for a long time through hydrolysis and therefore it should be redistilled before use as well.

[3] Cinnamic acid has *cis*-and *trans*-isomers, the product prepared usually is *trans*-formed with a melting point of 135.6℃.

IR Spectrum

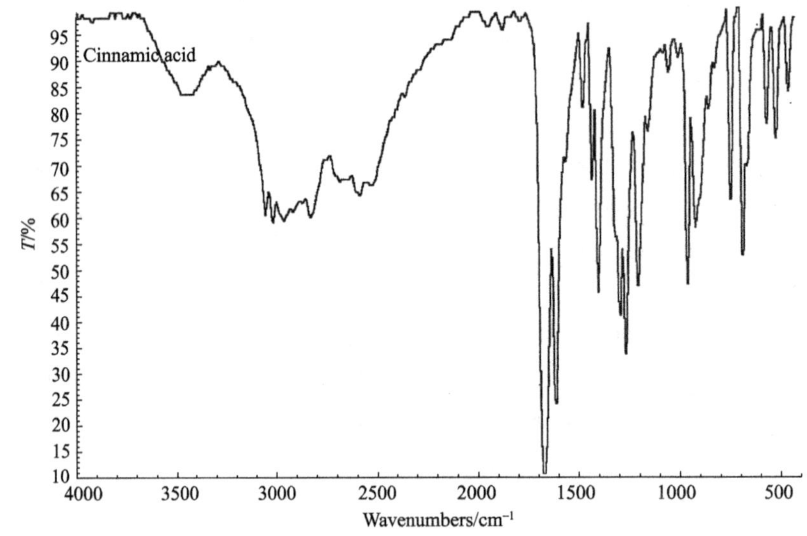

Questions

(1) What compound is removed by using steam distillation? Why can steam distillation purify the crude product?

(2) What can we get from the reaction of benzaldehyde with propionic anhydride in the presence of anhydrous potassium carbonate?

3.9 Preparation of Acetylsalicylic Acid

Principle

Acetylsalicylic acid (aspirin) is one of the most widely used over-the-counter non-prescription drugs[1]. It can be prepared from Salicylic acid (o-hydroxybenzoic acid), acetic anhydride and an acid catalyst, like sulfuric or phosphoric acid, to speed up the reaction.

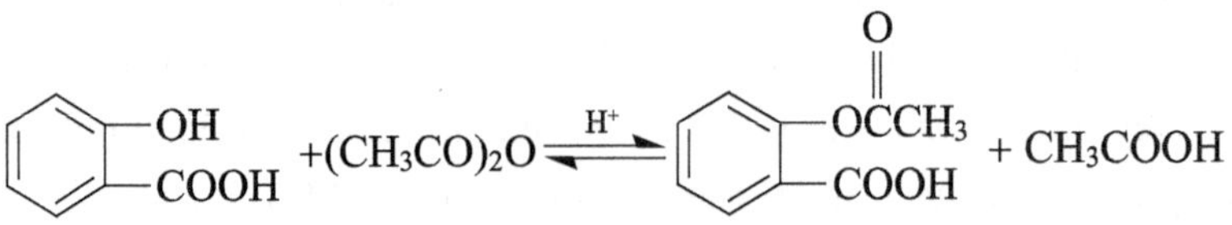

Apparatus and Materials

Materials		
salicylic acid	3.2g (0.023mol)	m.p.159 ℃
acetic anhydride	5g (about 5mL, 0.05mol) $d = 1.0820^{20/4}$ g/mL	b.p.139.6 ℃
concentrated sulfuric acid (98%)	5 drops	
commercial aspirin tables		
95% ethanol		
1% ferric chloride		

Time 4h

Procedure

(1) Take 3.2g (0.023mol) of salicylic acid and place it in a 100mL Erlenmeyer flask. Carefully add 5mL (0.05mol) of acetic anhydride[2], and then while swirling, add 5 drops of concentrated sulfuric acid.

(2) Place the flask in the boiling water bath, heat for 15min[3]. The solid will completely dissolve. Swirl the solution occasionally.

(3) Remove the Erlenmeyer flask from the bath and let it cool to approximately room temperature. Then slowly pour the solution into a 200mL beaker containing 50mL of ice-water[4], mix thoroughly, and place the beaker in an ice-water bath.

(4) Collect the crystals by vacuum filtration and wash the crystals with two 8mL portions of ice- water, and dry the crude products.

(5) Recrystallize the crude product using a mixed solvent of ethanol and water[5].

(6) Dry the solid, determine the melting point and calculate the percentage yield.

Pure acetylsalicylic acid is a white crystal, m.p.136℃.

Brief Summary

1. Objectives

(1) Illustrate the preparation of the drug aspirin.

(2) Use a chemical test to determine the purity of the preparation.

2. Notes

[1] Aspirin behaves as an antipyretic drug (it reduces fever) and an anti-inflammatory agent capable of reducing swelling. It is also an effective agent in preventing strokes and heart attacks due to its ability to act as an anti-coagulant.

[2] Acetic anhydride will irritate your eyes, so handle it with care. Dispense in the hood.

[3] Salicylic acid is a bifunctional compound. It is a phenol and a carboxylic acid. The reaction temperature should be controlled to around 70℃ to prevent the following by-products formed.

[4] The water destroys any unreacted acetic anhydride and will cause the insoluble aspirin to precipitate from solution.

[5] You can use the following method to determine the purity of the aspirin. The purity of the sample will be tested with 1% ferric chloride and compared with a commercial aspirin and salicylic acid.

(a) Label three test tubes 1, 2 and 3; place a few crystals of salicylic acid into test tube no.1, a small sample of your aspirin to test tube no.2, and a small sample of a crushed commercial aspirin into test tube no.3. Add 5mL of distilled water to each test tube and shake to dissolve the crystals.

(b) Add 10 drops of 1% aqueous ferric chloride to each test tube.

(c) Compare and record your observations. The formation of a purple color indicates the presence of salicylic acid. The intensity of the color qualitatively tells how much salicylic acid is present.

IR Spectrum

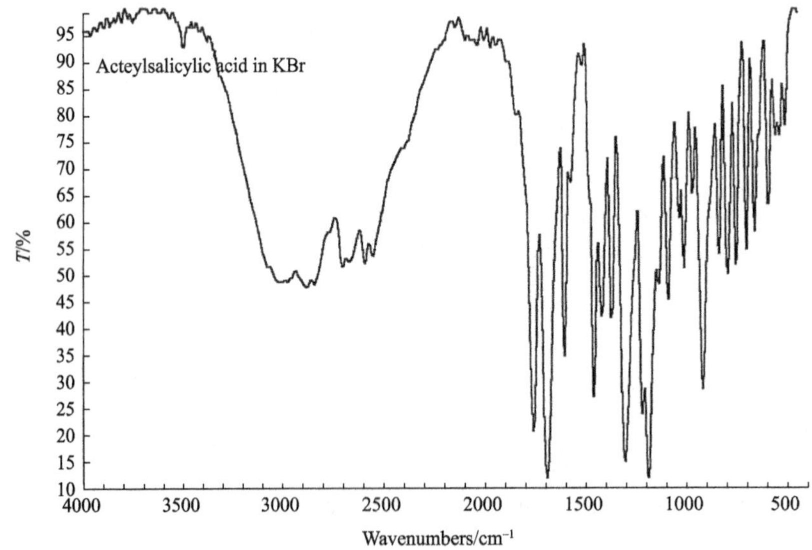

Questions

(1) What is the purpose of the concentrated sulfuric acid used in the acetylation?

(2) What is the product when salicylic acid reacts with excess ethanol in the presence of the concentrated sulfuric acid?

3.10 Preparation of *n*-Butyl Acetate

Principle

n-Butyl acetate can be prepared with acetic acid and 1-butanol by a single step reaction using a catalytic amount of concentrated sulfuric acid.

$$CH_3COOH + CH_3(CH_2)_2CH_2OH \underset{}{\overset{H_2SO_4}{\rightleftharpoons}} CH_3COO(CH_2)_3CH_3 + H_2O$$

Apparatus and Materials

Apparatus	reflux with a water separator	
Materials		
1-butanol	11.5mL (9.3g, 0.125mol) $d = 0.8098^{20/4}$g/mL	b.p.117.2℃
glacial acetic acid	7.2mL (7.5g, 0.125mol) $d = 1.049^{20/4}$g/mL	b.p.118℃
concentrated sulfuric acid	$d = 1.841^{20/4}$g/mL	
10% sodium carbonate solution		
anhydrous magnesium sulfate		

Time 4～5h

Procedure

(1) Add 1-butanol 11.5mL (9.3g, 0.125mol), acetic acid 7.2mL (7.5g, 0.125mol) and concentrated sulfuric acid (0.5mL) [1,2] to a dried 100mL round-bottom flask with a water separator and stir the mixture.

(2) Install the water separator and the condenser. Put some water into the discharging side of the separator and make it lower than the level of the branch nozzle. Make a mark there.

(3) Heat slowly the mixture on an asbestos pad. Keep the temperature at 80℃ for 15min, then heat to reflux for an additional 25min. When heating the mixture, you should remember to remove the water produced in the reaction system to keep the water level in the separator unchanged[3].

(4) When no more water is produced, stop heating and write down the amount of water separated[4].

(5) When the mixture is cooled to room temperature, discharge the condenser. Then combine the liquid in the separator and the reaction liquid in the round-bottom flask, and pour the mixture into a separate funnel and remove the water phase.

(6) Wash the organic phase with 10% sodium carbonate (10mL), keeping the pH at 7, and remove the water layer.

(7) Wash the organic layer with water again (10mL), and remove the water layer.

(8) Pour the organic phase into a dried cone-shaped flask. Dry it with the proper amount of anhydrous magnesium sulfate. Stir it to make the organic phase transparent.

(9) Pour the dried *n*-butyl acetate into a dried 50mL distillation flask. Distill the ester. Collect the fraction boiling between 124～126℃. Yield: 68%～75%.

Pure *n*-Butyl acetate is a colorless, transparent liquid, b.p. 126.3℃, d_4^{20} 0.8825, n_D^{20} 1.3947.

Brief Summary

1. Objectives

(1) Learn the principle and method of preparing *n*-butyl acetate by direct esterification of acetic acid and 1-butanol.

(2) Master the techniques of distillation, extraction and reflux with a water separator.

2. Notes

[1] The concentrated sulfuric acid is a catalyst in this reaction, but the amount of the sulfuric acid is very important in the reaction. You must not use too much, just a catalytic amount.

[2] The sulfuric acid should be added dropwise or the experiment will fail.

[3] The reaction can proceed smoothly by azeotropic removal of the water formed in the reaction.

[4] There are two ways to judge whether the reaction has finished: ①there are no more water drops sinking; ②compare the amount of the water from the separator with the theoretical amount of the water produced in the reaction.

IR Spectrum

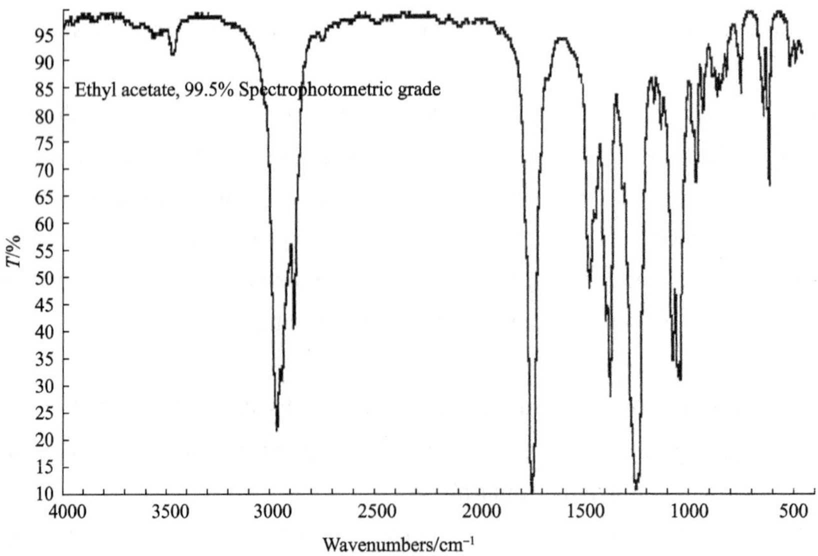

Questions

(1) What principles and methods does this experiment adopt to improve the production rate of *n*-butyl acetate?

(2) What principles does this experiment employ to remove the water? Why must the water be removed?

3.11 Preparation of *n*-Dibutyl Phthalate

Principle

n-Dibutyl phthalate can be prepared with phthalic anhydride and 1-butanol by a two-step reaction using a catalytic amount of concentrated sulfuric acid. The first reaction is very quick, and the second reaction is reversible. In order to shift the equilibrium reaction to the right, a water separator is employed to remove the water from the reaction mixture.

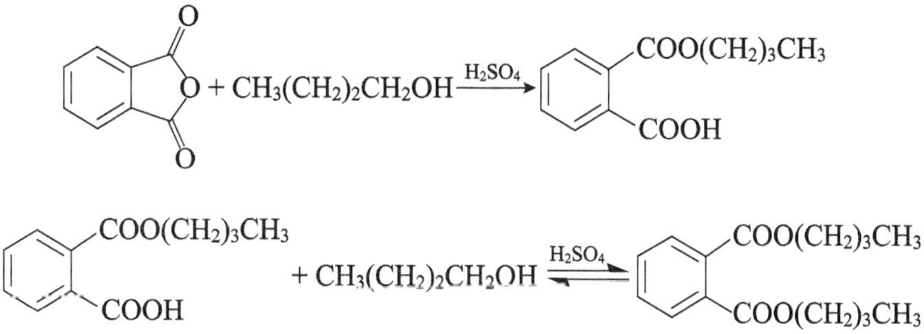

Apparatus and Materials

Apparatus reflux with a water separator, vacuum distillation		
Materials		
1-butanol	13mL (0.14mol)	b.p.117.2℃ $d = 0.8098^{20/4}$g/mL
phthalic anhydride	6g (0.04mol)	m.p.131℃ $d = 1.527^{20/4}$g/mL
concentrated sulfuric acid	0.2mL	$d = 1.841^{20/4}$g/mL
5% sodium carbonate solution		

Time 4～5h

Procedure

(1) Place phthalic anhydride (6g, 0.04mol), 1-butanol (13mL, 0.14mol) and concentrated sulfuric acid 0.2mL into a dried 100mL three-neck flask or two neck flask. Shake or swirl and mix

them fully, and add a boiling stone into the flask.

(2) Set up the apparatus according to Fig. 3.1. A thermometer is placed in one neck while a water separator is placed in another neck. On the top, a condenser is fitted.

(3) Add 1-butanol into the discharging side of the separator and make it lower than the level of the branch nozzle.

(4) Heat slowly the mixture on an asbestos pad. After the solid phthalic anhydride disappears, an azeotrope[1] of 1-butanol-water is evaporated and gathered in the water separator. As the reaction proceeds, the temperature of reaction solution in the flask rises slowly. When the temperature rise to 140℃[2], stop heating. The total reaction time needed is about 1.5h.

(5) When the mixture is cooled to 70℃, discharge the condenser. Then combine the liquid in the separator and the reaction liquid in the round-bottom flask, and pour the mixture into a separate funnel and remove the water layer.

(6) Wash the organic phase with 5% sodium carbonate (10～15mL)[3], and remove the water layer.

(7) Wash the organic layer with warm saturated brine again (15mL×2), keeping the pH at 7.

(8) Remove 1-butanol by simple distillation, and then distill the residue under reduced pressure to afford 5.3g of the product. The yield is 63%.

Pure *n*-dibutyl phthalate is a colorless, oily liquid, b.p.340℃ (175～176℃/665.5Pa), n_D^{20} 1.4911.

Brief Summary

1. Objectives

(1) Learn the principle and method of preparing *n*-dibutyl phthalate by the esterification of phthalic anhydride and *n*-butyl alcohol.

(2) Master the techniques of vacuum distillation, extraction and reflux with a water separator.

2. Notes

[1] See notes [1] of exp. 3.4, Synthesis of Dibutyl Ether.

[2] Comparing the amount of the water from the separator helps one to judge whether the reaction has finished. In acid condition, *n*-dibutyl phthalate is easily decomposed when the reaction temperature exceeds 180℃.

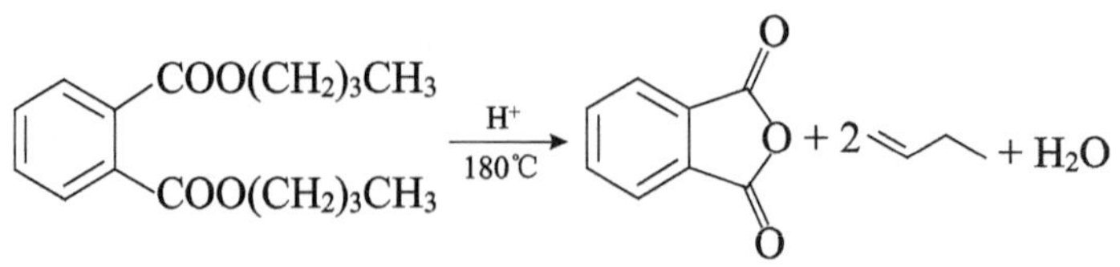

[3] When the reaction mixture is neutralized, the temperature should not exceed 70℃, and a highconcentration of base is also inadvisable. Sodium hydroxide can not be used. Otherwise, the

saponification reaction of the ester occurs easily. Using the saturated brine instead of water to wash the reaction mixture may reduce the loss of the ester. In addition it prevents emulsification. After handled like this, the dryness of the organic phase no need.

IR Spectrum

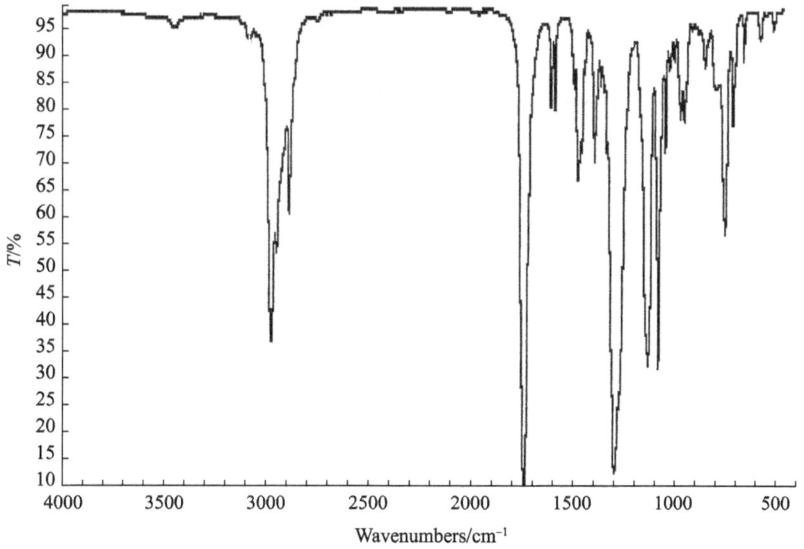

Questions

(1) When 1-butanol is heated to high temperature in presence of concentrated sulfuric acid, which side reaction may occur? What is the unexpected effect of the reaction if the amount of concentrated sulfuric acid is excessive?

(2) This reaction should be carried out by heating gently. What is the unexpected effect of the reaction if heated quickly?

3.12 Preparation of Acetanilide

Principle

Acetanilide can be prepared from aniline in several ways, using acetyl chloride, acetic anhydride or glacial acetic acid as starting materials. Acetyl chloride reacts very vigorously. Acetic anhydride is preferred for a laboratory synthesis because its rate of hydrolysis is low enough to allow the acetylation of amine to be carried out in aqueous solution. It gives a product of high purity and in good yield. The procedure with glacial acetic is of commercial interest since it is economical, but it requires long heating. In the present experiment, we can use either of the following methods to prepare the acetanilide.

Method 1

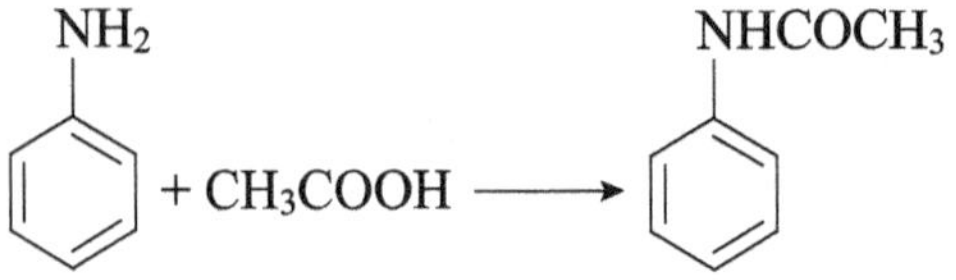

Method 2

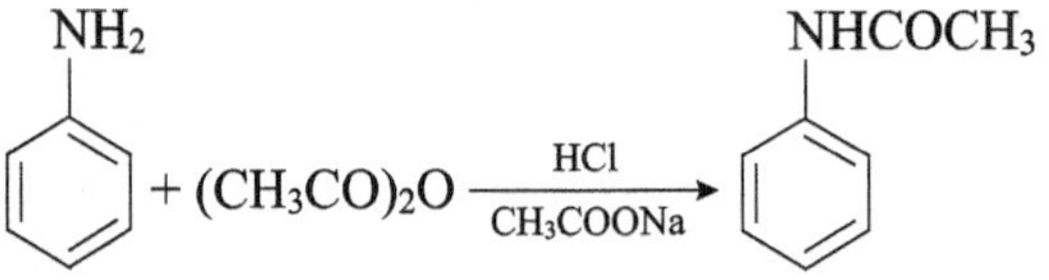

Acetylation is often used to "protect" a primary or a secondary amine functional group. The amine group can be regenerated readily by hydrolysis in acid or base.

Apparatus and Materials

Apparatus　fractional distillation

Materials

aniline	10mL 10.2g (0.11mol)	b.p.184℃ $d = 1.0217^{20/4}$g/mL
glacial acetic acid	17mL 17.8g (0.26mol)	b.p.118 $d = 1.049^{20/4}$g/mL
zinc power	0.1g	
acetic anhydride	5.2mL (5.6g, 0.055mol)	b.p.139.55℃ $d = 1.0820^{20/4}$g/mL
sodium acetate	4.51g (0.055mol)	m.p.324℃ $d = 1.528$g/mL
concentrated hydrochloride acid (36%)	4.5mL	$d = 1.18$g/mL

Time　3h

Procedure

Method 1

(1) Measure 10mL (10.2g, 0.11mol) of aniline[1] into a 100mL round-bottom flask, add 17mL (17.8g, 0.30mol) of glacial acetic acid and 0.1g of zinc powder[2] to the flask.

(2) Assemble a fractional column with a thermometer, and use a 50mL Erlenmeyer flask as a collector.

(3) Put the round-bottom flask on an asbestos pad and heat the mixture to reflux, The flame must be controlled to keep the temperature of the distilling vapor being about 105℃[3].

(4) After 1h, the reaction has finished. With stirring, the hot solution is poured into a beaker with 250mL of cooled water. In a few seconds a copious precipitate of acetanilide forms.

(5) Collect the product by suction filtration, wash it with ice-cold water, and recrystallize from water[4].

(6) Record the mass and melting range of the acetanilide obtained, calculate the percentage yield[5].

Pure acetanilide is a colorless shaped crystal, m.p.114.3℃.

Method 2

(1) Put 125mL of water in a 250mL Erlenmeyer flask. Add 4.5mL of concentrated hydrochloride acid, and swirl the flask a couple of times, and then add 4.6mL (4.65g, 0.05mol) of aniline[1] and swirl the mixture.

(2) In a separate container, add 4.51g (0.055mol) of sodium acetate to 25mL of water, Measure into a graduated cylinder 5.2mL (5.61g, 0.055mol) of acetic anhydride[6].

(3) Warm the aniline hydrochloride solution to 50℃ on a hot-water bath, then add the acetic anhydride. Swirl the flask to dissolve the anhydride, and add the sodium acetate prepared in step 2 quickly in one portion[7]. Swirl the flask again and set it in an ice-water bath.

(4) After 20min, collect the product by suction filtration, wash it with a small amount of ice-cold water, and recrystallize from water[4].

(5) Record the mass and calculate the percentage yield.

(6) Determine the melting point of acetanilide.

Pure acetanilide is a colorless sheet shaped crystal, m.p.114.3℃.

Brief Summary

1. Objectives

(1) Learn the principle and method of preparing acetanilide by acetic anhydride and glacial acetic acid as the acetylating reagent.

(2) Master the experimental technique of recrystallization.

2. Notes

[1] Aniline is a toxic substance, and it can be absorbed through the skin. Care should be need in handling it.

[2] In order to prevent the aniline from being oxidized during the reaction, zinc powder should be added.

[3] At this temperature, the water formed during the reaction can be removed and the glacial acetic acid will remain in the reaction flask.

[4] If the solution has color, then add a small amount of activated charcoal, swirl the mixture and allow it to boil gently for a few minutes, and filter out the carbon.

[5] You will obtain about 10g of acetanilide, the estimated yield is about 61%~68%.

[6] The synthesis takes place in an aqueous environment, because aniline is soluble only to the extent of the 3.4g/100mL, but it can be made more soluble by converting it to its hydrochloride salt. But the presence of the acid reduces the nucleophilicity of the anilide. You can circumvent this

problem by buffering the solution with sodium acetate and keeping the concentration of aniline low enough to maintain solubility in water.

[7] You must make aniline react with the anhydride without delay. Therefore add sodium acetate as soon as the anhydride dissolves in the reaction mixture, because the acetic anhydride will react with water to yield acetic acid.

IR Spectrum

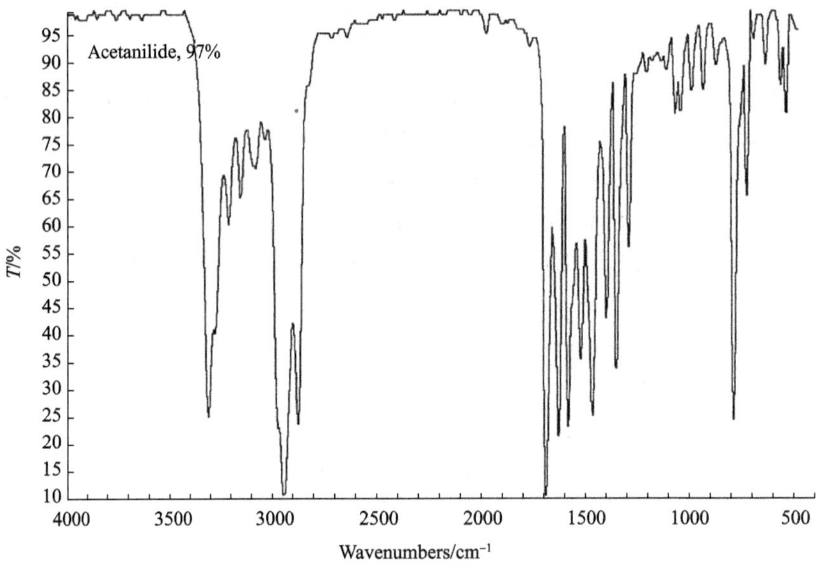

Questions

(1) In method 1, why must the temperature of the distilling vapor be controlled to about 105℃?

(2) In method 2, why must sodium acetate be added immediately after the acetic anhydride is dissolved? What is the function of sodium acetate?

(3) Why is the ice-cold water rather than room temperature water used to wash the final product?

3.13 Preparation of 4-Nitroaniline

Principle

Primary reaction

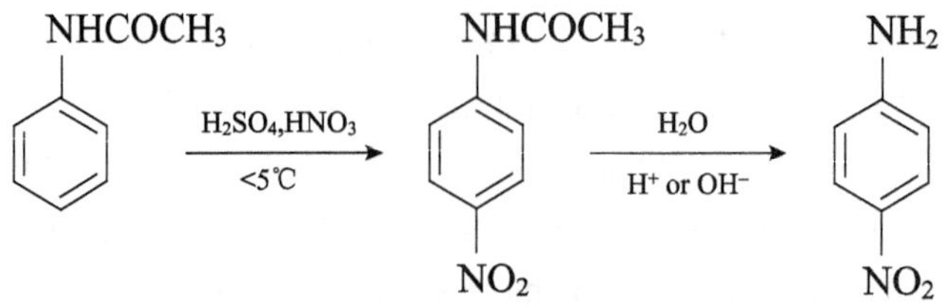

Side reaction

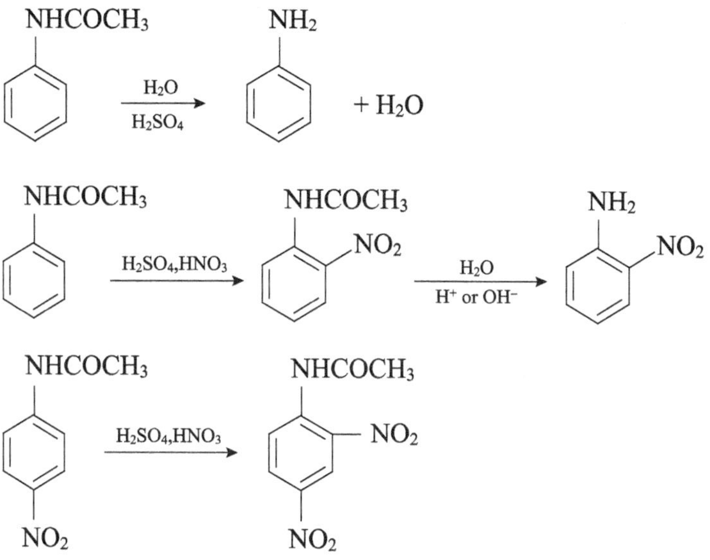

Apparatus and Materials

Apparatus reflux		
Materials		
acetanilide	5g (0.037mol)	m.p. 114.3℃
concentrated sulfuric acid	1.4mL	d=1.841$^{20/4}$g/mL
concentrated nitric acid	2.2mL (0.032mol)	d=1.503$^{20/4}$g/mL
glacial acetic acid	5mL (5.25g,0.087mol)	b.p. 118℃ d=1.049$^{20/4}$g/mL
20% sodium hydroxide		

Time 3~5h

Procedure

1. Preparation of 4-Nitroacetanilide

(1) 2.2mL of concentrated nitric acid[1] and 1.4 mL of concentrated sulfuric acid are mixed in a conical flask to prepare a mixed acid solution and the solution is then cooled in an ice-salt bath[1] for reserve demand.

(2) 5g of acetanilide and 5mL of glacial acetic acid[2] are added into a 100mL conical flask[2] and then cooled in an ice-water bath. 10mL of concentrated sulfuric acid is slowly added into the conical flask under shaking. After the dissolution of acetanilide, clear solution is obtained and then cooled to 0～2℃ in an ice water bath.

(3) The mixed acid (prepared in step 1) is slowly dropped into the flask through a dropper under shaking. It is noteworthy to make sure the temperature of reaction won't exceed 5℃[3].

(4) Take the conical flask out from the ice water and keep it at room temperature for about

30min, shaking it intermittently.

(5) The mixture obtained above is slowly poured into the beaker containing 20mL water and 30g crushed ice, while 4-nitroacetanilide soon appears as a light yellow solid. Then it is set side.

(6) After filtration, the solid is washed with 10ml ice water for 3 times to obtain the crude product. It is used to prepare for the next step directly without further purification.

2. Preparation of 4-Nitroaniline[4]

(1) 4g 4-nitroacetanilide (prepared in step 1)、20mL 7% sulfuric acid[5] and a boiling stone are added in a 100mL round-flask equipped with a reflux condenser. The mixture is heated and refluxed for 40min until clear solution is finally obtained.

(2) The clear solution above is poured into the beaker containing 50g crushed ice. The solution is alkalified by 20% sodium hydroxide solution until the solution is alkaline. After a few seconds, a copious precipitate 4-nitroanilide will be formed.

(3) The solution is filtered after cooling, and washed with cold water to remove lye. The crude 4-nitroaniline is recrystallized by water[6], then dried and weighed. Finally, the yield should be calculated.

(4) Pure 4-nitroaniline is a yellow monoclinic acicular crystal, with m.p. 147.5℃. It is so poisonous that 4-nitroaniline can be absorbed through the skin to poison people. It is easily decomposed to explode when heated.

Brief Summary

1. Objectives

(1) Learn the theory and method of the synthesis 4-nitroaniline through the nitration of 4-nitroacetanilide.

(2) Master the experimental technique of reflux and recrystallization.

2. Notes

[1] To prevent the by-products of multi-nitration, the amount of nitric acid cannot be large, the yield in this experiment is calculated according to the dosage of nitric acid.

[2] After the nitration in glacial acetic acid, the main product is para-position product. (if in acetic anhydride, the main product is ortho product), in addition, glacial acetic acid can accelerate the dissolution of acetanilide in sulfuric acid.

[3] Acetanilide react with mixed acid at below 5℃, para-position product is given as the main product, if the temperature is higher than 5℃, ortho-position by-products will increase.

[4] 4-Nitroacetanilide can also be hydrolyzed in alkaline conditions, refluxing with 35% sodium hydroxide for 2.5～3h. Alkaline cannot be strong, and reflux time should not be long, otherwise it prone to partial hydrolysis reaction, which will affect yields.

[5] 7% sulfuric acid preparation method: during shaking and cooling, 12mL concentrated sulfuric acid was carefully added to 9mL cold water as a thin stream, take 20mL this solution when use.

[6] The solubility of 4-nitroaniline in the water is 0.08g/(100mL) at 18.5℃; 2.2g/100mL at 100℃.

IR Spectrum

The IR spectrum of 4-nitroaniline is shown as follow:

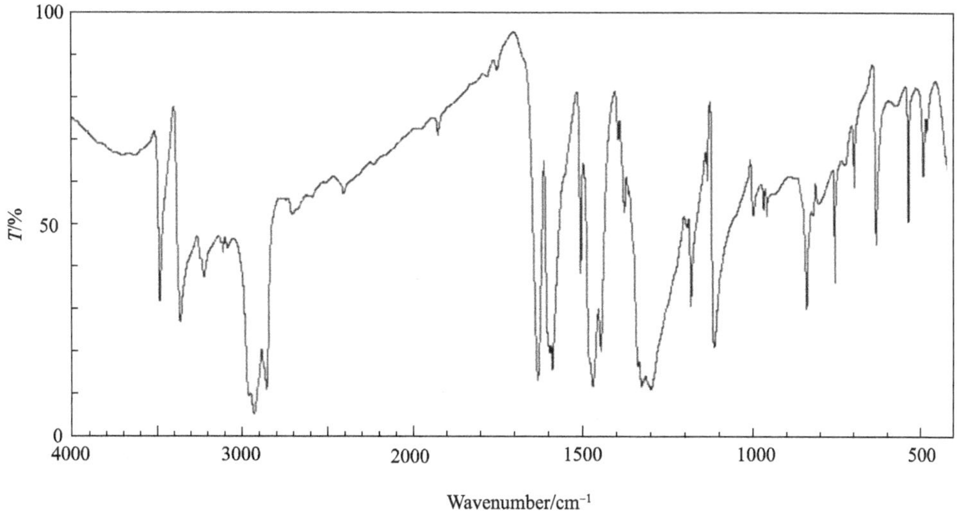

Questions

(1) Can 4-nitroaniline be prepared directly from aniline? why?

(2) What is the clear solution obtained after refluxing under acidic conditions of 4-nitroacetanilide? After adding 20% sodium hydroxide solution, why the 4-nitroaniline is precipitated out? And why do we need to add alkali to make the solution alkaline?

3.14 Isolation of Caffeine From Tea Leaves

Principle

Caffeine[1] can be isolated from tea leaves by means of microwave-assisted extraction as well as traditional soxhlet extraction.

Caffeine belongs to a group of alkaloid compounds called the xanthines. Its chemical name is 1, 3, 7-trimethyl-2, 6-dioxopurine and it is a derivative of purine as shown below:

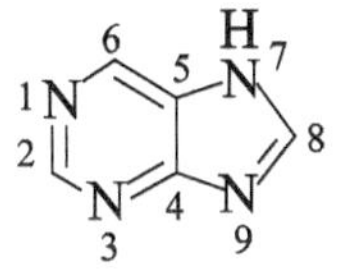

Purine

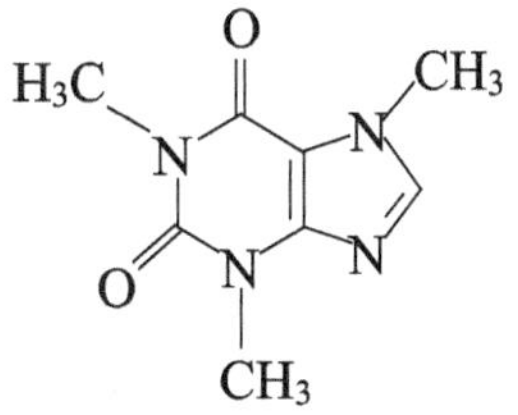

Caffeine, 1, 3, 7-trimethyl-2, 6-dioxopurine

Apparatus and Materials

Apparatus home microwave; soxhlet extractor; sublimation	
Materials	
tea leaves[2]	7.0～10g
95% ethanol	120mL, 60mL
CaO powder	2.5g

Time 3h or 6h

Procedure

1. The method of microwave-assisted extraction[3]

(1) Place 10g black tea leaves into a 250mL iodimetric flask. Add 120mL of 95% ethanol, as well as some boiling stones.

(2) Put the iodimetric flask into a home microwave, adjust microwave power up to some 320W, radiate for 50～60s[4], and then take the flask out and cool it down.

(3) Repeat the above procedures three or four times[5], and then filter to remove the tea leaves from the ethanol solution.

(4) Place the filtrate in a distillation apparatus with a water bath and distill out most of the solvents, which can be reused afterwards, until the residual liquid in the flask is 5～8mL.

(5) Pour the residue into an evaporating dish, wash the flask with small amounts of distilled ethanol three times, and then add them to the residue in the evaporating dish together.

(6) Add 2.5g CaO powder[6] into the evaporating dish and stir the mixture continuously. Then put it on a boiling water bath and evaporate to dryness.

(7) Move the evaporating dish onto the asbestos pad, and heat the crude caffeine with a low, moderate flame.

(8) Pierce many small holes in a large round filter paper and cover over an appropriately sized glass funnel with it. Put a small amount of cotton batting into the neck of the funnel and place on the evaporating dish.

(9) Sublime the caffeine[7] with a small flame[8] at first, and then stop heating as soon as some brown oil substances appear on the wall of glass funnel. Cool and collect the caffeine crystals on the filter paper.

(10) Re-sublime the residue of caffeine twice with a slightly larger flame after stirring completely. Afterwards put all sublimated products together. Weigh and calculate the yield (70～80mg). Pure caffeine is a white or slightly yellow needle-shaped crystal, m.p.238℃.

2. The method of tradtional soxhlet extraction

(1) Place 7g of tea leaves into a suitable filter cylinder, then put it into a soxhlet extractor (Fig. 2.14).

(2) Add 60mL of 95% ethanol and put boiling stones into a round-bottom flask. Prepare a reflux apparatus with a water bath.

(3) Reflux continuously and extract for 2h until the colour of extracted liquid is very light. Stop heating instantly[9] once the liquid just siphons back to the flask from the soxhlet.

(4) The rest of the steps will follow the procedures mentioned in microwave-assisted extraction from No.4 to No.10[10].

Brief Summary

1. Objectives

(1) Learn two different method of extraction including main principles and basic operations.

(2) Be familiar with the process of sublimation.

2. Notes

[1] Caffeine is used as a cardiac, respiratory, and mental stimulant. It is also often used as a vascular analgesic, especially for migraine headaches. Overuse can lead to increased tolerance and mild addiction. Caffeine, some flavonoid pigments, green chlorophyll, and tannins are all extracted from tea leaves, in which the content of caffeine and tannins is 1%～3% and 11%～12%, respectively. On the whole, the caffeine content in black tea leaves is higher than one in green tea leaves.

Hydrated Caffeine is fairly soluble in 80℃ hot water, or acetone, or ethanol, or chloroform and so on. It can lose crystal water at 100℃, and start sublimating. The process of sublimation can go fast when the temperature is above 178℃.

[2] Any popular brand tea leaves may be purchased from a supermarket; loose tea may also be used. Dry black tea leaves may be preferred in this experiment.

[3] Microwave-assisted extraction can save more than 2h, compared with other methods of extraction.

[4] Do not boil vigorously or boil to dryness during microwave heating.

[5] Cool down before repeating microwave heating.

[6] Neutralize with CaO to remove acidic substances such as tannic acid.

[7] If the mixture is not completely dry, there exists small water drops on the wall of glass funnel at the beginning of sublimation. If so, move the flame away, wipe water drops off, and continue with sublimation.

[8] Controlling temperature is the key step during the process of sublimation which has a direct influence on the quality and yield of caffeine. Too high a temperature results in a charred substance or makes caffeine yellow.

[9] The filter paper must be tightly close to the wall of soxhlet. Its height is not higher than the one of siphon arm with soxhlet extractor.

[10] The yield of caffeine is 30～40mg.

IR Spectrum

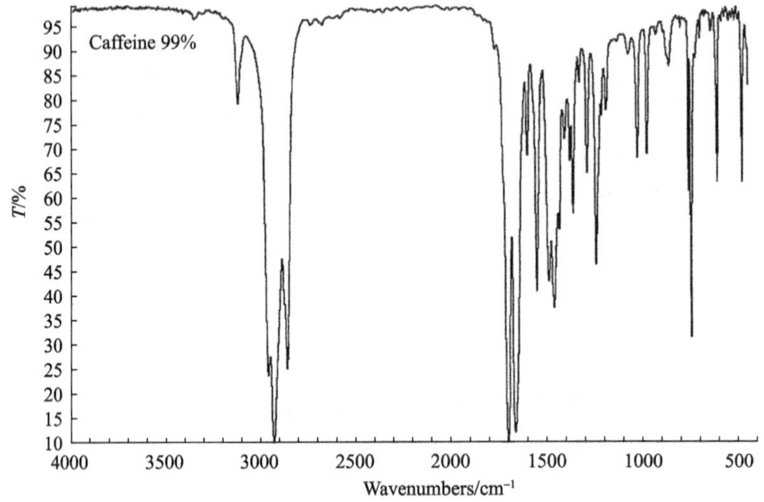

Questions

(1) Assume that your crude caffeine is nearly pure caffeine. How does the percentage yield of crude caffeine obtained in this experiment compare with the expected value of 3% caffeine in tea leaves? If there is a discrepancy between your result and the normal value, give a feasible explanation.

(2) Try to make a comparison between microwave-assisted and soxhlet extraction and describe their features.

3.15 Preparation of 2-Furanmethanol and 2-Furancarboxylic Acid

Principle

2-Furanmethanol and 2-furancarboxylic acid are prepared through the Cannizzaro reaction.

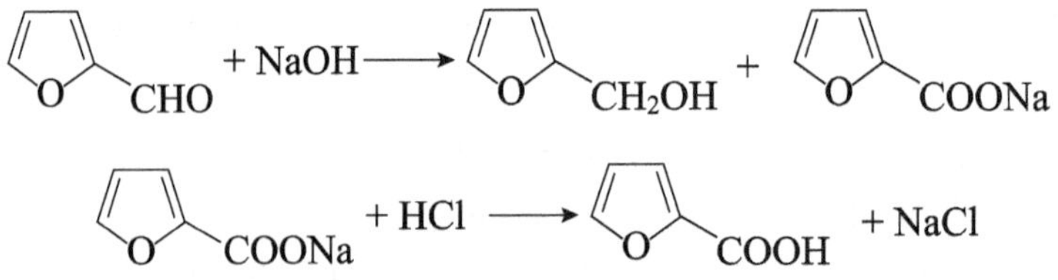

Apparatus and Materials

Apparatus vacuum distillation		
Materials		
2-furaldehyde	10mL (11.6g, 0.12mol),	b.p.161.7℃, $d = 1.1594^{20/4}$g/mL
43% sodium hydroxide solution	9mL	
diethyl ether	b.p.34.5℃,	$d = 0.7138^{20/4}$g/mL
hydrochloride acid		$d = 1.18$g/mL
polyethylene glycol (400)	2g	
anhydrous magnesium sulfate		

Time 6h

Procedure

(1) Measure 9mL of 43% NaOH and 2g of polyethylene glycol (its relative molecular weight 400) [1] in a 100mL beaker. Shake the mixture to a uniform consistency. Put the beaker in the ice water bath to cool it down to about 5℃.

(2) With ceaseless stirring, add 10mL (11.6g, about 0.12mol) of freshly distilled 2-furaldehyde[2] through the dropping funnel slowly, finish adding within 15min with a well-controlled rate. Meanwhile, maintain reaction temperature between 8～12℃[3]. When accomplished, keep on stirring for about 25min at room temperature, then a primrose yellow paste-like mixture is seen, which indicates the reaction is completed.

(3) With stirring, add 15mL of water just to dissolve the precipitate completely[4]. The solution turns a dark red or dim brown colour.

(4) Transfer the solution to the separating funnel, extract it four times with 10mL diethyl ether each.

(5) Combine the ether solutions; dry it with 2g anhydrous magnesium sulfate.

(6) Distill the ether away in a water bath before vacuum distillation of 2-furanmethanol, and collect the distillation cut between 169～172℃. The yield is about 68%～84%.

(7) The residual solution after ether extraction contains furan sodium formate. Acidify it with 25% hydrochloric acid (about 18mL) to make the pH between 2～3[5].

(8) Cool down the mixture sufficiently to separate out 2-furancarboxylic acid thoroughly, filter and wash it with some water.

(9) Recrystallize the raw product from water to get the white needle-like crystalloid. The yield is about 68%. The melting point of pure 2- furancarboxylic acid is 133～134℃.

Brief Summary

1. Objectives

(1) Study the principle and method of preparing 2-furanmethanol and 2-furancarboxylic acid from 2-furaldehyde by the Cannizzaro reaction.

(2) Master the techniques of vacuum distillation and recrystallization.

2. Notes

[1] As the reaction takes place between two phases, use the polyethylene glycol (400) as the phase transition catalysts.

[2] If stored for too long, the 2-furaldehyde will turn into chocolate brown, and possibly contains water. So just distill to purify it before use. Collect the distillation cut between 155～162℃. Vacuum distillation is recommend. Collect the distillation cut between 54～55℃/2.3kPa. The freshly distilled 2-furaldehyde is colorless or a straw yellow liquid.

[3] At the beginning of the reaction the temperature will go up slowly. But after reaching 10℃ it increases quickly. So add dropwise slowly when temperature is near 10℃ and pause dropwise addition when temperature is beyond 10℃.

[4] The furan sodium formate can be separated out during the reaction, just adding some water to dissolve it and turn the paste-like mixture into solution. The water should not be more than required in order to avoid partial loss of the product.

[5] The amount of acid must be sufficient to let the pH remain between 2~3, and dissociate the 2-furancarboxylic acid thoroughly, which is the key step of getting high yield.

IR Spectrum

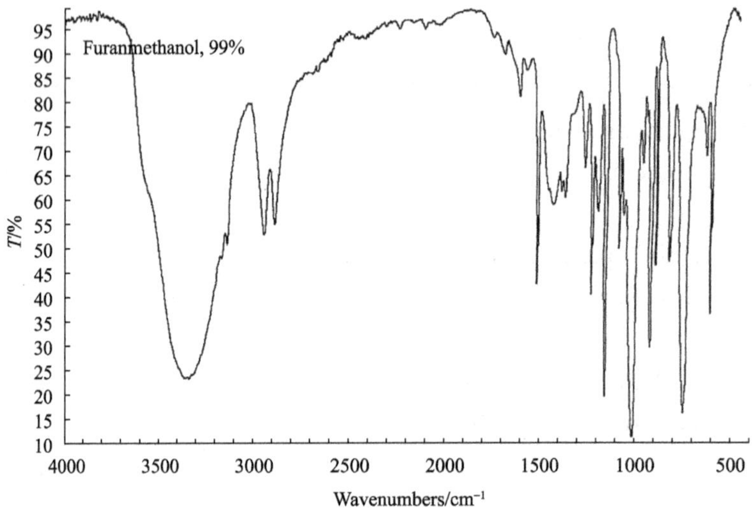

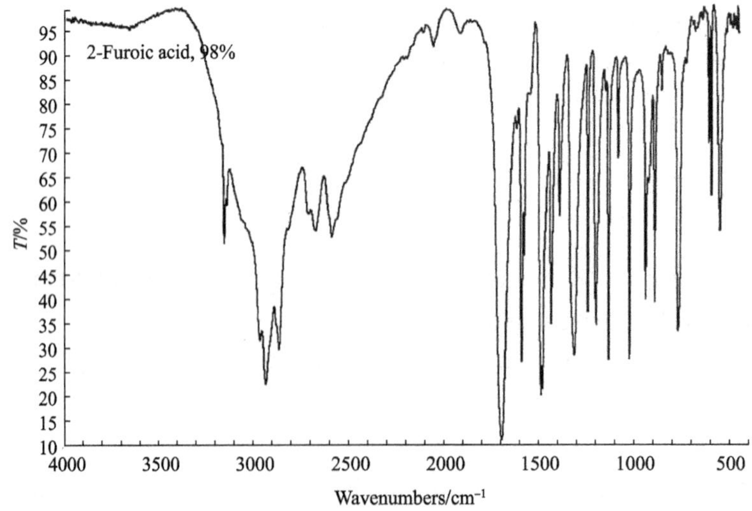

Questions

(1) In this experiment, why should newly-distillated 2-furaldehyde be used?

(2) Why should the reaction solution be extracted with diethyl ether four times? What product is to be extracted?

3.16 Preparation of 8-Quinolinol

Principle

8-Quinolinol is prepared through the Skraup reaction.

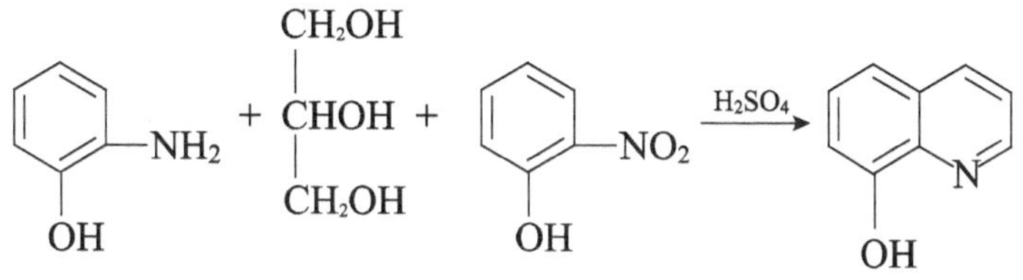

Apparatus and Materials

Apparatus steam distillation

Materials

2-nitrophenol	1.8g (0.013mol)	
2-aminephenol	2.8g (0.025mol)	
anhydrous glycerol	7.5mL (9.5g, 0.1mol)	$d = 1.260^{20/4}$g/mL
concentrated sulfuric acid	4.5mL (98%)	
sodium hydroxide solution	7mL (1 : 1)	
saturated aqueous sodium carbonate	5mL	

Time 6h

Procedure

(1) In a dry 100mL 3-neck round-bottom flask[1], place 1.8g (0.013mol) of 2-nitrophenol, 2.8g (0.025mol) of 2-aminephenol, 7.5mL (9.5g, 0.1mol) of anhydrous glycerol[2]. Shake the flask vigorously until a homogenous mixture is formed. Then carefully add 4.5mL of concentrated sulfuric acid (98%) dropwise while cooling in an ice water bath.

(2) Install the condenser, and heat the mixture using an asbestos pad until the mixture begins to reflux gently for about 15min. Remove the heating source.

(3) Then heat the mixture again and bring the mixture to a gentle boil and reflux it for 1h.

(4) Turn off the heating source and allow the mixture to cool. Then add 15mL of water. Rearrange a steam distillation apparatus to distill the 2-nitrophenol until the color of distillate change to colorless.

(5) Afterward cool down the reaction mixture, and add 7mL of sodium hydroxide solution into the flask. Carefully add 5mL of saturated aqueous sodium carbonate until the pH = 7[3].

(6) Add 20mL of water and rearrange a steam distillation apparatus to distill the 8-Quinolinol.

(7) Cooling down the mixture, then filter and wash and dry to get the raw product 3g.

(8) Recrystallize the raw product from an ethanol-water mixture (volume ratio = 4 : 1) to get the white needle-like crystalloid. The melting point of pure 8-Quinolinol is 72～74℃.

Brief Summary

1. Objectives

(1) Study the principle and method of preparing 8-Quinolinol through the Skraup reaction.

(2) Master the techniques of steam distillation and recrystallization.

2. Notes

[1] The chemicals and apparatus employed in this experiment must be dried adequately.

[2] The amount of water in glycerol must be less than 0.5%. This is an exothermic reaction, so just add the reagent slowly to avoid explosion caused by too fierce a reaction.

[3] The 8-Quinolinol will dissolve in both the acid and the base, and change to the salt, distillation of the salt is difficult, thus the pH of the solution must be brought to 7～8.

IR Spectrum

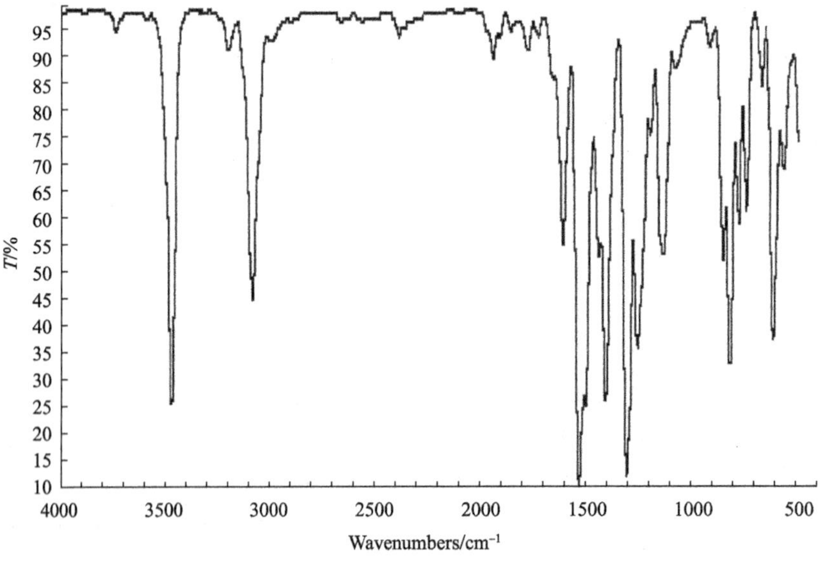

Questions

(1) In this experiment, why should the steam distillation be used in acidic condition at the first time and in neutral condition at the second time?

(2) If 4-methyl-2-aminophenol replaces the 2-aminophenol as starting materials, what kind of product can be obtained?

3.17 Preparation of Acetylferrocene

Principle

Primary reaction

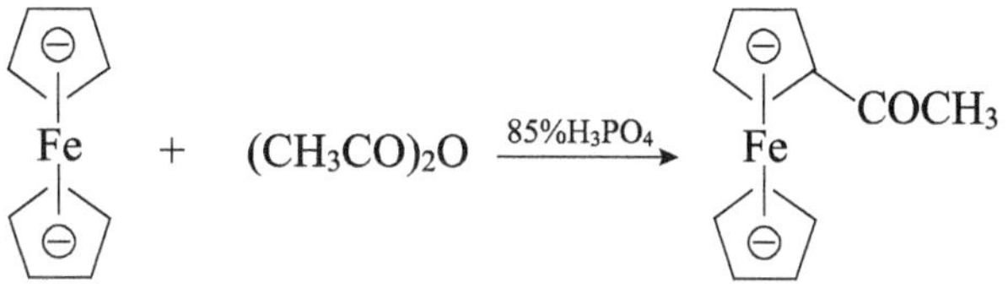

Apparatus and Materials

Apparatus: vacuum filtration

Materials

ferrocene	1g (0.0054mol)	m.p. 173℃
acetic anhydride	10mL (10.8g, 0.10mol)	b.p.139.6℃ d=1.0820$^{20/4}$g/mL
85% phosphoric acid	2mL	

petroleum ether (60～90℃); sodium bicarbonate (solid); ethanol; benzene; ice.

silica gel G plates (3cm×1cm): several blocks

Time 4~6h

Procedure

1. Preparation of Acetylferrocene

(1) 1g ferrocene and 10mL acetic anhydride are added in a 100mL round flask[1], 2mL 85% phosphoric acid is slowly dropped into the flask through a dropper under shaking. Then plug the flask by a stopper equipped with a calcium chloride drying tube[1]. The reaction mixture is heated on a boiling water bath for 40min with intermittent shaking.

(2) The mixture is poured into a 400mL beaker containing 40g crushed ice, and the flask is washed with 10mL cold water, then put the rinse lotion into the beaker.

(3) With stirring, add about 20～25g of solid sodium bicarbonate into the beaker until the solution is neutral[2]. The reactant after neutralization was cooled in an ice-water bath for about 25min.

(4) After vacuum filtration, the orange solid is collected and washed with 50mL ice-water twice, and finally dried in the air.

(5) The crude product is recrystallized by petroleum ether (60～90℃). The weight of the products is 0.3g, with melting point 84～85℃ (the melting point of pure acetylferrocene is 85℃).

2. Identification Acetylferrocene by Thin Layer Chromatography (TLC)

(1) A little of dried crude acetylferrocene is dissolved in benzene, and then spotted on the TLC

plate. 3 : 1 petroleum ether / ethyl acetate (volume ratio) is used as the developing solvent, and the TLC plate from top to bottom presents yellow, orange and red three points. representing ferrocene, acetylferrocene and by-product 1,1'-diacetyl ferrocene, respectively.

(2) 0.1g recrystallized acetylferrocene is dissolved in about 3mL benzene to identify sample purity[3] by thin layer chromatography and determine the R_f of acetylferrocene.

Brief Summary

1. Objectives

(1) Learn the theory and method of the synthesis of acetylferrocene through the acetylation of ferrocene.

(2) Master the experimental technique of TLC.

2. Notes

[1] The flask must be dried, calcium chloride drying tube should be used to avoid the water in the air enters the flask.

[2] Large amount of carbon dioxide escape during the process of neutralization, leading to a large number of bubbles, so it should be handled with care. It is better to use a pH testing paper to test the pH of solution, if the color of reaction mixture is dark for the use of pH testing paper, sodium bicarbonate can be used, the disappearance of bubble will indicate the completion of neutralization.

[3] If only one point left on the plate after chromatography, it indicates the acetylferrocene sample is pure after recrystallization.

IR Spectrum

The IR spectrum of acetylferrocene is shown as follow:

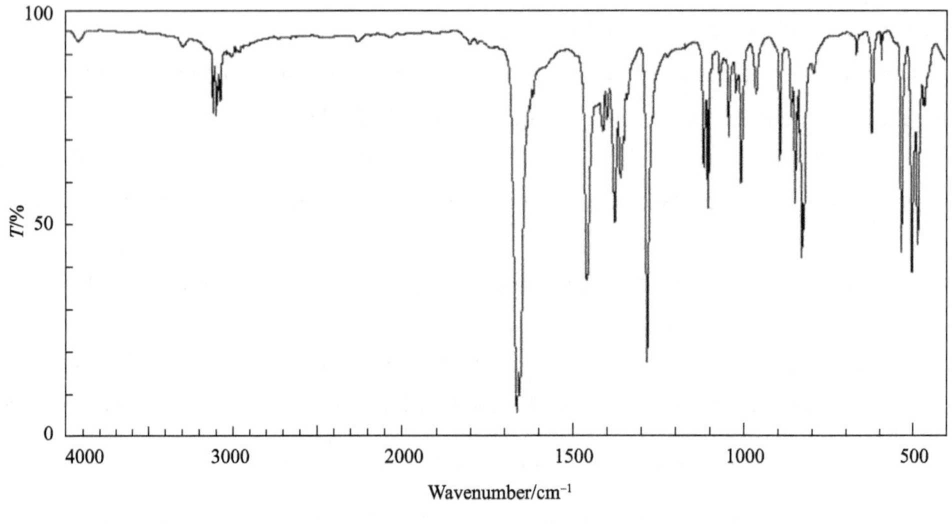

Questions

(1) Why do we need to use a dried flask and a calcium chloride drying tube? If the water goes into the flask, what will be the influence on the reaction? Why?

(2) Upon ferrocene acylation, if side product (diacylferrocene) is generated, which the cyclopentadienyl anion ring would enter the second acyl group? Why?

(3) Why is the ferrocene very stable, with aromaticity? Try to give some explains from the structure of ferrocene.

3.18 Biological Synthesis of Ethanol

Principle

This experiment adopts the method of sucrose fermentation to prepare ethanol[1]. Through the action of dry yeast and Pasteur salt solution[2], sucrose is fermented for one week at room temperature to get the fermentation broth containing 8%～10% ethanol. The fermentation broth is fractionated to obtain 95% ethanol (namely general industrial alcohol).

The main chemical reactions of sucrose fermentation are:

$$\underset{\text{sucrose}}{C_{12}H_{22}O_{11}} \longrightarrow \underset{\text{glucose}}{C_6H_{12}O_6} + \underset{\text{fructose}}{C_6H_{12}O_6} \longrightarrow \underset{\text{ethanol}}{4CH_3CH_2OH} + 4CO_2$$

Biochemical processes of sucrose fermentation are mainly as follows: first, the sucrose is hydrolyzed into glucose and fructose, the 1, 6-diphosphate fructose is generated by the activation of glucose and fructose, after degradation of the 1, 6- diphosphate fructose to form glyceraldehyde 3-phosphate, it is oxidized to generate pyruvic acid. Under anaerobic conditions, decarboxylation of pyruvic acid leads to acetaldehyde and CO_2, acetaldehyde is reduced to ethanol at the final stage. Each of the above step requires a miracle enzyme as a catalyst, but also need some common inorganic ions (such as magnesium), and phosphates.

Sucrose fermentation biochemical processes can be expressed as follows:

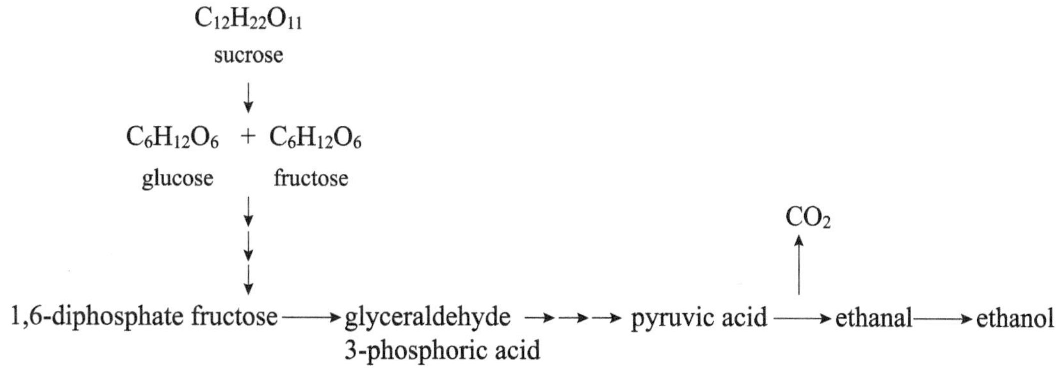

Apparatus and Materials

Apparatus: stinging fractionating column	
sucrose	40g (0.12mol)
dry yeast	1.5g
potassium phosphate:	2g; calcium phosphate: 0.2g; magnesium sulfate: 0.2g; ammonium

tartrate: 10g; disodium hydrogen phosphate: 0.25g; saturated lime water; celite.

Time 6h

Procedure

(1) In 500mL conical flask, 40g (0.12mol) sucrose is dissolved in 350mL water. At room temperature, 35mL Pasteur salt solution[2] and 1.5g dry yeast are added with violently shaking to mix it completely.

(2) Insert a single-hole rubber plug with a bent glass tube on the bottle. The lower end of the glass tube is immersed in the saturated lime water[3]. The mixture is set aside for a week at room temperature (25~35℃) until carbon dioxide stop escaping, which indicates the completion of fermentation.

(3) After fermentation, the conical flask is moved to the desktop with care to make sure that the bottom sediments will not float. then the liquid is decanted into a 500mL round bottom flask with care by a group of cotton or glass wool.

(4) Add some grains of zeolite into the round bottom flask. Mount a stinging fractionating column and a condenser pipe to the flask. The solution is distilled in an asbestos online to collect 60mL of distillate, finally the residual liquid in the bottle is discarded.

(5) The distillate is transferred to a 100mL round bottom flask, using the same fractionation unit, the following boiling range of distilled fractions are collected: A: 78~82℃; B: 82~88℃; C: 88~95℃. Discard the fusel oil remaining in the bottle[4].

(6) Measure the volume of each fraction, if the collected fraction A is less than 15mL, collected fraction should be merged to perform re-distillation.

(7) Measure the density of fraction A and B, and convert them into the content of ethanol, finally calculate the yield of ethanol.

Brief Summary

1. Objectives

(1) Learn the theory and method about the synthesis of ethanol by the sucrose room temperature fermentation.

(2) Master the experimental technique of fermentation and fractionation.

2. Notes

[1]Fermentation is a series of biochemical processes of natural organic compounds catalyzed by the bio-catalysis, enzymes. It has been widely used in industry and daily life. Yeast fermentation is an enzyme-catalyzed biochemical process. Zymase is a complex with highly selective. Its activity is greatly affected by temperature and pH .

[2]The preparation of Pasteur salt solution: 2.0g potassium phosphate, 0.2g calcium phosphate, 0.2g magnesium sulfate and 10g ammonium tartrate are dissolved in 860mL water. It can also use 0.25g disodium hydrogen phosphate in place of Pasteur salt solution to perform fermentation, it does not need to add any other salts, but yield of this method is low, the separation of yeast residue is relatively difficult.

[3]The role of lime water is to prevent air from entering the flask, while allowing the gas to escape from the bottle. A balloon can be used to replace lime water, during fermentation, the gas (CO_2) is released to make the balloon expand. If the oxygen is continuously exposed to the fermentation solution, ethanol will be further oxidized to acetic acid, or oxidized to carbon dioxide and water.

[4]The high boiling point fractions are fusel oil, the fusel oil are $C_3 \sim C_5$ alcohols mixture, such as 1-propanol, 2-propanol, 1-butanol, 2-methyl-2-propanol, 3-methyl-1-butanol. The composition of the mixture depends on the raw materials used, it is not formed by fermentation of glucose, but formed by transformation of the proteins present in the feed and yeast.

Questions

(1) Why does distillation only get 95.6% ethanol? How do we prepare the anhydrous ethanol by the conventional ethanol?

(2) Testing the density of the solution can determine the percentage of water in the ethanol, why?

Chapter 4 All-around Experiments

4.1 Synthesis and Characterization of Ethyl Acetate and Ethyl Acetoacetate

4.1.1 Synthesis and Characterization of Ethyl Acetate

Principle

Ethyl acetate is prepared by the direct esterification of acetic acid with ethanol. The reaction is reversible, and equilibrium is reached rapidly through the use of the sulfuric acid catalyst. The yield of the ester can be increased by using an excess of ethanol or by removing one of the products, usually water.

$$CH_3COOH + CH_3CH_2OH \xrightleftharpoons{H_2SO_4} CH_3COOCH_2CH_3 + H_2O$$

Apparatus and Materials

Apparatus reflux, simple distillation

Materials

glacial acetic acid	9mL (9.0g, 0.15mol)	b.p.118℃ $d = 1.049^{20/4}$g/mL
anhydrous ethanol	14.5mL (13.8g, 0.30mol)	b.p.78.4℃ $d = 0.7893^{20/4}$g/mL
concentrated sulfuric acid	3.8mL	$d = 1.841^{20/4}$g/mL
saturated aqueous sodium carbonate		
saturated aqueous sodium chloride	7.5mL	
saturated aqueous calcium chloride	7.5mL	
anhydrous magnesium sulfate		

Time 4h

Procedure

(1) In a dry 50mL round-bottom flask, place 14.5mL (13.8g, 0.30mol) of anhydrous ethanol, 9mL (9.0g, 0.15mol) of glacial acetic acid. Then carefully add 3.8mL of concentrated sulfuric acid (98%) dropwise. Swirl the solution to mix and add two boiling stones.

(2) Attach the flask to a reflux assembly using a water cooled condenser. On the top of the condenser is a calcium chloride drying tube.

(3) Heat the mixture gently with a heating mantle or with an oil bath. Bring the mixture to a gentle boil and reflux it for 45min.

(4) At the end of the reflux, remove the heating source and allow the mixture to cool slightly.

(5) Rearrange a simple distillation apparatus to distill the ethyl acetate formed during the reaction. Collect the fraction boiling at approximately 75～85℃.

(6) Slowly add saturated aqueous sodium carbonate to the distillate[1]. Swirl the mixture gently until carbon dioxide gas is no longer evolved[2].

(7) Transfer the solution to a separatory funnel. Place the separatory funnel on a ring clamp and allow it to stand for 5min.

(8) Draw off the lower aqueous layer. Add 7.5mL of saturated aqueous sodium chloride[3] to the organic layer contained in the separatory funnel, stir the mixture gently without shaking. Carefully separate the lower aqueous layer and discard it.

(9) Wash the organic layer with 7.5mL of saturated aqueous calcium chloride, and then wash it again with some water.

(10) When the water has been removed, pour the crude ester from the top of the separatory funnel into a dry flask. Add about 0.3g anhydrous magnesium sulfate to dry the ester.

(11) Transfer the crude ester to a clean, dry 50mL round-bottom flask, add two boiling stones.

(12) Assemble a simple distillation apparatus. Dry all glassware thoroughly before use.

(13) Distill the ester. The receiver must be cooled in an ice bath. Collect the fraction boiling between 73～78℃.

(14) Weigh the product and calculate the percentage yield.

(15) Identify the product by UV spectrum.

Pure ethyl acetate is a colorless liquid, b.p.77.06℃, d_4^{20} 0.9003, n_D^{20} 1.3723.

Brief Summary

1. Objectives

(1) Demonstrate direct esterification by the preparation of ethyl acetate.

(2) Master the distillation and extraction techniques.

2. Notes

[1] The crude ester in the distillate contains some acetic acid, which can be removed by neutralization with saturated aqueous sodium carbonate.

[2] Check to see whether it is basic to litmus. If it is not basic, add additional base until the solution is basic.

[3] Wash with saturated aqueous sodium chloride to aid in layer separation.

IR Spectrum

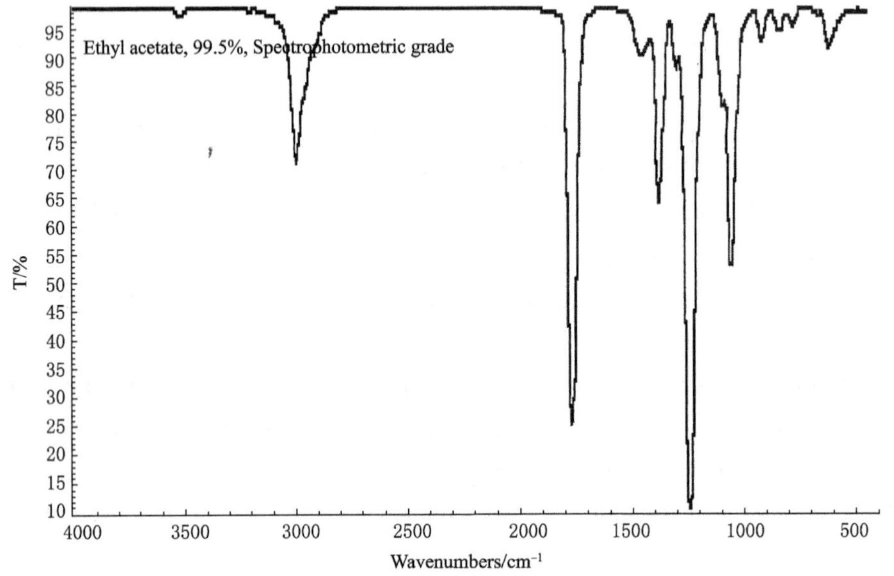

Questions

(1) What methods can be used to shift the equilibrium in the esterification in order to favor products?

(2) Which impurities may be contained in the crude ester, and how can they be removed?

4.1.2 Synthesis and Characterization of Ethyl Acetoacetate

Principle

Ethyl acetoacetate is usually prepared by the Claisen condensation of ethyl acetate.

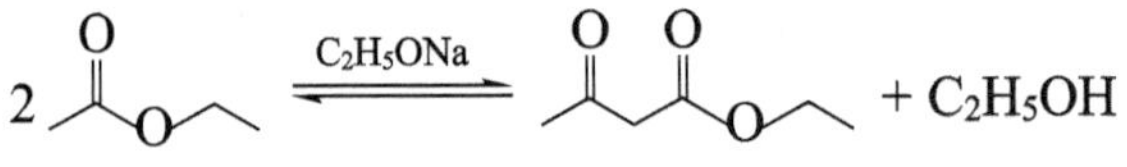

Apparatus and Materials

Apparatus reflux, vacuum distilltion

Materials

ethyl acetate	9.8mL (8.8g, 0.10mol) $d = 0.9003^{20/4}$ g/mL	b.p.77.06℃ n_D^{20} 1.3723
sodium metal	1g (0.04mol)	
50% acetic acid		
saturated aqueous sodium chloride		
5% aqueous sodium carbonate		
anhydrous magnesium sulfate		

Time 6h

Procedure

(1) In a dry 50mL round-bottom flask[1], place 9.8mL (8.8g, 0.1mol) of anhydrous ethyl acetate prepared above, then quickly add 1g of sodium hydroxide-free sodium metal as thin flakes[2, 3].

(2) Place the flask in a reflux apparatus with a warm-water bath as the heat source. At the top of the condenser fit a drying tube containing anhydrous calcium choride.

(3) Heat the reaction mixture under reflux gently until the sodium metal disappears (about 2h). The solution will be clear red.

(4) Turn off the heating source and allow the mixture to cool.

(5) Add 50% acetic acid[4] until the solution is just slightly acid to blue litmus paper (pH = 5～6) with stirring slowly.A solid may appear, but it dissolves in acid conditions.

(6) Transfer the reaction mixture to a separatory funnel, add an equal volume of saturated aqueous sodium chloride, shake it thoroughly and let it stand for a few minutes.

(7) Separate the ester layer, extract the aqueous layer with 5mL of ethyl acetate and mix it with the ester layer.

(8) Wash the organic layer with 5% Na_2CO_3 until the solution is neutral to pH paper.

(9) Save the organic layer in a small Erlenmeyer flask, dry the crude product using a small amount of anhydrous magnesium sulfate.

(10) Decant the clean liquid into a dry distilling flask. Remove the ethyl acetate from the ethyl acetoacetate by distilling on a water-bath.

(11) Set up an apparatus for reduced pressure distillation. Vacuum-distill the product at about 931Pa (7mmHg), at which pressure the product is collected between 54～55℃[5].

(12) Weigh the product and calculate the percentage yield.

(13) Identify the product by UV spectrum.

Pure ethyl acetoacetate is a colorless liquid, b.p.180.4℃ (decomposition), d_4^{20} 1.0282, n_D^{20} 1.4194.

Brief Summary

1. Objectives

(1) Learn the principle and method of preparing ethyl acetoacetate by Claisen condensation of ethyl acetate.

(2) Master the technique of vacuum distillation.

2. Notes

[1]All the glassware using in this experiment must be thoroughly dry and the reagents must be absolutely anhydrous.

[2]It is necessary to remove any oxide at the surface of the sodium and cut the sodium into small pieces for speeding up the condensation.

[3]The reaction starts immediately. If it gets too violent, immerse the flask in a cold-water bath to stem the reaction. If the reaction does not start, heat the reaction mixture to promote the reaction, and then, remove the heat source.

[4]Be careful when adding 50% acetic acid, because it reacts violently with unreacted sodium.

[5]The relationship between the boiling point of the ethyl acetoacetate and the pressure is shown in the following table.

Pressure	mmHg	12	14	18	20	30	40	60	80	760
	kPa	1.6	1.87	2.4	2.67	4	5.33	8	10.67	101.33
b.p.	℃	71	74	78	82	88	92	97	100	181

IR Spectrum

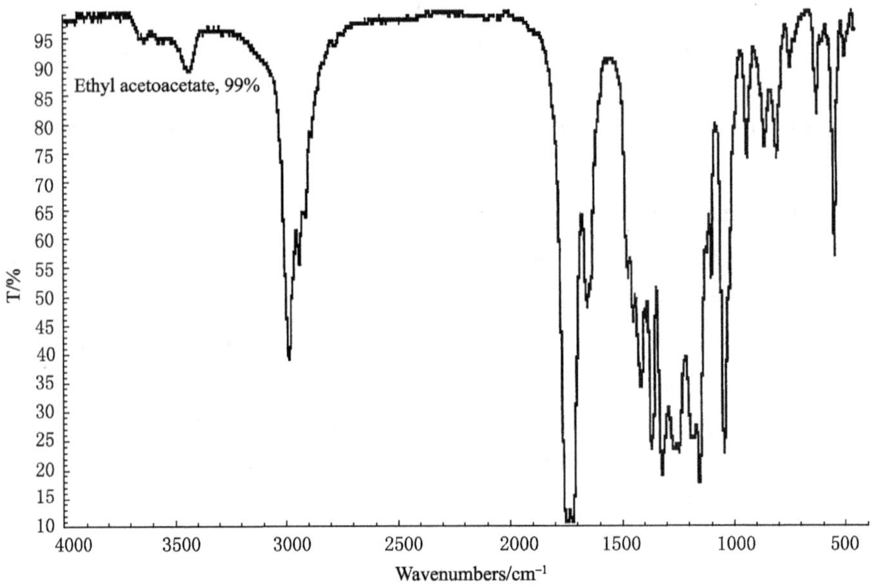

Questions

(1) All the glassware and reagents using in this experiment must be dry and absolutely anhydrous, Why?

(2) In the work up procedure for ethyl acetoacetate, what are the purposes of adding 50% acetic acid and saturated aqueous sodium chloride?

4.2　Synthesis of Sulfanilic Acid and Methyl Orange

4.2.1　Synthesis of Sulfanilic Acid

Principle

Sulfanilic acid (4-aminobenzenesulfonic acid) is one of the important intermediates for the synthesis of dyes and is also used to make methyl orange. It will be prepared by the sulfonation of aniline[1].

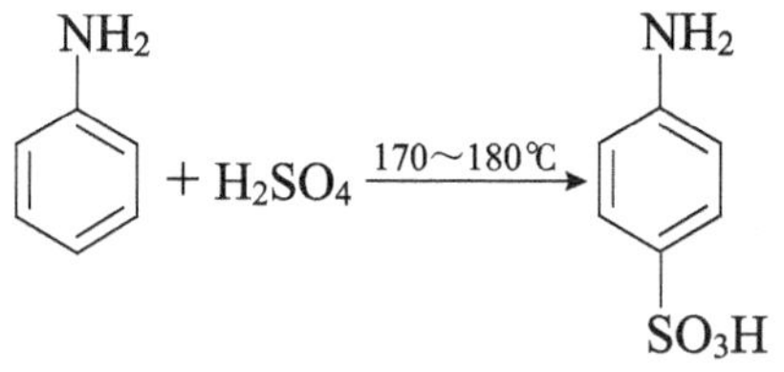

Apparatus and Materials

Apparatus reflux with a thermometer		
Materials		
aniline	10mL (10.2g, 0.11mol)	$d = 1.021^{20/4}$ g/mL
concentrated sulfuric acid	18mL (0.34mol)	$d = 1.841^{20/4}$ g/mL

Time 4h

Procedure

(1) Place 10mL (10.2g, 0.11mol) of aniline in a 250mL three neck flack fitted with a reflux condenser and a thermometer.

(2) Slowly and cautiously add 18mL of concentrated sulfuric acid (d = 1.84g/mL) to the flask through the unused neck, and than replace the stopper.

(3) Heat the mixture gently to 170～180℃[2] with a heating mantle or an oil bath and reflux for 2～2.5h.

(4) Allow the mixture to cool to about 50℃[3], and pour it into a beaker containing 100mL of ice water. Using a glass rod, stir the resulting viscous mass vigorously.

(5) Collect the product by vacuum filtration, wash it with a very cold water.

(6) Recrystallize the crude sulfanilic acid from boiling water[4]. Decolorization will probably be necessary.

(7) The mother liquid from the crystallization should be concentrated in volume[5], decolorized and crystallized to provide a second crop of crystals.

(8) Compare the color of the second crop of material to that of the first crop, and calculate the total yield.

Because sulfanilic acid is a salt, it does not give a definite melting point. Rather, it chars at a temperature between 280～290℃.

Brief Summary

1. Objectives

(1) Learn the principle and method of preparing sulfanilic acid by the sulfonation of aniline.

(2) Master the purification technique of recrystallizing solids.

2. Notes

[1] In acid solutions, the amino group is often protonated and becomes a meta directing group in the substitution reactions. In this experiment, three factors lead to predominantly para

substitution. First, under the high temperature conditions of this reaction, aniline is converted to its sulfonamide derivative. The sulfonamide group is an ortho, para directing group. Finally, as the sulfonamide group is quite large, the amount of ortho substitution is much diminished due to steric hindrance. Sulfonation of aniline at 170℃, therefore, proceeds mainly at the para position. At the end of the reaction, the sulfonyl group is removed by hydrolysis, to give sulfanilic acid. The mechanism of the sulfonation of aniline is shown as follows:

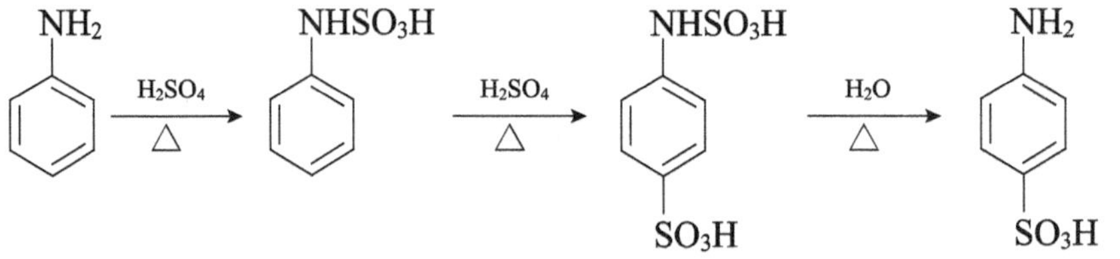

[2] The temperature should be controlled rather carefully. Black and viscous substance will be produced when the temperature is above 190℃.

[3] Below this temperature, the reaction mixture may become viscous and solidify, making it rather difficult to remove from the flask.

[4] The solubility of sulfanilic acid in water is 6.67g/100mL at 100℃ and 1.08g/100mL at 20℃.

[5] Since sulfanilic acid is still quite soluble in water at 20℃, a good deal of material remains in the mother liquors from the crystallization.

IR Spectrum

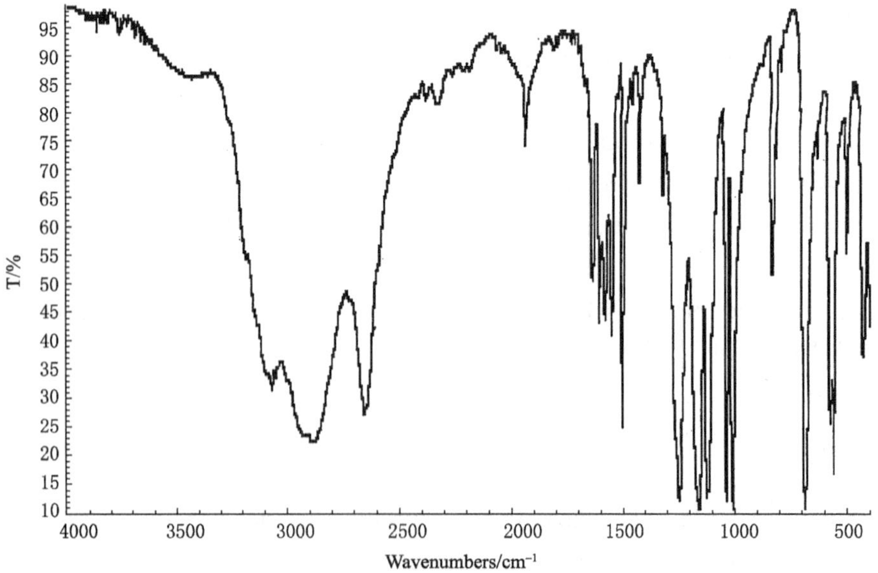

Questions

(1) Although sulfanilic acid is quite soluble in water, it is not appreciably soluble in benzene or ether, Explain.

(2) Draw a mechanism for the sulfonation of aniline.

4.2.2 Synthesis of Methyl Orange

Principle

Methyl orange is commonly used as an acid-base indicator. In this experiment it will be prepared by the diazo coupling reaction from diazotized sulfanilic acid and *N, N*-dimethylaniline.

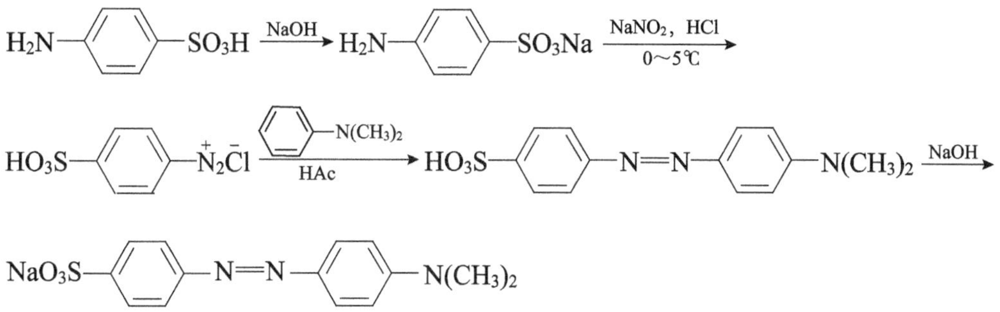

Methyl Orange

Materials

sulfanilic acid	2.1g (0.01mol)	m.p.288℃
N, N-dimethylaniline	1.3mL (1.2g, 0.01mol) $d = 0.9557^{20/4}$g/mL	b.p.193℃
sodium nitrite	0.8g (0.011mol)	m.p.271℃
10% aqueous sodium hydroxide solution	25mL	
glacial acetic acid	1mL $d = 1.049^{20/4}$g/mL	b.p.118℃,
concentrated hydrochloride acid (36%)	$d = 1.18$g/mL	
sodium choride		

Time 5h

Procedure

1. Diazotization

(1) Place 2.1g (0.01mol) of sulfanilic acid prepared above in a 100mL beaker, add 10mL of 5% aqueous sodium hydroxide solution[1].

(2) Stir the mixture with a glass rod and warm it in a hot water bath until it dissolves.

(3) Allow the solution to cool to room temperature, add 0.8g (0.011mol) of sodium nitrite and stir until it dissolves.

(4) Pour slowly this solution batchwise, with stirring[2], into a 250mL beaker containing 13mL of water and 2.5mL of concentrated hydrochloric acid. During the reaction, the temperature should be controlled below 5℃[3].

(5) Keep the mixture in an ice-salt bath for about 15min to complete the reaction[4].

2. Coupling reaction

(1) In a test tube containing 1.3mL (1.2g, 0.01mol) of *N*, *N*-dimethylaniline and 1mL of glacial acetic acid, mix the solution thoroughly by swirling the test tube.

(2) Slowly, with stirring, add this solution to the cooled diazotized sulfanilic acid in the 250mL beaker. Stir the mixture vigorously with a stirring rod.

(3) Keep the mixture in an ice bath for about 15min to make sure the coupling reaction is completed.

(4) Add 15mL of a 10% aqueous sodium hydroxide solution[5]. Check with litmus or pH paper to guarantee the solution is basic. If not, add extra base. The color of solution turns to orange. The crude methyl orange is precipitated with fine-granular shape.

(5) Heat the mixture with a boiling water bath for 5min to dissolve most of the newly formed methyl orange.

(6) When all (or most) of methyl orange is dissolved, add 5g of sodium chloride, cool the mixture to room temperature and put it in an ice bath. The methyl orange will restart to be crystallized and isolated.

(7) When the precipitation appears completely, collect the product by vacuum filtration using a Buchner funnel.

(8) Rinse the beaker with two cold portions of a saturated sodium chloride solution (5mL each) and wash the filter cake with these rinse solutions.

(9) Purify the product by recrystallizing the crude methyl orange from boiling water.

(10) Allow the product to dry, weigh it, and calculate the percentage yield. (About 75%).

Pure methyl orange is a orange slice-shaped crystal, with no definite melting point[6], pH = 3.1 (red) ~4.4 (orange).

Brief Summary

1. Objectives

(1) Study the principle and method of preparing methyl orange from sulfanilic acid and *N*, *N*-dimethylaniline by the diazo coupling reaction.

(2) Master the technique of recrystallization.

2. Notes

[1] Sulfanilic acid, insoluble in acid solution and soluble in basic solution, is an amphoteric compound. Its acidity is slightly stronger than its basicity. It is nevertheless necessary to carry out diazotization reaction in an acid (HNO_2) solution. To resolve this problem, sulfanilic acid is first dissolved in basic solution, not in acidic solution.

[2] Continuous stirring is important to this diazotization. In a short time the diazonium salt of sulfanilic acid should separate as a finely divided white precipitate.

[3] Temperature is important in this reaction. If the temperature of the reaction is above 5℃, the diazonium salt will be hydrolyzed to a phenol, thus reducing the yield of the desired product.

[4] At this moment the solution is weak alkaline. If neutral, the small amounts of alkaline liquid should be added until the solution just appears alkaline. If strongly alkaline, the resin-like polymer, not desired product, will be formed easily.

[5] The colour of wet methyl orange can deepen quickly when exposed in the natural light. So the ordinary crude methyl orange is a red-purplish (mauve) crystal. It will dry quickly if washed first with alcohol and then ether.

[6] The product is salt. Since salts do not generally have well-defined melting points, the determination of melting point should not be attempted.

IR Spectrum

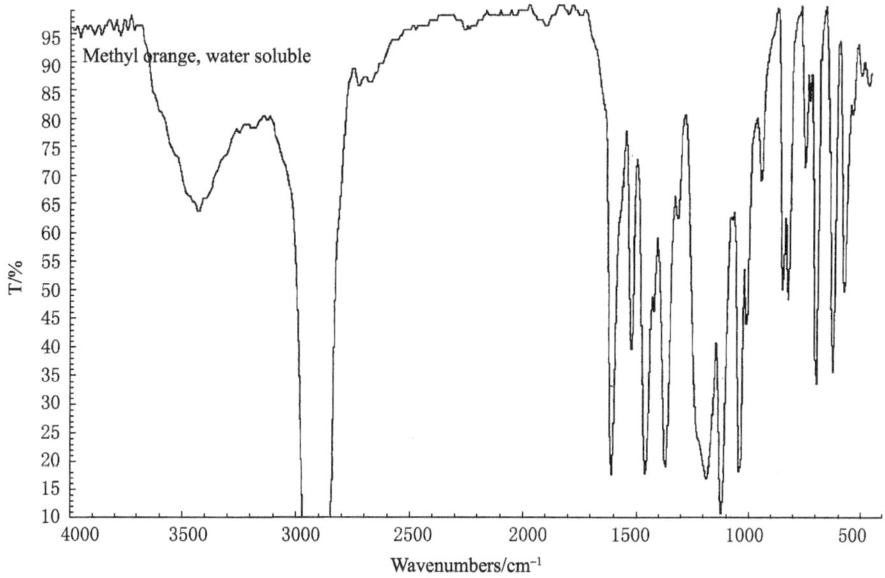

Questions

(1) In this experiment, why should the temperature of procedure 4 be controlled below 5℃?

(2) Why is the dimethylaniline coupling with diazonium salt formed a para-position product?

(3) What would the result be if cuprous chloride were added to the diazonium salt prepared in this reaction?

4.3 Extraction and Separation Spinach Leaf Pigments

Principle

Petroleum ether : ethanol = 2 : 1 (volume ratio) is used as extraction agent in this experiment. The spinach leaf pigments[1] are exacted , such as chlorophyll, lutein and β-carotene. According to different solubilities and polarities of the chlorophyll, lutein and β-carotene, silica gel G is used as adsorbent, benzene : acetone : petroleum ether = 2 : 1 : 2 (volume ratio) as the eluent in this experiment and these three above components are separated by TLC.

Apparatus and Materials

Apparatus: TLC means		
benzene	b.p. 80℃	$d = 0.8786^{20/4}$g/mL
propanone	b.p. 56℃	$d = 0.7899^{20/4}$g/mL
petroleum ether (60～90℃)		
absolute ethanol	b.p. 78℃	$d = 0.7893^{20/4}$g/mL
anhydrous sodium sulfate; silica gel G; fresh spinach		

Time 6h

Procedure

1. Preparation of Plate

(1) 3g silica gel G and 7mL distilled water are added in a mortar, and fully grounded into a paste. Put onto the clean, dry, smooth glass slides (10mm × 30mm ×2.5mm). The entire plate surface is coated rapidly by mortar bar. Then hold one end of a glass slide and gently shake at the edge of the table, so that silica gel G can be evenly coated on a glass slide to form a smooth surface [2].

(2) Placed the glass slide horizontally and dry it naturally for 30min, then place it in an oven for activation at 105～110℃ about 30min, finally put in a desiccator after cooling.

2. Extraction

(1) 10g spinach leaves are weighed and cut into pieces, then placed it in a mortar, adding 15mL of 2 : 1 (volume ratio) in petroleum ether-absolute ethanol solution. It should be ground to a dark green liquid.

(2) The extract is transferred into a separatory funnel by a dropper, then an equal volume of saturated sodium chloride solution is added and then washed [3]. It should stand for a while for liquid separation.

(3) The organic layer is retained and washed with a small amount of distilled water twice, the organic layer is dried in a conical flask, add appropriate amount of solid anhydrous sodium sulfate, then set them aside for later use.

3. Separation

1) Spotting

The above extracting solution is extracted by capillary syringe, then dropped carefully and slowly from about 1.5cm at one end of the sheet. Spot repeatedly for several times until the sample point become dark green, and it should control to keep the spot diameter within 2mm. The distance between two parallel sample points is about 1cm.

2) Expand

10mL of the eluent (benzene : petroleum ether : acetone=2 : 1 : 2) is added in a dry chromatography tank. The sample plate is put into the chromatography tank (spotted end down), and then cover the tank with the lid. When the distance between solvent front and the upper end of the sheet is about 1～2cm, the plate should be removed, and the position of the solvent front should be marked with a pencil. After drying, the distance between the solvent front and the sample point, as well as the distance between the solvent front and each dot[4] should be measured.

4. Calculate R_f value of each pigment

Calculate R_f value of each pigment according to the formula.

Brief Summary

1. Objectives

(1) Learn the theory and method of extraction and separation spinach leaf pigments.
(2) Master the experimental technique of TLC.

2. Notes

[1] The primary pigments of spinach leaves are chlorophyll and carotenoids. In the chlorophyll, the content ratio of chlorophyll a (blue) and chlorophyll b (yellow-green) is 3 : 1, in carotenoids, the content ratio of lutein (orange) and β- Carotene (yellow) is 2 : 1. These dyes are soluble in petroleum ether, ethanol, benzene and acetone, the polar order: lutein > chlorophyll b > chlorophyll a > β- carotene.

[2] The coating should be uniform, there should be no lines or pellets, sheets should be clean, flat and uniform. Preparation of plates, spotting and expand can refer to the section 2.10.3 of this book.

[3] The samples are washed with saturated sodium chloride solution to remove water-soluble substances contained.

[4] The order of the R_f value of the four main pigment should be: β-carotene > chlorophyll a > chlorophyll b > lutein.

Questions

(1) When performing the expanding, if the sample point submerged below the surface of the eluent, what are the consequences?

(2) If the proportion of acetone in the expansion agent is increased, how does the R_f value of each pigment change with it?

4.4 Extraction, Separation and Identification Capsanthin and β-Carotene

Principle

According to the different polarity of capsanthin[1], capsorubin and β-carotene, this experiment regards silica gel G as adsorbent, dichloromethane as extraction solvent, 1 : 1 petroleum ether-dichloromethane (volume ratio) solution as the eluent. The above three components containing in the red pepper are separated by column chromatography, and capsanthin is identified by UV, β-carotene is identified by IR.

Apparatus and Materials

Apparatus: chromatography column (20cm×1cm), reflux and evaporation apparatus (rotary evaporator recommended)

Test equipment: ultraviolet spectrometer, infrared spectrometer

Materials

dichloromethane b.p. 39.75℃

dried red pepper: 2g; petroleum ether (60~90℃); silica gel G (100~200 mesh): 8~8.5g; silica gel plate (3cm×1cm): several blocks; quartz sand: a little.

Time 4~5h

Procedure

1. Extract

(1) 2g dried and crushed red pepper[2] and 30mL dichloromethane, as well as some boiling stones are added in a 50mL round-flask equipped with a reflux condenser. Then the reflux is heated in water bath for 20min[3].

(2) After the extractive is cooled to room temperature, the solid should be removed by a pump suction, and then the solvent is evaporated[4] to collect the pigment mixture.

2. Spotting

(1) A 200mL jar is used as a chromatography groove and dichloromethane is used as a developing agent. A small amount of the dye mixture is added in a small beaker, and 2~3 drops of dichloromethane are added to dissolve it.

(2) The sample is spotted on a silica gel plate and then it is placed into the chromatography groove to perform chromatography.

(3) Calculate the R_f value [5] of each kind of pigments.

3. Packing [6]

(1) Take a chromatography column of diameter 20cm × 1cm, whose bottom is filled with cotton wool and covered with a thin layer of quartz sand. The eluent (petroleum ether : dichloromethane = 1 : 1, volume ratio) is added into the three-quarters of the chromatography column. Then the piston is opened to release some eluent.

(2) 8~8.5g silica gel G (100~200 mesh) and moderate tune petroleum ether (10~12mL) are stirred into a paste. And then add it to the column through a funnel, gently tapping column to make the adsorbent packed tightly. Subsequently a layer of 0.5cm quartz sand is added on the layer of silica gel.

(3) Close the piston after the eluent falls to upper quartz sand.

4. Separation

(1) The dye mixture (prepared in step 1) is dissolved in 1~2mL of petroleum ether:

dichloromethane = 1 : 1 (volume ratio) solution, and then the solution is added along the walls of the column by a long dropper. At the same time, the piston should be opened immediately.

(2) When the solution flows to the surface of quartz sand, the colored sticky substance on the walls should be washed with 0.5mL petroleum ether : dichloromethane = 1 : 1 solution. Repeat this step twice. Then the eluant (petroleum ether : dichloromethane = 1 : 1) is slowly added into the column, and the pigment crude product is separated through column chromatography[4].

(3) The eluents are collected by test tubes (each 2mL), and each segment of eluate should be tested by thin layer chromatography (TCL).

(4) The eluents of the same R_f are merged, and then concentrated respectively to obtain pigment products of each component.

5. Identification

1) Capsanthin identification with UV

5 drops of capsanthin solution (obtained in step 4) are dropped into a test tube containing 5mL *n*-hexane. Subsequently the ultraviolet scanning is performed, regarding *n*-hexane as blank sample, to find the λ_{max}. With *n*-hexane as the reference, λ_{max} for capsanthin is 470nm.

2) *β*-Carotene is identified by IR

Take moderate amount of *β*-carotene solution to test by infrared spectrometer, the obtained spectra is compared with the standard IR spectra of *β*-carotene.

Brief Summary

1. Objectives

(1) Learn the theory and method about extraction, separation and identification for capsanthin with *β*-carotene.

(2) Master the experimental technique of column chromatography.

2. Notes

[1] Red pepper contains several kinds of bright color pigment, such as capsanthin, capsorubin, *β*-carotene. The red parts, whose polarity is larger, are capsanthin and capsorubin, which accounts for 50% ~ 60%, the less polar yellow component is *β*-carotene. They contain four terpenoids consisted of eight isoprene units, which are insoluble in water and ethanol, but soluble in petroleum ether, chloroform and dichloromethane.

capsanthin, $C_{40}H_{56}O_3$, molecular structure:

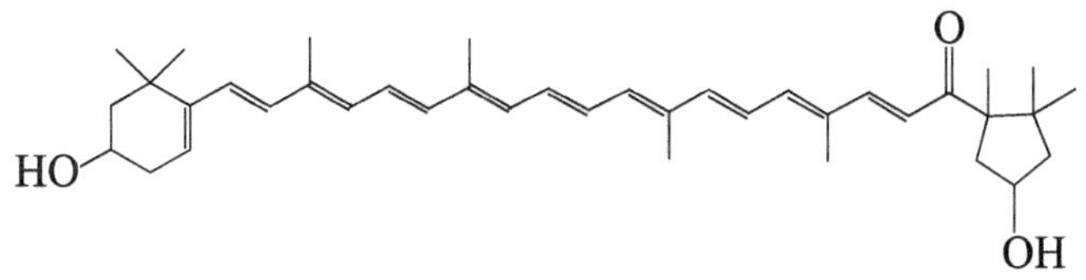

capsorubin, $C_{40}H_{56}O_4$, molecular structure:

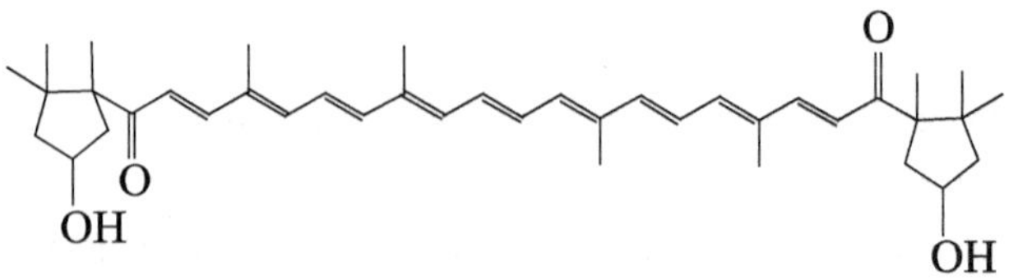

β-carotene, $C_{40}H_{56}$, molecular structure:

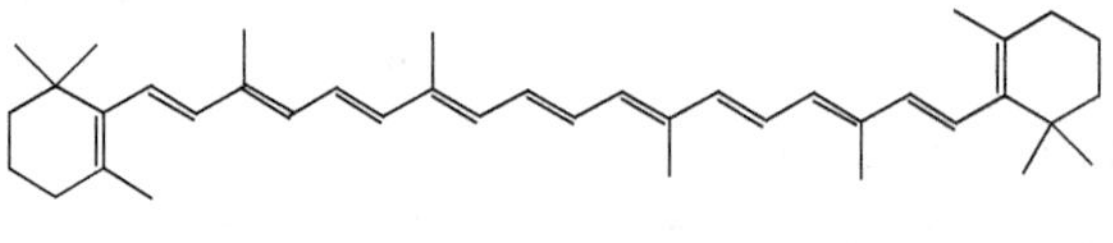

Capsanthin has bright color, high color scale, strong tinctorial strength and high usage security. It has been validated by the United States FAO, Britain, Japan, EEC, WHO, China and international organizations as unrestricted natural food additives, so its international market demand is very high.

[2] Red pepper should be dried and porphyrized.

[3] Reflux rate should not be too high, in case the soaking extraction is insufficient.

[4] Evaporation and column operation should be carried out in a fume cupboard, during the evaporation of filtrate, the solvent should be evaporated as much as possible, better with rotary evaporator.

[5] The large red spot with R_f =0.6 represent capsanthin, the small red spot with $R_f < 0.6$ represent capsorubin, the yellow spot with the maximum R_f stands for β-carotene.

[6] This experiment can use wet or dry method to pack. Column packing operations is referred to the section 2.10.2 of this textbook and 2.10.2 of the corresponding Chinese part.

IR Spectrum

The standard infrared spectra of β-carotene is shown below.

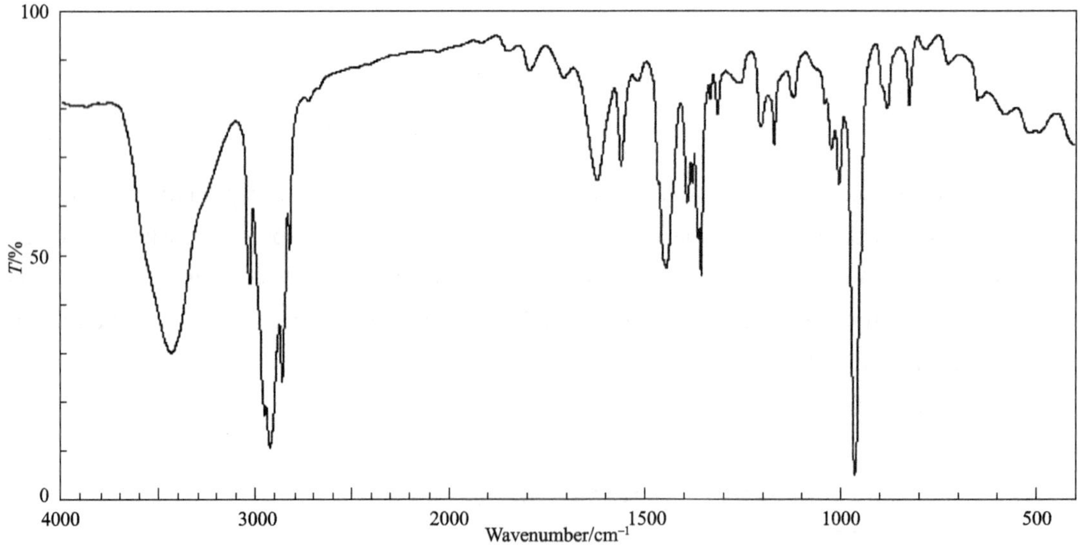

Questions

(1) If the column is filled with bubbles or uneven, how does this influent the separation? How to avoid this situation?

(2) There might be a "tailing" phenomenon when separating samples by thin layer chromatography, why? What's its influence on chromatography? and how to prevent it?

4.5 Coenzyme Preparation and Characterization of Benzoin

Principle

In this experiment, a benzoin condensation of benzaldehyde will be carried out using a biological coenzyme, vitamin B_1, as the catalyst.

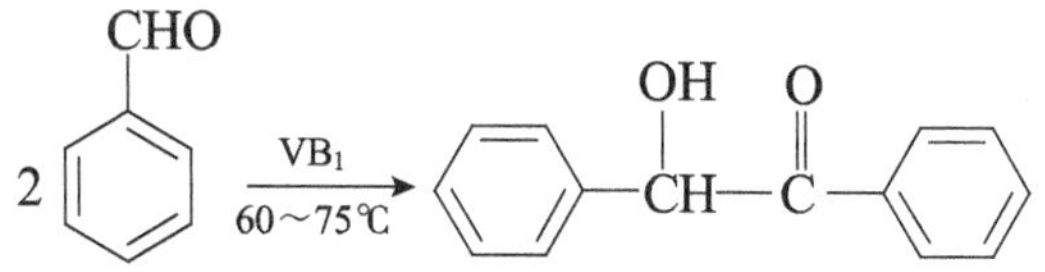

The same reaction can be accomplished using cyanide ion, a hypertoxic reagent, as the catalyst. The vitamin B_1 used as an alternative catalyst to catalyze the reaction is a environmentally benign method. The mechanism of vitamin B_1 accomplishing the reaction is listed below.

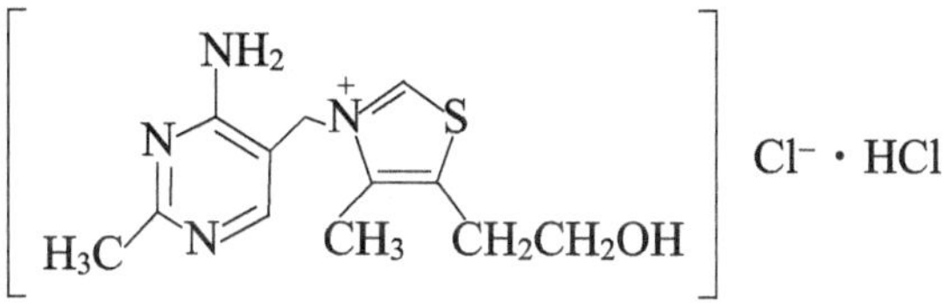

Vitamin B_1

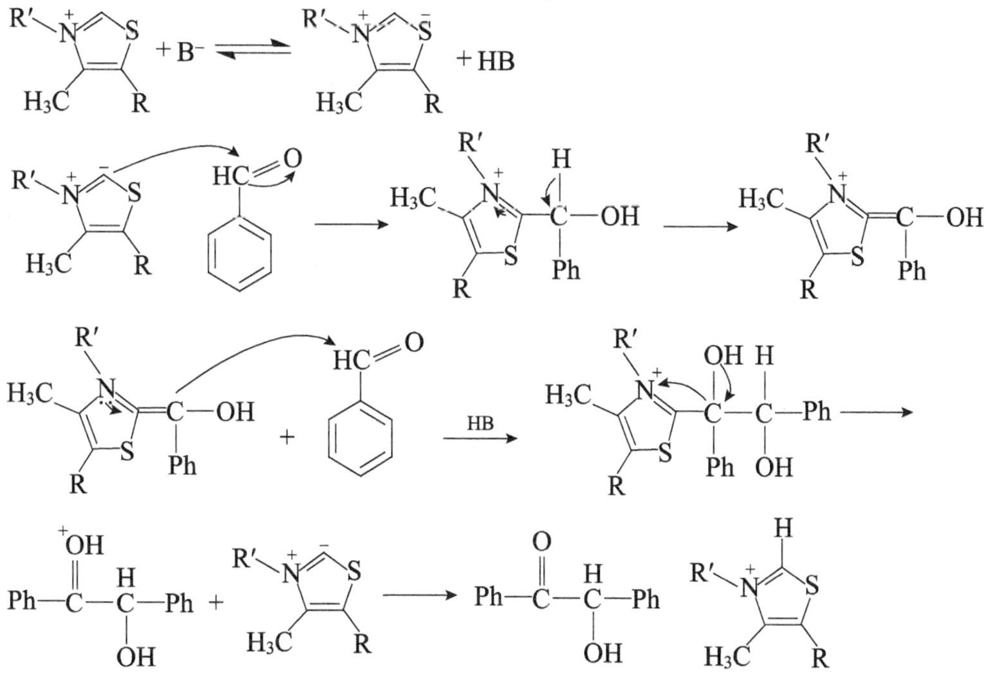

Apparratus and Materials

Apparatus reflux			
Materials			
Benzaldehyde	10.4g (10mL)	b.p.178～179℃	$d = 1.045^{20/4}$ g/mL
Vitamin B_1	1.8g		
95% ethanol			
10% sodium hydroxide			

Time 5h

Procedure

(1) Dissolve 1.8g of vitamin B_1[1] in 5mL of distilled water in a 100mL round-bottom flask. Add 15mL of 95 % ethanol and cool the solution by swirling the flask in an ice-water bath until the temperature is down to about 0℃.

(2) Meanwhile, place 5mL of 10% sodium hydroxide solution into a test tube and cool it for 15min in an ice-water bath.

(3) Carefully add the cooled solution of 10% sodium hydroxide dropwise to the cooled solution of vitamin B_1, keeping the pH of solution between 9～10, The process needs about 20min[2].

(4) After removing the ice-water bath, 10mL (10.4g, 0.1mol) of freshly distilled benzaldehyde[3] is added into the flask. Attach it to a reflux assembly using a water cooled condenser. Add a boiling stone into the flask and heat the mixture gently on a water bath, maintaining the reaction temperature between 65～75℃ for 90min.

(5) Allow the mixture to cool to room temperature, and then induce crystallization of the benzoin by cooling the mixture in an ice-water bath. Collect the product by vacuum filtration using a Buchner funnel, and wash it with ice-water (2×15mL). Recrystallize the crude product from 95% ethanol to get the white needle-like crystalloid (5g). The melting point of pure benzoin is 134～136℃.

(6) Determine the IR spectrum of the benzoin as a KBr mull and point out the most characteristic absorptions.

Brief Summary

1. Objectives

(1) Study the principle and method of preparing benzoin from benzaldehyde as catalyzed by the coenzyme VB_1.

(2) Master the characteristic technique of obtaining an IR spectrum.

2. Notes

[1] The vitamin B_1 should be preserved in icebox, for it is easy to lose bioactivity at room temperature.

[2] After half of the solution of 10% sodium hydroxide (2.5 mL) has been added, the color of

the solution changes from colorless to pale yellow.

[3] Benzaldehyde is oxidized easily in the air, if stored for too long. Crystals of benzoic acid are often visible in the bottom of the reagent bottle, so it should be distilled to purify it before use.

IR Spectrum

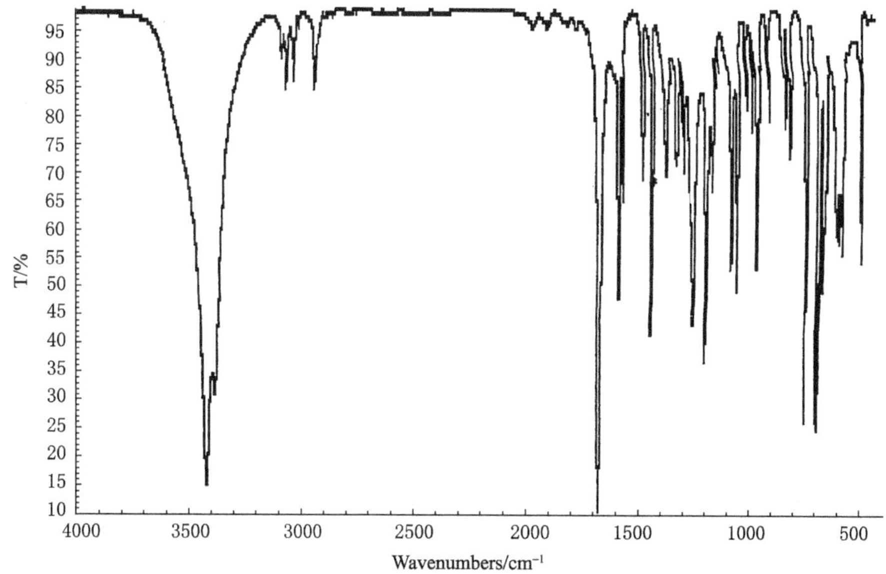

Questions

(1) Why should the 10% sodium hydroxide solution should be added to the solution of vitamin B_1?

(2) Why should the pH value of the mixture be kept between 9~10 after adding benzaldehyde? What would the result be if the pH value of the mixture is below 9?

4.6 Preparation and Characterization of Benzilic Acid

Principle

In this experiment benzilic acid will be prepared via the rearrangement of the α-diketone, benzil. Benzil is obtained through the oxidation of benzoin with the sodium bromate. The driving force for the reaction is provided by the formation of the stable carboxylate salt (sodium benzilate). Once this salt is produced, acidification yields benzilic acid. The reaction proceeds in the following way:

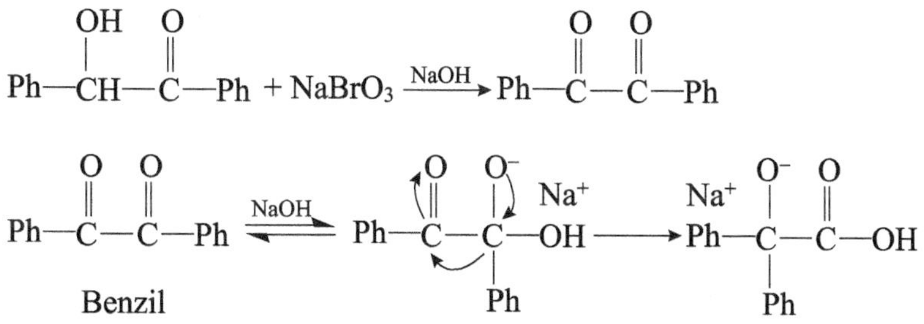

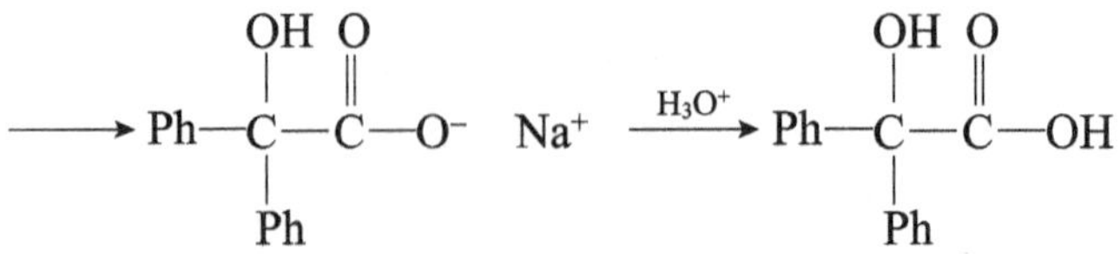

Sodium Benzilate　　Benzilic acid

The benzilic acid rearrangement reaction can generally be used to convert aromatic α-diketones to aromatic α-hydroxyacids. In certain cases, some aliphatic α-diketones will also undergo a benzilic acid type rearrangement.

Materials

benzoin	1.1g (0.005mol)	m.p.134～136℃
sodium hydroxide	1.25g (0.03mol)	
sodium bromate	0.3g (0.002mol)	
40% sulfuric acid		

Time 5h

Procedure

(1) Dissolve 1.25g (0.03mol) of sodium hydroxide and 0.3g (0.002mol) of sodium bromate in 3.0mL of water in a 100mL beaker.

(2) Place the beaker in a warm-water bath at 85～90℃[1]. With stirring, 1.1g (0.005mol) dried benzoin is added in small portions. Continue to heat and to stir until a test portion is completely water-soluble, this process needs about 1.5h.

(3) Dilute the reaction mixture with 25mL of water, cool it down in a crushed ice bath, and filter the solution into a 50mL beaker[2].

(4) Using magnetic stirring, 40% sulfuric acid solution is added slowly into the pink filtrate until the pH value of the mixture is between 2～3[3].

(5) Filter the solid and wash it with ice-water (2×15mL), The practically pure white solid should weigh about 1.0 g. The melting point of pure benzilic acid is 148～149℃.

(6) Determine the IR spectrum of the product, point out the most characteristic absorptions, and compare it with the IR spectrum of the benzoin.

Brief Summary

1. Objectives

(1) Study the principle and method of preparing of benzilic acid from benzil by a benzilic acid type rearrangement.

(2) Master the method of identifying the structure of benzilic acid by its IR spectrum.

2. Notes

[1] Do not overheat the reaction mixture, if the temperature is above 90℃, the by-product diphenylmethanol will be formed.

[2] To filter off any by-product diphenylmethanol formed during the reaction.

[3] At this time, flocculent precipitate will be formed.

IR Spectrum

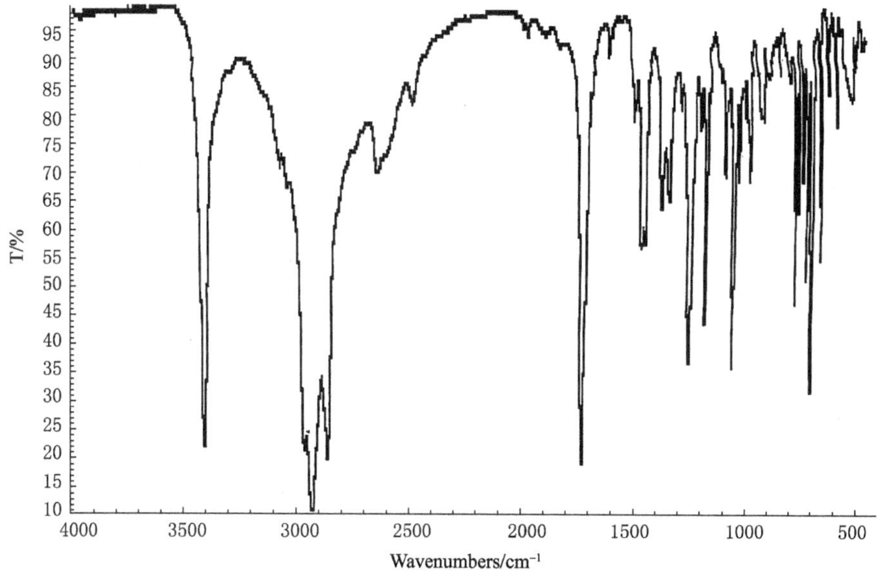

Questions

How to prepare the following compounds starting from the appropriate aldehyde.

(1) 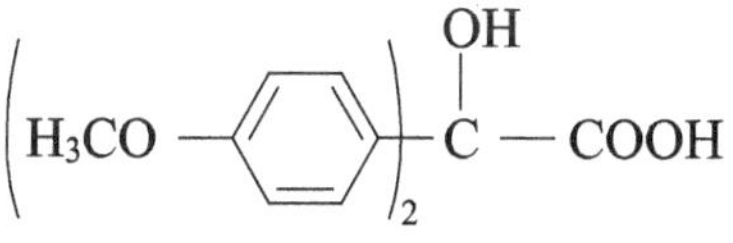

(2) 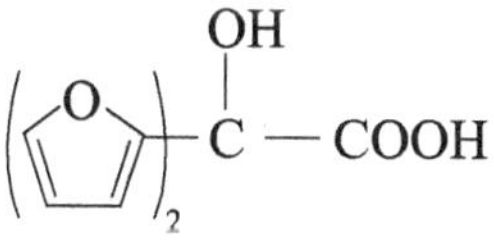

4.7 Microwave-Assisted Preparation and Characterization of 2-Substitutedphenyl Benzoxazole

Principle

In this experiment, 2-substitutedphenyl benzoxazole were synthesized under microwave-assisted using the condensation of 2-aminophenol and substituted benzoic acid catalyzed by polyphosphoric acid.

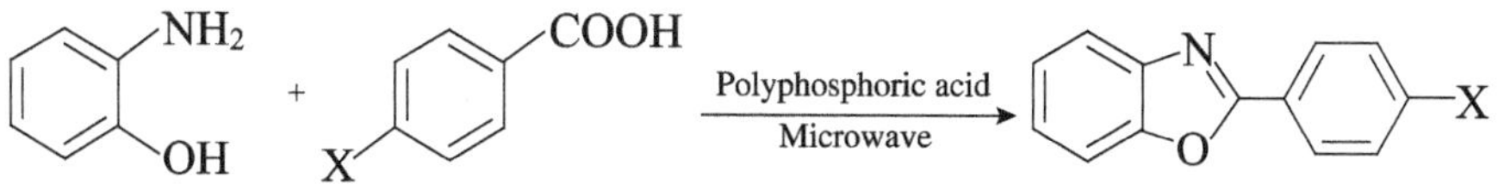

X=Cl, Br

Apparatus and Materials

Apparatus home microwave; reflux		
Materials		
2-aminophenol	1.091g (0.01mol)	m.p.170～175℃
4-bromobenzoic acid	2.01g (0.01mol)	m.p.252～254℃

4-chlorobenzoic acid	1.566g (0.01mol)	m.p.238~241℃
polyphosphoric acid	15mL	
90% ethanol		
10% aqueous sodium bicarbonate		

Time 3h

Procedure

(1) Mix 1.091g (0.01mol) of 2-aminophenol and 2.01g (0.01mol) of 4-bromobenzoic acid [or 1.57g (0.01mol) of 4-chlorobenzoic acid] in a 100mL round-bottom flask, 15mL of polyphosphoric acid is added with stirring.

(2) Put the reaction flask into a microwave oven and attach an air condenser, adjust microwave power up to 260W, radiate intermittently for 5min and then take the flask out.

(3) Under stirring, pour the warm mixture on to 80g of crushed ice, and filter the solid product. Wash it with 30mL of 10% aqueous sodium bicarbonate and then with 30mL of water.

(4) Recrystallize the product from 90% ethanol to obtain 1.8g of 2-(4-chlorophenyl)-benzoxazole or 2.0g of 2-(4-bromophenyl)-benzoxazole, determine the melting point. Pure 2-(4-chlorophenyl)-benzoxazole, m.p.153~154℃. Pure 2-(4-bromophenyl)-benzoxazole, m.p.142~143℃.

(5) Determine the ^{1}H NMR spectra of the products with $CDCl_3$ as solvent, and point out the chemical shift of the corresponding hydrogen.

Brief Summary

Objectives

(1) Master the technique of microwave-assisted synthesis of 2-substitutedphenyl benzoxazole.

(2) Master the characteristic method of ^{1}H NMR.

Chapter 5 Experiments from Literature

5.1 A Microscale Synthesis of the Diastereomers of 2, 3-Dibromosuccinic Acid

Principle

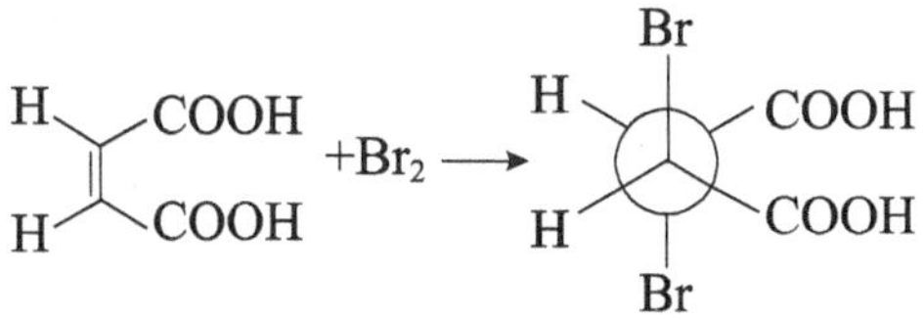

(1)

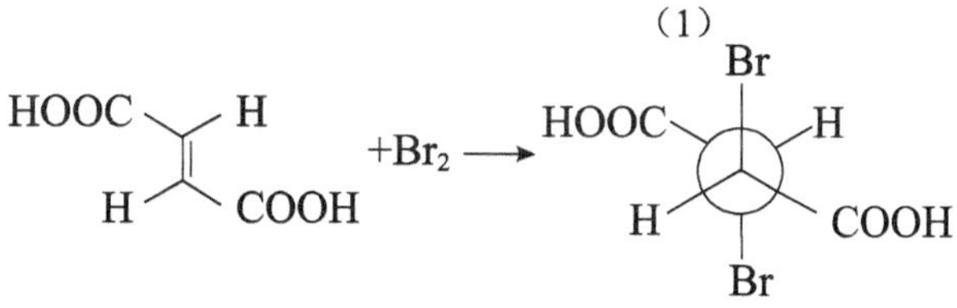

(2)

Procedure

1. Preparation of Meso-2, 3-Dibromosuccinic Acid(2)

A stock solution of bromine (7.75g) and potassium bromide (6.25g) in 10mL of water is prepared in a 25mL volumetric flask and diluted to the mark with water. CAUTION: bromine is moderately toxic by vapor inhalation and poisonous by ingestion. Its vapor is extremely corrosive. It should be used in a good fume hood and protective gloves should be worn when handling it(3a). Fumaric acid (200mg) is weighed into a 25mL Erlenmeyer flask and 2.5mL of the stock bromine solution[1] is added. CAUTION: Fumaric acid is mildly toxic by ingestion and is a skin and eye irritant(3b). The contents of the flask are mixed and the flask is placed in a boiling water bath. Within a minute some bromine vapor is expelled and a clear orange solution forms. After 6～10min a white precipitate forms and the solution color fades to a light yellow. Heating is continued for a total of 10～12min. If the solution becomes colorless, a few drops of the stock solution are added and the heating is continued for several more minutes. The flask is removed from the bath and cooled in an ice-water bath. The mixture is vacuum filtered and the product is washed with ice water and then dried in an oven at 100℃. If desired, the product can be recrystallized from water. Without recrystallization, the meso-2, 3-dibromosuccinic acid weighed between 280～360mg(51%～62% yield) and had a melting point of 261～266℃(lit. 255～256℃; c.a.280℃). The IR spectrum should match that of an authentic sample of meso-2, 3-dibromosuccinic acid.

2. Preparation of Racemic-2, 3-Dibromosuccinic Acid(1)

CAUTION: All equipment and reagents must be dry[2].

Maleic acid (200mg) is weighed into a test tube and 2mL of anhydrous ether is added. CAUTION: Maleic acid is moderately toxic by ingestion and can be absorbed through the skin. It is a severe skin and eye irritant. It should be handled carefully avoiding skin contact or inhalation. Ethyl ether is moderately toxic by ingestion and mildly toxic by inhalation. It is a very dangerous fire and explosion hazard. It forms explosive peroxides when exposed to air. All possible sources of ignition should be removed from the area where ether is being used.

On a balance, 310mg of bromine[3] is added dropwise to the test tube and the contents are mixed thoroughly. A small exotherm will result, and as the ether gently boils the solid will slowly dissolve. If any solid either remains or forms, it indicates that the reaction mixture was contaminated with water. Should this occur, it is usually best to abort the reaction, dispose of the reactants properly, and redo the experiment. If no precipitate forms, the solution is allowed to sit for 10～15min; the deep orange color should fade to pale orange or yellow. The ether is removed by placing the test tube in a beaker of warm water in a good fume hood, leaving a pale orange or yellow solid. The test tube is cooled in an ice-water bath for a few minutes, petroleum ether is added, and a glass rod is used to break up the solid. The solid is vacuum filtered, rinsed with a few milliliters of petroleum ether, and dried in air. Yields of racemic-2, 3-dibromosuccinic acid range from 440 to 450mg (95%～96%), with a melting point of 168～170℃ (lit.166～167℃).

Notes

[1]The synthesis of meso-2, 3-dibromosuccinic acid by adding bromine to a suspension of fumaric acid in boiling water(2) gives very poor yields on the microscale level. The yield is raised by adding KBr to comple the bromine.

[2]Contamination of the reactants by water produces hydrogen bromide, which rapidly isomerizes the maleic acid to the less reactive and less soluble fumaric acid. The product isolated in these cases consists of mixtures of the product (racemic-dibromosuccinic acid) and fumaric acid.

[3]Pyridinium hydrobromide perbromide as a safer and more conveniently handled alternative to liquid bromine is also cited as possessing greater stereospecificity than bromine. For these reactions, however, the products are contaminated with pyridine hydrobromide and are not stereochemically pure. The racemic isomer especially (from maleic acid) contains at least 50% of the meso product.

(Abstracted from: *Journal of Chemical Education.* 1999, Vol.76, 73)

5.2 A Grignard-like Organic Reaction in Water

Principle

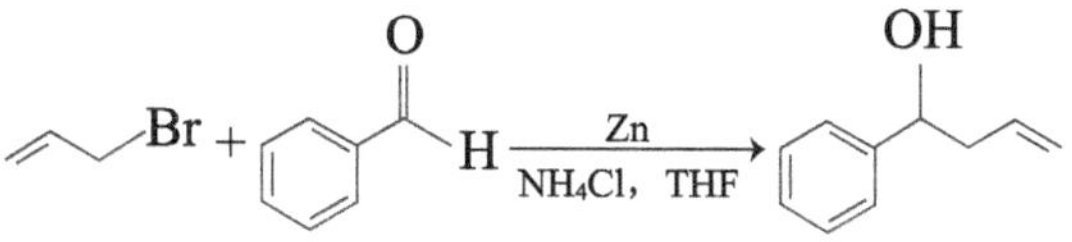

Experimental Procedure

CAUTION: Allyl bromide is a toxic, flammable liquid. Gloves should be worn at all times during its handling, and all manipulations should be carried out in an efficient hood.

To a mixture of 0.078g(1.20mmol) of untreated, commercially available zinc powder and 1mL of a saturated aqueous NH_4Cl solution is added a solution is added a solution of 0.102mL (1.00mmol) of benzaldehyde in 0.5mL of THF. This mixture is stirred vigorously in a 25mL round-bottomed flask fitted with a condenser while 0.104mL (1.20mmol) of allyl bromide is added dropwise via a calibrated pipet, through the condenser [1, 2] .An immediate reaction takes place, with loss of the zinc powder. The mixture is stired for 0.5h, and 1mL of ether is added. The mixture is filtered through a plug of glass wool to remove excess zinc and any precipitate(zinc salts) that may have formed. The precipitate is rinsed with 1mL of fresh ether. The organic phase is separated, and the aqueous phase is washed once with a fresh aliquot(1mL) of ether. The combined organic phases are dried over Na_2SO_4, filtered, and concentrated to afford 0.126g [85% yield (typical yields of 70%~85%)] of 1-phenyl-3-buten-1-ol as a colorless liquid. (The product from some runs may be contaminated with small amounts of residual benzaldehyde, but is generally suitable for spectroscopic analysis.) $n^{21.5}$ = 1.5284(lit. $n^{21.5}$ = 1.5289); IR(neat)cm^{-1}: 3360, 3050, 2890, 1037, 905, 690; ^{1}H-NMR (60MHz, $CDCl_3$) δ: 7.05 (s, 5H), 5.95~5.30 (m, 1H), 5.19~4.80 (m, 2H), 4.60(t, J = 6Hz, 1H), 2.44 (t, J = 6Hz, 2H), 2.06(br, s, 1H, OH).

(Abstracted from: *Journal of Chemical Education.* 1998, Vol.75, 85)

5.3 An Efficient Microscale Procedure for the Synthesis of Aspirin

Experimental Procedure

To 138mg (0.001mol) of salicylic acid in a dry reaction tube is added 0.1mL of pyridine (just sufficient to dissolve it) while the tube rests in a cold water bath. One-tenth milliliter of acetyl chloride (slight excess over 0.001mol) is added in one portion. The mixture becomes viscous at this stage. The reaction tube is allowed to stand in the cold water bath for 15min. Then 5mL of cold water is added and the mixture is shaken vigorously. It turns cloudy. Shaking is continued until white product begins to appear and at once separates. Crystals are filtered, washed with cold water, and air dried. Recrystallization from aqueous ethanol(50%) gives a yield of 33%, m.p. 133～135℃.

(Abstracted from: *Journal of Chemical Education.* 1998, Vol.75, 770)

5.4 A Solvent-Free Claisen Condensation Reaction

Principle

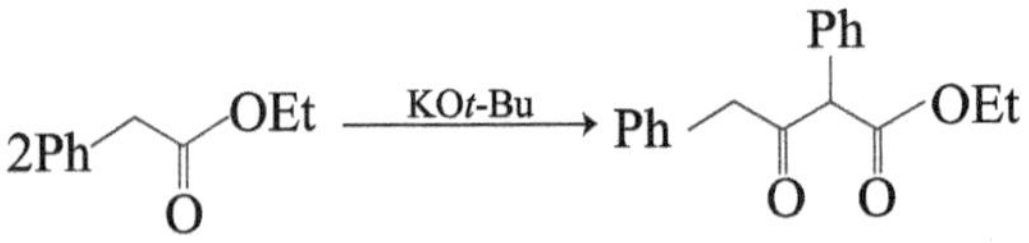

Experimental Procedure

A mixture of 1.57g (14mmol) of KO*t*-Bu and 3.28g(20mmol) of ethyl phenylacetate were added to a 25mL round bottom flask. The resulting mixture was stirred vigorously with a spatula until the contents appeared homogeneous. A reflux condenser was attached and the flask placed in a preheated hot water or steam bath at 100℃. After 0.5h, the flask was removed from the heat source. The mixture was cooled to room temperature and neutralized by the slow addition of 15mL of 1mol/L HCl. The residue was extracted with 2×15mL portions of ether. The organic extracts were combined, dried with $MgSO_4$, filtered, and the solvent removed by rotary evaporation. Trituration of the oily residue with 7mL of cold pentane[1] produced a white solid. Recrystallization of the product from hot hexanes afforded 2.25g of 2, 4-diphenyl acetoacetate(80%), m.p. 75～78℃. Purity of the product was assessed through melting point determinations. Typical student yields are in the 50%～80% range.

(Abstracted From: *Journal of Chemical Education.* 2003, Vol.80, 1446)

5.5 The Preparation of a Fluorescent Dye: A Microscale TLC Experiment

Experimental Procedure

Technical grade 4-chloro-1, 8-naphthalic anhydride (5～10mg) is weighed into a 3mL vial to which 1mL of toluene is added. The mixture is stirred(spin bar) and 1-hexylamine (500μL) is added to the reaction mixture by syringe. The contents of the vial are stirred and heated under reflux for 45min or until all the solid has dissolved. At the end of the heating period, the reaction mixture is allowed to cool. It is then analyzed by TLC on silica gel using two solvent systems: 20% ethyl acetate in hexane, and toluene.

Observations

The reaction is accompanied by several readily observable changes during the course of formation of the final product. The chemical reactions are shown in the following scheme:

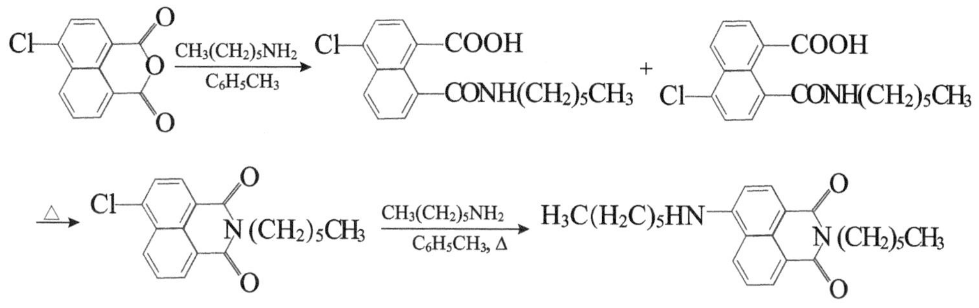

When the eluting solvent is 20% ethyl acetate in hexane, most students observe four to six spots evenly spaced and easily visible, with R_f values typically falling between 0.8~0.3. In this eluting system, the colors of the four fluorescent bands observed by every strdent alternate, a blue band having the highest R_f. When six bands are observed, yellow bands with R_f's near 0.8 and 0.1 are seen. Using toluene as eluting solvent, all strdents again observe four bands with R_f values between 0.5~0.05; some strdents observe up to seven spots.

When the eluting solvent is toluene, the elution order changes: the blue bands have the highest R_f's and the yellow bands have the lower R_f's. That not every student observes the maximum number of spots can be attributed to variations in spot size of the original spot and adsorbent activity. Typical R_f values for the four universally observed spots are collected in Table 5.1.

Table 5.1 R_f Values of the Four Compounds

Solvent	Color of Fluorescence	R_f
Ethyl acetate-hexane 1 : 5 (volume ratio)	Blue	0.74±0.04
	Yellow	0.60±0.04
	Blue	0.49±0.04
	Yellow	0.35±0.04
Toluene	Blue	0.41±0.06
	Blue	0.27±0.06
	Yellow	0.20±0.05
	Yellow	0.14±0.04

(Abstracted from: *Journal of Chemical Education.* 1999, Vol.76, 82 ~ 83)

5.6 Microwave Microscale Experiment: 2-Naphthyl Acetate from 2-Naphthol

Principle

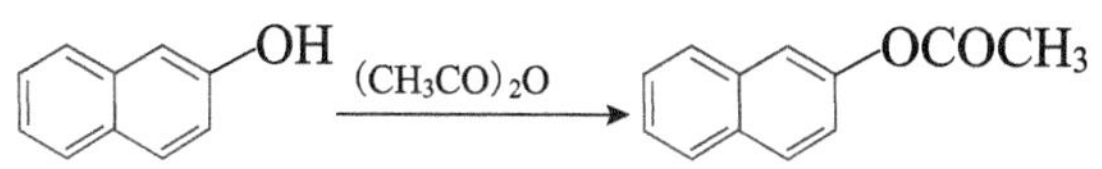

Experimental Procedure

2-Naphthol (288mg, 2mmole) and 1mL of acetic anhydride are mixed in a 50mL beaker. The beaker is covered with a watch glass and irradiated in the microwave for 4min at 50% power. The reaction mixture is poured into 20mL of water. After the mixture has been stirred to hydrolyze the excess acetic anhydride, the solid is collected and recrystallized in 50% ethanol to give a 60%~80% yield of product(mp 67.0~67.5℃).

(Abstracted from: *Journal of Chemical Education.* 1996, Vol.73, A105)

Chapter 6 Appendix

6.1 List of the Element with Their Symbols and Atomic Masses*

Element	Symbol	Atomic Number	Atomic Mass†
Actinium	Ac	89	(227)
Aluminum	Al	13	26.98
Americium	Am	95	(243)
Antimony	Sb	51	121.8
Argon	Ar	18	39.95
Arsenic	As	33	74.92
Astatine	At	85	(210)
Barium	Ba	56	137.3
Berkelium	Bk	97	(247)
Beryllium	Be	4	9.012
Bismuth	Bi	83	209.0
Boron	B	5	10.81
Bromine	Br	35	79.90
Cadmium	Cd	48	112.4
Calcium	Ca	20	40.08
Californium	Cf	98	(249)
Carbon	C	6	12.01
Cerium	Ce	58	140.1
Cesium	Cs	55	132.9
Chlorine	Cl	17	35.45
Chromium	Cr	24	52.00
Cobalt	Co	27	58.93
Copper	Cu	29	63.55
Curium	Cm	96	(247)
Dysprosium	Dy	66	162.5
Einsteinium	Es	99	(254)
Erbium	Er	68	167.3
Europium	Eu	63	152.0
Fermium	Fm	100	(253)
Fluorine	F	9	19.00

* All atomic masses have four significant figures. These values are recommended by the Committee on Teaching of Chemistry, International Union of Pure and Applied Chemistry.

Continued

Element	Symbol	Atomic Number	Atomic Mass†
Francium	Fr	87	(223)
Gadolinium	Gd	64	157.3
Gallium	Ga	31	69.72
Germanium	Ge	32	72.59
Gold	Au	79	197.0
Hafnium	Hf	72	178.5
Hahnium	Ha	105	(260)
Hassium	Hs	108	(265)
Helium	He	2	4.003
Holmium	Ho	67	164.9
Hydrogen	H	1	1.008
Indium	In	49	114.8
Iodine	I	53	126.9
Iridium	Ir	77	192.2
Iron	Fe	26	55.85
Krypton	Kr	36	83.80
Lanthanum	La	57	138.9
Lawrencium	Lr	103	(257)
Lead	Pb	82	207.2
Lithium	Li	3	6.941
Lutetium	Lu	71	175.0
Magnesium	Mg	12	24.31
Manganese	Mn	25	54.94
Meitnerium	Mt	109	(266)
Mendelevium	Md	101	(256)
Mercury	Hg	80	200.6
Molybdenum	Mo	42	95.94
Neodymium	Nd	60	144.2
Neon	Ne	10	20.18
Neptumium	Np	93	(237)
Nickel	Ni	28	58.69
Nielsbohrium	Ns	107	(262)
Niobium	Nb	41	92.91
Nitrogen	N	7	14.01
Nobelium	No	102	(253)
Osmium	Os	76	190.2
Oxygen	O	8	16.00
Palladium	Pd	46	106.4

Continued

Element	Symbol	Atomic Number	Atomic Mass†
Phosphorus	P	15	30.97
Platinum	Pt	78	195.1
Plutonium	Pu	94	(242)
Polonium	Po	84	(210)
Potassium	K	19	39.10
Praseodymium	Pr	59	140.9
Promethium	Pm	61	(147)
Protactinium	Pa	91	(231)
Radium	Ra	88	(226)
Radon	Rn	86	(222)
Rhenium	Re	75	186.2
Rhodium	Rh	45	102.9
Rubidium	Rb	37	85.47
Ruthenium	Ru	44	101.1
Rutherfordium	Rf	104	(257)
Samarium	Sm	62	150.4
Scandium	Sc	21	44.96
Seaborgium	Sg	106	(263)
Selenium	Se	34	78.96
Silicon	Si	14	28.09
Silver	Ag	47	107.9
Sodium	Na	11	22.99
Strontium	Sr	38	87.62
Sulfur	S	16	32.07
Tantalum	Ta	73	180.9
Technetium	Tc	43	(99)
Tellurium	Te	52	127.6
Terbium	Tb	65	158.9
Thallium	Tl	81	204.4
Thorium	Th	90	232.0
Thulium	Tm	69	168.9
Tin	Sn	50	118.7
Titanium	Ti	22	47.88
Tungsten	W	74	183.9
Uranium	U	92	238.0
Ununbium	Uub	112	(277)
Ununbexium	Uuh	116	(289)
Ununnilium	Uun	110	(269)
Ununoctium	Uuo	118	(293)

Continued

Element	Symbol	Atomic Number	Atomic Mass†
Ununquadium	Uuq	114	(285)
Unununium	Uuu	111	(272)
Vanadium	V	23	50.94
Xenon	Xe	54	131.3
Ytterbium	Yb	70	173.0
Yttrium	Y	39	88.91
Zinc	Zn	30	65.39
Zirconium	Zr	40	91.22
Ionization constants of monoprotic acids			

† Approximate values of atomic masses for radioactive elements are given in parentheses.

Katherine J, Derniston et al. General. Organic, and Biochemistry 3rd ed. Published by Mc.Graw-Hill Companies, Inc., New York. NY10020, 1997. (www.mhhe.com)

6.2 Main Families of Organic Compounds

Family	Specific Example	IUPAC Name	Common Name	General Formula	Functional Group
Alkane	CH_3CH_3	Ethane	Ethane	RH	C—H and C—C bonds
Alkene	$CH_2{=}CH_2$	Ethene	Ethylene	$RCH{=}CH_2$ $RCH{=}CHR$ $R_2C{=}CHR$ $R_2C{=}CR_2$	$>C{=}C<$
Alkyne	$HC{\equiv}CH$	Ethyne	Acetylene	$RC{\equiv}CH$ $RC{\equiv}CR$	$—C{\equiv}C—$
Arene		Benzene	Benzene	ArH	Aromatic Ring
Haloalkane	CH_3CH_2Cl	Chloroethane	Ethyl chloride	RX	—C—X
Alcohol	CH_3CH_2OH	Ethanol	Ethyl alcohol	ROH	—C—OH
Ether	CH_3OCH_3	Methoxy methane	Dimethyl ether	ROR	—C—O—C—
Amine	CH_3NH_2	Methanamine	Methylamine	RNH_2 R_2NH R_3N	—C—N—

Continued

Family	Specific Example	IUPAC Name	Common Name	General Formula	Functional Group
Aldehyde	$CH_3\overset{O}{\overset{\Vert}{C}}H$	Acetaldehyde	Acetaldehyde	$R\overset{O}{\overset{\Vert}{C}}H$	$-\overset{O}{\overset{\Vert}{C}}-H$
Ketone	$CH_3\overset{O}{\overset{\Vert}{C}}CH_3$	Propanone	Acetone	$R\overset{O}{\overset{\Vert}{C}}R$	$-\overset{\vert}{\underset{\vert}{C}}-\overset{O}{\overset{\Vert}{C}}-\overset{\vert}{\underset{\vert}{C}}-$
Carboxylic Acid	$CH_3\overset{O}{\overset{\Vert}{C}}OH$	Ethanoic Acid	Acetic acid	$R\overset{O}{\overset{\Vert}{C}}OH$	$-\overset{O}{\overset{\Vert}{C}}-OH$
Ester	$CH_3\overset{O}{\overset{\Vert}{C}}OCH_3$	Methyl acetate	Methyl acetate	$R\overset{O}{\overset{\Vert}{C}}OR$	$-\overset{O}{\overset{\Vert}{C}}-O-\overset{\vert}{\underset{\vert}{C}}-$
Amide	$CH_3\overset{O}{\overset{\Vert}{C}}NH_2$	Acetamide	Acetamide	$R\overset{O}{\overset{\Vert}{C}}NH_2$ $R\overset{O}{\overset{\Vert}{C}}NHR$ $R\overset{O}{\overset{\Vert}{C}}NR_2$	$-\overset{O}{\overset{\Vert}{C}}-\underset{\vert}{N}-$

第 1 章　有机化学实验的一般知识

有机化学实验是一门以实验为基础的学科，随着新的实验技术不断出现，这门实验课程正在向用量少、效率高、绿色化的方向发展。通过有机化学实验课程的学习，使学生能够掌握有机化学实验的基本原理，有机化合物的合成、分离、鉴定的一般方法；加深对有机化学理论知识的理解，培养学生养成“预习(包括查阅文献)—准备—实验—记录—总结”的实验习惯，以及严谨的科学态度和计算机的使用能力。

1.1　有机化学实验的基本规则

为使有机化学实验有条不紊、安全地进行，必须遵循以下规则：

(1) 熟悉实验室的安全规则，学会正确使用水、电、煤、通风橱、灭火器等，了解实验事故的一般处理方法。做好实验的预习工作，了解所用药品的危害性及安全操作方法，按操作规程，小心使用有关实验仪器和设备，若有问题应立即停止使用。

(2) 实验前，认真清点、检查玻璃仪器；实验中，安全合理的使用玻璃仪器；实验后，洗净并妥善保管玻璃仪器，尤其应学会玻璃仪器的洗涤方法。

(3) 实验时，要保持实验室和桌面的清洁，认真操作，遵守实验纪律，严格按照实验中所规定的实验步骤、试剂规格及用量来进行。若要改变，需经教师同意方可进行。

(4) 实验药品使用前，应仔细阅读药品标签，按需取用，避免浪费；取药品后要迅速盖上瓶塞，避免搞错瓶塞，污染药品。不要任意更换实验室常用仪器(如天平、干燥器、折光仪等)和常用药品的摆放位置。

(5) 整个实验操作过程中要集中思想，避免大声喧哗，不要在实验室吃东西。

(6) 实验中和实验后，各类固体废物和液体废物应分别放入指定的容器中。

(7) 离开实验室前，应检查水、电、煤是否安全关闭。

1.2　有机化学实验的一般安全知识

有机化学实验很大程度上由玻璃仪器、实验试剂和电器设备等组成，如果操作不当，会对人体、环境造成伤害。实验试剂往往具有易燃、易爆、易挥发、易腐蚀、毒性高等特点，玻璃仪器与电器设备使用不当也可能发生意外。因此，有机化学实验室是一个潜在的、高危险性的场所。

1.2.1　防火

实验操作要规范，实验装置要正确，对易燃、易爆、易挥发的实验药品要远离明火，不可随意丢弃，实验后应专门回收。一旦发生火灾，应先切断电源和煤气，移去易燃易爆试剂，再采取其他适当方法灭火，如灭火器、石棉网或黄沙覆盖，或用水冲等。

1.2.2　防爆

仪器装置要正确，常压蒸馏及回流时，整个系统不能密闭。若在加热后发现未放沸石，应停止加热，冷却后再补加。减压蒸馏时，应事先检查玻璃仪器是否能承受系统的压力，冷凝水要保持畅通。

有些有机物遇氧化剂会发生猛烈的爆炸或燃烧，操作或存放时应格外小心。

1.2.3　防中毒

绝大多数有机实验试剂都有不同程度的毒性，对有刺激性或者产生有毒气体的实验，应尽量安排在通风橱，或在有排风系统的环境中进行，或采用气体吸收装置。有毒或有较强腐蚀性的药品应严格按照有关操作规程进行，不能用手直接接触这类化学药品，不得入口或接触伤口，也不可随便倒入下水道。

实验中若发现有头晕、头痛等中毒症状，应立即转移到空气新鲜的地方休息，严重者应立即送医院。

1.2.4　防化学灼伤

强酸、强碱和溴等化学药品接触皮肤均可引起灼伤，使用时应格外小心。一旦发生这类情况应立即用大量水冲洗，再用以下方法处理：

酸灼伤：眼睛灼伤用 1% $NaHCO_3$ 溶液清洗；皮肤灼伤用 5% $NaHCO_3$ 溶液清洗。

碱灼伤：眼睛灼伤用 1% 硼酸溶液清洗；皮肤灼伤用 1%～2% 乙酸溶液清洗。

溴灼伤：立即用酒精洗涤，再涂上甘油，或敷上烫伤油膏。

灼伤较严重者经急救后速去医院治疗。

1.2.5　防割伤和烫伤

在玻璃仪器的使用和玻璃工的操作中，常因操作或使用不当而发生割伤和烫伤现象。若发生此类现象，可用以下方法处理：

割伤：先要取出玻璃片，用蒸馏水或双氧水清洗伤口，涂上红药水，再用纱布包扎；若伤口严重，应在伤口上方用纱布扎紧，急送医院。

烫伤：轻者涂烫伤膏，重者涂烫伤膏后立即送医院。

1.3　有机化学实验废物的处置

有机化学实验往往会产生各种固体、液体等废物，为提倡环境保护，遵守国家的环保法规，减少对环境危害，可采用以下处理方法：

(1) 所有实验废物应按固体、液体，有害、无害等分类收集于不同的容器中，对一些难处理的有害废物可送环保部门专门处理。

(2) 少量的酸（如盐酸、硫酸、硝酸等）或碱（如氢氧化钠、氢氧化钾等）在倒入下水道之前必须先中和，并用水稀释。

(3) 有机溶剂必须倒入带有标签的废物回收容器中，并存放在通风处。

(4) 对无害的固体废物，如滤纸、碎玻璃、软木塞、氧化铝、硅胶、硫酸镁、氯化钙等可直接倒入普通的废物箱中，不应与其他有害固体废物相混；对有害固体废物应放入带有标签的广口瓶中。

(5) 对能与水发生剧烈反应的化学品，处置之前要用适当的方法在通风橱内进行分解。

(6) 对可能致癌的物质，处理起来应格外小心，避免与手接触。

1.4 常用的玻璃仪器和实验装置

1.4.1 常见玻璃仪器及实验装置

参见英文部分 Fig. 1.1～Fig. 1.7。

1.4.2 使用玻璃仪器的注意事项

(1) 使用时要轻拿轻放，以免弄碎。

(2) 除烧杯、烧瓶和试管外，均不能用火直接加热。

(3) 锥形瓶、平底烧瓶不耐压，不能用于减压系统。

(4) 带活塞的玻璃器皿用过洗净后，在活塞与磨口之间垫上纸片，以防粘连而打不开。

(5) 温度计的水银球玻璃很薄，易碎，使用时应小心。不能将温度计当搅拌棒使用；温度计使用后应先冷却再冲洗，以免破裂；测量范围不得超出温度计刻度范围。

1.4.3 安装实验装置的注意事项

(1) 所用玻璃仪器和配件要干净，大小要合适。

(2) 搭建实验装置时应按照从下向上、从左到右的原则，逐个装配。

(3) 拆卸时，则按从右到左，从上到下的原则，逐个拆除。

(4) 常压下进行的反应装置，应与大气相通，不能密闭。

(5) 实验装置要求做到严密、正确、整齐、稳妥。磨口连接处要紧密连接。

1.4.4 玻璃仪器的清洗

玻璃仪器用毕后应立即清洗，一般的清洗方法是将玻璃仪器和毛刷淋湿，蘸取肥皂粉或洗涤剂，洗刷玻璃器皿的内外壁，除去污物后用水冲洗；当洁净度要求较高时，可依次用洗涤剂、蒸馏水（或去离子水）清洗；也可用超声波振荡仪来清洗。

必须反对盲目使用各种化学试剂或有机溶剂来清洗玻璃器皿，这样不仅造成浪费，还可能带来危险，对环境产生污染。

1.4.5　玻璃仪器的干燥

干燥玻璃仪器的方法通常有以下几种：

自然干燥：将仪器倒置，使水自然流下，晾干。

烘干：将仪器放入烘箱内烘干，仪器口朝上；也可用气流干燥器烘干或用电吹风吹干。

有机溶剂干燥：急用时可用有机溶剂助干，用少量 95%乙醇或丙酮荡涤，把溶剂倒回至回收瓶中，然后用电吹风吹干。

附：简单玻璃工操作

玻璃管的切割、弯制及毛细管的制作等都是有机化学实验中最基本的操作。

1. 切割玻璃管和玻璃棒

(1) 用小的砂轮片在所需截断的地方垂直于玻璃管(棒)，向一个方向锉一个稍深的凹痕(注意不要来回锉，另外玻璃管应是干燥的)。

(2) 两手握住玻璃管(棒)，用大拇指顶住锉痕背面的两边，轻轻向前推，同时双手向两边拉，玻璃管(棒)即可平整断开[注意：折断玻璃管(棒)时，应远离眼睛]。

(3) 断口处必须淬火，圆口，即把断口处放在煤气灯的火焰上来回旋转几下，以除去断口面的快口[1]。

2. 弯玻璃管

(1) 将干燥的玻璃管倾斜一定角度，放在煤气灯的强火焰上灼烧，双手均匀地向一个方向转动。

(2) 当加热部位呈红色开始软化时，即从火焰中取出，轻轻弯成所需的角度。

(3) 加热或弯曲管子时不能扭动，以避免弯管不在同一个平面上的现象。

(4) 弯管时要避免弯角内侧出现瘪陷，弯好后应检查角度是否正确，整个弯管是否在同一平面上[2]，然后放在石棉网上冷却(不要直接放在桌面上)。

3. 实验

(1) 取数根废旧的玻璃管练习切割、加热、转动、弯制等操作，掌握操作要点。

(2) 搅拌棒的制作：取一根直径为 5mm，长度约 20cm 的玻璃棒，两端分别在火焰上烧圆，作为搅拌棒。

(3) 玻璃管的弯制：取两根直径为 7mm 的玻璃管，弯成 90°、75°角的玻璃管各一支[3]。

4. 注释

[1]有时断口面不平整，易割伤手，要小心。

[2]玻璃管弯好后，也可在小火上进行退火，然后再放于石棉网上。

[3]玻璃管长度视用途而定。

1.5　干燥与干燥剂

干燥是有机化学实验中非常普通且十分重要的基本操作。干燥的方法大致有物理方法和化学方法两种。物理方法主要有吸附、分子筛脱水等；化学方法是用干燥剂去水，根据去水原理不同可分为两类：①与水结合生成水合物；②与水起化学反应，例如：

$$CaCl_2+6H_2O \rightleftharpoons CaCl_2 \cdot 6H_2O\text{（第一类）}$$

$$2Na+2H_2O \rightleftharpoons 2NaOH+H_2\uparrow\text{（第二类）}$$

1.5.1　液体有机物的干燥

1. 干燥剂的选择

液体有机物的干燥通常是将干燥剂直接放入有机物中，因此选择干燥剂要考虑以下因素：①与被干燥的有机物不能发生化学反应；②不能溶于该有机物中；③吸水量大、干燥速度快、价格便宜。常用干燥剂的性能参见英文部分 Table 1.1。各类有机物常用干燥剂参见英文部分 Table 1.2。

2. 干燥剂的用量

干燥剂的用量是根据干燥剂的吸水量和水在有机物中的溶解度来估算的，一般用量比理论值要高一些。当然也要考虑分子结构，含亲水性基团的化合物用量稍多些。干燥剂的用量要适当，用量少干燥不完全；用量过多，因干燥剂表面吸附而造成被干燥有机物的损失。一般用量为 10mL 液体约加 0.5～1g 干燥剂。

3. 操作方法

干燥前要尽可能地把有机物中的水分除去，加入干燥剂后，振荡，静置观察，若干燥剂黏附在瓶壁上，则应再加些干燥剂。若干燥前液体呈浑浊，干燥后为澄清，可认为水分基本除去。反之，则说明水分太多，要先除水。干燥剂颗粒大小要适当，太大吸水慢；太小吸附有机物较多。

1.5.2　固体有机物的干燥

晾干：将固体样品放在干燥的表面皿或滤纸上，摊开，再用一张滤纸覆盖，放在空气中晾干。

烘干：将固体样品置于表面皿中放在水浴上烘干，也可用红外灯或烘箱烘干。必须注意样品不能遇热分解，加热温度要低于样品的熔点。

其他干燥方法：干燥器干燥，减压恒温干燥器干燥等。

1.6　加热与冷却

加热与冷却是有机化学实验中常用的一项基本操作技能。

1.6.1　加热

有机化学实验常用的热源有煤气、酒精和电能。加热方式有直接加热和间接加热。为避免直接加热可能带来的问题，根据实际情况可选用以下间接加热的方式。

(1)空气浴加热：利用热空气间接加热的原理，对沸点在 80℃以上的液体均可采用。实验中常用的方法有石棉网上加热和电热套加热。

(2)水浴加热：加热温度在 80℃以下时，可用水浴加热。将容器浸于水中，使水的液面高于容器内液面。

(3)油浴：油浴的加热范围为 100～250℃，油浴所能达到的最高温度取决于所用油的品种。实验室常用的油有植物油(200～220℃)、液体石蜡(220℃)等。油浴加热要注意安全，防止着火，防止溅入水滴。

(4)沙浴：当要求加热温度较高时，采用沙浴。沙浴温度可达 350℃。

1.6.2　冷却

冷却是有机化学实验要求在低温下进行的一种常用方法，根据不同的要求，可选用不同的冷却方法：

一般情况下的冷却，可将盛有反应物的容器浸在冷水中；在室温以下冷却，可选用冰或冰水混合物；在 0℃以下冷却，可用碎冰和某些无机盐按一定比例混合作为冷却剂。常用冰盐冷却剂参见英文部分 Table 1.3，干冰(固体二氧化碳)和丙酮、氯仿等溶剂混合，可冷却到−78℃；液氮可冷却到−196℃。

必须注意的是当温度低于－38℃时，不能使用水银温度计，而应使用装有有机液体的低温温度计。

1.7　实验记录和实验报告

参见英文部分 1.7：Experimental Record and Laboratory Report。

1.8　有机化学的文献资料

有机化学的文献资料非常丰富，现作简单介绍。

1.8.1　工具书

(1)*CRC Handbook of Chemistry and Physics*：这是美国(CRC Press, Boca Raton, FL)出版的一本化学与物理英文手册，它每年出版一次。该书内容分六个方面：数学用表、元素和无机化合物、有机化合物、普通化学、普通物理常数和其他。在“有机化学”部分包含约 15 000 个有机化合物及它们的物理性质，并按照有机化合物英文名字的字母顺序排列。查阅时可以根据英文名称，也可以根据该书提供的分子式索引(Formula Index)进行查找。

(2)*Merck Index of Chemicals and Drugs*(12th)：该书由美国(Merck and Co., Rahway, NJ)

出版的一本辞典，它主要介绍有机化合物和药物，共收集了 1 万余种化合物的物理常数、制备、用途、毒性及参考文献等，并提供分子式索引和主题索引。

(3) *Beilstein Handbook of Organic Chemistry*：该书内容较全，提供了有关有机化合物的来源、制备方法、物理性质、化学性质、生理作用、用途和分析方法等，并附有原始文献资料的出处。该书可根据其编排原则进行查找，也可根据分子式索引或主题索引进行查找。

(4) 化工辞典(4th)：这是综合性的化工工具书，收集了有关化学、化工名词 16 000 余条，列出了化学物质名称的分子式、结构式，基本的物理化学性质和有关数据，并有简要的制法和用途说明。

1.8.2 期刊

(1) 中文期刊：与化学有关的中文期刊非常多，重要的有：《中国科学》、《化学学报》、《化学通报》、《高等学校化学学报》、《有机化学》等。

(2) 英文期刊：与化学有关的英文期刊非常多，重要的有：

Journal of the Chemical Society (*Perkin Transactions*)；

Journal of American Chemical Society；

Journal of Organic Chemistry；

Angewandte Chemie International Edition;

Chemical Reviews、*Tetrahedron*、*Tetrahedron Letters*、*Journal of Chemical Education* 等。

1.8.3 化学文摘

化学文摘是将大量的、分散的各种文字的文献加以收集、摘录、分类整理而出版的一种期刊。在众多的文摘性刊物中美国化学文摘(*Chemical Abstracts*，简称 CA)最重要。CA 创刊于 1907 年，现在每年出两卷，每周一期。CA 的索引系统比较完善，有期索引、卷索引、每十卷有累积索引。累积索引主要有分子式索引(Formula Index)、化学物质索引(Chemical Substance Index)、普通主题索引(General Subject Index)、作者索引(Author Index)、专利索引(Patent Index)等。

1.8.4 网上资源

由于互联网技术的迅速发展，从网上查找有关资料变得非常方便、迅速。从网上获取化学信息的途径很多，这里只作简单的介绍。

(1) 网上图书馆：Internet 上的图书馆是获取图书、杂志资料的重要途径之一。例如：

中国国家图书馆：http://www.nlc.gov.cn/

清华大学图书馆：http://www.lib.tsinghua.edu.cn/

北京大学图书馆：http://www.lib.pku.edu.cn/html

(2) 中国期刊网：http://www.chinajournal.net.cn/

中文科技期刊数据库：http://www.cqvip.com/

(3) 专利文献。

IBM Intellectual Property Network: http://www.patents.ibm.com/

中国专利信息网：http://patent.com.cn/

中国专利网：http://cnpatent.com/

(4)数据库资源：有关化学信息数据库中，化学结构数据库占有很高的比例，但也不乏一些范围较小的专业数据库，例如：

有机化合物数据库：http://www.colby.edu/chemistry/cmp/cmp.html

化合物基本性质数据库：http://www.chemfinder.camsoft.com/

上海有机化学研究所的红外光谱数据库：http://www.sioc.ac.cn/lccdeb/sjk.htm

网络中有些资源可免费查阅，而有些资源的使用则需收费。

(5)其他网站。

http://www.acs.org/(美国化学会)

http://www.ccs.ac.cn/(中国化学会)

http://www.chemsoc.org/(ChemSoc，英国皇家化学会)

http://www.csir.org/(化学软件与信息资源)

http://www.organicchem.com/(有机化学网)

http://chemnet.com.cn/(中国化工网)

http://www.reagent.com.cn/(中国试剂网)

http://www.chemonline.net/(化学在线)

第 2 章　有机化学实验的基本操作

2.1　熔点的测定

2.1.1　实验目的

(1) 了解熔点测定的意义和应用。
(2) 掌握熔点测定的操作方法。

2.1.2　实验原理

熔点是固体化合物在 101.325kPa 下固—液两相处于平衡时的温度。纯净的固体有机物一般都有固定的熔点，一个纯化合物从开始熔化(初熔)至完全熔化(全熔)的温度范围称为熔程或熔距，其熔程一般不超过 0.5～1℃。当含有杂质时，熔点会有显著的变化，会使其熔点下降，熔程延长。因此，可以通过测定熔点来鉴定有机化合物，并根据熔程的长短来判断有机化合物的纯度。

2.1.3　实验方法

1. 毛细管法

实验步骤如下：

1) 样品的填装

取少量干燥样品用研钵研细[1]，放在干净的表面皿或玻璃片上，堆成一小堆，将熔点管的开口端插入样品堆中，使样品挤入管内。然后把熔点管开口一端向上，轻轻在桌子上顿几下，使样品掉入管底(参见 Fig. 2.2)，以同样方式重复取样几次。再取一支长约 45cm 的玻璃管垂直于表面皿或玻璃片上，将熔点管从玻璃管上端自由落下，重复多次，使样品装填紧密，高度约为 2～3mm。填装时操作要迅速，防止样品吸潮，装入的样品要结实。

2) 仪器装置

毛细管法中最常用的仪器是 Thiele 管(又称 b 型管或熔点测定管)。取一支 b 型管，固定在铁架台上，装入导热液(导热液一般用液体石蜡、硫酸或硅油等)至略高于支管口上沿。管口配一插有温度计的开槽塞子(也可将温度计悬挂)，毛细管通过导热液紧附在温度计上，样品部分位于温度计水银球中部。并用橡皮圈将毛细管缚在温度计上(橡皮圈不能浸入导热液中)。调整温度计位置，使其水银球恰好在 Thiele 管两侧管的中部[2](参见 Fig. 2.3)。

3) 熔点测定

测定时，先加热 Thiele 管，若测定已知样品的熔点，可先以较快速度加热，在距离熔点 15～20℃时，应控制加热速度，使温度每分钟上升 1～2℃[3]至测出熔程；若测定未知样品，要先粗测熔点范围，再用上述方法细测。

当毛细管中的样品开始塌落，并有小液滴出现时，表明样品已开始融化即初熔(或始熔)，记下此温度。继续观察，待固体样品恰好完全溶解成透明液体即全熔时再迅速记下温度。这个温度范围即为样品化合物的熔程。在测定过程中，还要观察和记录是否有萎缩、变色、发泡、升华及碳化等现象。

熔点测定至少要有两次重复数据，每一次测定都必须用新的熔点管新装样品，不能使用已测过的熔点管[4]。同时必须待导热液温度冷至待测物熔点以下 15℃时才能再进行测定。

测定完成后，必须将导热液冷至室温后方可倒回试剂瓶里。刚用完的温度计不能立即用水冲洗，待其冷却后用纸擦去导热液，再用水冲洗，以避免温度计炸裂。

2. 数字熔点测定仪

使用数字熔点仪进行测定，方便、准确、易于操作。以 WRS-1 数字熔点仪为例。该熔点仪采用光电检测，数字温度显示等技术，具有初熔、全熔自动显示，可与记录仪配合使用，可进行熔化曲线自动记录。该仪器采用集成化的电子线路，能快速达到设定的起始温度，并具有六挡可供选择的线性升、降温速率自动控制，初熔、全熔读数可自动储存，无需监管。该熔点仪采用毛细管作样品管。

操作步骤如下：

(1)开启电源开关，稳定 20min。

(2)通过拨盘设定起始温度，再按起始温度按钮，输入此温度，此时预置灯亮。

(3)选择升温速度，把波段开关旋至所需位置。

(4)当预置灯熄灭时，可插入装有样品的毛细管，此时初熔灯也熄灭。

(5)把电表调至零，按升温按钮，数分钟后初熔灯先亮，然后出现全熔读数显示。

(6)按初熔按钮，显示初熔读数，记录初、全熔温度。

(7)按降温按钮，使温度降至室温，最后切断电源。

2.1.4 实验内容

采用毛细管法，分别用乙酰苯胺、苯甲酸、尿素、肉桂酸，以及混合物(以纯样品按不同的比例配制)作为样品，研细，进行熔点测定的练习。

2.1.5 注释

[1]样品一定要研得极细，才能使装样结实，这样受热时才均匀，如果有空隙，不易传热，影响结果。

[2]此处导热液对流循环好，样品受热均匀。

[3]有充分时间让热量从熔点管传至毛细管内，减少观察上的误差。

[4]避免在融化过程中晶型改变或分解引起熔点的改变。

2.1.6 思考题

(1)用毛细管法测定一纯净有机化合物的熔点时，哪些错误操作会导致下列现象的发生？

(a)实测值低于正确熔点。

(b)实测值高于正确熔点。

(c)熔程较宽(跨越好几度)。

(2)试判断下列说法是否正确？如果是错误的，试解释原因。

(a)杂质的存在总是会降低有机化合物的熔点。

(b)有机物的敏锐熔点总是意味着它是一纯净的单一物质。

(c)若在化合物 X 中加入化合物 A 后熔点并未降低，则 X 与 A 为同一物质。

(d)若在化合物 X 中加入化合物 A 后熔点降低，则 X 与 A 为不同的物质。

2.2 重 结 晶

2.2.1 实验目的

(1)学习重结晶提纯固体有机化合物的原理和方法。

(2)掌握重结晶的实验操作。

2.2.2 实验原理

重结晶是利用混合物中各组分在某种溶剂中的溶解度不同，或在同一溶剂中不同温度时的溶解度不同，而使它们相互分离的方法，它是提纯固体有机化合物常用的方法之一。

2.2.3 重结晶提纯法的一般操作

(1)选择适宜的溶剂(选择方法具体见英文部分 2.2.2:2)。

(2)将粗产品溶于适宜的热的溶剂中制成饱和溶液(具体见英文部分 2.2.2:3)。

(3)趁热过滤除去不溶性杂质。如溶液的颜色深，则应先脱色，再进行过滤(具体见英文部分 2.2.2:4)。

(4)冷却溶液，或蒸发溶剂，使之慢慢析出结晶而杂质则留在母液中，或者杂质析出而欲提纯的化合物则留在溶液中(具体见英文部分 2.2.2:5)。

(5)抽气过滤分离母液，分出结晶体或杂质(具体见英文部分 2.2.2:6)。

(6)洗涤结晶，除去附着的母液(具体见英文部分 2.2.2:6)。

(7)干燥结晶(具体见英文部分 2.2.2:6)。

2.2.4 实验内容

用重结晶法提纯粗品乙酰苯胺

(1)称取 4g 粗乙酰苯胺，放在 250mL 三角烧杯中，加入 50mL 纯水，加热至沸腾至乙酰苯胺溶解，若不溶解，可适量添加少量热水，搅拌并热至接近沸腾，使乙酰苯胺溶解。

(2)稍冷后,加入适量(约 0.1g)活性炭于溶液中,煮沸 5～10min,趁热用热水漏斗[Fig. 1.7(b)]或折叠式滤纸(折叠方法见 Fig. 2.5)过滤，用三角烧杯收集滤液，在过滤过程中，热水漏斗和溶液均应用小火加热保温[Fig. 1.7(a)，(b)]，以免冷却。

(3) 滤液放置冷却后，有乙酰苯胺结晶体析出，抽气过滤(抽气过滤装置见 Fig. 2.4)，抽干后用玻璃钉或玻璃瓶塞压挤晶体[Fig. 1.7 (c)]，继续抽滤，尽量除去母液。

(4) 进行晶体的洗涤工作，即先把橡皮管从抽滤瓶上拔出，关闭抽气泵，将少量蒸馏水(作溶剂)均匀地撒在滤饼上，浸没晶体，用玻璃棒小心均匀地搅拌晶体，接上橡皮管，抽滤至干，如此重复洗涤两次。

(5) 取出晶体，放在表面皿上晾干，或在 100℃以下烘干，称重。

纯乙酰苯胺 m.p.114℃。乙酰苯胺在水中的溶解度：5.5g/100mL (100℃)，0.53g/100mL (0℃)。

2.2.5　思考题

(1) 重结晶操作包括哪几个步骤？每一步骤的目的各是什么？

(2) 为什么重结晶时溶剂的用量不能过多也不能过少？应如何确定正确的溶剂用量？

(3) 为什么重结晶时溶剂的实际用量要少于计算值？为什么溶剂需逐滴加入至被重结晶的化合物中，直至固体在溶剂沸点时全部溶解？

2.3　蒸馏与分馏

2.3.1　实验目的

(1) 学习普通蒸馏和分馏的原理及其应用。

(2) 掌握实验室常用的蒸馏和分馏的操作。

2.3.2　普通蒸馏

1. 实验原理

蒸馏是分离和纯化液体有机化合物常用的方法之一。当液体物质被加热时，该物质的蒸气压达到液体表面大气压时，液体沸腾，这时的温度称为沸点。常压蒸馏就是将液体加热到沸腾状态，使该液体变成蒸气，又将蒸气冷凝后得到液体的过程。

每个液态的有机化合物在一定的压力下均有固定的沸点。利用蒸馏可将两种或两种以上沸点相差较大(>30℃)的液体混合物分开。但是应该注意，某些有机物往往能和其他组分形成二元或三元恒沸混合物，它们也有固定的沸点，因此具有固定沸点的液体，有时不一定是纯化合物。纯液体化合物的沸程一般为 0.5～1℃，混合物的沸程则较长。可以利用蒸馏来测定液体化合物的沸点。

2.　实验操作

(1) 按 Fig. 2.6 将实验装置按从下往上，从左到右的原则安装完毕，注意各磨口之间的连接。选一个大小适宜的烧瓶，使待蒸馏的液体量不超过它的一半。温度计经套管插入蒸馏头中，并使温度计的水银球的上缘恰好位于蒸馏头支口的下缘，使它们在同一水平线上，见 Fig. 2.6。

(2) 将待蒸馏的液体经漏斗加入蒸馏烧瓶中，放入 1～2 粒沸石[1]，然后通冷凝水[2]。

(3) 最初小火加热，然后慢慢加大火力，使之沸腾，开始蒸馏。

(4) 调节火源，控制蒸馏速度为 1～2 滴/秒，记下第一滴馏出液的温度[3]。

(5) 维持加热速度，继续蒸馏，收集所需温度范围的馏分。当不再有馏分蒸出且温度突然下降时，停止蒸馏[4]。

(6) 蒸馏完毕，关闭热源，停止通水，拆卸实验装置，其顺序与安装时相反。

3. 实验内容

用无水乙醇为样品，水浴加热，进行蒸馏操作实验。

4. 注释

[1]加沸石可使液体平稳沸腾，防止液体过热产生暴沸；一旦停止加热后再蒸馏，应重新加沸石；若忘了加沸石，应停止加热，冷却后再补加。

[2]冷凝水从冷凝管支口的下端进，上端出。

[3]此时的温度就是馏出液的沸点。

[4]切勿蒸干，以防意外事故发生。

5. 思考题

(1) 为什么不能将沸石加至热的液体中？

(2) 为什么蒸馏装置的尾端要有一个开口通大气？

2.3.3　分馏

1. 实验原理

分馏也是分离提纯液体有机化合物的一种方法，适用于沸点相差较小的液体有机物的分离提纯，分离效果比蒸馏好。

分馏通常是在蒸馏的基础上用分馏柱来进行的。利用分馏柱进行分馏，实际上就是让分馏柱内的混合物进行多次气化与冷凝。当上升的蒸气与下降的冷凝液互相接触时，上升的蒸气部分冷凝放出热量使下降的冷凝液部分气化，两者之间发生了热量交换，其结果是上升蒸气中易挥发组分增加，而下降的冷凝液中高沸点组分增加。每进行一次这样的热量交换即相当于进行了一次蒸馏，如果继续多次，就等于进行了多次的气液平衡，即达到了多次蒸馏的效果。这样，靠近分馏柱顶部易挥发物质的组分比率高，而烧瓶里高沸点组分的比率高。当分馏柱的效率足够高时，在分馏柱顶部出来的蒸气就接近于纯低沸点的组分，高沸点组分则留在烧瓶里，最终便可将沸点不同的物质分离开来。

2. 实验操作

(1) 选一根分馏柱，按 Fig. 2.7[也可参见 Fig. 1.3 (c)]将实验装置安置完毕，注意各磨口之间的连接。

(2) 将待分馏液放入烧瓶中，加入 1～2 粒沸石，通冷凝水。

(3)控制加热速度，使馏出速度为 1～2 滴/秒[1]。

(4)分段收集馏分[2]，分别记下各馏分相应的温度，分别称量。

3. 实验内容

乙醇-水混合物的分馏

(1)在 100mL 的圆底烧瓶中放入约 70%的乙醇水溶液 60mL，加入 2～3 粒沸石，安装好分馏装置。

(2)通冷凝水，水浴加热，控制加热速度[3]，收集前馏分。

(3)当温度达到 78℃时，调换接收器，收集馏出液，馏出速度控制在 1～2 滴/秒，记下温度[4]。

(4)当温度持续下降时[5]，即可停止加热。记录馏出液、前馏分和残余液的体积，并测定馏出液的质量分数[6]。

4. 注释

[1]馏出速度太快，产物纯度下降；馏出速度太慢，馏出温度易上下波动。为减少分馏柱内热量散失，可用石棉绳将其包裹起来。

[2]注意切不可蒸干。

[3]使蒸气慢慢上升到柱顶。

[4]由于温度计误差，实际温度可能略有差异。

[5]分馏要结束时，由于乙醇蒸气不足，温度计水银球不能被乙醇蒸气包围，因此温度出现下降。

[6]用乙醇比重计测定，一般可达 89%～94%。

5. 思考题

(1)什么是共沸混合物？为什么分馏也不能将共沸混合物分离？

(2)试说明简单蒸馏与分馏各有什么特点。

2.4　水蒸气蒸馏

2.4.1　实验目的

(1)学习水蒸气蒸馏的原理及其应用。

(2)掌握水蒸气蒸馏的装置和操作方法。

2.4.2　实验原理

水蒸气蒸馏也是分离提纯液体有机化合物的一种方法。它是将水蒸气通入不溶或难溶于水、有一定挥发性的有机化合物中，使该有机化合物随水蒸气一起蒸馏出来。

根据分压定律，混合物的蒸气压应该是各组分蒸气压之和。当各组分的蒸气压之和等于大气压力时，混合物开始沸腾。混合物的沸点要比单个物质的正常沸点低，这意味着该有机化合物可在比其正常沸点低的温度下被蒸馏出来。在馏出物中，有机物的质量(W_A)与水的质量之比(W_A/W_{H_2O})等于两者的分压(p_A和p_{H_2O})分别和两者的相对分子质量(M_A和M_{H_2O})的乘积之比，见英文部分2.4.1中方程式(1)。

水蒸气蒸馏常在以下几种情况下使用：①常压蒸馏易分解的高沸点有机化合物；②混合物中含有大量固体，蒸馏、过滤、萃取等方法都不适用；③混合物中含有大量树脂状的物质或不挥发杂质，用蒸馏、萃取等方法难以分离。

被提纯物质应具备的条件：①不溶于或难溶于水；②共沸腾下与水不反应；③100℃时必须有一定的蒸气压。

2.4.3　实验操作

(1)按Fig. 2.8和Fig. 2.9，将实验装置安装完毕[也可参见Fig. 1.3(d)]，注意各磨口之间的连接，Fig. 2.8和Fig. 2.9之间用一个T形管连接，T形管下端连接一个带有夹子的短橡皮管。

(2)将蒸馏物倒入圆底烧瓶中，其量不超过烧瓶容量的1/3，确保所有实验装置连接紧密。

(3)开始蒸馏前将T形管的夹子打开，通冷凝水，加热水蒸气发生器，当T形管支管有蒸气冲出时，夹紧夹子，使蒸气通入烧瓶中[1]。

(4)调节火源，控制馏出速度1～2滴/秒[2]。

(5)当馏出物澄清透明时，即可停止蒸馏。

(6)先打开夹子，再移去火源[3]，拆除装置。

2.4.4　实验内容

从中药徐长卿中提取丹皮酚[4]

(1)称取中药徐长卿5g于250mL烧瓶中，加水20mL。安装好水蒸气蒸馏实验装置，打开T形管夹子，通冷凝水。

(2)加热水蒸气发生器[5]，当有水蒸气从T形管的支管冲出时，夹紧夹子，让水蒸气导入三颈烧瓶中。

(3)调节火源和蒸气流量，控制馏出速度1～2滴/秒，当馏出液由混浊液变为澄清透明时，可停止蒸馏。

(4)打开T形管的夹子，移去火源。

(5)嗅一下馏出物的气味，取一滴馏出液于小块滤纸上，待其挥发后，观察滤纸上是否留有油迹。

(6)取馏出液1～2mL，搅匀，加入1% $FeCl_3$乙醇溶液2～4滴，观察现象。

2.4.5　注释

[1]此时瓶内的混合物不断翻滚，不久有机物和水的混合物馏出。

[2]为使水蒸气不致在烧瓶中过多而冷凝，可在烧瓶底下用小火加热。要随时注意安全管中水柱的情况，若有异常，立刻打开T形管夹子，移去热源，排除故障后方可继续。

[3]以防止倒吸。

[4]从徐长卿中提取挥发油，其主要成分为丹皮酚，结构式见英文部分 2.4.4 Note[4]。

[5]水蒸气发生器中的水不能太满，以占容器的 2/3 为宜，否则沸腾时水将会冲出来，导致热烧伤。

2.4.6 思考题

(1)水蒸气蒸馏的基本原理是什么?

(2)T 形管和安全管的作用各是什么?

(3)如何判断水蒸气蒸馏已完成?

2.5 减压蒸馏

2.5.1 实验目的

(1)学习减压蒸馏的原理和应用。

(2)掌握减压蒸馏的仪器安装和操作。

2.5.2 实验原理

高沸点的有机化合物，或在常压下蒸馏易发生分解，氧化或聚合的有机化合物，常可采用减压蒸馏进行分离，提纯。沸点大于 200℃的液体一般需用减压蒸馏提纯。

液体的沸点随外界压力变化而变化，若系统的压力降低了，液体的沸点温度也随之降低。在进行减压蒸馏之前，应先从文献中查阅欲提纯的化合物在所选择压力下的相应沸点，若文献中无此数据，可用下述经验规则推算，即若系统的压力接近大气压时，压力每降低 1.33kPa(10mmHg)，则沸点下降 0.5℃；若系统在较低压力状态时，压力降低一半，沸点下降 10℃。例如，某化合物在 20mmHg(2.67kPa)的压力下，沸点为 100℃，压力降至 10mmHg(1.33kPa)时，沸点为 90℃。

更精确一些的压力与沸点的关系可以用 Fig. 2.10 的压力温度关系图来估算。已知某化合物在某一压力下的沸点便可近似地推算出该化合物在另一压力下的沸点。具体的使用方法请参照英文部分 2.5.1。

2.5.3 实验操作

(1)按 Fig. 2.11 或 Fig. 2.12 把仪器安装完毕后[1]，检查系统的气密性。若使用 Fig. 2.11 的减压蒸馏装置时，先旋紧毛细管上的螺旋夹子，关闭安全瓶上的二通旋塞，然后开泵抽气，观察能否达到要求的真空度且保持不变[若用水泵减压，一般可达 20mmHg(2.67kPa)的压力；若用油泵抽气，压力则会更低]。若发现有漏气现象，则需分段检查各连接处是否漏气，必要时可在磨口接口处涂少量真空脂密封。待系统无明显漏气现象时，慢慢打开安全瓶上的活塞，使系统内外压力平衡。

(2)在蒸馏烧瓶中倒入待蒸馏的液体[2]，其量控制在烧瓶容积的 1/3～1/2，关闭安全瓶上的活塞，开泵抽气[3]，通过螺旋夹调节毛细管导入空气，使能冒出一连串小气泡为宜。

(3) 当达到所要求的低压且压力稳定后，开启冷凝水，开始加热。热浴温度一般比瓶内温度高 20～30℃。蒸馏过程中，密切注意蒸馏的温度和压力，若有不符，则应调节。控制馏出速度 1～2 滴/秒。待达到所需的沸点时，更换接收器[4]。若用多头接收器[5]，只需转动接引管的位置，使馏出液流入不同的接收器中。

(4) 蒸馏完毕时，撤去热源，慢慢打开毛细管上的螺旋夹，并缓缓打开安全瓶上的活塞[6]，平衡体系内外压力，然后关闭油泵(或水泵)。

(5) 拆除装置，清洗仪器。

2.5.4 实验内容

粗呋喃甲醛(糠醛)的纯化

在 50mL 的梨形瓶中加入 20mL 粗呋喃甲醛，装好仪器，进行减压蒸馏。

呋喃甲醛的沸点为：161.8℃/101.33kPa；103℃/13.33kPa；67.8℃/2.67kPa；18.5℃/0.133kPa。

2.5.5 注释

[1]在减压蒸馏系统中切勿使用有裂缝的或薄壁的玻璃仪器，尤其不能使用不耐压的平底瓶如锥形瓶，以防引起爆炸。

[2]待减压蒸馏的液体中若含有低沸点组分，应先进行普通蒸馏，尽量除去低沸物，以保护油泵。

[3]使用水泵时应特别注意因水压突然降低，会使水泵不能维持已达到的真空度，蒸馏系统内的真空度比水泵所产生的真空度高，因此水会流入蒸馏系统玷污产品。为此，需在水泵与蒸馏系统间安装一个安全瓶。

[4]更换接受瓶时的操作同操作步骤 4。换上新的接受瓶后再按操作步骤 2 和 3 进行减压蒸馏。

[5]多用接收器请见本书英文部分 Fig. 2.13。

[6]减压蒸馏结束后，安全瓶上的活塞一定要缓慢打开，如果打开太快，系统内外压力突然变化，使水银压力计的压差迅速改变，可导致水银柱破裂。

2.5.6 思考题

(1) 利用 Fig. 2.10 估计 1, 6-己二醇[沸点 132℃(10mmHg, 1.33kPa)]在常压下(760mmHg)的沸点是多少？

(2) 为什么在减压蒸馏前需检查系统的气密性。

2.6 萃取与洗涤

2.6.1 实验目的

(1) 学习萃取和洗涤的原理和应用。

(2) 掌握萃取和洗涤的操作方法。

2.6.2　实验原理

萃取是分离和提纯有机化合物常用的基本操作之一。设溶液由有机化合物 X 溶解于溶剂 A 而成，现如要从其中萃取 X，我们可选择一种对 X 溶解度极好，而与溶剂 A 不相混溶和不起化学反应的溶剂 B。把溶液放入分液漏斗中，加入溶剂 B，充分振荡。静置后，由于 A 与 B 不相混溶，故分成两层。此时 X 在 A、B 两相间的浓度比，在一定温度和压力下为一常数，称为分配系数，以 K 表示，这种关系称为分配定律。用下面的公式表示：

$$\frac{\text{X在溶剂A中的浓度}}{\text{X在溶剂B中的浓度}}=K(\text{分配系数})$$

注意：分配定律是假定所选用的溶剂 B 不与 X 起化学反应时才适用的。

依照分配定律，要节省溶剂而提高萃取的效率，用一定分量的溶剂一次加入溶液中萃取，则不如把这个量的溶剂分成几份多次来萃取好，可用计算式来说明(参见英文部分 2.6.1)。

洗涤是从混合物中提取出不需要的少量杂质，所以洗涤实际上也是一种萃取。

2.6.3　实验步骤

本实验用乙醚从乙酸水溶液中萃取乙酸为例来说明实验步骤。

1. 一次萃取法

用移液管准确量取 10mL 冰醋酸与水的混合液(冰醋酸与水以 1∶19 的体积比相混合)，放入分液漏斗中[1-3]。用 30mL 乙醚萃取[4]，注意近旁不能有火，否则易引起火灾。加入乙醚后，加盖玻璃活塞。先用右手食指的末节将漏斗上端的玻璃塞顶住，再用大拇指及食指和中指握住漏斗。这样漏斗转动时可用左手的食指和中指蜷握在活塞的柄上，使振摇过程中[如图 Fig. 2.15(a)]玻璃塞和活塞均夹紧，上下轻轻摇振分液漏斗，每隔几秒钟将漏斗倒置(活塞朝上)，小心打开活塞，以平衡内外压力[如 Fig. 2.15(b)]，重复操作 2～3 次，然后再用力振摇，使互不相溶的乙醚和乙酸水溶液充分接触，提高萃取效率，若振摇时间太短，则会影响萃取效率。

将分液漏斗置于铁圈上，当溶液分成两层后，小心旋开活塞，放出下层水溶液至三角烧瓶内，加入 3～4 滴酚酞作指示剂，用 0.2mol/L 标准氢氧化钠溶液滴定，记录用去氢氧化钠的毫升数。计算：①留在水中的乙酸量及质量百分数；②留在乙醚中的乙酸量及质量百分数。

2. 三次萃取法

准确量取 10mL 冰醋酸与水的混合液(体积比同上)于一分液漏斗中，用 10mL 乙醚如上法萃取，分去乙醚溶液。水溶液再用 10mL 乙醚萃取，再分出乙醚溶液后，水溶液仍用 10mL 乙醚萃取。如此前后共计三次。最后将用乙醚第三次萃取后的水溶液放入 50mL 的三角烧瓶内，用 0.2mol/L 标准氢氧化钠溶液滴定，计算：①留在水中的乙酸量及质量百分数；②留在乙醚中的乙酸量及质量百分数。

根据上述两种不同萃取法所得数据，比较萃取乙酸的效率。

2.6.4　实验内容

混合物的分离

实验室有一混合物待分离提纯，已知其中含有乙酸乙酯、苯胺与苯甲酸，根据其性质和溶解度选择合适溶剂，设计合理方案，从该混合物中经萃取、分离、纯化后得到纯净的乙酸乙酯、苯胺和苯甲酸。

参考方案

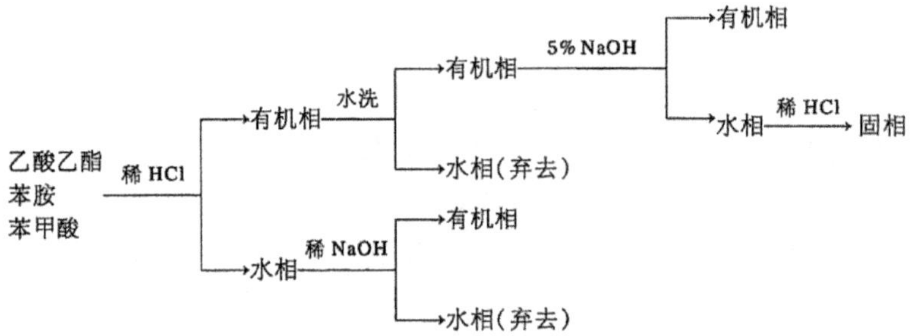

实验操作

取 52mL 混合物[5]，充分搅拌下滴入 4mol/L HCl 使混合液 pH = 3，将其分液，水相放入锥形瓶中待处理，向有机相中加入适量的水，洗去附着的酸，并分离。边振荡边向有机相中滴加 5% NaOH，使 pH = 9～10，分出有机相于一干燥的锥形瓶中，用适量无水 $CaCl_2$ 干燥，常压蒸馏得一无色透明液体，约 17mL，测沸点，为何物质?

被分出的水相，置于一小烧杯中，滴加 4mol/L HCl，至 pH = 3，此时有白色沉淀，过滤，选择合适溶剂重结晶，干燥，称重，测熔点，为何物质?

将上述第一次置于锥形瓶中待处理的水相，边振荡边加入 6mol/L NaOH，使 pH = 10，分离，将有机相置于圆底烧瓶中，用乙醚萃取，分离，用粒状 NaOH 干燥，蒸馏，得一无色透明液体约 12～13mL，测沸点，是何物质?

2.6.5　注释

[1]常用的分液漏斗有球形、锥形和梨形三种，在有机化学实验中，分液漏斗主要应用于:

(a)分离两种分层而不起作用的液体。

(b)从溶液中萃取某种成分。

(c)用水或碱或酸溶液洗涤某种产品。

(d)用来滴加某种试剂(代替滴液漏斗)。

[2]分液漏斗价格昂贵而且易碎。务必不要把分液漏斗倒置，应把它放在一个铁圈上或放在漏斗支撑架或其他一些稳定装置上。

[3]溶液体积应该少于分液漏斗体积的 3/4，如果分液漏斗上有一个玻璃活塞，玻璃表面必须润滑以阻止黏结、渗漏或结冰；如果用的是一个塑料活塞，因为它本身就具有一定的润滑作用，可以不加润滑剂。

用完分液漏斗后，应用水冲洗干净，注意！玻璃塞应用薄纸包裹后再塞回去。使用分液漏斗需注意:①不能把活塞上附有凡士林的分液漏斗放在烘箱内烘干；②不能用手拿住分液漏斗来分离液体；③上口玻璃塞打开后才能开启活塞；④上层的液体不能由分液漏斗的下方放出。

[4]通常每个实验都有一定的步骤和特定的萃取剂用量。如果没有，通常可用与被萃取液等体积的萃取剂，萃取剂至少应分为两部分使用。

[5] 52mL 的混合物由 30mL 乙酸乙酯，20mL 苯胺和 2g 苯甲酸组成。

2.6.6　思考题

(1)影响萃取效率的因素有哪些？如何选择合适的溶剂？

(2)使用分液漏斗的目的是什么？使用时要注意哪些事项？

(3)有两种互不溶解的液体存在于同一分液漏斗中，相对密度大的在哪一层？下层的液体应从哪里放出来？放出液体时为了使其不要流得太快，应该如何操作？留在分液漏斗中的上层液体，应从哪里倾入另一容器中？

2.7　升　　华

2.7.1　实验目的

(1)了解升华的原理和意义。

(2)掌握实验室常用的升华方法。

2.7.2　实验原理

升华是提纯固体有机化合物的方法之一。某些物质在固态时有相当高的蒸气压，当加热时，不经过液态而直接气化，蒸气受到冷却又直接冷凝成固体，这个过程称为升华。若固态混合物具有不同的挥发度，则可应用升华法提纯。升华得到的产品一般具有较高的纯度。此法特别适用于纯化易潮解的物质。升华法只能用于在不太高的温度下有足够大的蒸气压力(在熔点前高于 266.6Pa)的固态物质，因此具有一定的局限性。

2.7.3　实验步骤

在蒸发皿中盛粉碎了的样品，上面用一个直径小于蒸发皿的漏斗覆盖，漏斗颈用玻璃棉塞住，防止蒸气逸出，两者用一张穿有许多小孔(孔刺向上)的滤纸隔开。调节吸气量，避免样品蒸气在漏斗颈或橡皮管内冷凝聚集。用沙浴(或其他热浴)加热，小心调节火焰，控制浴温(低于被升华物质的熔点)，而让其慢慢升华。蒸气通过滤纸小口，冷却后凝结在滤纸上或漏斗壁上。为了加快升华速度，可在减压下进行升华，减压升华法特别适用于常压下其蒸气压不大或受热易分解的物质。

2.7.4　实验内容

见实验 3.14 从茶叶中提取咖啡因。

2.8　液体有机化合物折光率的测定

2.8.1　实验目的

(1)了解测定折光率对研究有机化合物的实用意义。

(2)掌握使用阿贝折光仪测定液体有机化合物折光率的方法。

2.8.2　原理

折光率是液体化合物一个有用的物理常数。通过测定折光率可以判断有机化合物的纯度和鉴定未知物。

光在不同的介质中传播的速度是不同的，光从介质 A(空气)射入另一介质 B 时，入射角 α 与折射角 β 的正弦之比称为折光率(n)，见 Fig. 2.18。

$$n=\frac{\sin\alpha}{\sin\beta}$$

对于一个确定的化合物，其折光率常受温度和光线的波长等因素的影响。所以表示折光率时必须注明测定时的温度和光线的波长。一般以钠光作为光源(波长为 589nm，以 D 表示)，在 20℃时测定化合物的折光率，如某物质的折光率表示如下：

$$n_{\mathrm{D}}^{20}=1.4892$$

一般温度升高 1℃，液体化合物的折光率降低 3.5×10^{-4}～5.5×10^{-4}。为了便于不同温度下折光率的换算，一般采用 4.5×10^{-4} 为温度常数，用下列式子进行粗略计算：

$$n_{\mathrm{correct}}=n_{\mathrm{observed}}+0.000\,45\times(t-20.0)$$

式中，t 为测量时的温度。

例如，乙酸在 16℃时测量的折光率为 1.373 17，20℃时的折光率为：

$$n_{\mathrm{D}}^{20}=1.373\,17+0.000\,45\times(16.0-20.0)=1.371\,37$$

2.8.3　阿贝折光仪及操作步骤

测定液体化合物折光率常用的仪器是阿贝(Abbe)折光仪，其结构见 Fig. 2.19。

操作步骤

(1)开启恒温水浴，通入恒温水(一般为 20℃或 25℃)，若未连接恒温水浴，此项操作可免去。

(2)当恒温后，松开锁钮，开启下面棱镜，使其镜面处于水平位置，滴入 1～2 滴乙醇或甲醇于镜面上，合上镜面，促使难挥发的污物移走，再打开棱镜，用丝巾或擦镜纸轻轻擦拭镜面。

(3) 轻轻打开棱镜，用滴管将 2～3 滴待测液均匀地滴在下面的磨砂面棱镜上[1, 2]，要求液体无气泡并充满视场，关紧棱镜。若测定易挥发样品，可用滴管从棱镜间小槽滴入。

(4) 调节反光镜和小反光镜，使两镜筒视场最亮。

(5) 旋转棱镜转动手轮，使在目镜中观察到明暗分界线。若出现色散光带，可调节消色散棱镜手轮，使明暗清晰，然后再旋转棱镜转动手轮，使明暗分界线恰好通过目镜中“×”字交叉点，如 Fig. 2.20 所示。记录从镜筒中读取的折光率[3]，读至小数点后四位，同时记下温度。重复测定 2～3 次，取其平均值为样品的折光率。

(6) 仪器用毕后用沾有少量乙醇或乙醚的擦镜纸擦拭干净，晾干两镜面，然后合紧两镜面，用仪器罩盖好或放入木箱内。

2.8.4　实验内容

(1) 测定无水丙酮和无水乙醇的折光率，分别各测三次，取平均值，并记录测定时的温度。

(2) 有两份未贴标签的样品各 0.5mL，已知其中 1 份是乙酸正丁酯 (n_D^{20} 1.3940)，另一份是苯甲酸乙酯 (n_D^{20} 1.5454)，试通过测定它们的旋光度，并换算成比旋光度后将两者区分。

2.8.5　注释

[1]操作时要特别小心，严禁触及棱镜，特别是油手，汗手及滴管的末端等。

[2]测定有毒样品的折光率时，应在通风橱内操作。

[3]若使用数显折光仪，可直接从荧光屏上读取数据。

2.8.6　思考题

(1) 某化合物在 17.5℃的折光率为 1.3698，计算其在 20℃的折光率。

(2) 通常用乙醇或甲醇而不用丙酮清洁折光仪的玻璃表面，理由是什么?

(3) 写出使用 Abbe 折光仪的具体步骤。

2.9　旋光度的测定

2.9.1　实验目的

(1) 了解旋光仪的构造，掌握使用旋光仪测定物质的旋光度的方法。

(2) 学习比旋光度的计算。

2.9.2　原理

某些手性化合物具有使偏光振动平面旋转的性质。偏光振动平面旋转的角度称为旋光度。偏光振动平面是由光源通过 Nicol 棱镜产生的。

物质的旋光度与溶液的质量浓度、溶剂的性质、温度、旋光管的长度和所用光源的波长等都有关系。因此，常用比旋光度来表示各物质的旋光性。

比旋光度是物质特有的性质。它可用于某些手性物质的识别，研究分子的构型和研究某些化学反应的机理等。

用$[\alpha]_{\lambda}^{t}$表示物质的比旋光度，计算式如下：

纯液体的比旋光度 $$[\alpha]_{\lambda}^{t}=\frac{\alpha}{l\times d}$$

溶液的比旋光度 $$[\alpha]_{\lambda}^{t}=\frac{\alpha\times 100}{l\times c}(\text{溶剂})$$

式中，$[\alpha]_{\lambda}^{t}$表示旋光性物质在t℃、光源的波长为λ时的比旋光度；t为测定时的温度；λ为光源波长；α为标尺转动角度的读数(旋光度)；d为纯液体的密度；l为旋光管的长度(单位：dm)；c为样品的质量浓度(100mL 溶液中所含有样品的质量)，单位为 g/mL；溶剂指配制溶液使用的溶剂。

2.9.3 实验操作

(1)接通电源，让光源稳定 5min 后，开始测定[1]。

(2)将样品管充满蒸馏水或待测样品的溶剂，观察视场是否与零点视场一致，如不一致说明零点有误差，应在测量读数中加上或减去这一偏差值。

(3)选择长度适宜的样品管，充满待测液[2,3]，放入旋光仪内。旋转粗调和微调，所得读数与零点之间的差值即为样品的旋光度。重复测试三次，取平均值。

(4)根据公式计算样品的比旋光度。

2.9.4 实验内容

准确称取 2.5g 样品(如葡萄糖)放在 10mL 容量瓶中配成溶液，依照上述方法测定其旋光度。这时所得的读数与零点之间的差值即为该物质的旋光度。记下样品管的长度及溶液的温度，然后按公式计算其比旋光度。

2.9.5 注释

[1]旋光仪一定要先预热，使之稳定。

[2]样品液一定要充满样品管，勿有气泡。

[3]样品管的螺丝帽一定要旋好，勿漏液体；也不宜旋得过紧，以免影响读数。

2.10 色谱技术

2.10.1 实验目的

(1)学习柱色谱，薄层色谱，气相色谱和液相色谱的原理和应用。

(2)掌握柱色谱和薄层色谱的操作方法。

色谱法是一种建立在相分配原理基础上的分离、提纯和鉴定有机化合物的实验方法。

色谱法一般要将样品溶解在流动相中，流动相可以是液体，也可以是气体，然后流经固定相。固定相可以是色谱柱或是固体表面。各组分与固定相相互作用的时间足够长，它们就能被分开。

色谱法按照固定相和流动相可分为气固色谱、液固色谱、气液色谱及液液色谱。固相可以使用硅胶、氧化铝或离子交换树脂等多种材料，液相可以在一些如硅胶、多孔玻璃珠或是聚合物等材料的担体上涂布固定液制成。气固色谱和液固色谱的原理是吸附作用。吸附色谱法是以分析物与固定相之间直接的相互吸附作用为基础。气液色谱和液液色谱的原理是分配作用。

液固和液液色谱可以在柱子或板上进行，前者亦称为柱色谱，后者通常有两种类型：纸色谱和薄层色谱。气固色谱和气液色谱只能使用柱色谱，通常称为 GC。

2.10.2　柱色谱

1. 实验原理

柱色谱是分离、提纯复杂有机化合物的重要方法，可用于分离较大量的有机物。其原理参见英文部分 2.10.2:1 Introduction。

2. 吸附剂

(1) 在柱色谱中常用的固定相是硅胶和氧化铝。作为流动相的洗脱液是非极性或具有适中极性的溶剂。目前使用的吸附剂大多是硅胶，因为它能用于分离极性范围很广的样品。与氧化铝相比，它会很少与被分离的样品发生化学反应。氧化铝极性更强一些，因此它对极性大的有机化合物的吸附力强，要用极性更强的溶剂才能进行洗脱。活性氧化铝商业上有售，分为中性(pH 7)，碱性(pH 10)和酸性(pH 4)三种，它们的吸附能力有很大的差异。

(2) 极性特别强的化合物的分离需要吸附能力比硅胶和氧化铝还小的吸附剂，在这种情况下通常使用反相色谱。反相色谱需要使用极性比流动相小的吸附剂为固定相，而极性大的样品先被洗脱出来，此时，极性小的样品在固定相上的吸附力更强。

3. 洗脱剂

(1) 在柱色谱中，非极性化合物在固体吸附剂上的吸附力小，很容易用非极性的溶剂洗脱。极性化合物在金属氧化物上有很强的吸附力，因此必须用极性溶剂洗脱。

(2) 将非极性的洗脱液正己烷与中等极性的乙醚进行对比，前者与氧化铝的作用是弱的范德华力，后者与氧化铝是偶极-偶极和配位作用。所以乙醚在氧化铝上的吸附力更强。

(3) 吸附剂的吸附力和溶剂的极性决定样品在柱子里的洗脱速度。样品洗脱得太快，分离效率就低，同样，吸附剂太强或溶剂极性太弱也是如此。相反，如果洗脱太慢，则需要选择有效的极性溶剂和温和的吸附剂。

(4) 一些常见溶剂的洗脱能力顺序：烷烃(石油醚、正己烷、环乙烷)<四氯化碳<甲苯<二氯甲烷<乙醚<氯仿<丙酮<乙酸乙酯<乙醇<甲醇。

4. 选柱和装柱

(1) 选好吸附剂后，还需确定其用量多少。这取决于被分离的样品的量和柱子的直径。

样品在细长的柱子里比在短粗的柱子里待的时间更长。一般来说，吸附剂的用量是样品用量的 20～30 倍。吸附剂的高度与柱子直径之比是 10 : 1 或 15 : 1。

(2) 氧化铝的密度是 1g/cm^3，而硅胶的密度大约是 0.3g/cm^3。例如，20g 氧化铝填充到直径为 1.5cm 的层析柱时，高度达到 11cm；若用 20g 硅胶作吸附剂，则应使用短粗的色谱柱。

(3) 在选好色谱柱并称好吸附剂后，就可以装柱了。色谱柱的装填与吸附剂、洗脱液的选择同样重要，如果装填的吸附剂有裂缝或有流通渠道，吸附剂平面不规整，均会造成极差的分离效果。

(4) 将色谱柱垂直固定在铁架台上，加入计划使用的第一种洗脱剂或极性小的溶剂至柱子的 1/2 处。用玻璃棉将柱子下端塞住，再铺上 6mm 厚的石英沙，以防止吸附剂堵塞柱子底部的尖端。在充满溶剂的柱子里慢慢加入吸附剂粉末时，柱子下端的活塞必须关闭。吸附剂要装填紧实，但也不能装得过紧，否则洗脱液的流速会很慢。在将吸附剂加入到溶剂中时，要轻轻敲打柱子的边沿以防止吸附剂中出现气泡。吸附剂的顶部必须是平整的，加完吸附剂后再小心加入 4mm 厚的石英沙，该沙层可以防止新加入溶剂时对吸附剂平面的影响。

(5) 色谱柱一旦装好，就不能干枯。而且溶剂液面不允许低于吸附剂的上层水平面。

5. 洗脱技术

1) 溶解样品

加样时，通常是把混合物溶解在溶剂中，然后加到柱子里。溶液的浓度要尽可能大一些，体积一般不超过 5mL。如果样品不溶解在开始用的洗脱溶剂中，可以用少量极性更大的溶剂进行溶解。

2) 加样品溶液

加样前让柱子里的溶剂流出，待溶剂液面刚好流在石英沙上面时，关闭柱子下端的活塞。加入样品溶液，然后打开活塞，等样品液面刚好流至石英沙面时，再关闭活塞。将柱子加满洗脱液，打开活塞进行洗脱。

3) 洗脱化合物

(1) 首先用极性小的溶剂把极性小的化合物先洗脱出来，然后换成极性大的溶剂洗脱有极性的化合物。如果样品中的成分有颜色，随着洗脱的进行，会分离成不同的色带。

(2) 有时也用混合溶剂进行洗脱。例如，开始用已烷洗脱时，没有样品流出，然后改用含有 10%或 20%乙醚的已烷溶液，必要时甚至换成纯的乙醚来进行洗脱。

(3) 薄层层析可以为柱层析选取合适的洗脱液，应该使用与柱层析相同的吸附剂，被分离混合物中各组分的 R_f 最大值应约为 0.3。

(4) 洗脱液的液面越高，流速越快。比较理想的流速可控制为 2mL/min。流速太快则不能达到吸附平衡，分离会不完全，但流速太慢则会因为样品色带的自然扩散而导致分离失败。可以在柱子的顶部安置一个储存洗脱液的溶剂球，以维持洗脱液液面具有一定高度。

(5) 每份洗脱液收集多少取决于特定的实验，一般的范围是 25～150mL。如果分离的化合物是有颜色的，则分别收集不同色带的洗脱液；若为无色物质，应使用薄层层析法跟踪鉴定多份洗脱液，再合并相同组分的洗脱液。

4) 收集洗脱的化合物

通常使用旋转真空蒸发仪蒸发收集到的洗脱液，可得到各组分的纯的化合物。

6. 实验内容

(1)用柱色谱法从顺式和反式偶氮苯的混合物中分离得到纯的反式偶氮苯。装柱和柱层析法见英文部分 2.10.2:7 Experiment。

(2)本教材实验 4.4 从红辣椒中提取、分离和鉴定辣椒红素和 β-胡萝卜素。

2.10.3　薄层色谱法

1. 原理

薄层色谱法是以薄层板作为载体，让样品溶液在薄层板上展开而达到分离的目的，故称为薄层层析。它是快速分离和定性分析少量物质的一种广泛使用的实验技术，可用于精制样品、化合物鉴定、跟踪反应进程和柱色谱的先导(为柱色谱摸索最佳条件)等方面，详见英文部分 2.10.3:1 Principle。

2. 薄层板材料

见英文部分 2.10.3:2 Material of Plates。

3. 薄层色谱的展开和显色

见英文部分 2.10.3:3 Developing and Visualization of Thin-layer Chromatography。

4. R_f 的测定

R_f(比移值)表示物质移动的相对距离，即样品点到原点的距离和溶剂前沿到原点的距离之比，常用分数表示(Fig. 2.25)。R_f 值与化合物的结构、薄层板上的吸附剂、展开剂、显色方法和温度等因素有关。但在上述条件固定的情况下，R_f 值对每一种化合物来说是一个特定的数值。当两个化合物具有相同的 R_f 值时，在未做进一步的分析之前不能确定它们是不是同一个化合物。在这种情况下，简单的方法是使用不同的溶剂或混合溶剂来展开样品，以做进一步的检验。

5. 薄层层析常用的吸附剂

硅胶和氧化铝是薄层层析常用的固相吸附剂。化合物极性越大，它在硅胶和氧化铝上的吸附力越强。所有的吸附剂均制成活性精细粉末，活化通常是加热粉末以脱去水分。硅胶是酸性的，用来分离酸性或中性的化合物。氧化铝有酸性、中性和碱性三种，可用于分离极性或非极性的化合物。商用薄层板可以买到，这些薄板常用玻璃或塑料制成。展开剂在薄层板上爬升的距离越长，混合物的分离效果越好。宽的薄层板可用于多个样品的分离鉴定。厚度为 1～2mm 的大板可用于 50～1000mg 样品的分离制备。

6. 样品的制备与点样

样品必须溶解在挥发性的有机溶剂中，浓度最好是 1%～2%。溶剂应具有高的挥发性以利于立即蒸发。丙酮、二氯甲烷和氯仿是常用的有机溶剂。分析固体样品时，可将 20～40mg 样品溶到 2mL 的溶剂中。在距薄层板底端 1cm 处，用铅笔画一条线，作为起点线。用毛细管(内径小于 1mm)吸取样品溶液，垂直地轻轻接触到薄层板的起点线上。样品量不能太多，否则易造成斑点过大，互相交叉或拖尾现象，不能得到很好的分离效果。

7. 展开

将选择好的展开剂放在层析缸中，使层析缸内溶剂蒸气达到饱和状态，再将点好样品的薄层板放入层析缸中进行展开。使用足够的展开剂以使薄层板底部浸入溶剂 3～4mm。但溶剂不能太多，否则样点在液面以下，溶解到溶剂中，不能进行层析。当展开剂爬升到薄层板的前沿(离顶端 5～10mm 处)或各组分已明显分开时，取出薄层板，用铅笔画出展开剂前沿的位置后，放平晾干即可显色。

8. 显色

如果化合物本身有颜色，就可直接观察它的斑点。但是很多有机物本身无色，可在紫外灯下观察有无荧光斑点。另外一种方法是待薄层板溶剂晾干后，放在含有 0.5g 碘的密闭容器中，许多有机物都能和碘形成黄棕色斑点。也可在溶剂蒸发前用显色剂喷雾显色。根据 R_f 值的不同对各组分进行鉴别。

9. 实验内容

(1)用薄层色谱法鉴别邻硝基苯胺与间硝基苯胺(或鉴别邻硝基苯胺与对硝基苯胺)的两种异构体。

实验步骤

(a)在老师的指导下，制备好 2～4 块薄层板。将 5mg 邻硝基苯胺和 5mg 间硝基苯胺分别溶于约 0.5mL 丙酮中。

(b)将二氯甲烷加入层析缸中，厚度约为 0.6～0.8cm。

(c)在 2.5cm×7.0cm 的硅胶板上离底边 1cm 处用铅笔画一条直线，用一根干净的毛细管吸取邻硝基苯胺样品溶液，在薄板的铅笔线上左侧点样，样品点的直径约 1～2mm，若一次点样不够，则应等样点干后，在同一圆心上点样第 2 次、第 3 次[1]。另取一支干净的毛细管吸取间硝基苯胺溶液，在薄板的铅笔线上距左侧点 1cm 处用同样的方法点样。

(d)将点好样的薄板放入层析缸中[Fig. 2.26(b)]，薄层板展开至溶剂前沿离顶部约 0.5～1cm 时结束。

(e)取出薄层板，在溶剂挥发前迅速将溶剂前沿标出，然后让溶剂挥发至干。

(f)通常在溶剂挥发干后，可以观察到薄板上的样品点。如果将薄层板置于碘缸中或紫外灯下，样点将更明显。

(g)分别计算两种硝基苯胺的 R_f 值。

注释

点样的次数依样品浓度而定，一般为 2～5 次。若样品量太少时，有的样品组分不易显出；若样品量太多时，易造成斑点过大，互相交叉或拖尾，影响分离效果。

(2)本教材实验 4.3 从菠菜叶中提取和分离叶色素。

10. 思考题

(1)TLC 实验中，为什么样品点的位置必须在展开剂液面之上？

(2)根据薄层层析的结果，分别计算两种硝基苯胺的 R_f 值，并排出两种硝基苯胺的极性大小顺序。

2.10.4　气相色谱

1. 原理

气相色谱是以气体作为流动相，根据固定相状态的不同可分为气固色谱和气液色谱，统称为 GC。

2. 仪器

气相色谱仪的示意图见 Fig. 2.27。气相色谱系统的不同在于使用不同的载气、进样系统、色谱柱和检测器。

3. 载气

常用的载气有氮气，一些惰性气体如氦气、氩气和二氧化碳也常作为载气使用。

4. 进样系统

在分析气体样品时，样品直接注射入载气流中，液体和固体样品则必须经闪蒸器气化。汽化温度通常要比混合样品中最难挥发的组分的沸点高 50℃。进样系统可以加热，并将载气流和色谱柱连在一起。它的入口处用硅橡胶膜片封住，进样时必须刺穿隔膜进入系统。这种进样操作必须要将蒸气迅速推进，进样速度太慢会使色谱峰变宽，由此引起结果不正确。

5. 填充色谱柱和加热箱

分离色谱柱可由不锈钢、玻璃或熔凝硅石制成。熔凝硅石作为一种色谱柱材料逐渐被广泛使用。由聚酰胺制得的色谱柱具有可靠的强度。色谱柱要在炉中预热。填充色谱柱和毛细管色谱柱之间是有区别的。填充柱是填充粒状担体作为固定相。填料通过漏斗流进内径约 3～8mm，长约 1～3m 的柱中。毛细管色谱柱是空心的，固定液直接涂在毛细管柱内壁。一种方法是将配制好的一定浓度的固定液匀速推进色谱柱中；另外一种方式是将色谱柱中装满极度稀释的溶液，然后用真空泵将溶剂抽掉。毛细管色谱柱最长能达到 100m，内径在 0.15～1mm。短的填充柱一般是直形的或 U 形的。长填充柱和毛细管柱制成直径 10～30cm 的螺旋形管。使用前色谱柱必须通载气，放在色谱加热箱内充分加热以除去溶剂残留物或活化硅胶单体和分子筛。

6. 检测器

在气相色谱中，广泛使用的检测器有热导池检测器和火焰离子化检测器，对于检测特殊化合物也会使用特定的检测器。

2.10.5　高效液相色谱

1. 原理

高效液相色谱(HPLC)不同于普通的液相色谱。普通的液相色谱，色谱柱的内径为 1～5cm，填充剂粒度的平均直径为 100～250μm，只需要很小的柱前压，液流速度很慢(大约

0.1mL/min 或更小），所需的分析时间很长。如果加快液流速度，则会降低柱效和分离效果。普通液相色谱的优点在于能够用于较大量的制备性实验，填充剂的价格便宜，操作简单。

减小填充剂的粒度是提高柱效的最有效途径。高效液相色谱中常用填充剂颗粒直径小于 75μm，而柱径很小（小的柱径既能大大降低溶剂用量又能提高检测浓度），因此阻力很大。为了达到快速、高效的分离，必须有很高的柱前压力，以获得高速的液流。载液在色谱柱内的流速较之经典液相色谱高得多，一般可达 0.5～5mL/min。高效液相色谱的柱效通常要比经典液相色谱高 10～100 倍，而且分离时间大大缩短。

2. 仪器

高效液相色谱仪由贮液管、高压泵、进样器、色谱柱、检测器、数据处理系统组成，见 Fig. 2.28。正庚烷常用于正相色谱中，而在逆相色谱中，常使用甲醇、乙腈、水和它们以不同比例混合的溶剂。常使用短的预分离柱来保护分离色谱柱或进行预分离。色谱柱是高效液相色谱仪中最重要的部分，分离效率主要由它决定。我们可以根据化合物的性质来选择色谱柱。检测器有很多种，使用最广泛的是紫外可见光检测器，它具有很高的灵敏度，但是如果化合物对于 200nm 以上的光无吸收，则无法用此检测器来分析。

2.11 有机化合物的光谱鉴定

通过重结晶、蒸馏、色谱分离等技术得到纯净的产物后，接下来的问题是如何表征这些化合物的结构。鉴定有机化合物的结构有四种常用的光谱技术，即紫外吸收光谱（UV）、红外吸收光谱（IR）、核磁共振波谱（NMR）和质谱（MS）。本节将主要介绍前三种光谱技术。Fig. 2.29 是按波长由短到长排列而成的电磁波谱。从 X 射线到无线电波，几乎电磁波谱中的每一波段都被用于原子和分子的结构鉴定。

当电磁波照射某一有机物时，如果将某波段的电磁波的波长不断变化，物质就会吸收某一定能量的光子，使分子内部发生某种能级的变化。能级的跃迁是量子化的，能级跃迁所需的能量 E 与被吸收光子波长之间的关系，可简单地按下式计算：

$$E = hc/\lambda$$

式中，h 为普朗克常量；c 为光速；λ 为被吸收光子的波长。

2.11.1 紫外与可见光谱

1. 实验原理

如果用一束具有连续波长的紫外或可见光照射有机化合物，这时紫外或可见光中某些波长的光辐射就可以被该化合物的分子所吸收。吸收光线的多少取决于入射光的波长和化合物的结构。紫外与可见光吸收光谱是由分子中价电子能级跃迁所产生的。

在不同类型的电子跃迁中，能产生紫外与可见光吸收谱的主要有 $n\rightarrow\pi^*$，$\pi\rightarrow\pi^*$，$n\rightarrow\sigma^*$ 和 $\sigma\rightarrow\sigma^*$ 跃迁。$\sigma\rightarrow\sigma^*$ 跃迁的能量最高，吸收的波长都在 150nm 以下。这样波长的紫外光因能被空气中的氧所吸收，只能在真空中进行工作，因此称为真空紫外。由于真空紫外的测定操作不便，而且仪器复杂，在实际工作中不常使用。$n \rightarrow \sigma^*$跃迁的吸收波长通常为 150～250nm，含有带 n 电子的杂原子(如氧、氮、硫、卤素等)的饱和分子会有这类跃迁。$n \rightarrow \pi^*$跃迁和 $\pi \rightarrow \pi^*$跃迁的吸收波长位于近紫外和可见光区(180～700nm)，这两类跃迁在紫外光谱中最为常见，也最具实际意义。

尽管有些电子跃迁所需的能量较低，但在谱图中没有吸收带或显示弱的吸收带。如羰基化合物中的 $n \rightarrow \pi^*$跃迁，在紫外或可见光区有不太强的吸收，其原因可以从羰基的轨道结构来解释。由于 n 轨道的电子与 π 电子处在不同的空间，跃迁的可能性很小，即跃迁的概率不大，因此 $n \rightarrow \pi^*$跃迁的吸收带较弱。通常 $\pi \rightarrow \pi^*$跃迁概率很大，相应吸收光谱的强度很高，可以用于低浓度化合物的定量测定。

进行紫外光谱测定时，大多数采用溶液或液体试样。辐射被吸收的程度遵循朗伯-比尔定律。

$$A = \log I_0/I = \varepsilon cl$$

式中，I_0 为入射光强度，I 为透过光强度；c 为物质的浓度，单位为 mol/L；l 为液层厚度，单位为 cm；ε 为摩尔吸光系数，它是浓度为 1mol/L 的溶液在 1cm 的吸收池中，在一定波长下测得的吸光度(A)，表示物质对光能的吸收强度。

Fig. 2.30 是对甲苯乙酮的紫外光谱图。可以看到对甲苯乙酮的图谱中于 225nm 到 275nm 之间有一个较宽的吸收带，最大吸收波长是 250nm。在紫外吸收光谱中常以吸收带最大吸收处波长 λ_{max} 和该波长下的摩尔吸收系数 ε_{max} 来表征化合物的吸收特征。

凡是能导致化合物在紫外及可见光区产生吸收的基团称为生色基团。一般不饱和的基团都是生色基团(如 C═C、C═O、N═N、叁键、苯环等)。助色基团是指那些本身不会使化合物分子产生颜色或者在紫外及可见光区不产生吸收的一些基团，但这些基团与发色基团相连时却能使发色基团的吸收带波长移向长波，同时使吸收强度增加。通常，助色基团是由含有孤对电子的元素所组成(如—NH_2，—NR_2，—OH，—OR，—Cl 等)，这些基团借助 p-π 共轭使发色基团增加共轭程度，从而使电子跃迁的能量下降。

由于有机化合物分子中引入了助色基团或其他发色基团而产生结构的改变，或者由于溶剂的影响使其紫外吸收带的最大吸收波长向长波方向移动的现象称为红移。与此相反，如果吸收带的最大吸收波长向短波方向移动，则称为蓝移。与吸收带波长红移及蓝移相似，由于化合物分子结构中引入取代基或受溶剂的影响，使吸收带的强度即摩尔吸光系数增大或减少的现象称为增色效应或减色效应。

因为不同的生色团有不同的最大吸收波长，有时可以将某样品的 λ_{max} 与几种已知化合物的 λ_{max} 进行对照，从而对化合物进行鉴定。但仅仅根据紫外光谱来推断未知有机分子是否含有某一生色团，不是十分可靠。如果未知物是几种已知化合物中的一种，并且这几种已知化合物的最大吸收波长最少相差 10nm 以上，那么未知物的紫外光谱就可用于定性分析。

2. 仪器和吸收池

紫外-可见光分光光度计的工作波长大多数为 190～750nm。分光光度计有很多型号，但各类光谱分析仪器均由光源、单色器、吸收池、检测器和显示系统等五个部分构成。提供入射光的光源主要有两种。钨灯(卤钨灯)发光波长 360～1000nm 适用于可见光区。氢(氘)灯波长范围 180～375nm 适用于紫外区。单色光被分为两束交替通过样品池和参比池。由于样品的吸收，两束光强度不同，经光电倍增管检测，即给出相应的电信号，驱动马达记录下光谱。

吸收池用石英玻璃制成，可用于 190nm 以上波段的测定。

操作方法：

(1)调节波长。

(2)打开试样室(光门自动关闭)，调节“0”旋钮，使数字显示为“0% T”。

(3)将参比溶液置于光路中，调节透光率“100”旋钮，使数字显示为“100% T”。

(4)将样品溶液置于光路中，数字表上显示出被测溶液的透光率，吸光度或被测溶液相应的浓度值。

2.11.2　红外光谱

1. 实验原理

红外光谱(IR)就是由分子吸收红外光后，引起分子振动能级的跃迁而产生的特征光谱。中红外区的波数范围一般在 4000～650cm^{-1}。波长(μm)和波数(cm^{-1})两者可以互换，即 $\bar{\nu} = 1/\lambda(cm^{-1})$。红外光谱可用于鉴定化合物的官能团，如 NH_2，COOH，OH，$CONH_2$，叁键(C≡C、C≡N)，芳环，羰基(C═O)和双键(C═C、C═N、N═N)。

有两种分子振动能够产生红外吸收，即伸缩振动和弯曲振动。伸缩振动为沿键轴的有规律运动，原子间距离增大或缩小。弯曲振动是键角发生变化的振动。

振动光谱通常是吸收带而不是吸收线，这是由于振动能量变化通常伴随许多转动能级的变化。因此，红外光谱又称为振转光谱。波数主要取决于原子相对质量，键的力常数和原子几何形状。显然短而强的键其伸缩振动能级比长而弱的键要高。例如，C≡C、C≡N 叁键和 C═O、C═N、C═C 双键的吸收波数分别处在 2300～2000 和 1900～1500cm^{-1}。含较轻原子的价键比含重原子的振动能级高。吸收带的强度可以用 T(透光率)或 A(吸光度)表示，通常使用前者。透光率(T)表示透射光的强度(I)与入射光的强度(I_0)之比。

$$T = I/I_0$$

峰强度也可用吸光度(A)表示，A 是透光率倒数的对数：

$$A = \lg(1/T)$$

在实际应用中峰的强度很少定量表示，而是用强峰(s)、中峰(m)、弱峰(w)简单描述。理论上说，一个非常简单的分子也会产生很复杂的谱图。事实上，凡具有相同官能团的化合物不管分子的其他部分结构如何，该官能团的吸收峰都出现在一定的波数范围内，如羰基(C═O)出现在 1900～1600cm^{-1}。化学工作者可以根据红外光谱中的特征吸收峰而判断分子中含有哪些官能团。总之，从化合物的红外谱图可获得有关其官能团的信息。

2. 仪器简介

除有关元件必须与相应的电磁辐射能级范围匹配外，红外光谱仪的基本构造与紫外光谱仪相同。除常用的 NaCl、KCl 和 NaBr、KBr 外，很少有物质在 IR 整个波长范围内是透明的。液体池窗口通常采用 NaCl 晶片，液体可在 NaCl 晶片上做成薄膜加以检测。常用的溶剂为氯仿或四氯化碳，但这些溶剂在远红外区有多处较强吸收，干扰化合物光谱分析。固体物质可与液体石蜡研磨成均匀糊状物来进行检测，石蜡油仅在特定的红外区域中有吸收。固体样品也可以和 KBr 或 KCl 拌匀后压成透明的薄片来进行检测。一般近似地认为，重要红外生色团在固态和液态下有相同的吸收频率。

3. 基团吸收频率

一个分子的红外光谱是由许多吸收带组成的，分子结构的微小变化对吸收带位置，形状和强度都有较大影响。但在 4000～1500cm^{-1} 区域内的官能团特征吸收带受分子中其他结构影响较小，容易辨认。一些重要官能团的峰位波数总结如下：

1) 4000～3000cm^{-1}

羟基(—OH)，包括醇(ROH，强吸收)、酚(ArOH，强吸收)和羧酸(RCOOH，强吸收)；氨基(NH)，包括酰胺(RC(═O)—NHR^1，强吸收)，芳胺(Ar—NH—R^2，中等强度吸收)，脂肪胺(R—NH—R^1，弱吸收)；和叁键(C≡C—H)相连的 C—H 有中强吸收；和双键(C═C—H)相连的 C—H 有较弱吸收。

2) 3000～2800cm^{-1}

饱和 C—H 键在此范围内有吸收。

3) 2800～2700cm^{-1}

醛的费米振动出现在 2720cm^{-1} 处，为弱峰，可作为醛基官能团的特征吸收带。

4) 2700～2500cm^{-1}

巯基(—SH)在此区域有弱吸收带。

5) 2400～1900cm^{-1}

叁键如 C≡C(弱吸收)，C≡N(弱吸收)，N≡N(弱吸收)及连二烯型 C═C═C(弱吸收)，N═C═O(强吸收)，N═C═S(强吸收)在此区域有吸收。

6) 1900～1600cm^{-1}

含有羰基官能团的化合物如酰氯、酸酐、酯、酮、醛、羧酸和酰胺在此区域有较强吸收；双键如 C═C，C═N 和 N═N 在此区域有弱吸收。此外，N—H 键的弯曲振动吸收频率也落在此区域。

7) 1600～1500cm^{-1}

芳环和—NO_2 官能团在此区域有特征吸收带。

以上有机化合物重要官能团的特征吸收频率(cm^{-1})总结在本教材英文部分 2.11.2 的 Fig. 2.31 中。

2.11.3　核磁共振谱

1. 实验原理

核磁共振(NMR)是磁性原子核在外磁场中产生能级跃迁的一种物理现象。它揭示了有机化合物结构中的许多细节，特别是相连的氢原子和碳原子的相互关系。

凡是原子序数为单数的原子核，由于自旋而具有磁性。中子数均为奇数，或质子数和中子数中有一个是奇数的原子核，如 ^{1}H、^{13}C、^{19}F、^{31}P 等都有自旋。而质子数、中子数均为偶数，质量数也为偶数的核，如 ^{12}C、^{16}O、^{34}S 等则没有。当自旋量子数为 I 的原子核放入一个均匀的磁场中时，可以产生 $2I+1$ 种取向。例如，$I=1/2$ 的原子核有两种取向，一种与外加磁场同向，形成一个低能级；另一种与外加磁场反向，形成一个高能态。两个能级间的能量差 ΔE 为

$$\Delta E = h\gamma/2\pi \cdot H_0 \tag{1}$$

式中，γ 为核的磁旋比；H_0 为外加磁场强度。这就简单地说明了 ΔE 和磁场强度 H_0 之间的关系。

质子在一个磁场强度固定的外磁场中产生两个不同能级后，受到频率为 v 的电磁波辐射，当电磁波的能量等于两个能级的能量差时，即

$$\Delta E = hv \tag{2}$$

能量将被质子吸收，质子将由低能级跃迁到高能级，这种现象称为核磁共振。因此，从方程(1)和(2)可以得出质子的共振频率为：$v = \gamma/2\pi \cdot H_0$

NMR 信号与结构的关系，主要反映在以下三个主要参数上：峰面积积分高度、化学位移(δ)、峰的裂分和偶合常数(J)。

在 NMR 谱中，峰面积与原子核数目有关，即峰面积越大，则代表此峰的原子核数越多。各峰的面积常用积分线高度来表示。例如，在 CH_3CH_2OH 的氢谱中，三组信号的积分线高度之比为 3：2：1。

由于不同质子共振时的外磁场强度的差别极其微小，不同信号之间的照射频率之差也很小，同时这种差距与外加磁场的强度成正比，也与该磁场相匹配的辐射频率成正比。为了克服以上两个问题，引入了化学位移(δ)的定义。

$$\delta = (\text{某种质子的共振频率} - \text{参考物质的共振频率}) \times 10^6/\text{所用外磁场的共振频率}$$

很多情况下，NMR 谱中的吸收峰有“精细结构”(存在裂分的现象)。这是自旋的氢核之间相互干扰的结果，这种现象称为自旋-自旋偶合。质子峰裂分的多重性由邻近质子数决定。$n+1$ 规律和 Pascal's 三角形分别用来预测峰的裂分数和各裂分小峰的强度。$n+1$ 规律是指一个信号的分裂峰数决定于邻接碳上磁等同的质子数，如该数是 n，则分裂峰数为 $n+1$。由 $n+1$ 规律所得到的各裂分小峰，其强度比例系数为展开二项式的系数呈 Pascal's 三角形。分裂峰中各小峰之间的距离称为偶合常数(J)，它的大小反映了核之间自旋偶合的有效程度，与相偶合的质子间的结构关系是密切相关的。

2. 各种有机化合物的核磁共振数据

化学位移值反映了分子结构，因此它可以用于获取结构信息。^1H 周围的电子云密度或空间分布的改变将会引起化学位移的变化。Table 2.2 和 Table 2.3 给出了有机化合物中 ^1H 的化学位移值(见英文部分)。值得注意的是 OH，NH_2(C═O)的质子没有特征的化学位移值范围，它们的值随着测定条件如温度、浓度等改变而改变。值得庆幸的是，它们可以通过重水交换，使其在谱图中消失来确认。

3. NMR 谱仪简介

核磁共振谱仪主要由超导磁体，谱仪，探头，计算机工作站和软件等主要部分组成。超导磁体是整个仪器中最基本的部分，它是由超导材料组成的线圈浸泡在液氦中，使其处于超导

状态，然后对线圈施加电流，由于没有电阻，撤去电源后，电流仍在线圈中作恒定流动，因而产生了恒定的磁场。谱仪的主要工作是对样品发射一定的射频脉冲，它通过由频率发生器，功率放大器等组成的射频通道发射射频脉冲。探头是核磁共振谱仪的关键部分，因为对样品发射射频脉冲和接受原子核磁化强度的感应信号都是通过 NMR 探头中的线圈进行的。也就是说，核磁共振过程及信号检测是发生在线圈部分的。计算机负责数据储存，数据处理和总体控制(英文部分 Fig. 2.32)。

4. 仪器和试剂

试剂：氘代试剂($CDCl_3$等)。

仪器：样品管(核磁管)，微量注射器。

5. 常规液体 NMR 实验——^{1}H 谱实验操作步骤

1)样品的制备

测定有机化合物氢谱时，通常将样品配制成 2%～10%的溶液，将样品装在内径为 5mm，长 200mm 的核磁管中，一般要求溶液的高度至少在 3.5～4cm 以上。选择氘代溶剂时，应考虑样品溶解度的大小，通常越大越好。极性较小的样品用 CCl_4，$CDCl_3$或氘代苯为溶剂，极性较大的样品则用 D_2O、CD_3COCD_3、DMSO-d_6为溶剂。

2)实验操作

下面简单介绍布鲁克公司生产的 AVANCE AV 400MHz 傅里叶数字化核磁共振谱仪的常规液体 NMR 实验——^{1}H 谱实验操作步骤。

用单脉冲序列 zg 测常规的 ^{1}H 谱是做得最多的实验，其脉冲序列如下：

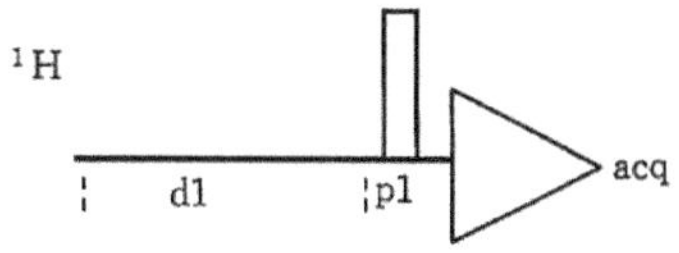

(1)样品的配制：选择合适的溶剂使样品能够均匀地溶解于整个溶液，尽量去除悬浮的固体颗粒，一般要求样品溶液的高度至少在 3.5～4.0cm 以上，以优化匀场。(此步骤可先于实验完成)

(2)用 edc 命令建立一个新的实验数据目录。

(3)键入 rpar 命令，选择 PROTON、再选择 acqu 和 proc，然后按 COPY。(也可选择所有的采样、处理和作图参数，但打印机的名字可能与所用的不同)。

(4)键入 edasp 命令，检查采样通道(F1)是否设置成 ^{1}H，OSFH1 中的数值是否为通常 ^{1}H 谱的 O1 值，(如果不知道具体数值，可以先保留标准参数中的数值)。按 SAVE 钮退出。

(5)键入 eda 命令设置和样品及图谱有关的参数：

TD　32K

SW　30ppm (即使 O1 设定值不是最合适数值，较大的谱宽也能包括所有的谱峰)

NS　8

DS　0

(6)键入 ased 命令设置与脉冲序列有关的参数：

PULPROG　zg

D1　2s（一般设置为 1～5 倍的 T1 时间）

P1　3μs（通常设置成 30°～45°的脉宽）

PL1　（^{1}H 在采样通道的 90°脉宽所对应的功率）

（7）按照装样程序将核磁管放入磁体中，选择合适的氘代试剂锁场，然后进行匀场。

（8）键入 wobb 调节探头的 tuning 和 matching，调谐完毕键入 stop。

（9）键入 acqu 进入采样窗口，再键入 zg 命令开始采样。观察第一次采样得到的 FID 数据，确定参数 rg 的设置是否合适，或在键入 zg 命令前，先键入 rga 命令，由程序自动确定参数 rg 的最佳值。

采样结束后，键入 ft 命令得到 ^{1}H 图谱，并作相位和基线校正。观察发射中心 O1 和谱宽 SW 的设置是否合适。如果不合适，可用鼠标选择合适的谱宽范围显示在数据窗口上，点击 SW-SFO1 按钮，此时程序自动地将显示的谱宽数值设置到 SW 中；显示的发射中心频率（数据窗口中谱宽的中心）设置到 O1 中。再键入 zg 命令时，程序将采用新的 SW 和 O1 值采样。

3）实验内容

（1）乙苯标样的测定。

按以上实验操作步骤对标样进行测定。

（2）合成有机物的测定。

（a）取 10～20mg 样品，装入盛有 0.5mL $CDCl_3$ 的小试管中，溶解后小心地装入核磁样品管中（高约 4.5～5cm），再滴加两滴 TMS，摇匀后盖上盖子。

（b）按以上实验操作步骤进行测定。

第 3 章　有机化合物的制备

3.1　环己烯的制备

【实验原理】

环己烯通常由环己醇在浓硫酸或浓磷酸催化下脱水制备，由于浓硫酸在反应中易炭化，本实验以浓磷酸作脱水剂制备环己烯。

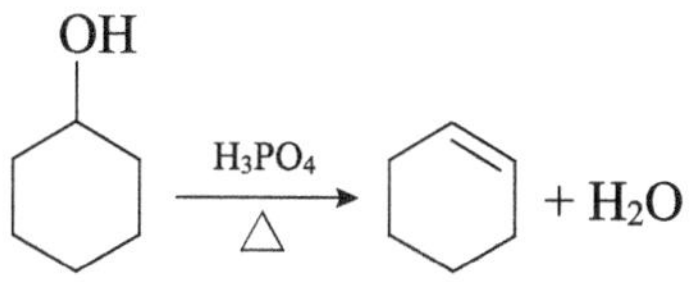

【主要试剂及实验装置】

分馏(短分馏柱)装置				
环己醇	10.4mL	10g(0.1mol)	b.p.116℃	$d = 0.9642^{20/4}$g/mL
85%磷酸	4mL			
氯化钠	1g			
5%碳酸钠溶液				
无水氯化钙				

【实验时间】

4h

【实验步骤】

(1)在 50mL 的圆底烧瓶中，加入 10.4mL(10g，0.10mol)环己醇，4mL 85%的磷酸和几粒沸石，充分振荡使之混合均匀。

(2)如 Fig. 2.7 安装分馏装置[1]，使用短分馏柱，用 50mL 的三角烧瓶作接收器，并置于冰水浴中，以免环己烯挥发而损失。

(3)用石棉网小火加热反应混合物至沸腾，控制分馏柱顶部的温度不要超过 90℃[2]，慢慢地蒸出生成的环己烯和水。

(4)当烧瓶中只剩下少量的残留物时，即可停止加热，全部蒸馏时间约需 1h。

(5)将馏出液用 1g 固体氯化钠饱和，并轻轻地振摇烧瓶[3]。

(6)将馏出液倒入一分液漏斗中，加入 3～4mL 5%碳酸钠溶液(或用 0.5mL 20%的氢氧化钠溶液）[4]。轻轻振摇分液漏斗直至漏斗放气时无气体逸出。

(7) 放出下层的水层，上层的粗产物从分液漏斗的上口倒入一个小的三角烧瓶中。加入1～2g 无水氯化钙，回荡反应瓶，直至溶液成为澄清[5]。

(8) 将干燥后的环已烯滤入一个干燥的 50mL 圆底烧瓶中，加入几粒沸石后，用水浴加热蒸馏[6]，用一称重的 50mL 圆底烧瓶作接收器，将烧瓶置于冰水浴中。

(9) 收集 80～85℃的馏分，称重产品，计算产率。

纯的环已烯为无色液体，b.p.82.98℃，n_D^{20} 1.4465，d_4^{20} 0.808。

【注释】

[1]将生成的环已烯不断从反应体系中蒸馏出来，有利于反应平衡向产物方向移动。

[2]环已烯的沸点为 83℃，环已烯与水共沸，沸点为 70.8℃，原料环已醇也与水形成共沸物，沸点为 97.8℃，因此蒸馏温度需仔细控制，使其不超过 90℃。

[3]加精盐的目的是减少产物在水中的溶解度，达到更好地分离的目的。

[4]少量的磷酸也会与产物共沸，所以需用碳酸钠水溶液洗涤除去。

[5]干燥后的溶液应澄清，若仍混浊，可补加 0.5g 干燥剂，回荡后再干燥 10min。

[6]在精制产品时，蒸馏所用的仪器需在 110℃的烘箱内进行干燥，约需 10min。

【思考题】

(1) 在制备环已烯的过程中为什么要控制分馏柱顶部的温度，使其不超过 90℃？

(2) 在中和与分液前加入精盐的目的是什么？

(3) 为什么反应混合物中存在的少量磷酸必须在蒸馏环已烯前用碳酸钠中和除去？

3.2　1-溴丁烷的制备

【实验原理】

1-溴丁烷是由正丁醇与溴化钠、浓硫酸共热制得的。

主反应

$$NaBr + H_2SO_4 \longrightarrow HBr + NaHSO_4$$

$$n\text{-}C_4H_9OH + HBr \underset{}{\overset{\triangle}{\rightleftharpoons}} n\text{-}C_4H_9Br + H_2O$$

副反应

$$CH_3CH_2CH_2CH_2OH \xrightarrow[\triangle]{H_2SO_4} CH_3CH_2CH{=}CH_2 + CH_3CH{=}CHCH_3$$

$$2CH_3CH_2CH_2CH_2OH \xrightarrow[\triangle]{H_2SO_4} CH_3CH_2CH_2CH_2OCH_2CH_2CH_2CH_3$$

【主要试剂及实验装置】

带气体吸收装置的回流装置			
正丁醇	9.3mL(7.4g，0.12mol)	b.p.117.2℃	$d = 0.8098^{20/4}$g/mL
溴化钠	12.5g(0.12mol)		
浓硫酸	14.5mL(0.27mol)		$d = 1.841^{20/4}$g/mL
10%氢氧化钠溶液			
无水氯化钙			

【实验时间】

5h

【实验步骤】

(1)在 100mL 的圆底烧瓶中加入 12.5g(0.12mol)溴化钠，12mL 水和 9.3mL(7.4g，0.12mol)正丁醇，充分振摇[1]。

(2)将烧瓶置于冰水浴中，在不停地回荡下，慢慢加入 14.5mL 浓硫酸，再加入几粒沸石。

(3)装上回流冷凝管，在冷凝管上端接一气体吸收装置，如 Fig. 1.6(a)，用 5%的氢氧化钠水溶液作吸收剂。

(4)在石棉网上小火加热回流混合物约 0.5h，在此过程中，要经常摇动烧瓶[1]。

(5)冷却后，改装蒸馏装置。

(6)在石棉网上加热蒸馏混合物至馏出液完全溶于水(或变为澄清)[2]，此时 1-溴丁烷已全部蒸出，停止蒸馏。

(7)将馏出液小心转入分液漏斗中，用 15mL 水洗涤，并静置分层。

(8)将有机层(哪一层？1-溴丁烷和水的密度各为多少？)[3]转入到另一个干燥的分液漏斗中。

(9)有机层用 6mL 浓硫酸洗涤，并尽量分去硫酸层(哪一层？)[4]。

(10)有机层依次用 15mL 水，15mL 10%氢氧化钠和 15mL 水洗涤，用 pH 试纸检验是否已达中性，否则重复水洗[5]。

(11)将产物移入一干燥的小三角烧瓶中，加入少量的无水氯化钙干燥，间歇摇动，直至液体透明。

(12)将干燥后的产物小心转入到一个干燥的蒸馏烧瓶中，在石棉网上加热蒸馏，收集 99～103℃的馏分。称重产物，计算产率[6]。

纯的 1-溴丁烷为无色透明液体，b.p.101.6℃，d_4^{20} 1.2758，n_D^{20} 1.4401。

【注释】

[1]在加料和反应过程中需经常振摇烧瓶，否则将影响反应的产率。

[2]取一支试管加入 0.5mL 水，再收集一滴馏出液，检验其是否溶于水。

[3]仔细判断哪一层为有机层，1-溴丁烷的密度（$d = 1.27$g/mL）。

[4]浓硫酸用来洗去粗品中少量未反应的正丁醇和副产物 1-丁烯，2-丁烯和丁醚等杂质。否则正丁醇和 1-溴丁烷可以形成共沸物（b.p.98.6℃，含正丁醇 13%）而难以除去。

[5]在后处理过程中，经历 5 次洗涤，为保证不将产物丢弃，需将每次分液后的液体保留并做好标记，直至反应结束后再丢弃。

[6]本实验 1-溴丁烷的产量约为 7g，产率约 52%。

【思考题】

（1）本实验中硫酸起了多种作用，请一一说明。

（2）请用反应方程式说明丁醚、1-丁烯和 2-丁烯等反应的副产物是如何用硫酸除去的？

（3）为什么在蒸馏 1-溴丁烷前需用无水氯化钙干燥？

（4）为什么在用 10% NaOH 洗涤前要先用水洗涤？

3.3　三苯甲醇的制备

【实验原理】

三苯甲醇可以通过 Grignard 反应来制备。

方法一

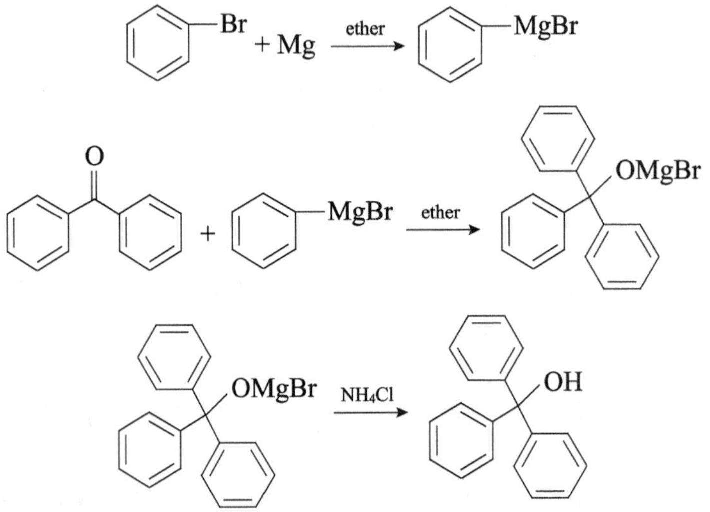

方法二

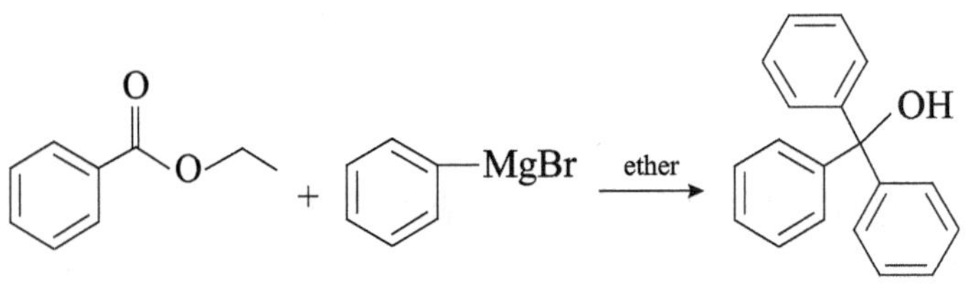

副反应

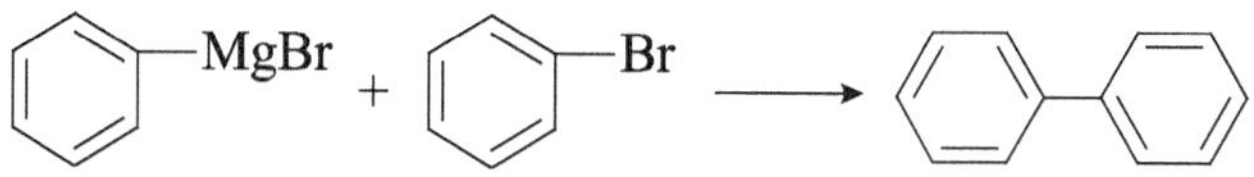

【主要试剂及实验装置】

带滴加和回流的搅拌装置			
溴苯	5.3mL (7.85g，0.05mol)	b.p.156℃	$d = 1.495^{20/4}$g/mL
无水乙醚	20mL	b.p.34.5℃	$d = 0.7138^{20/4}$g/mL
镁屑或镁条	1.4g (0.055mol)		
二苯甲酮	9g (0.05mol)	m.p.49℃	$d = 1.0975^{20/4}$g/mL
苯甲酸乙酯	1.4mL (1.5g，0.01mol)	b.p.213℃	$d = 1.0458^{20/4}$g/mL
饱和氯化铵溶液	40mL		
石油醚	20mL	b.p.60～90℃	
碘	一小粒		

【实验时间】

7～8h

【实验步骤】

1. *方法一*

(1) 在一干净、干燥的 250mL 三颈烧瓶上分别装置搅拌器，回流冷凝管和滴液漏斗[1]。

(2) 在滴液漏斗和冷凝管的上面装置氯化钙干燥管，冷凝管中通入冷凝水。

(3) 向反应瓶内投入 1.4g (0.055mol) 镁屑[2]和一小粒碘[3]。

(4) 在滴液漏斗中加入 5.3mL (0.05mol) 溴苯和 20mL 无水乙醚，混匀，从滴液漏斗中滴入 4～5mL 混合液至三颈瓶中。

(5) 将烧瓶置于热水浴 (45～50℃) 中，乙醚开始沸腾，棕色的溶液褪色[4]，移去热水浴。

(6) 开动搅拌器，继续滴加其余的溴苯乙醚溶液，控制滴加速度，使反应保持中等回流的速度[5]。

(7) 滴加完毕，用温水浴 (45～50℃) 搅拌回流 30min，使镁屑几乎作用完全。

(8) 将反应瓶置于冰水浴中，搅拌下从滴液漏斗中缓缓加入 9g (0.05mol) 二苯甲酮和 25mL 无水乙醚的混合液。

(9) 加毕，用温水浴 (45～50℃) 回流 30min，使反应完全。

(10) 在冰水浴中，搅拌下由滴液漏斗滴入 40mL 氯化铵溶液[6]。

(11) 将反应装置改成简单蒸馏装置，用水浴加热慢慢蒸馏乙醚。

(12) 向烧瓶中加入 20mL 低沸点的石油醚 (60～90℃)，并搅拌数分钟[7]。

(13) 冷却，抽滤得粗产品。

(14) 粗产品用 2∶1 的石油醚 (60～90℃)-95%乙醇进行重结晶。

(15)干燥后，测熔点，称重并计算产率[8]。

纯的三苯甲醇为白色晶体，m.p.164.2℃。

2. 方法二

(1)在一干燥的 100mL 三颈瓶上，分别装上回流冷凝管和滴液漏斗，在冷凝管和滴液漏斗的上面装置氯化钙干燥管[1]。

(2)在烧瓶内放入 0.5g(0.02mol)镁屑[2]和一小粒碘[3]。

(3)在滴液漏斗中加入 2.1mL(3.14g，0.02mol)溴苯和 10mL 无水乙醚，混匀，从滴液漏斗中滴入 2～3mL 此溶液至三颈烧瓶中[9]。

(4)当棕色的溶液褪色，乙醚开始沸腾，说明反应已经开始，将剩余的溶液缓缓滴入烧瓶中，控制滴加速度，使反应保持中等回流速度[5]。

(5)加毕，在温水浴上回流 30min，使镁几乎作用完。

(6)将反应物冷至室温，在振摇下自滴液漏斗中慢慢滴入 1.4mL(1.5g，0.01mol)苯甲酸乙酯和 5mL 无水乙醚的混合液。

(7)加毕，用温水浴回流 30min。

(8)烧瓶用冷水冷却，在搅拌下自滴液漏斗慢慢滴加氯化铵溶液(由 2.5g 氯化铵和 20mL 水配成)[6]。

(9)水浴上蒸去乙醚至三苯甲醇晶体生成，向烧瓶中加入 15mL 低沸点石油醚(60～90℃)，搅拌数分钟[7]。

(10)冰浴冷却，抽滤，收集产品。

(11)用方法一中叙述的方法进行重结晶。

(12)干燥，测定熔点，称重，计算产率[10]。

纯的三苯甲醇为白色晶体，m.p.164.2℃。

【注释】

[1]在实验前必须充分干燥所用的玻璃仪器和试剂。在格氏试剂的制备和反应过程中需保持干燥条件。

[2]光亮的镁条可以代替镁屑，用细纱纸磨去镁条两面的氧化膜，并将其剪切成 5mm 左右的小碎条。

[3]加一小粒碘可促使非均相反应在镁的表面发生，诱导反应开始。

[4]这些现象表明反应已经开始。

[5]滴加速度应加以控制，使回流环不超过冷凝管内管的一半高度。若反应过于激烈，会增加副产物联苯的生成。

[6]滴加饱和氯化铵溶液是使加成物水解成三苯甲醇。

[7]粗产物中含有三苯甲醇和副产物联苯，联苯易溶于石油醚而被除去。

[8]用方法一可得到 4～5g 产品，产率约为 35%。

[9]必要时可用热水浴(45～50℃)温热烧瓶，诱导反应发生。

[10]用方法二，反应的产率为 48%。

【思考题】

(1)制备格氏试剂和进行格氏反应时均应保持无水条件，若反应体系进水，将会发生什么反应？

(2)请提出用格氏反应制备下列化合物的方法。

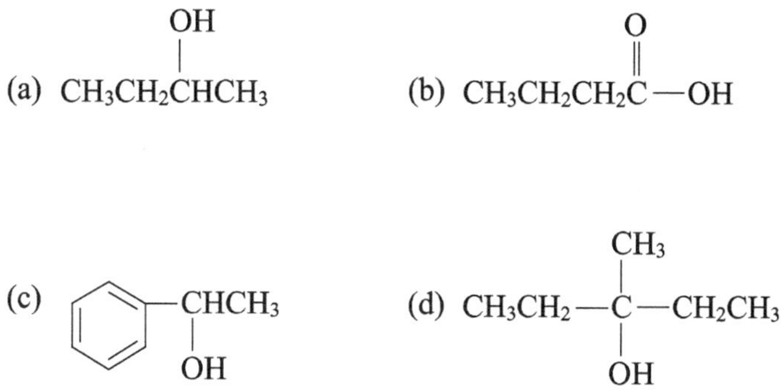

3.4　正丁醚的制备

【实验原理】

正丁醚常采用浓硫酸催化正丁醇进行分子间脱水的方法制备。

主反应

$$2CH_3CH_2CH_2CH_2OH \xrightleftharpoons{H_2SO_4,\ 134\sim135℃} CH_3CH_2CH_2CH_2OCH_2CH_2CH_2CH_3 + H_2O$$

副反应

$$CH_3CH_2CH_2CH_2OH \xrightleftharpoons[>135℃]{H_2SO_4} C_4H_8 + H_2O$$

【主要试剂及实验装置】

带分水器的回流装置			
正丁醇	25g(31mL，0.34mol)	b.p.117.2℃	$d = 0.8098^{20/4}$g/mL
硫酸	8g(4.5mL)		$d = 1.841^{20/4}$g/mL
无水氯化钙			

【实验时间】

5h

【实验步骤】

(1)在 100mL 两颈或三颈烧瓶中，加入 25g(31mL，0.34mol)正丁醇和约 8g(4.5mL)浓硫

酸，摇动使混合均匀，并加入几粒沸石。

(2) 在三颈瓶的一瓶口装上温度计，另一瓶口装上分水器，分水器上端接回流冷凝管(如图 Fig. 3.1)。

(3) 在分水器中放置(*V*−3.5) mL 水[1]，然后将烧瓶在石棉网上用小火加热，回流。

(4) 继续加热到瓶内温度升高到 134～135℃(约需 20min)。待分水器已全部被水充满时，表示反应已基本完成[2,3]。

(5) 冷却反应物，将它连同分水器里的水一起倒入内盛 50mL 水的分液漏斗中，充分振摇，静止，分出粗产物正丁醚。

(6) 用 25mL 50%硫酸[4]洗涤两次，再用 25mL 水洗涤一次，然后用无水氯化钙干燥。

(7) 干燥后的产物倒入蒸馏烧瓶中，蒸馏收集 139～142℃馏分，产量 7～8g，产率约为 50%。

纯正丁醚为无色液体，b.p.为 142℃，d_4^{20} 0.769，n_D^{20} 1.3992。

【注释】

[1] *V* 为分水器的容积，(*V*−3.5) 是指所加水量比分水器容积少 3.5mL。

[2] 反应中分水器内液面增加，这是由于反应生成的水以及未反应的正丁醇，经冷凝管冷凝后聚积于分水器内，由于比重不同，水在下层，正丁醇浮于水面而流回到反应瓶中。

[3] 若继续加热，则溶液变黑，并有大量副产物丁烯生成。

[4] 丁醇溶于 50%硫酸中，而正丁醚则很少溶解，以此除去正丁醇。

【思考题】

(1) 为什么在制备正丁醚的反应中要使用分水器?

(2) 你是如何知道反应已基本完成?

3.5　苯甲酸和苯甲醇的制备

【实验原理】

通过 Cannizzaro 反应制备苯甲酸和苯甲醇。

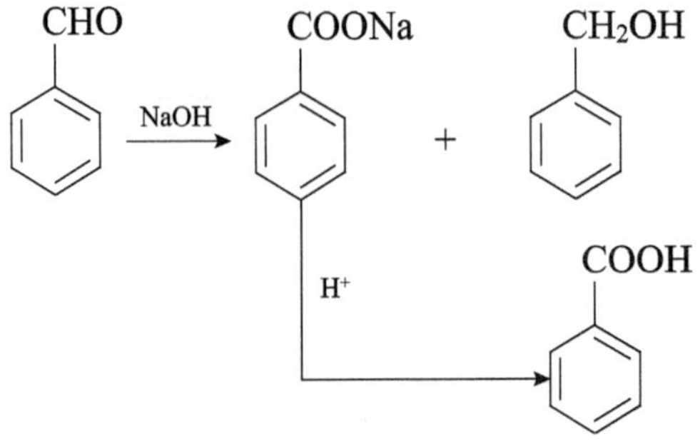

【主要试剂及实验装置】

蒸馏装置	
苯甲醛	20.5mL (21.3g，0.20mol)，b.p.179.2℃，$d = 1.0415^{20/4}$g/mL
NaOH	17.5g (0.44mol)
乙醚	b.p.34.5℃，$d = 0.7138^{20/4}$g/mL
浓盐酸	$d = 1.18$g/mL
饱和亚硫酸氢钠溶液；无水硫酸镁；10%碳酸钠溶液。	

【实验时间】

5h

【实验步骤】

(1) 在 250mL 的锥形瓶或烧杯中加入 17.5g (0.44mol) 氢氧化钠[1]和 17.5mL 水，充分振荡，使其完全溶解。

(2) 将 20.5mL (21.3g，0.20mol) 新蒸馏过的苯甲醛分批加入，充分摇动，使其成蜡状[2]。

(3) 放置过夜后或放置至下一次实验，加入 60～70mL 水，充分摇动，如还不溶，补加少量水或温热使其全溶[3]。

(4) 冷却后将混合物倒入分液漏斗中，分别用 48mL 乙醚分三次萃取[4]。水相备用。合并乙醚相，依次用 8mL 饱和 $NaHSO_3$ 溶液洗涤、16mL 10% Na_2CO_3 溶液和 16mL 冷水洗涤。乙醚提取液用无水硫酸镁干燥[5]。

(5) 水浴蒸去乙醚。将冷凝管中的水放掉，继续蒸馏收集 198～204℃馏分[6]，即为苯甲醇。

(6) 称重。计算产率。

(7) 在搅拌下将保留的水层以细流倒入 65mL 浓盐酸、65mL 水和 40g 冰的混合物中，冷却析出苯甲酸。

(8) 抽滤，洗涤，干燥，称重，计算产率。

(9) 纯苯甲醇为无色液体，b.p.205.3℃，d_4^{20} 1.0419，n_D^{20} 1.5396。纯苯甲酸为无色针状晶体，m.p.122.13℃。

【注释】

[1]这里为浓碱，操作需小心，尽量不要沾到皮肤上，若沾上，必须及时冲洗。

[2]苯甲醛必须是新蒸馏过的，且分批加入，每加一次都应用软木塞塞紧瓶塞，用力振荡，若温度过高，可将反应瓶放入冷水浴中冷却，如此反复至反应物成白色蜡状，可放置过夜。

[3]将烧瓶安置在铁架台上，在微热条件下加水，使瓶内蜡状物溶解，如不溶，则继续边搅拌边加水，加至所有的固体溶解。

[4]乙醚易燃，使用时远离明火。

[5]乙醚萃取液可用无水 $MgSO_4$ 干燥，也可用无水 K_2CO_3 干燥。

[6]乙醚回收后剩下的溶液也可改用空气冷凝管，蒸馏收集 198～204℃馏分（苯甲醇 b.p.205.4℃）。

【思考题】

(1) Cannizzaro 反应在浓 NaOH 溶液中容易进行，为什么？

(2) 本反应用饱和 $NaHSO_3$ 溶液洗涤来除去未反应的苯甲醛，这是根据什么反应原理？

3.6　环己酮的制备

【实验原理】

本实验分别用次氯酸钠和铬酸作氧化剂，将环己醇氧化成环己酮。

方法一

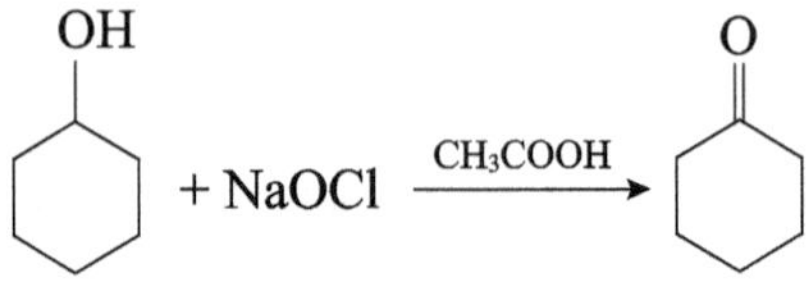

方法二

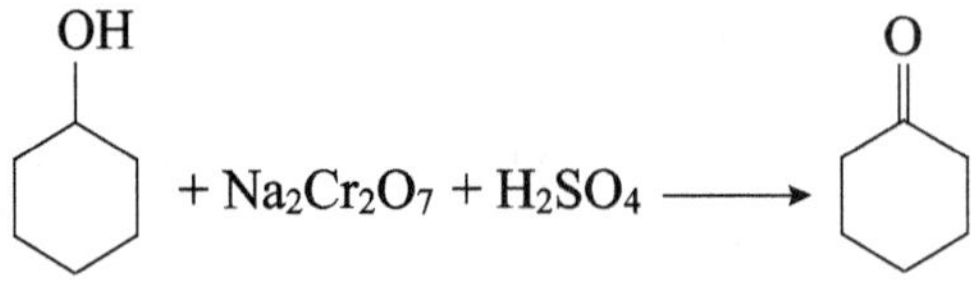

【主要试剂及实验装置】

带有回流冷凝管和滴液漏斗的搅拌装置			
环己醇	5.2mL (5g，0.05mol)	b.p.161.5℃	$d = 0.9642^{20/4}$ g/mL
冰醋酸	25mL	b.p.118℃	$d = 1.049^{20/4}$ g/mL
次氯酸钠 (1.8mol/L)	38mL (0.07mol)		
饱和亚硫酸氢钠溶液			
氯化铝	3g		
无水碳酸钠			
无水硫酸镁			
淀粉碘化钾试纸			
重铬酸钠	20g (0.268mol)		
浓硫酸			
乙醚			
氯化钠			

【实验时间】

4h

【实验步骤】

1. 方法一

(1) 向装有搅拌器、滴液漏斗和温度计的 250mL 三颈烧瓶中依次加入 5.2mL (5g, 0.05mol) 环己醇和 25mL 冰醋酸，将反应液置于冰水浴中冷却。

(2) 开动搅拌器，在冰水浴冷却下，将 38mL 次氯酸钠水溶液 (1.8mol/L)，通过滴液漏斗加入反应瓶中，控制滴加速度，使瓶内温度维持在 30～35℃，滴加完毕后，继续搅拌 5min。

(3) 用碘化钾淀粉试纸检验反应液呈蓝色，否则需要补加 5mL 次氯酸钠溶液[1]。

(4) 在室温下继续搅拌 30min，加入饱和亚硫酸氢钠溶液至反应液对碘化钾淀粉试纸不显蓝为止[2]。

(5) 向反应混合液中加入 30mL 水和 3g 氯化铝[3]，在石棉网上加热蒸馏至馏出液无油珠滴出为止。

(6) 在搅拌下向馏出液分批加入无水碳酸钠至反应液呈中性 (无 CO_2 气体逸出) 为止[4]，然后加入精制食盐使之变成饱和溶液[5]。

(7) 将混合液倒入分液漏斗中，分出有机层。用无水硫酸镁干燥。

(8) 蒸馏收集 150～155℃馏分。称重，计算产率 (产量约为 3.0～3.4g，产率：61%～69%)。

纯环己酮为无色液体，b.p.155℃，n_D^{20} 1.4507。

2. 方法二

(1) 向装有搅拌器，回流冷凝管和滴液漏斗的三颈烧瓶中加入 5.2mL (5g，0.05mol) 环己醇和 25mL 乙醚，摇匀，在冰水浴中冷却至 0℃。

(2) 在 250mL 的烧杯中，溶解 20g (0.066mol) $Na_2Cr_2O_7 \cdot 2H_2O$ 于 60mL 水中，搅拌下慢慢加入 26.8g (14.8mL，0.268mol) 98%的浓硫酸，最后稀释至 100mL，并将此溶液冷却至 0℃。

(3) 在剧烈搅拌下，将 50mL 已冷却至 0℃的上述铬酸溶液经滴液漏斗滴入反应瓶中，控制滴加速度，使滴加在 10min 内完成，滴加完毕后继续剧烈搅拌 20min。

(4) 将反应液倒入分液漏斗中，分出醚层。水层用乙醚萃取 2 次 (每次 15mL)，合并醚层，用 15mL 5%的碳酸钠溶液洗涤 1 次，然后用 4×15mL 水洗涤。无水硫酸镁干燥。

(5) 水浴加热蒸馏乙醚后，将冷凝管中的水放掉，继续加热蒸馏，收集 150～155℃的馏分。称重，计算产率 (产量约为 3.2～3.6g，产率：66%～72%)。

纯的环己酮为无色液体，b.p.155℃，n_D^{20} 1.4507。

【注释】

[1]在反应过程中次氯酸钠需过量。

[2]加入饱和亚硫酸氢钠溶液是为了除去过量的次氯酸钠。

[3]加氯化铝可预防蒸馏时发泡。

[4]加入无水碳酸钠是为了中和存在于反应混合物中的乙酸。

[5]31℃时环己酮在水中溶解度为 2.4g/100mL，用食盐饱和将减少环己酮的溶解度，有利于分层。

【思考题】

(1)方法一中，为什么在反应的混合液中要加入饱和亚硫酸氢钠溶液?

(2)方法一中，为何要向馏出液中加入无水碳酸钾至其呈中性(无 CO_2 气体逸出)?

3.7　己二酸的制备

【实验原理】

己二酸是合成尼龙-66 的主要原料之一。本实验用硝酸氧化环己醇制备己二酸。

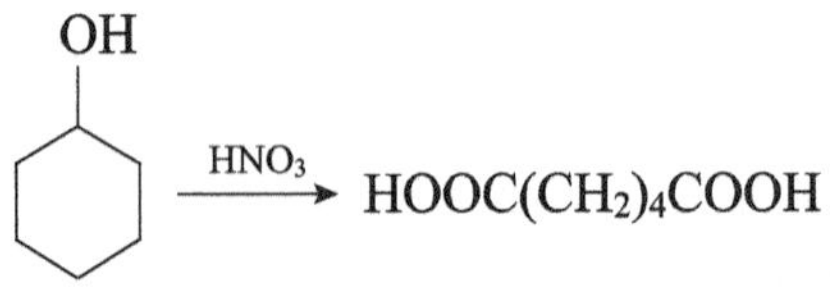

【主要试剂及实验装置】

带滴液漏斗和温度计的回流装置。
环己醇　　5.2mL(0.05mol)，b.p.161.5℃，$d = 0.9642^{20/4}$g/mL
50%硝酸　　16mL(0.17mol)
10% NaOH 溶液

【实验时间】

5h

【实验步骤】

(1)在 125mL 的三颈烧瓶上装置滴液漏斗，温度计和回流冷凝管。在冷凝管上端接一气体吸收装置，用 10%的氢氧化钠溶液吸收反应过程中产生的二氧化氮气体[1]。

(2)在三颈烧瓶中加入 16mL 50%的硝酸[2, 3]。

(3)用水浴预热硝酸溶液到 80℃，振荡下滴加一滴环己醇，温度迅速升至 90℃。待温度回到 85℃时，再滴加第二滴，维持反应体系的温度在 85℃左右，慢慢滴加环己醇至总量为 5.2mL(5g，0.05mol)[4]。滴加过程中需经常摇动反应瓶，控制滴加速度，使瓶内温度维持在 85～90℃[5]。

(4)滴加结束后，继续振荡并用 80～90℃的水浴加热约 15 分钟，至几乎无红棕色气体放出为止。

(5)冷却反应瓶，使固体析出。

(6)抽滤，用 3mL 冷水洗涤固体，压干水分[6]。

(7) 干燥，称重，计算产率。

纯己二酸为白色棱状晶体，m.p.153℃。

【注释】

[1] NO_2 吸收装置的导气管不能直接插入液面，否则会倒吸。

[2]注意！环己醇与浓硝酸切不可用同一量筒量取，两者相遇会发生剧烈反应，甚至发生意外。

[3]二氧化氮气体有毒，装置应严密不漏气，且反应最好在通风橱内进行。

[4]此反应为强放热反应，滴加速度要慢，以免反应过于剧烈，引起爆炸。

[5]温度过高可用冷水浴冷却，过低时可用水浴加热。

[6]必要时可用热水作溶剂进行重结晶纯化。若产物经重结晶纯化，建议测其熔点。

【思考题】

为什么必须严格控制氧化反应的温度？

3.8 肉桂酸的制备及结构表征

【实验原理】

利用 Perkin 反应，将苯甲醛与酸酐混合后在相应的羧酸盐存在下加热，可以制得 α，β-不饱和酸。本反应用碳酸钾代替 Perkin 反应中的乙酸钾，反应时间短、产率高。

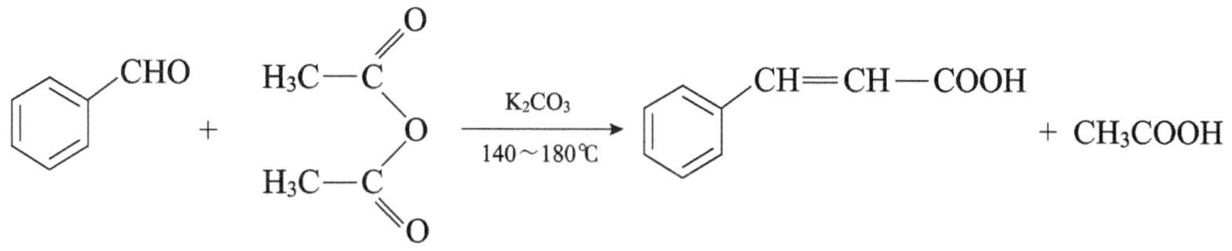

【主要试剂及实验装置】

回流和水蒸气蒸馏装置			
苯甲醛	3mL (3.15g，0.03mol)	b.p.179.2℃	$d = 1.0415^{20/4}$g/mL
乙酸酐	8mL (8.64g，0.085mol)	b.p.139.6℃	$d = 1.0820^{20/4}$g/mL
无水碳酸钾	4.2g (0.03mol)		
浓盐酸			$d = 1.18$g/mL
10%氢氧化钠溶液	20mL		

【实验时间】

6h

【实验步骤】

(1)在 250mL 圆底烧瓶中放入 3mL(3.15g，0.03mol)新蒸过的苯甲醛[1]，8mL(8.64g，0.085mol)新蒸过的乙酸酐[2]以及研细的 4.2g 无水碳酸钾，在石棉网上加热回流 45min[3]。

(2)待反应物冷却后，加入 20mL 水，将瓶内生成的固体尽量捣碎(小心！)，用水蒸气蒸馏蒸出未反应完的苯甲醛。

(3)再将烧瓶冷却，加入 10%氢氧化钠溶液 20mL，以保证所有的肉桂酸成钠盐而溶解。

(4)抽滤，将滤液倾入 250mL 烧杯中，冷却至室温，在搅拌下用浓盐酸酸化至刚果红试纸变蓝(pH 为 2～3)。

(5)冷却，抽滤，用少量水洗涤沉淀，抽干，自然晾干，产量约 3g(产率 65%～70%)。粗产品可用热水或 3∶1 的水-乙醇重结晶。

(6)测定产品的红外光谱，对产品进行表征。

纯肉桂酸(反式)为无色晶体，m.p.为 135～136℃[4]。

【注释】

[1]苯甲醛放久了，由于自动氧化而生成较多量的苯甲酸，这不但影响反应的进行，而且苯甲酸混在产品中不易除干净，将影响产品的质量。故本反应所需的苯甲醛要事先蒸馏，截取 170～180℃馏分供使用。

[2]乙酸酐放久了因吸潮和水解将转变为乙酸，故本实验所需的乙酸酐必须在实验前进行重新蒸馏。

[3]由于有二氧化碳放出，反应初期有泡沫产生。

[4]肉桂酸有顺反异构体。通常制得的是其反式异构体。

【思考题】

(1)用水蒸气蒸馏除去什么？为什么能用水蒸气蒸馏纯化产品？

(2)苯甲醛与丙酸酐在无水碳酸钾存在下反应将得到什么产物？

3.9　乙酰水杨酸(阿司匹林)的制备

【实验原理】

水杨酸与乙酸酐在 H^+ 催化下反应生成乙酰水杨酸。

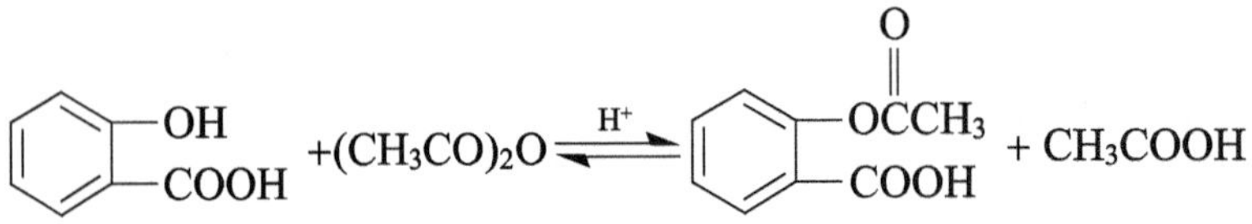

【主要试剂及实验装置】

实验装置			
水杨酸	3.2g (0.023mol)	m.p.159℃	
乙酸酐	5g (约 5mL，0.05mol)	b.p.139.6℃	$d = 1.0820^{20/4}$g/mL
浓硫酸(98%)	5 滴		
阿司匹林药片			
乙醇(95%)			
三氯化铁(1%)			

【实验时间】

4h

【实验步骤】

(1) 3.2g (0.023mol) 水杨酸放入 100mL 锥形瓶中，加入 5mL (0.05mol) 乙酸酐[1]，然后加入 5 滴浓硫酸，充分摇匀。

(2) 水浴加热，水杨酸立即溶解，维持 15min[2]，并时加振摇。

(3) 稍冷后，在不断搅拌下倒入 50mL 冰水中，并用冰水浴冷却[3]。

(4) 抽滤，分别用 8mL 冰水洗涤两次，将初产物干燥。

(5) 用水和乙醇的混合溶剂重结晶，干燥产品，称重，计算产率[4]。

纯的乙酰水杨酸(aspirin)为白色晶体，熔点为 136℃。

【注释】

[1]乙酸酐会刺激眼睛，要在通风橱内倒试剂，小心操作。

[2]水杨酸是一个双官能团的化合物，反应温度应控制在 70℃左右，以防下述副产物的生成。

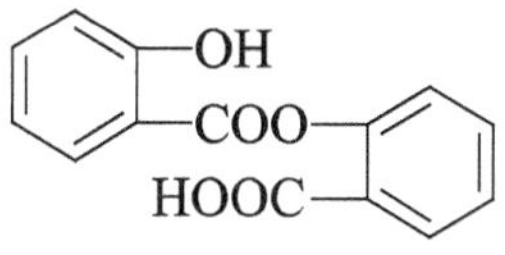

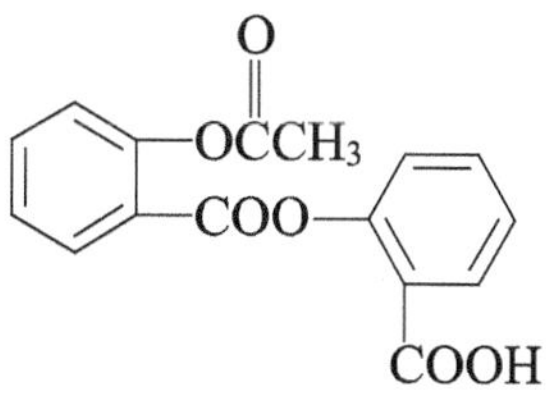

[3]水能除去未反应的乙酸酐，并使不溶于水的产物阿司匹林沉淀析出。

[4]经重结晶后的产品是否纯，可用 1% $FeCl_3$ 溶液进行实验，实验方法参考英文部分注释[5]。

【思考题】

(1) 为什么在水杨酸的乙酰化反应中要使用浓硫酸？

(2) 水杨酸与过量乙醇在酸催化下反应的产物是什么？

3.10　乙酸正丁酯的制备

【实验原理】

由冰醋酸与正丁醇在浓硫酸存在下经酯化反应制得乙酸正丁酯。

$$CH_3COOH+CH_3(CH_2)_2CH_2OH \xrightleftharpoons{H_2SO_4} CH_3COO(CH_2)_3CH_3+H_2O$$

【主要试剂及实验装置】

带分水器的回流装置			
正丁醇	11.5mL (9.3g, 0.125mol)	b.p.117.2℃	$d = 0.8098^{20/4}$g/mL
冰醋酸	7.2mL (7.5g, 0.125mol)	b.p.118℃	$d = 1.049^{20/4}$g/mL
浓硫酸			$d = 1.841^{20/4}$g/mL
10%碳酸钠溶液			
无水硫酸镁			

【实验时间】

4～5h

【实验步骤】

(1) 在干燥的 100mL 圆底烧瓶中加入 11.5mL (9.3g，0.125mol) 正丁醇、7.2mL (7.5g，0.125mol) 冰醋酸和 3～4 滴浓硫酸[1, 2]，充分振摇，混合均匀。加入几粒沸石。

(2) 安装分水器及回流冷凝管，在分水器放水口一侧预先加水至略低于支管口，并做好记号。

(3) 在石棉网上加热，于 80℃左右加热 15min，然后再升高温度，回流约 25min。与此同时，要不断地从分水器放水口处放出反应生成的水[3]，保持分水器中水层液面在原来的高度。

(4) 不再有水生成时，表示反应完毕[4]。停止加热，记录分出的水量。

(5) 冷却后拆卸回流冷凝管，将分水器中的液体和圆底烧瓶中的反应液合并后一起倒入分液漏斗，分出水层。

(6) 用 10mL 10%碳酸钠水溶液洗涤有机层，使有机层 pH 等于 7。分去水层。

(7) 再用 10mL 水洗涤一次，分去水层。

(8) 将有机层倒入一个干燥的小锥形瓶中，用适量无水硫酸镁干燥。摇动，至有机层透明。

(9) 将干燥后的乙酸正丁酯倒入干燥的 50mL 蒸馏烧瓶中，常压蒸馏，收集 124～126℃的馏分。产率约 68%～75%。

乙酸正丁酯是无色透明液体，b.p.126.3℃，d_4^{20} 0.8825，n_D^{20} 1.3947。

【注释】

[1]浓硫酸在反应中作催化剂，只需少量，不宜过多。

[2]滴加浓硫酸时，应边加边摇，必要时可用冷水冷却，以免局部炭化。

[3]本实验利用共沸混合物除去酯化反应中生成的水。共沸物的沸点为：乙酸正丁酯-水 90.7℃，正丁醇-水 93℃，乙酸正丁酯-正丁醇 117.6℃，乙酸正丁酯-正丁醇-水 90.7℃。

[4]可根据以下两种现象判断反应终点：①分水器中不再有水珠下沉；②分水器中分出的水量与理论分水量进行比较，判断反应完成的程度。

【思考题】

(1)本实验采用什么原理和方法来提高乙酸正丁酯的产率？

(2)本实验根据什么原理移去反应中生成的水？为什么水必须被移去？

3.11　邻苯二甲酸二正丁酯的制备

【实验原理】

邻苯二甲酸二正丁酯一般是由苯酐与正丁醇在浓硫酸存在下经酯化反应制得。反应分两步进行。第一步反应迅速完全，第二步是可逆反应。为使反应向生成二丁酯的方向进行，需利用分水器将反应过程中生成的水不断地从反应体系中移去。

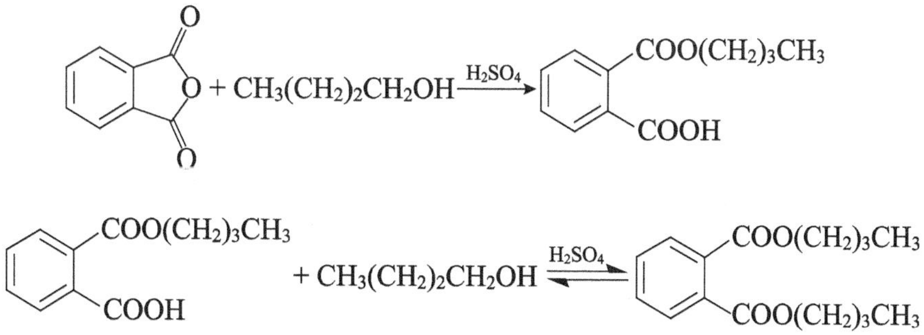

【主要试剂及实验装置】

带分水器的回流装置和减压蒸馏			
正丁醇	13mL(0.14mol)	b. p.117.2℃	$d = 0.8098^{20/4}$g/mL
苯酐	6.0g(0.04mol)	m. p.131℃	$d = 1.527^{20/4}$g/mL
浓硫酸	0.2mL		$d = 1.841^{20/4}$g/mL
5%碳酸钠溶液			

【实验时间】

4～5h

【实验步骤】

(1)在干燥的 100mL 三颈烧瓶侧口插入一温度计，它的水银球应位于烧瓶底 0.5～1cm 处，向三颈烧瓶中加入 13mL (0.14mol) 正丁醇、6g (0.04mol) 苯酐和 0.2mL 浓硫酸。充分振摇，混合均匀，加入几粒沸石。

(2) 如 Fig.3.1 所示安装分水器及回流冷凝管，在分水器放水口一侧预先加入正丁醇至略低于支管口。

(3) 在石棉网上小火加热，待苯酐固体消失后，很快就有正丁醇-水的共沸物[1]蒸出，在分水器中可看到有小珠逐渐沉入底部。随着反应的进行，瓶内反应液的温度缓慢升高，当上升至 140℃时可停止反应[2]。反应时间约需 1.5h。

(4) 待反应液冷却至 70℃时，将其转入分液漏斗中，用 10～15mL 5%碳酸钠水溶液洗涤中和[3]。

(5) 再用 10～15mL 温热的食盐水洗涤 2～3 次，使有机层 pH 等于 7。

(6) 将洗过的有机层先用蒸馏除去过量的正丁醇，最后减压蒸馏收集产品，产量约 5.3g (产率 63%)。

纯邻苯二甲酸二正丁酯是无色油状液体，b.p 340℃ (175～176℃/665.5Pa)，n_D^{20} 1.4911。

【注释】

[1]见实验 3.4，正丁醚的制备注释[1]。

[2]可根据从分水器中分出的水量来判断反应进行的程度。邻苯二甲酸二正丁酯在酸性条件下，当温度超过 180℃时易发生分解反应。

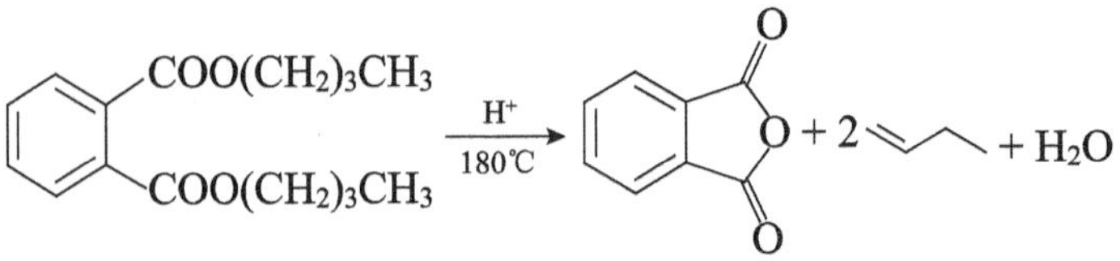

[3]中和时温度不宜超过 70℃，碱的浓度也不宜过高，氢氧化钠也不宜使用。否则，易发生皂化反应。用饱和食盐水代替水来洗涤有机层，一方面是为了尽可能减少酯的损失，同时也是为了防止在洗涤过程中乳化现象的发生。另外，这样处理后，不必进行干燥即可进行下一步操作。

【思考题】

(1) 正丁醇在浓硫酸存在下加热到高温时可能会有哪些副反应发生？若浓硫酸的量过多会有什么不良影响？

(2) 该反应在加热时必须用小火且缓慢进行，若加热过快，过猛会有什么不良影响？

3.12　乙酰苯胺的制备

【实验原理】

乙酰苯胺可以通过苯胺与乙酰氯、乙酸酐或冰醋酸等试剂作用制得。本实验可用下面任何一种方法制备乙酰苯胺。

方法一

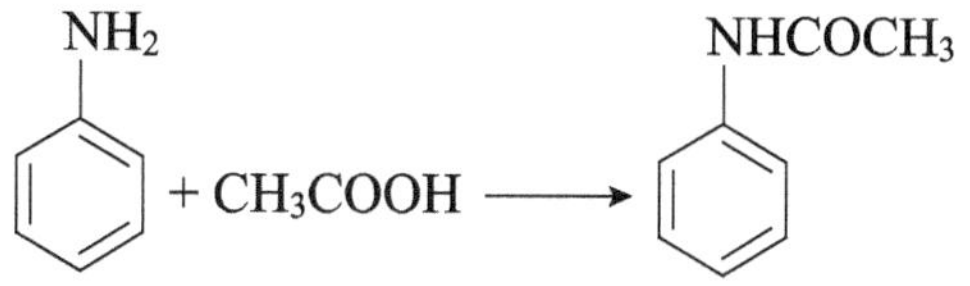

方法二

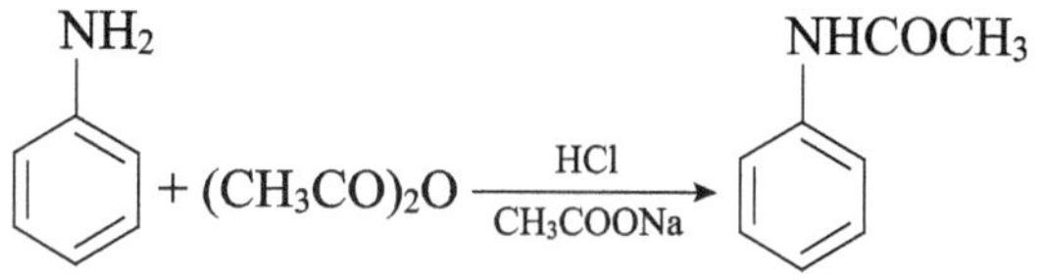

【主要试剂及实验装置】

分馏装置			
苯胺	10mL (10.2 g, 0.11mol)	b.p.184℃	$d = 1.0217^{20/4}$g/mL
冰醋酸	17mL (17.8 g, 0.26mol)	b.p.118℃	$d = 1.049^{20/4}$g/mL
锌粉	0.1g		
乙酸酐	5.2mL (5.6g, 0.055mol)	b.p.139.55℃	$d = 1.0820^{20/4}$g/mL
乙酸钠	4.51g (0.055mol)	m.p.324℃	$d = 1.528$g/mL
浓盐酸(36%)	4.5mL		$d = 1.18$g/mL

【实验时间】

3h

【实验步骤】

1. 方法一

(1) 量取 10mL 苯胺[1]，倒入 50mL 圆底烧瓶中，加入 17mL 冰醋酸和 0.1g 锌粉[2]。

(2) 在圆底烧瓶上装置一分馏柱，插上温度计，用一个 50mL 的锥形瓶作接收器。

(3) 用石棉网小火加热至反应混合物回流，然后控制加热速度，保持蒸馏的气温在 105℃左右[3] (温度计读数在 105℃左右)。反应生成的水及少量冰醋酸可被蒸出。

(4) 反应经 1h 后结束。搅拌下趁热将反应物倒入盛有 250mL 冷水的烧杯中，乙酰苯胺生成。

(5) 抽滤，用冰冷的水洗涤，并用水重结晶[4]。

(6) 记录产量和乙酰苯胺的熔程，并计算产率[5]。

纯的乙酰苯胺为无色片状晶体，m.p.114.3℃。

2. 方法二

(1) 在一个 250mL 的锥形瓶中倒入 125mL 水，加入 4.5mL 浓盐酸，振荡烧瓶，混匀，然后加入 4.6mL (4.65g，0.05mol) 苯胺，摇匀。

(2) 在另一容器中放入 25mL 水，再加入 4.51g (0.055mol) 乙酸钠，并用量筒量取 5.2mL (5.6g，0.055mol) 乙酸酐[6]。

(3) 用水浴加热苯胺盐酸盐溶液至 50℃后，加入乙酸酐，回荡烧瓶，使乙酸酐溶解，尽快一次性加入步骤 2 中配制的乙酸钠溶液[7]，回荡烧瓶，并将其置于冰水浴中。

(4) 20min 后，抽滤产品，用少量冰水洗涤，用水重结晶[4]。

(5) 记录产量，计算产率。测定乙酰苯胺的熔点。

纯的乙酰苯胺为无色片状晶体，m.p.114.3℃

【注释】

[1]苯胺有毒，它能经皮肤被吸收，使用时需小心。

[2]加入少量锌粉的目的是防止苯胺在反应过程中被氧化。

[3]控制此温度是为了尽量除去反应中生成的水，而防止原料冰醋酸被蒸出。

[4]若溶液有颜色，可加入少量活性炭，回荡反应混合物，并使其平稳沸腾几分钟，抽滤除去活性炭。

[5]用方法一将能得到大约 10g 产品，产率约为 61%～68%。

[6]反应在水溶液中进行，苯胺在水中的溶解度为 3.4g/100mL，加入浓盐酸，使其成为铵盐而增加在水中的溶解度，而在酸性条件下苯胺的亲核性下降，为此加入乙酸钠，铵盐部分被中和，使苯胺既有一定的亲核性又在水中有一定的溶解度。

[7]苯胺与乙酸酐的反应应尽快发生，以防止乙酸酐与水反应生成乙酸，为此，乙酸酐一旦溶解，就应立即将乙酸钠加入反应瓶中。

【思考题】

(1) 方法一中，为什么在反应时要控制蒸馏气体的温度在 105℃？

(2) 方法二中，为什么乙酸酐溶解后就应立即一次性加入乙酸钠，乙酸钠的作用是什么？

(3) 为什么洗涤产品时要用冰冷的水？

3.13　4-硝基苯胺的制备

【实验原理】

主反应：

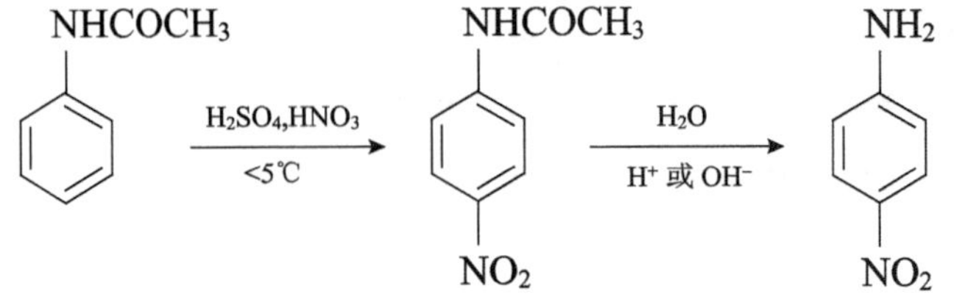

副反应：

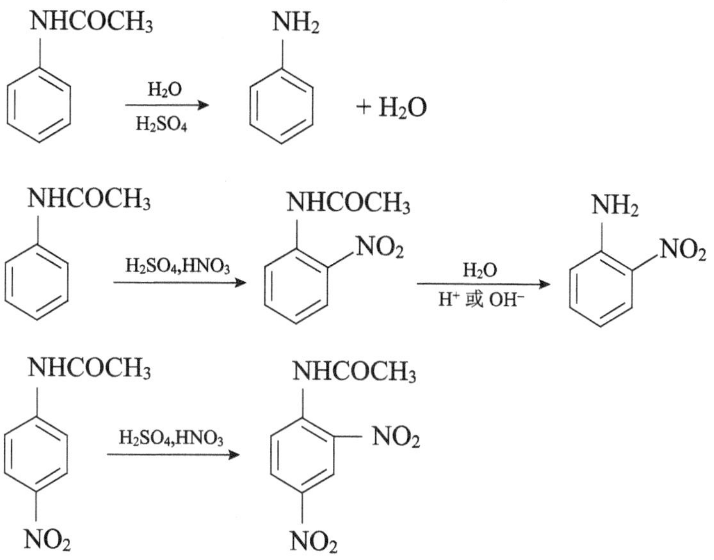

【主要试剂及实验装置】

回流和抽滤装置			
乙酰苯胺	5g (0.037mol)	m.p. 114.3℃	
浓硫酸	1.4mL		$d=1.841^{20/4}$g/mL
浓硝酸	2.2mL (0.032mol)		$d=1.503^{20/4}$g/mL
冰醋酸	5mL (5.25g, 0.087mol)	b.p. 118℃	$d=1.049^{20/4}$g/mL
20%氢氧化钠			

【实验时间】

3～5h

【实验步骤】

1. 4-硝基乙酰苯胺制备

(1) 在冰盐浴中配制 2.2mL 浓硝酸[1]和 1.4mL 浓硫酸的混酸，置于冰盐浴中冷却，备用。

(2) 将 5g (0.037mol) 乙酰苯胺和 5mL (0.087mol) 冰醋酸[2]放入 100mL 锥形瓶内，用冰水冷却，边摇动锥形瓶，边缓慢加入 10mL 浓硫酸，乙酰苯胺逐渐溶解，将所得透明溶液放入冰水中冷却至 0～2℃。

(3) 边振摇锥形瓶，边用滴管缓慢滴入上步制备的混酸至锥形瓶中，注意反应温度应低于 5℃[3]。

(4) 从冰水中取出锥形瓶，室温放置 30min，间歇振荡。

(5) 搅拌下把此反应混合物以细流缓慢倒入盛有 20mL 水和 30g 碎冰的烧杯中，4-硝基乙酰苯胺立即成淡黄色固体析出。放置约 10min。

(6) 抽滤，用冰水洗涤三次，每次 10mL，得到粗产品，不必精制，直接用于下步合成。

2. 4-硝基苯胺的制备[4]

(1)在一个 100mL 圆底烧瓶中加入步骤 1 制备的 4g 4-硝基乙酰苯胺粗品和 20mL7%硫酸[5]，投入沸石，装上回流冷凝管，加热回流 40min，得透明溶液。

(2)将透明的热溶液倒入盛有 50g 碎冰的大烧杯中，加入过量的 20%氢氧化钠溶液至呈碱性，4-硝基苯胺沉淀析出。

(3)冷却后抽滤，滤饼用冷水洗去碱液，用水重结晶[6]，干燥，测定熔点，称量，计算产率。

4-硝基苯胺为黄色单斜针状晶体，熔点 147.5℃。有毒，能经皮肤吸收使人中毒。受热易分解，发生爆炸。

【注释】

[1]为防止生成多硝化的副产物，硝酸的用量不能多，本实验按此硝酸用量来计算产率。

[2]本实验在冰醋酸中硝化，产物以对位产物为主(若在乙酐中硝化，则以邻位产物为主)，此外，加入冰醋酸还可以加速乙酰苯胺在硫酸中的溶解。

[3]乙酰苯胺与混酸在 5℃以下反应，对位产物为主；若温度高于 5℃，邻位副产物会增多。

[4]4-硝基乙酰苯胺也可以在碱性条件下水解，碱性水解可在 35%氢氧化钠中回流 2.5～3h，碱性不宜强，回流时间不宜长，否则易部分水解而影响产率。

[5]7%硫酸配制方法：在振荡和冷却下，将 12mL 浓硫酸小心地以细流形式加入 9mL 冷水中，使用时取 20mL。

[6]4-硝基苯胺在 100g 水中的溶解度：18.5℃，0.08g；100℃，2.2g。

【思考题】

(1)是否可以从苯胺直接硝化制备 4-硝基苯胺？为什么？

(2)4-硝基乙酰苯胺在酸性条件下回流后得到的透明溶液是什么？为何加入 20%氢氧化钠溶液后，4-硝基苯胺沉淀析出？又为何要求加碱至使溶液呈碱性？

3.14 从茶叶中提取咖啡因

【实验原理】

咖啡因的提取既可用微波萃取法也可用传统的索氏提取法。

咖啡因又名咖啡碱，属杂环化合物嘌呤的衍生物，它的化学名称为 1，3，7-三甲基-2，6-二氧嘌呤，结构如下：

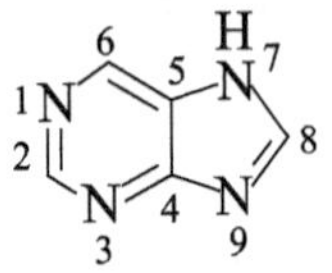

Purine

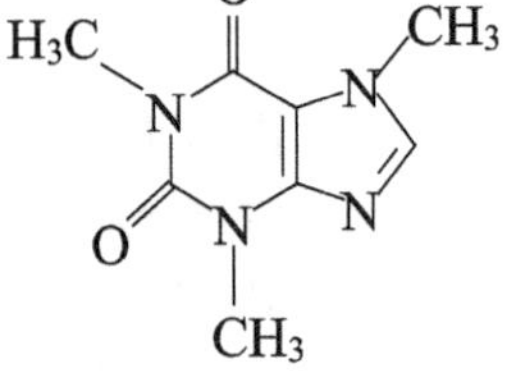

Caffeine 1, 3, 7-Trimethyl-2, 6-dioxopurine

【主要试剂及实验装置】

微波炉、索氏提取装置、升华装置	
茶叶[1]	7.0～10g
95%乙醇溶液	120mL，60mL
生石灰粉	2.5g

【实验时间】

3h 或 6h

【实验步骤】

1. 方法一：微波萃取法[2]

(1)称取研细的红茶末 10g，置于 250mL 碘量瓶中，加入 120mL 95%的乙醇溶液，放入沸石。

(2)将碘量瓶放于普通微波炉中，调节功率约 320W，辐射约 50～60s[3]，取出冷却。

(3)重复上述步骤 3～4 次[4]，过滤，去除红茶末。

(4)冷却后改用水浴蒸馏装置，蒸出提取液中的大部分乙醇(可回收利用)，提取液的残液为 5～8mL。

(5)将残液倒入蒸发皿中，并用蒸出的乙醇对蒸馏烧瓶稍作洗涤，一并倒入蒸发皿中。

(6)加 2.5g 生石灰粉[5]，不断搅拌，并将蒸发皿置于水蒸气浴上蒸干溶剂。

(7)将蒸发皿移至石棉网上，用小火加热，不断焙炒至干[6]。

(8)取一张稍大些的圆形滤纸，罩在大小适宜的玻璃漏斗上，刺上小孔且孔刺向上，再盖在蒸发皿上，漏斗颈部塞入少许棉花。

(9)用小火慢慢加热升华[7]，当有棕色油状物在玻璃漏斗壁上生成时，立刻停止加热，冷却，收集滤纸上的咖啡因晶体。

(10)残渣经充分搅拌后，用略大的火再升华 1～2 次，合并数次升华产物，称重，产量约 70～80mg。咖啡因为白色或略带微黄色的针状晶体，m.p.238℃。

2. 方法二：索氏萃取法

(1)称取红茶叶末 7g，置于合适的滤纸筒中，然后放入索氏提取器内(Fig. 2.14)[8]。

(2)取 60mL 95%乙醇于圆底烧瓶中，放入沸石，安装好回流提取装置，水浴加热。

(3)连续回流提取 2h 左右，直至提取液颜色较淡，当溶液刚好虹吸回流至烧瓶中时，即可停止加热[9]。

(4)其余步骤按方法一中的第 4～10 条操作[10]。

【注释】

茶叶中含有咖啡因、茶碱、丹宁酸、色素、纤维素等多种物质，其中咖啡因的含量约为 1%～5%，丹宁酸约为 11%～12%。咖啡因具有强心、兴奋、利尿等药理功能，是常见的中枢神经兴奋剂。丹宁酸易溶于 H_2O 和乙醇。通常红茶中咖啡因的含量高于绿茶，本实验可以选用红茶末。

[1]因红茶中咖啡因的含量较高，本实验可选用红茶末。

[2]微波萃取法比其他方法所需的实验时间可缩短 2h 左右。

[3]微波辐射时间以不使溶液暴沸冲出为原则。

[4]在进行下一次微波辐射前要先冷却。

[5]生石灰起中和作用，以除去丹宁酸等酸性物质。

[6]若残留少量水分，则会在下一步升华开始时漏斗壁上呈现水珠。如有此现象，则应撤去火源，迅速擦去水珠，然后继续升华。

[7]升华操作直接影响到产物的质量与产量，升华的关键是控制温度。温度过高，将导致被烘物冒烟炭化，或产物变黄，造成损失。

[8]滤纸筒的大小要紧贴器壁，高度不要超过索氏提取器的虹吸管。

[9]控制回流速度，一般 2h 内虹吸 8～10 次。

[10]产量约为 30～40mg。

【思考题】

(1) 假设你得到的咖啡因粗品较纯，与茶叶中 3%的咖啡因含量相比，你的产率如何？若有差异，请给出可能的解释？

(2) 试比较微波辅助法和传统的索氏提取法在从茶叶中提取咖啡因的实验中的差别。

3.15 呋喃甲醇和呋喃甲酸的制备

【实验原理】

无 α-氢的醛与浓的强碱溶液作用，发生分子间的自身氧化还原反应，一分子醛被还原成醇，另一分子醛被氧化成酸，此类反应称为 Cannizzaro 反应。呋喃甲醇和呋喃甲酸就是由呋喃甲醛经 Cannizzaro 反应制得。

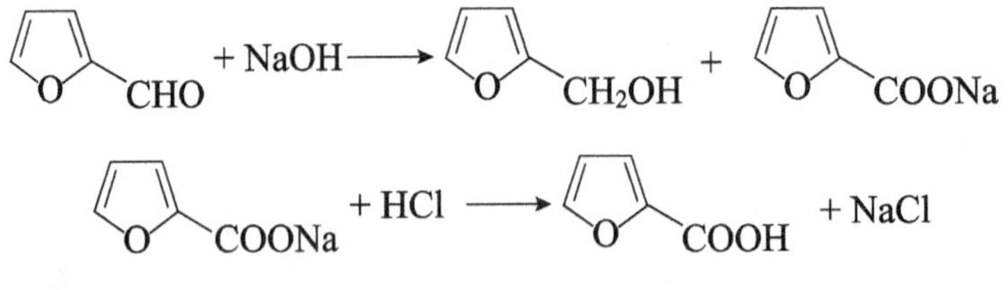

【主要试剂及实验装置】

减压蒸馏			
呋喃甲醛	10mL (11.6g, 0.12mol)	b.p.161.7℃	$d = 1.1594^{20/4}$g/mL
43%氢氧化钠溶液	9mL		
乙醚		b.p.34.5℃	$d = 0.7138^{20/4}$g/mL
盐酸			$d = 1.18$g/L
聚乙二醇(400)	2g		
无水硫酸镁			

【实验时间】

6h

【实验步骤】

(1) 在 100mL 烧杯中准确量取 9mL 43%的氢氧化钠溶液和 2g 聚乙二醇[1](相对分子质量为 400)，充分摇匀。将烧杯置于冰水浴中冷却至 5℃左右。

(2) 在不断搅拌下，由滴液漏斗慢慢滴入 10mL 新蒸过的呋喃甲醛[2]，控制滴加速度(约在 15min 内加完)，保持反应温度在 8～12℃[3]，加完后在室温下继续搅拌 25min，反应即可完成，得到淡黄色浆状物。

(3) 在搅拌下加入适量的水(约 15mL)，使沉淀恰好完全溶解[4]，此时溶液呈暗褐色或暗红色。

(4) 将反应液转入分液漏斗中，用乙醚萃取，每次用 10mL，重复萃取四次。

(5) 合并乙醚萃取液，用无水硫酸镁(约 2g)干燥。

(6) 先在水浴上蒸去乙醚，再蒸馏呋喃甲醇，收集 169～172℃的馏分，产率为 68%～84%。

(7) 乙醚萃取后的水溶液(主要含呋喃甲酸钠)，在搅拌下用 25%盐酸酸化，至刚果红试纸变蓝(pH = 3)[5]，约需 25%盐酸 18mL。

(8) 充分冷却，使呋喃甲酸析出完全，抽滤，用少量水洗涤。

(9) 粗产品用水重结晶，得白色针状结晶体呋喃甲酸。产率约 68%。

纯呋喃甲酸的熔点为 133～134℃。

【注释】

[1]反应在两相中进行，用聚乙二醇作相转移催化剂。

[2]呋喃甲醛存放过久会变成棕褐色，并可能带有水分。因此使用前需蒸馏提纯，收集 155～162℃的馏分。最好采用减压蒸馏，收集 54～55℃/2.3kPa 的馏分。新蒸过的呋喃甲醛为无色或浅黄色液体。

[3]反应开始后很剧烈，同时大量放热，溶液颜色变暗。若反应温度高于 10℃时，则反应温度极易升高，难以控制，致使反应液呈深红色。若低于 10℃时，则反应速度过慢，可能使部分呋喃甲醛积累，一旦反应发生，反应就会过于猛烈而使温度迅速升高，最终也可导致反应物变成深红色。

[4]加入适量的水使固态的呋喃甲酸钠溶解，若加水过量会导致部分产品损失。

[5]酸量一定要加足，保证酸化后 pH = 3，使呋喃甲酸充分游离出来。这是影响呋喃甲酸产率的关键。

【思考题】

(1) 本实验为什么要用新蒸馏的呋喃甲醛？

(2) 为什么反应液要用乙醚萃取四次？萃取的是什么产物？

3.16　8-羟基喹啉的制备

【实验原理】

以邻氨基酚、邻硝基酚、无水甘油和浓硫酸为原料合成 8-羟基喹啉。浓硫酸的作用是使甘油脱水生成丙烯醛，并使邻氨基酚与丙烯醛的加成物脱水成环。硝基酚为弱氧化剂，能将成环产物 8-羟基-1，2-二氢喹啉氧化成 8-羟基喹啉。

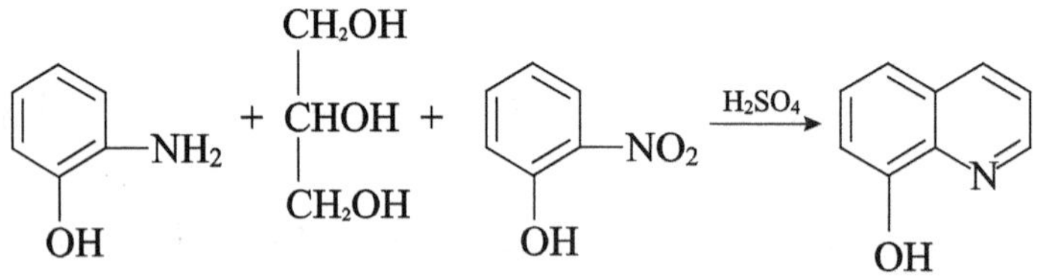

【主要试剂及实验装置】

水蒸气蒸馏		
邻硝基苯酚	1.8g(0.013mol)	
邻氨基苯酚	2.8g(0.025mol)	
无水甘油	7.5mL(9.5g, 0.1mol)	$d = 1.2620^{20/4}$g/mL
浓硫酸(98%)	4.5mL	
氢氧化钠溶液	7mL 1∶1(质量比)	
饱和碳酸钠溶液	5mL	

【实验时间】

6h

【实验步骤】

(1)在 100mL 的三颈烧瓶[1]中加入 1.8g(0.013mol)邻硝基苯酚，2.8g(0.025mol)邻氨基苯酚，7.5mL(9.5g，0.1mol)无水甘油[2]，剧烈振荡，使之混匀，在冷水浴下慢慢滴入 4.5mL 浓硫酸。

(2)装上回流冷凝管。用小火在石棉网上加热，约 15min 后溶液微沸，移开火源(此反应为放热反应，溶液呈微沸时，表示反应已经开始)。

(3)待反应缓和后，继续小火加热，保持反应物微沸反应 1h。

(4)冷却后加入 15mL 水，进行水蒸气蒸馏(约需 30min)，蒸去未反应的邻硝基苯酚，直至馏出液由浅黄色变成无色为止。

(5)待瓶内液体冷却后，慢慢加入 7mL 1∶1(质量比)氢氧化钠溶液，冷却，摇匀后，小心加入约 5mL 饱和碳酸钠溶液，使内容物呈中性(pH = 7～8)[3]，为什么？

(6)再加 20mL 水进行水蒸气蒸馏，蒸出 8-羟基喹啉(约需 25min)。

(7)冷却，结晶，抽滤，洗涤，干燥，粗产物约 3g。

(8)精制：粗产物用 25mL 4∶1(体积比)乙醇-水混合溶剂重结晶。
(9)测熔点：纯 8-羟基喹啉 m.p.72～74℃。

【注释】

[1]本实验使用的仪器必须先干燥。
[2]所用甘油含水量不要超过 0.5%($d = 1.26$g/mL)。此反应系放热反应，要严格控制反应温度，以免反应液冲出容器。
[3] 8-羟基喹啉既溶于碱又溶于酸而成盐，且成盐后不被水蒸气蒸馏，为此必须小心中和，严格控制在 pH = 7～8，当中和恰当时，瓶内析出的 8-羟基喹啉沉淀最多。

【思考题】

(1)为什么第一次水蒸气蒸馏要在酸性条件进行，第二次水蒸气蒸馏要在中性条件下进行?
(2)如果用 4-甲基-2-氨基苯酚代替 2-氨基苯酚为原料反应，将可得到什么产物?

3.17　乙酰二茂铁的制备

【实验原理】

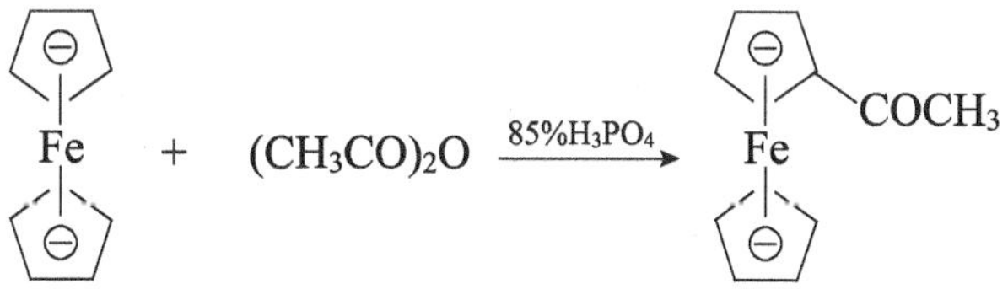

【主要试剂及实验装置】

抽滤装置			
二茂铁	1g（0.0054mol）	m.p. 173℃	
乙酸酐	10mL (10.8g, 0.10 mol)	b.p.139.6℃	d=1.0820$^{20/4}$g/mL
85% 磷酸	2mL		
石油醚(60～90℃)；碳酸氢钠(固体)；乙醇；苯；冰；硅胶 G 板(3cm × 1cm)：若干块。			

【实验时间】

4~6h

【实验步骤】

1. 乙酰二茂铁的制备

(1)在 100mL 圆底烧瓶[1]中，加入 1g(0.0054mol)二茂铁和 10mL(0.10mol)乙酸酐。在摇

荡下，用滴管慢慢加入 2mL 85%的磷酸。加完后用装有氯化钙干燥管的塞子塞住瓶口[1]，在沸水浴上加热 40min，并间歇振荡。

(2) 将反应混合物倾入盛有 40g 碎冰的 400mL 的烧杯中，用 10mL 冷水涮洗烧瓶，将涮洗液并入烧杯。

(3) 在搅拌下，分批加入固体碳酸氢钠，至溶液呈中性为止[2]，约需 20～25g 碳酸氢钠。将中和后的反应混合物置于冰水浴中冷却 25min。

(4) 抽滤，收集析出的橙黄色固体，每次用 50mL 冰水洗涤，洗涤两次，在空气中干燥。

(5) 用石油醚(60～90℃)重结晶，产物约 0.3g，熔点 84～85℃(纯乙酰二茂铁的熔点为 85℃)。

2. 用薄层色谱法鉴定乙酰二茂铁

(1) 取少许干燥后的粗产物溶于苯中，在硅胶 G 板上点样，用 3 : 1 的石油醚/乙酸乙酯(体积比)作展开剂，层析板上从上到下出现黄色、橙色和红色三个点，分别代表二茂铁、乙酰二茂铁和副产物 1，1′-二乙酰基二茂铁。

(2) 取 0.1g 重结晶后的乙酰二茂铁溶于 3mL 苯中，进行薄层层析，鉴定样品的纯度[3]，测定乙酰二茂铁的 R_f 值。

【注释】

[1]烧瓶要干燥，反应时需使用氯化钙干燥管，避免空气中的水进入烧瓶。

[2]中和时因逸出大量二氧化碳，出现激烈鼓泡，所以要小心操作！最好用 pH 试纸检验溶液的酸碱性，如果反应混合物颜色较深，用 pH 试纸检测有困难时，可以加碳酸氢钠至气泡消失作为中和完成的判断标准。

[3]若层析完成后，薄板上显示一个点，说明重结晶后得到的乙酰二茂铁样品较纯。

【思考题】

(1) 为什么反应需要使用干燥的烧瓶，并需使用氯化钙干燥管，若空气中的水进入烧瓶，对反应有什么影响？

(2) 二茂铁酰化时，若有副产物二酰基二茂铁生成，试问第二个酰基应进入哪个环戊二烯负离子环？为什么？

(3) 为什么二茂铁非常稳定，具有芳香性，试从二茂铁的结构给予说明。

3.18　生物法合成乙醇

【实验原理】

本实验采用蔗糖发酵法[1]制备乙醇。蔗糖在干酵母和 Pasteur 盐溶液[2]的作用下，室温发酵一周后得到含 8%～10%乙醇的发酵液，发酵液经分馏得到含量为 95%左右的乙醇，即普通的工业酒精。

蔗糖发酵的主要化学反应为：

$$\underset{\text{蔗糖}}{C_{12}H_{22}O_{11}} \longrightarrow \underset{\text{葡萄糖}}{C_6H_{12}O_6} + \underset{\text{果糖}}{C_6H_{12}O_6} \longrightarrow \underset{\text{乙醇}}{4CH_3CH_2OH} + 4CO_2$$

蔗糖发酵的生化过程主要为：蔗糖首先水解为葡萄糖和果糖，葡萄糖和果糖活化生成 1,6-二磷酸果糖，后者经降解得到 3-磷酸甘油醛，氧化得到丙酮酸，无氧条件下丙酮酸脱羧得到乙醛和 CO_2，乙醛在最后阶段还原为乙醇。上述每一步均需要一种特效的酶作催化剂，也需要一些常见的无机离子(如镁)，还有磷酸盐。蔗糖发酵的生化过程可表示如下：

【主要试剂及实验装置】

刺形分馏柱	
蔗糖	40g(0.12mol)
干酵母	1.5g

磷酸钾：2g；磷酸钙：0.2g；硫酸镁：0.2g；酒石酸铵：10g；磷酸氢二钠：0.25g；饱和石灰水；硅藻土。

【实验时间】

6h

【实验步骤】

(1)在 500mL 锥形瓶中将 40g(0.12mol)蔗糖溶于 350mL 水，室温下加入 35mL Pasteur 盐溶液[2]和 1.5g 干酵母，剧烈摇振，使其混合完全。

(2)在瓶口塞上插有弯玻璃管的单孔橡皮塞，玻璃管下端浸入盛于试管中的 10mL 饱和石灰水[3]的液面下，将混合物在室温下(25～35℃)放置一周，待气体(二氧化碳)停止放出时，表明发酵已经完全。

(3)完成发酵后，小心地将锥形瓶移至桌面，以免瓶底沉积物泛上，然后小心地将液体通过一团棉花或玻璃丝倾析到 500mL 圆底烧瓶中。

(4)加入几粒沸石，装上刺形分馏柱和冷凝管，在石棉网上蒸馏收集 60mL 馏出液，弃去留在瓶内的残液。

(5)将馏出液转入 100mL 圆底烧瓶，使用相同的分馏装置，蒸馏收集下列沸程的馏分：A(78～82℃)，B(82～88℃)，C(88～95℃)，弃去瓶内所含的杂醇残液[4]。

(6)测量各馏分的体积。如果馏分 A 的收集量小于 15mL，则应合并馏分重新蒸馏。

(7)测量 A 和 B 馏分的密度并换算成乙醇的含量，计算乙醇的产率。

【注释】

[1]发酵是天然有机物借助生物催化剂——酶进行的一系列生物化学变化的过程，在工业及日常生活中有着广泛的应用。1907 年 Büchner 证明了发酵过程没有任何酵母细胞，酵母的发酵是由非常高效的催化剂——酒化酶所催化的生化过程。酒化酶是一个复合物，有着高度的选择性，其反应活性受温度、pH 的影响很大。

[2]Pasteur 盐溶液由 2.0g 磷酸钾、0.2g 磷酸钙、0.2g 硫酸镁和 10g 酒石酸铵溶于 860mL 水配制而成。也可用 0.25g 磷酸氢二钠代替 Pasteur 盐溶液进行发酵，且不必加入其他任何盐类，但此法产率较低，酵母残渣分离较困难。

[3]此处石灰水起液封作用，防止空气进入锥形瓶，但允许瓶中的气体逸出。还可用一只气球代替石灰水液封装置，发酵时放出的气体(CO_2)使气球膨胀。液封和气球的作用都是防止空气及不需要的酶进入锥形瓶。若让氧气持续接触发酵溶液，乙醇会进一步氧化成乙酸，甚至氧化为二氧化碳和水。

[4]高沸点馏分为杂醇油，杂醇油是 1-丙醇、2-丙醇、1-丁醇、2-甲基-1-丙醇和 3-甲基-1-丁醇等 C_3～C_5 醇的混合物，其组成取决于发酵所用的原料，它不是葡萄糖发酵形成的，而是由存在于原料和酵母中的蛋白质转化而来的。

【思考题】

(1)为什么用蒸馏的方法只能得到 95.6%的乙醇？如何用普通乙醇来制备无水乙醇？

(2)通过测定含水乙醇溶液的密度可以得到该乙醇中水的百分含量？试说明它的依据是什么？

第 4 章　综合性实验

4.1　乙酸乙酯和乙酰乙酸乙酯的制备和结构表征

4.1.1　乙酸乙酯的制备及结构表征

【实验原理】

乙酸和乙醇在浓硫酸催化下直接酯化生成乙酸乙酯。

$$CH_3COOH + CH_3CH_2OH \overset{H_2SO_4}{\rightleftharpoons} CH_3COOCH_2CH_3 + H_2O$$

【主要试剂及实验装置】

回流和蒸馏装置			
冰醋酸	9mL (9.0g, 0.15mol)	b.p.118℃	$d = 1.049^{20/4}$g/mL
无水乙醇	14.5mL (13.8g，0.30mol)	b.p.78.4℃	
			$d = 0.7893^{20/4}$g/mL
浓硫酸	3.8mL		$d = 1.841^{20/4}$g/mL
饱和碳酸钠溶液			
饱和食盐水	7.5mL		
饱和氯化钙溶液	7.5mL		
无水硫酸镁			

【实验时间】

4h

【实验步骤】

(1) 在一干燥的 50mL 圆底烧瓶中放入 14.5mL (13.80g，0.30mol) 无水乙醇，9mL (9.0g，0.15mol) 冰醋酸。然后逐滴加入 3.8mL 浓硫酸 (98%)，混匀后，加入沸石，然后装上回流冷凝管，在冷凝管的上端安装一氯化钙干燥管。

(2) 用小火加热反应瓶，保持缓缓回流 45min。待瓶内反应物冷却后，将回流装置改成蒸馏装置，加热蒸出生成的乙酸乙酯，收集 75～85℃的馏分。

(3) 在馏出液中慢慢加入饱和碳酸钠溶液[1]，并不断振荡，直至不再有二氧化碳气体产生[2]，然后将混合液转入分液漏斗，静置 5min，分去下层水溶液。

(4) 有机层用 7.5mL 饱和食盐水洗涤[3]，再用 7.5mL 饱和氯化钙溶液洗涤，最后用水洗一次，分去下层液体。

(5) 有机层倒入一干燥的三角烧瓶中，用无水硫酸镁干燥。

(6) 将干燥后的有机层液体进行蒸馏，收集 73～78℃的馏分。

(7) 称重，计算产率。产量约 6.3g，产率约为 48%。

(8) 测定产品的紫外光谱，对产品进行表征。

纯的乙酸乙酯为无色液体，b.p.77.06℃，d_4^{20} 0.9003，n_D^{20} 1.3723。

【注释】

[1]在馏出液的粗酯中含有一些乙酸，用饱和碳酸钠溶液除去。

[2]或用检测溶液的 pH 至石蕊试纸不再显酸性的方法，来控制加入饱和碳酸钠溶液的量。

[3]加入饱和食盐水是为了帮助溶液更好的分层。

【思考题】

(1) 在本实验中采用什么方法使酯化反应尽量向产物方向进行?

(2) 蒸出的粗乙酸乙酯中主要有哪些杂质? 如何一一除去?

4.1.2　乙酰乙酸乙酯的制备及结构表征

【实验原理】

从乙酸乙酯出发经 Claisen 酯缩合反应制备乙酰乙酸乙酯。

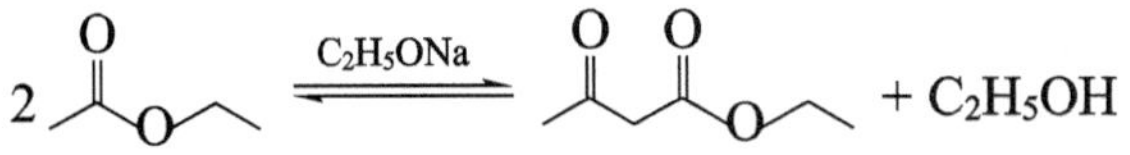

【主要试剂及实验装置】

回流和减压蒸馏装置			
乙酸乙酯	9.8mL (8.8g，0.10mol)	b.p.77.06℃	$d = 0.9003^{20/4}$g/mL
金属钠	1g (0.04mol)		
50%乙酸			
饱和食盐水			
5%碳酸钠水溶液			
无水硫酸镁			

【实验时间】

6h

【实验步骤】

(1) 50mL 干燥的圆底烧瓶中[1]投入 9.8mL (8.8g，0.10mol) 无水乙酸乙酯，然后迅速加入 1.0g (0.04mol) 切细的金属钠[2,3]。

(2) 安装回流装置，用水浴作热源，在回流冷凝管的上端安装一个氯化钙干燥管。

(3) 加热反应混合物，控制反应温度使其缓慢回流至金属钠全部反应完(约需 2h)，此时溶液呈透明红色。

(4) 停止加热，冷却后，搅拌下向反应混合物中加入 50%的乙酸[4]，至反应液呈弱酸性，此时溶液中所有的固体都已溶解。

(5) 将反应液倒入分液漏斗中，加入等体积的饱和食盐水，振摇，静置。

(6) 分出红色酯层，水层用 5mL 乙酸乙酯萃取，将萃取液与酯层合并后用 5%碳酸钠溶液洗至中性，用无水硫酸镁干燥。

(7) 将干燥后的液体倒入圆底烧瓶中，先用水浴蒸出乙酸乙酯，然后减压下蒸馏乙酰乙酸乙酯，b.p.54～55℃/931Pa[5]。

(8) 测定产品的紫外光谱，对产品进行表征。

纯的乙酰乙酸乙酯为无色液体，b.p.180.4℃(分解)，$d = 1.0282^{20/4}$g/mL，n_D^{20} 1.4194。

【注释】

[1]本实验所用仪器需充分干燥，试剂应绝对无水。

[2]除去金属钠表面的氧化物并将其切细，将加速缩合反应。

[3]反应立即发生，若过于激烈，可用冷水浴冷却，若反应不立即开始，可用小火直接加热，促使反应发生，然后将热源移开。

[4]加入乙酸时必须小心，以防止与未作用完的金属钠发生激烈反应。

[5]乙酰乙酸乙酯的沸点(℃)与压力(kPa，mmHg)的关系列于下表中。

压力	mmHg	12	14	18	20	30	40	60	80	760
	kPa	1.6	1.87	2.4	2.67	4	5.33	8	10.67	101.33
沸点	℃	71	74	78	82	88	92	97	100	181

【思考题】

(1) 本实验所用的仪器和试剂必须干燥和绝对无水，为什么？

(2) 在后处理乙酰乙酸乙酯时，加入 5%的乙酸和饱和食盐水的目的分别是什么？

4.2　对氨基苯磺酸和甲基橙的制备

4.2.1　对氨基苯磺酸的制备

【实验原理】

对氨基苯磺酸是合成染料的重要中间体，也是合成甲基橙指示剂的原料，可由苯胺的磺化制备[1]。

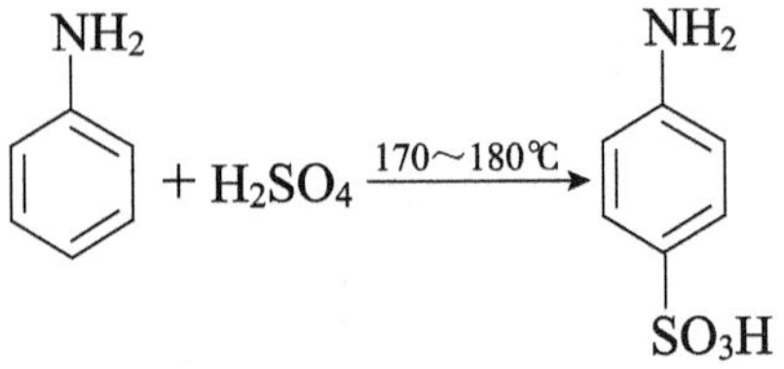

【主要试剂及实验装置】

回流装置		
苯胺	10mL(10.2g，0.11mol)	$d = 1.021^{20/4}$g/mL
浓硫酸	18mL(0.34mol)	$d = 1.841^{20/4}$g/mL

【实验时间】

4h

【实验步骤】

(1)在 250mL 的三颈瓶内加入 10mL(10.2g，0.11mol)苯胺，安装回流冷凝管和温度计，温度计应插入液面以下。

(2)缓慢地小心加入 18mL 浓硫酸($d = 1.84$g/mL)，将三颈瓶的瓶口塞紧。

(3)用油浴缓慢加热反应混合物至 170～180℃[2]，回流 2～2.5h。

(4)将反应混合物冷至 50℃[3]，在玻璃棒搅拌下，将其倒入盛有 100mL 冰水的烧杯中。

(5)抽滤，少量冷水洗涤。

(6)用热水重结晶，必要时需脱色[4]。

(7)结晶时的母液减压下脱溶[5]，浓缩后结晶，抽滤，洗涤，必要时脱色，得到第二部分的产品。

(8)将第二次得到的产品的颜色与第一次得到的产品进行比较，合并两次的产品，计算产率。

对氨基苯磺酸是一种盐，没有固定的熔点，不必测定熔点，温度达 280～290℃将炭化。

【注释】

[1]酸性溶液中苯胺易质子化而成为一间位定位基，本实验中苯胺磺化反应发生在对位是由三方面因素决定的：

(a)在高温下苯胺与浓硫酸反应生成磺酰苯胺。

(b)磺酰氨基是一个邻、对位定位基。

(c)由于磺酰氨基的位阻效应，使邻位产物很少，因此 170～180℃时苯胺磺化生成对磺酰氨基苯磺酸，后者在酸性条件下水解得到对氨基苯磺酸。

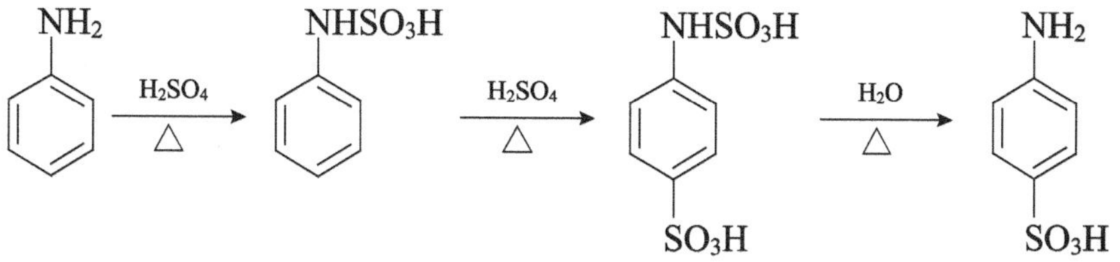

[2]反应温度需控制在 170～180℃，大于 190℃将生成黑色黏稠状物质。

[3]低于 50℃时反应混合物将变得黏稠和固化，使其不易从烧杯中倒出。

[4]对氨基苯磺酸在水中的溶解度是：6.678g/100mL，100℃；1.08g/100mL，20℃。

[5]由于 20℃时对氨基苯磺酸在水中有一定的溶解度，故需对结晶时的母液进行减压脱溶，浓缩等操作。

【思考题】

(1)为什么对氨基苯磺酸较易溶于水而不溶于苯和乙醚?

(2)写出本实验中苯胺磺化的反应机理。

4.2.2　甲基橙的制备

【实验原理】

甲基橙是一种指示剂，它是由对氨基苯磺酸的重氮盐与 *N*, *N*-二甲基苯胺的乙酸盐在弱酸性介质中偶合得到的。反应如下：

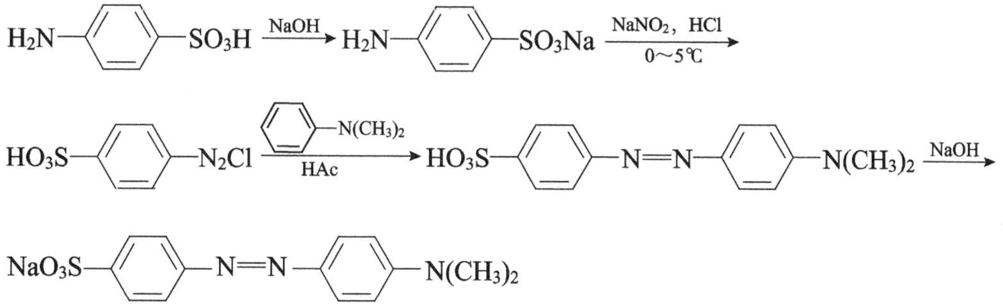

Methyl Orange

【主要试剂及实验装置】

实验装置略		
对氨基苯磺酸	2.1g (0.01mol)	m.p.288℃
N, *N*-二甲基苯胺	1.3mL (1.2g, 0.01mol)	b.p.193℃
	$d = 0.9557^{20/4}$g/mL	
亚硝酸钠	0.8g (0.011mol)	m.p.271℃
5%氢氧化钠溶液 10mL，10%氢氧化钠溶液 15mL；浓盐酸；冰醋酸。		

【实验时间】

5h

【实验步骤】

1. 重氮盐的制备

(1) 100mL 烧杯中放入 2.1g (0.01mol) 自制的对氨基苯磺酸晶体，加入 10mL 5%氢氧化钠溶液，玻璃棒搅拌下，在热水浴中温热使之溶解[1]。

(2) 冷至室温后加入 0.8g (0.011mol) 亚硝酸钠，使其溶解。

(3) 搅拌下[2]，将上述混合溶液分批滴入盛有 13mL 水和 2.5mL 浓盐酸的烧杯中，并控制温度在 5℃以下[3]。

(4) 滴加完后用淀粉-碘化钾试纸检验[4]。然后在冰盐浴中放置 15min，使重氮化反应完全。

2. 偶合反应

(1) 取一支试管，加入 1.3mL (1.2g，0.01mol) *N*, *N*-二甲基苯胺和 1mL 冰醋酸，振荡使之混合。

(2) 不断搅拌下将此溶液慢慢加到上述冷却的重氮盐溶液中，加完后继续搅拌 15min，使偶合反应进行完全。

(3) 搅拌下慢慢加入 15mL 10%氢氧化钠溶液，反应物变为橙色[5]，粗制的甲基橙呈细粒状沉淀析出。

(4) 将反应物在沸水浴上加热 5min，使沉淀溶解，冷却至室温后再置于冰水浴中冷却，甲基橙全部重新结晶析出。

(5) 抽滤，晶体用少量水洗涤，压干[6]。

(6) 若要制得纯度较高的产品，可用溶有少量氢氧化钠 (约 0.15g) 的沸水重结晶。

(7) 称重，计算产率。产量约 2g，产率约为 75%。

(8) 溶解少许产品于水中，加几滴稀盐酸，然后用稀氢氧化钠溶液中和，观察溶液颜色有何变化。

纯甲基橙是橙黄色片状晶体，没有明确熔点。pH 3.1 (红) ～pH 4.4 (橙黄)。

【注释】

[1]对氨基苯磺酸是两性化合物，其酸性略强于碱性，所以它能溶于碱中而不溶于酸中。

[2]为了使对氨基苯磺酸完全重氮化，反应过程必须不断搅拌。

[3]重氮化反应过程中控制温度很重要，若温度高于 5℃，则生成的重氮盐易水解成酚类，降低产率。

[4]若不显蓝色，尚需酌情补加亚硝酸钠溶液。若亚硝酸已过量，可用尿素水溶液使其分解。

[5]这时反应液呈弱碱性，若呈中性，则继续加入少量碱液至恰呈碱性，因强碱性又易生成树脂状聚合物而得不到所需的产物。

[6]湿的甲基橙在空气中受光照射后，颜色会很快变深，故一般得紫红色粗产物，如再依次用乙醇、乙醚洗涤晶体，可使其迅速干燥。

【思考题】

(1)为什么本实验第 4 步重氮化反应的温度需控制在 5℃以下？
(2)为什么 *N*, *N*-二甲苯胺与重氮盐偶合反应发生在氨基的对位上？
(3)在制备重氮盐时加入氯化亚铜将出现什么样的结果？

4.3 从菠菜叶中提取和分离叶色素

【实验原理】

本实验用石油醚：无水乙醇=2：1(体积比)溶液为萃取剂，提取菠菜叶[1]中含有的叶绿素、叶黄素及 β-胡萝卜素等色素。根据叶绿素、叶黄素及 β-胡萝卜素的溶解性和极性大小不同，以硅胶 G 为吸附剂，苯：丙酮：石油醚=2：1：2(体积比)为展开剂，用薄层色谱法将它们分离。

【主要试剂及实验装置】

薄层色谱装置		
苯	b.p.80℃	$d = 0.8786^{20/4}$g/mL
丙酮	b.p.56℃	$d = 0.7899^{20/4}$g/mL
石油醚（60～90℃）		
无水乙醇	b.p.78℃	$d = 0.7893^{20/4}$g/mL
无水硫酸钠		
硅胶 G		
新鲜菠菜		

【实验时间】

6h

【实验步骤】

1. 制备薄板

(1)称取 3g 硅胶 G 于研钵中，加入 7mL 蒸馏水，充分研磨成糊状，分倒在干净、干燥、光滑的载玻片(10mm×30mm×2.5mm)上，迅速用研杵涂布整块板面，然后手持载玻片的一端在桌边轻轻振摇，使硅胶 G 均匀地涂在载玻片上，形成光滑表面[2]。

(2)水平放置，自然晾干 30min。放入烘箱，在 105～110℃活化 30min，冷却，置于干燥器中备用。

2. 提取

(1)称取菠菜叶 10g，剪碎，置于研钵中，加入 2∶1(体积比)的石油醚-无水乙醇溶液 15mL，适当研磨至有深绿色液体出现。

(2)用滴管将提取液转入分液漏斗，加入等体积的饱和氯化钠溶液，洗涤[3]，静置，分液。

(3)保留有机层，用少量蒸馏水洗涤两次，有机层转移至干燥锥形瓶中，加适量无水硫酸钠固体干燥，待用。

3. 分离

1)点样

用点样毛细管吸取上述提取液，小心慢慢地滴在距薄板一端约 1.5cm 处，重复点样数次，至样品点呈深绿色，样品点直径控制在 2mm 以内。平行点两个样品点，两点间相距约 1cm。

2)展开

在干燥的层析缸中加入体积比为 2∶1∶2 的苯-丙酮-石油醚的展开剂 10mL，将已点好样品的薄板倾斜放入层析缸中(点样端向下)，盖好层析缸盖。当展开剂前沿上行到距薄板上端 1～2cm 时，取出薄板，立即用铅笔划出展开剂前沿位置。晾干后，分别测量溶剂前沿及各斑点到样品点的距离。

4. 计算各色素的 R_f 值

根据 R_f 计算公式算出各色素的 R_f 值[4]。

【注释】

[1]菠菜叶中含有的叶色素主要有叶绿素和类胡萝卜素，两者的含量比为 3∶1。叶绿素中叶绿素 a(蓝色)与叶绿素 b(黄绿色)的含量比为 3∶1，类胡萝卜素中叶黄素(橙黄色)与 β-胡萝卜素(黄色)的含量比为 2∶1。这些色素易溶于石油醚、无水乙醇、苯和丙酮等，极性大小顺序为叶黄素 > 叶绿素 b > 叶绿素 a > β-胡萝卜素。

[2]载玻片上涂层要均匀，不应有纹路或带团粒，薄板宜洁、平、匀。有关制板、点样和展开等操作，请参见本教材英文部分 2.10.3 小节和中文部分 2.10.3 小节。

[3]用饱和氯化钠溶液洗涤，除去含有的水溶性物质。

[4]四种主要色素的 R_f 大小顺序应为 β-胡萝卜素 > 叶绿素 a > 叶绿素 b > 叶黄素。

【思考题】

(1)进行展开操作时，若将薄板上的样品点浸入展开剂液面以下，会产生什么结果?

(2)若增加展开剂中丙酮的比例，各色素的 R_f 值会有什么变化?

4.4 从红辣椒中提取、分离和鉴定辣椒红素和 β-胡萝卜素

【实验原理】

根据红辣椒中含有的辣椒红素[1]、辣椒玉红素和 β-胡萝卜素的极性不同，本实验以硅胶

G 为吸附剂，二氯甲烷作萃取剂，1∶1 的石油醚-二氯甲烷(体积比)溶液为洗脱剂，用柱色谱分离红辣椒中的上述三种组分，并用紫外光谱鉴定分离得到的辣椒红素，红外光谱鉴定分离得到的 β-胡萝卜素。

【主要试剂及实验装置】

色谱柱(20cm×1cm)，回流和蒸发装置(最好使用旋转蒸发仪)
紫外光谱仪，红外光谱仪
二氯甲烷　　b.p. 39.75℃
干燥红辣椒(2g)；石油醚(60～90℃)；硅胶 G(100～200 目)：8～8.5g；硅胶板(3cm×1cm)若干块；石英砂少许。

【实验时间】

4～5h

【实验步骤】

1. 提取

(1)在 50mL 圆底烧瓶中，放入 2g 干燥并研碎的红辣椒[2]和两粒沸石，加入 30mL 二氯甲烷，装上回流冷凝管，水浴加热回流 20min[3]。

(2)待提取物冷却至室温，水泵抽滤，除去固体，然后蒸发溶剂[4]，收集色素混合物。

2. 点板

(1)以 200mL 广口瓶作层析槽，二氯甲烷作展开剂，取少量上述色素混合物于一小烧杯中，滴入 2～3 滴二氯甲烷使之溶解。

(2)在硅胶板上点样，置入层析槽中层析。

(3)计算每一种色素的 R_f 值[5]。

3. 装柱[6]

(1)取一直径 20cm×1cm 的层析柱，底部用脱脂棉塞上，并覆盖一薄层石英砂，加入洗脱剂(石油醚∶二氯甲烷=1∶1，体积比)至层析柱 3/4 高度，打开活塞，放出少许洗脱剂。

(2)称量硅胶 G(100～200 目)8～8.5g，用适量石油醚(10～12mL)调成糊状，通过漏斗加入到层析柱中，边加边轻轻敲击层析柱，使吸附剂装填致密。在硅胶上层加一层 0.5cm 的石英砂。

(3)当洗脱剂降至石英砂上层时，关闭活塞。

4. 分离

(1)将步骤 1 提取得到的色素混合物用 1～2mL 石油醚∶二氯甲烷=1∶1(体积比)的溶液溶解，用一根较长的滴管，沿柱壁加入色谱柱中，立即打开活塞。

(2)当此溶液流至接近石英砂面时，用 0.5mL 石油醚∶二氯甲烷=1∶1(体积比)的溶液洗下沾在管壁上的有色物质，如此操作 2 次，然后向色谱柱中缓缓加入洗脱剂(石油醚：二氯甲烷=1：1，体积比)，将色素粗品进行柱层析分离[4]。

(3)用试管分段(每段 2mL)收集洗脱液，各段洗脱液用薄层层析(TCL)检验。

(4)合并 R_f 相同的洗脱液，分别浓缩，得到各组分色素产品。

5. 鉴定

(1)用紫外光谱鉴定辣椒红素。

取步骤 4 分离得到的辣椒红素溶液 5 滴于一试管中，加入 5mL 正己烷，并以正己烷为空白进行紫外扫描，找出 λ_{max}，正己烷对照下，辣椒红素的 λ_{max}=470nm。

(2)用红外光谱鉴定 β-胡萝卜素。

取步骤 4 分离得到的 β-胡萝卜素溶液少许，在红外光谱仪上做红外光谱图，将所得图谱与 β-胡萝卜素的标准红外图谱作比较，标准红外图谱见本教材英文部分 4.4。

【注释】

[1]红辣椒中含有辣椒红素、辣椒玉红素和 β-胡萝卜素等几种色泽鲜艳的色素，其中极性较大的红色组分是辣椒红素和辣椒玉红素，占总量的 50%～60%，极性较小的黄色组分是 β-胡萝卜素，它们均属于由 8 个异戊二烯单位组成的四萜类化合物，难溶于水和乙醇，易溶于石油醚、氯仿和二氯甲烷。

辣椒红素(capsanthin，$C_{40}H_{56}O_3$，相对分子质量为 584.85)的结构式为

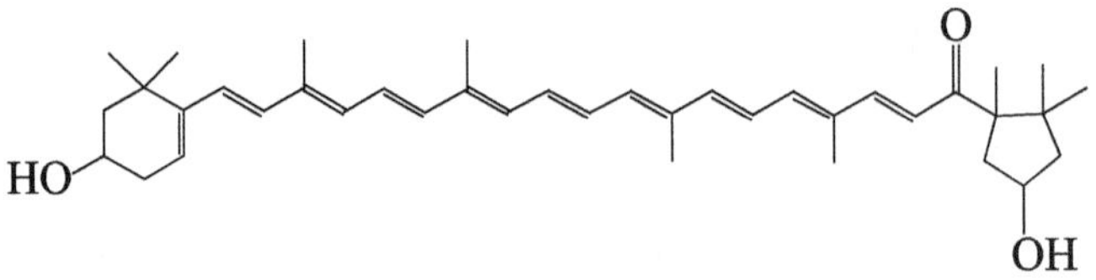

辣椒玉红素(capsorubin，$C_{40}H_{56}O_4$，相对分子质量为 600.85)的结构式为

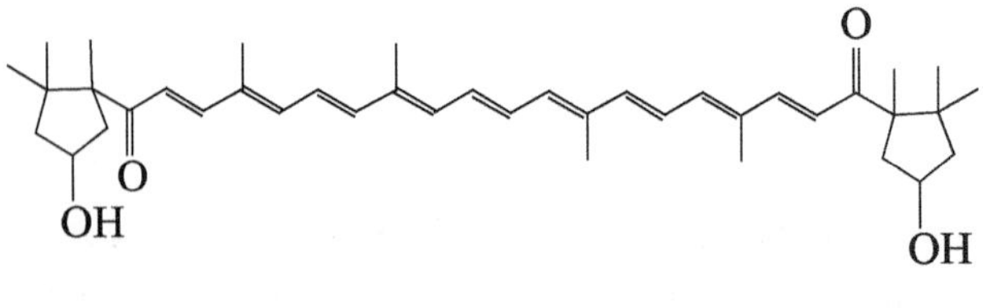

β-胡萝卜素(β-carotene，$C_{40}H_{56}$，相对分子质量为 536.88)的结构式为

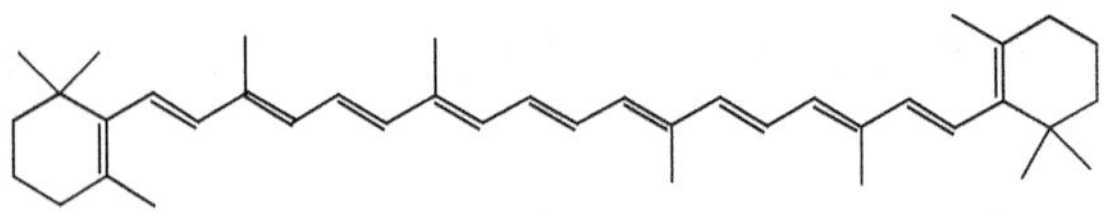

辣椒红素色泽鲜艳，色价高，着色力强，保色效果好，安全性高，已被美国 FAO、英国、日本、EEC、WHO 和中国国际等组织审定为无限性使用的天然食品添加剂，其国际市场十分紧俏。

[2]红辣椒要干燥且研细。

[3]回流速度不宜过快，以防止浸泡提取不够充分。

[4]蒸发和过柱操作都应在通风橱中进行；蒸发滤液时应尽量将溶剂蒸去，最好使用旋转蒸发仪。

[5]R_f约为 0.6 的较大的红色斑点代表辣椒红素，R_f值稍大于 0.6 的较小的红色斑点代表辣椒玉红素，R_f值最大的黄色斑点代表 β-胡萝卜素。

[6]本实验可以用湿法或干法装柱。装柱操作可参照本教材英文部分 2.10.2 小节和中文部分 2.10.2 小节。

【思考题】

(1)装柱时，若柱子中有气泡或填装不均匀，这将会给分离造成什么样的影响？应如何避免？

(2)用薄层色谱分离样品时，有时会出现“拖尾”现象，这是由什么原因造成的，它对层析有什么影响？应如何防止该现象的出现。

4.5　辅酶催化安息香的制备及结构表征

【实验原理】

安息香(二苯乙醇酮)是一重要的有机合成中间体，一般采用剧毒的氰化钾作催化剂，由安息香缩合反应制备。本实验利用生物活性辅酶维生素 B_1 代替氰化物催化苯甲醛发生安息香缩合反应制备安息香，这是一种环境友好的合成方法。

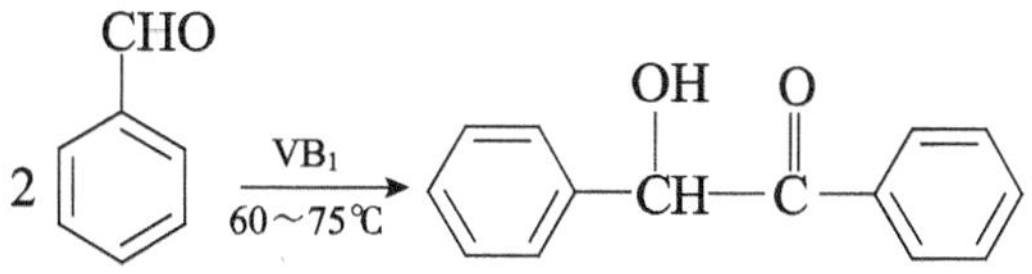

维生素 B_1 的结构及其催化安息香缩合反应的机理如下：

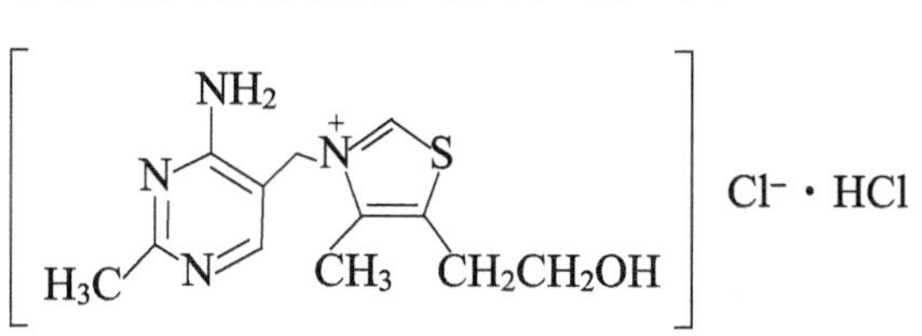

维生素B_1

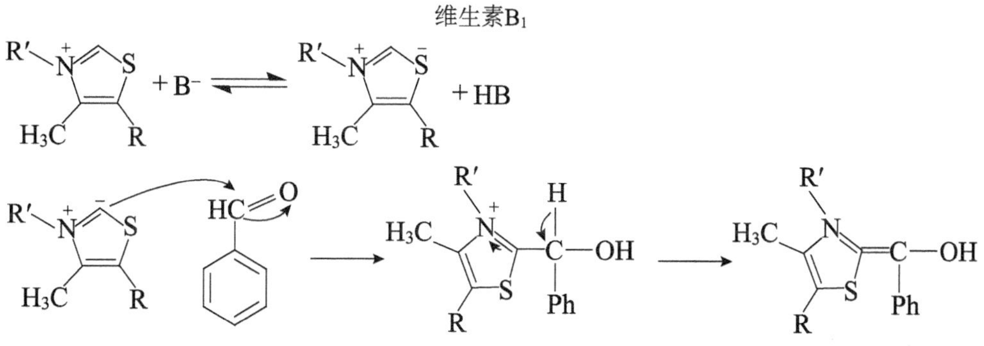

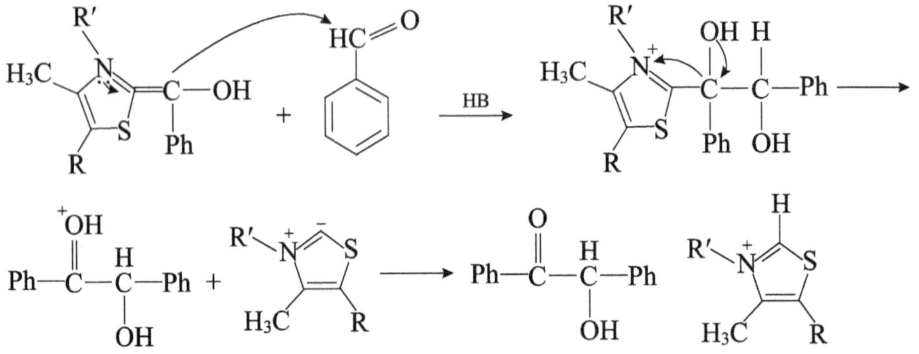

【主要试剂及实验装置】

回流装置			
苯甲醛	10.4g（10mL）	b.p.178～179℃	$d = 1.045^{20/4}$g/mL
维生素 B_1	1.8g		
95%乙醇溶液			
10%氢氧化钠溶液			

【实验时间】

5h

【实验步骤】

（1）将 1.8g 维生素 B_1[1]加入 100mL 圆底烧瓶中，用 5mL 蒸馏水溶解后，加入 15mL 95%乙醇溶液，将烧瓶置于冰水浴中冷却至 0℃。

（2）取 5mL 10%氢氧化钠溶液于一支试管中，也置于冰水浴中冷却，约需冷却 15min。

（3）在冰水浴冷却及搅拌下，将冷却的 10%氢氧化钠溶液逐滴加入盛有维生素 B_1 的烧瓶中，直到混合液体系的 pH 为 9～10，此过程约需 20min。当碱液加入一半（2.5mL）时溶液呈淡黄色。

（4）移去冰水浴，向烧瓶中加入 10mL（10.4g，0.1mol）新蒸的苯甲醛[2]，装上回流冷凝管。加入几粒沸石后置于 60～75℃水浴上缓慢加热，反应约 1.5h。

（5）将反应混合物冷却至室温，并将烧瓶置于冰水浴中，使晶体析出。抽滤并用 2×15mL 冰水洗涤。

（6）粗产物可用 95%乙醇溶液重结晶，得白色针状结晶产品 5g，测定熔点，纯安息香熔点为 134～136℃。

（7）测定产品的红外光谱并与安息香的标准红外光谱图对比，将各主要吸收峰进行一一归属。

【注释】

[1]维生素 B_1 受热易变质，将失去生物活性，应置于冰箱内保存，即用即取。

[2]苯甲醛极易被空气中的氧氧化，储存时间过长，将会氧化为苯甲酸固体。因此，使用前必须重新蒸馏。

【思考题】

(1)为什么要向维生素 B_1 的溶液中加入 10%的氢氧化钠溶液?

(2)为什么加入苯甲醛后，反应混合物的 pH 要保持在 9～10? 溶液的 pH 小于 9 会出现什么情况?

4.6　二苯基乙醇酸的制备及结构表征

【实验原理】

二苯乙二酮在氢氧化钠催化下经二苯乙醇酸重排，生成二苯乙醇酸。二苯乙二酮由安息香经溴酸钠氧化得到。此重排反应的主要推动力是形成了稳定的羧酸盐，羧酸盐一旦形成后，经酸化即生成二苯乙醇酸。

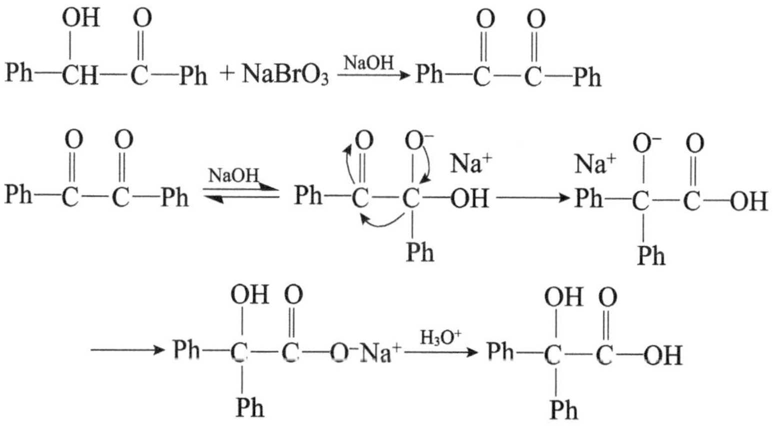

这一重排反应可普遍用于将芳香族 α-二酮转化为芳香族 α-羟基酸，某些脂肪族 α-二酮也可发生类似的二苯乙醇酸重排反应。

【主要试剂】

安息香(自制)	1.1g(0.005mol)	m.p. 134～136℃
氢氧化钠	1.25g(0.03mol)	
溴酸钠	0.3g(0.002mol)	
40%硫酸		

【实验时间】

5h

【实验步骤】

(1)在 100mL 的烧杯中，用 3mL 水溶解 1.25g(0.03mol)氢氧化钠和 0.3g(0.002mol)溴酸钠。

(2)将烧杯置于水浴上加热到 85～90℃[1]，在搅拌下分批加入 1.1g(0.005mol)安息香，加完后保持在此温度下反应，反应至取少量反应混合物于试管中，加水后几乎完全溶解为止，此过程约需 1.5h。在此过程中应不断补充少量的水，以免使反应液变得过于黏稠。

(3)用 25mL 水稀释反应混合物，置于冰水浴中冷却后滤去不溶物[2]。

(4)将粉红色滤液转入一 50mL 的烧杯中，在搅拌下，慢慢加入 40%硫酸(1∶3，体积比)，到 pH 为 2～3 为止(约需 3～4mL)。此时体系中有大量白色絮状沉淀产生。

(5)抽滤，滤饼用 30mL 冰水分两次洗涤，得白色纯净固体 1.0g，测定熔点，纯的二苯乙醇酸的熔点为 148～149℃。

(6)测定产品的红外光谱并与安息香的标准红外光谱图对比，指出其主要吸收峰的归属。

【注释】

[1] 温度过高将导致二苯乙醇酸的水解，生成副产物二苯甲醇。

[2] 此处过滤除去的是副产物二苯甲醇。

【思考题】

试用适当的醛为原料经二苯乙醇酸重排合成下列化合物：

(1) 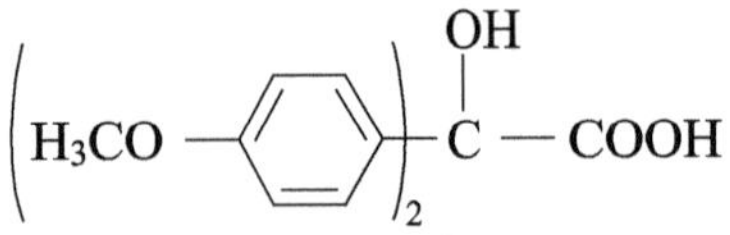

(2) 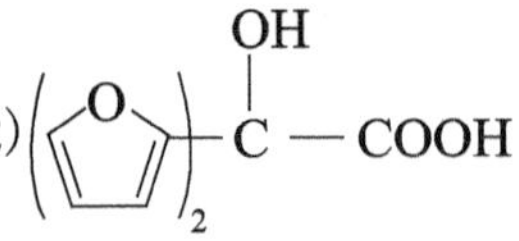

4.7　2-取代苯基苯并噁唑的微波法合成

【实验原理】

本实验在微波辐射下，以多聚磷酸为催化剂，邻氨基苯酚与取代苯甲酸经缩合反应合成 2-取代苯基苯并噁唑。

X=Cl，Br

【主要试剂及实验装置】

微波炉，回流装置		
邻氨基苯酚	1.091g(0.01mol)	m.p.170～175℃
对溴苯甲酸	2.01g(0.01mol)	m.p.252～254℃
对氯苯甲酸	1.566g(0.01mol)	m.p.238～241℃
多聚磷酸	15mL	
90%乙醇溶液		
10%碳酸氢钠溶液		

【实验时间】

3h

【实验步骤】

(1)在 100mL 的圆底烧瓶中依次加入邻氨基苯酚 1.091g(0.01mol)，4-氯苯甲酸 1.57g(0.01mol)或 4-溴苯甲酸 2.01g(0.01mol)，混合均匀后加入 15mL 多聚磷酸，搅拌均匀。

(2)将反应瓶放入微波炉中，加上空气冷凝管，功率 260W，间歇式辐射 5min，取出反应瓶。

(3)将反应液趁热倒入盛有 80g 碎冰的烧杯中，搅拌，抽滤，滤饼先用 30mL 10%的碳酸氢钠溶液洗涤，再用 30mL 水洗至中性。

(4)将干燥后的粗产品用 90%乙醇溶液重结晶，得到产品，测定熔点，纯的 2-(4-氯苯基)-苯并噁唑，m.p.153～154℃；纯的 2-(4-溴苯基)-苯并噁唑，m.p.142～143℃。

(5)以 $CDCl_3$ 为溶剂测试产物的 ^{1}H NMR 谱，并对图谱进行分析归属。

第5章　文献实验

5.1　非对映体的2, 3-二溴琥珀酸的微量合成

【实验原理】

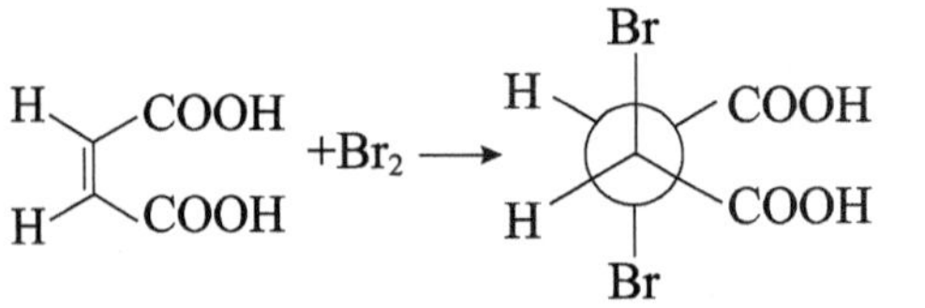

(1)

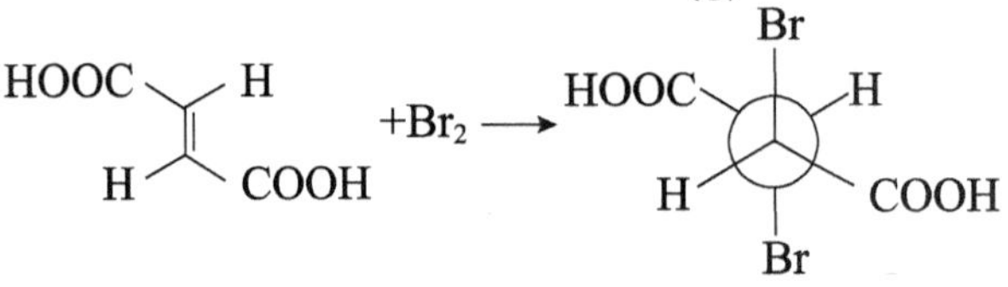

(2)

【实验步骤】

1. 内消旋-2, 3-二溴琥珀酸（2）的制备

将7.75g溴[1]和6.25g溴化钾溶于10mL水的溶液加入到25mL容量瓶中，用水稀释至刻度，备用。

25mL的锥形瓶中放入200mg富马酸(反丁烯二酸)[2]，加入2.5mL上述溴溶液，混匀。将锥形瓶置于沸水浴上，溴蒸气逸出，溶液呈橙色。6～10min后有白色固体生成，溶液褪色呈亮黄色。继续加热10～12min，若溶液呈无色，则再加入几滴上述溴溶液，继续加热几分钟。

反应混合液放在冰水浴中冷却，抽滤，用冰水洗涤，在100℃的烘箱内干燥，可得到内消旋的2, 3-二溴琥珀酸280～360mg。用水重结晶，测定熔点，m.p.261～266℃。(文献值：255～256℃)产率：51%～62%。用IR鉴定产品。

2. 外消旋2, 3-二溴琥珀酸（1）的制备

本实验所用仪器和试剂必须干燥。

在一干燥的试管中加入200mg马来酸(顺丁烯二酸)[3]和2mL无水乙醚。滴加310mg溴，充分混匀，反应少量放热。醚液沸腾，固体慢慢溶解。若固体不能溶解或有固体生成，说明反应混合物被水污染，此时应放弃该反应，而重做[4]。若无沉淀生成，将反应液放置10～15min，深橙色渐渐褪至浅橙色或黄色。在通风橱内将试管放入热水浴中，此时醚溶剂蒸发，剩下浅橙色或黄色的固体，用玻璃棒将固体捣碎，抽滤，少量石油醚冲洗，空气中干燥。得到外消

旋的2, 3-二溴琥珀酸440～450mg，测定熔点，m.p.168～170℃（文献值：166～167℃），产率：95%～96%。

【注释】

[1]溴有毒和强的腐蚀性，应避免吸入其蒸气，反应需在通风橱内进行，操作时应戴上手套。

[2]富马酸有中度毒性，对皮肤和眼睛有刺激作用。

[3]马来酸有中度毒性，能通过皮肤被吸收，对眼睛和皮肤有刺激作用。

[4]反应混合物若被水污染将生成溴化氢，溴化氢将使马来酸异构化为反应活性小且溶解性差的富马酸。

（摘自：*Journal of Chemical Education.* 1999, Vol.76, 73）

5.2 在水相中进行的类似 Grignard 反应

【实验原理】

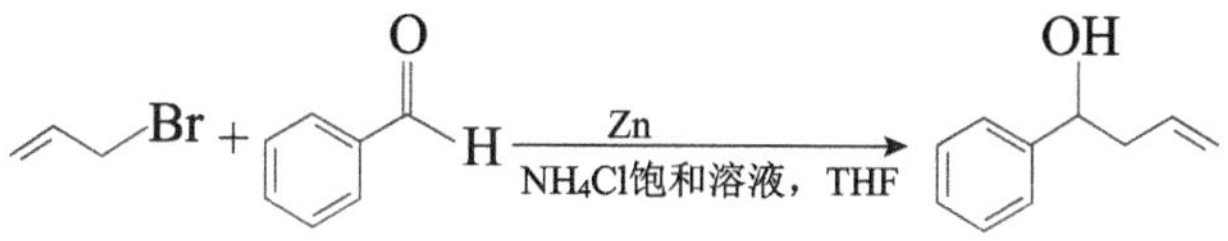

【实验步骤】

注意：烯丙基溴是一有毒、易燃的液体。本实验需戴手套并应在通风橱内进行反应。

在25mL的圆底烧瓶中加入0.078g（1.20mmol）锌粉与1mL饱和NH_4Cl水溶液，向此混合物中加入0.102mL（1.00mmol）苯甲醛溶于0.5mL THF的溶液。剧烈搅拌下，从回流冷凝管上端用注射器或校准吸移管滴入0.104mL（1.20mmol）烯丙基溴，反应立即发生。继续搅拌0.5h后，加入1mL乙醚。过滤除去过量的锌粉和锌盐沉淀，并用1mL乙醚冲洗沉淀。分出有机层，水层用1mL乙醚洗涤。合并有机层，用无水硫酸钠干燥，过滤，浓缩后得到0.126g 1-苯基-3-丁烯-1-醇的无色液体。（此产物中可能存有痕量未反应的苯甲醛，但已符合光谱分析要求）。

$n^{21.5}$ = 1.5284（文献值：n_{5D}^{21}=1.5289）; IR（cm^{-1}）: 3360, 3050, 2890, 1037, 905, 690; ^1H NMR（60MHz, $CDCl_3$）δ: 7.05（s, 5H）, 5.95～5.30（m, 1H）, 5.19～4.80（m, 2H）, 4.60（t, J = 6Hz, 1H）, 2.44（t, J = 6 Hz, 2H）, 2.06（br, s, 1H, OH）

（摘自：*Journal of Chemical Education.* 1998, Vol.75, 85）

5.3 微量法合成阿司匹林

【实验步骤】

在一干燥的试管中放入138mg（0.001mol）水杨酸，在冷水浴冷却下依次加入0.1mL吡啶和 0.1mL 乙酰氯，反应混合物呈黏稠状。继续在冷水浴上反应 15min 后，在剧烈振摇下加入 5mL 水，反应液变浑浊，继续振摇试管至白色的产物出现。抽滤，冷水洗涤，空气中干燥，用 50%的乙醇重结晶，得乙酰水杨酸（阿司匹林）。产率：33%, m.p.133～135℃。

（摘自：*Journal of Chemical Education.* 1998, Vol.75, 770）

5.4　无溶剂的 Claisen 缩合反应

【实验原理】

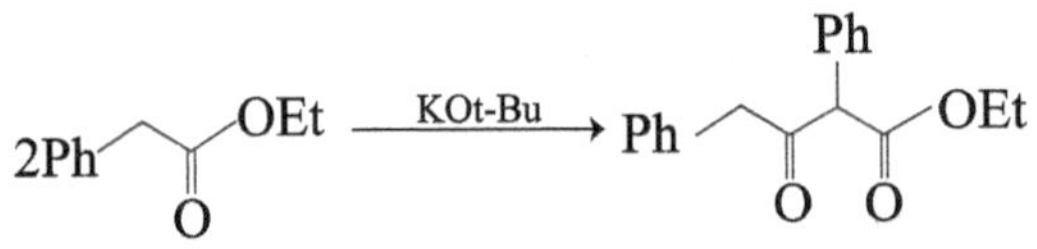

【实验步骤】

在 25mL 的圆底烧瓶中加入 1.57g（0.014mol）叔丁醇钾和 3.28g（0.02mol）苯乙酸乙酯，用刮勺剧烈搅拌使其混匀。装上回流冷凝管，在预热至 100℃的水浴或蒸汽浴上反应 0.5h。反应混合物被冷至室温后，用约 15mL 1M 的 HCl 慢慢中和。用 2×15mL 的乙醚萃取后，合并有机层，用无水硫酸镁干燥。溶剂经旋转蒸发除去，残余油状物加入 7mL 冷的戊烷研制后生成一白色固体。用热的己烷重结晶，得 2.25g 2, 4-二苯基乙酰乙酸乙酯，测定熔点，确证产品。纯的 2, 4-二苯基乙酰乙酸乙酯 m.p.75～78℃，产率：80%。

（摘自：*Journal of Chemical Education* 2003, Vol.80, 1446）

5.5　一种荧光染料的制备：微量 TLC 实验

【实验步骤】

在 5mL 的圆底烧瓶中依次加入 1mL 甲苯和 5～10mg 4-氯-1, 8-萘二酸酐，磁力搅拌下用注射器加入 500μL 1-己胺。反应混合物在搅拌下回流 45min 或回流至固体溶解，冷却至室温。

用荧光硅胶板对产物进行 TLC（薄层色谱）观察分析，分别使用乙酸乙酯∶己烷 = 1∶5（体积比）溶液和甲苯作展开剂。

TLC 观察分析实验

当用乙酸乙酯∶己烷 = 1∶5（体积比）溶液作展开剂时，可以观察到 4～6 个分开的点，R_f 值在 0.8～0.3。在这个展开剂体系中，四个荧光谱带的颜色交替出现，蓝色的谱带具有最高的 R_f 值。当能观察到 6 个谱带时，黄色谱带的 R_f 值分别为 0.8 和 0.1。

当用甲苯作展开剂时，可以在 R_f 值为 0.5～0.05 观察到四个点，有时还可以观察到 7 个点。这时蓝带具有最高的 R_f 值，黄带的 R_f 值比较小。常见的四个点的 R_f 值及颜色见表 5.1，化学反应如下：

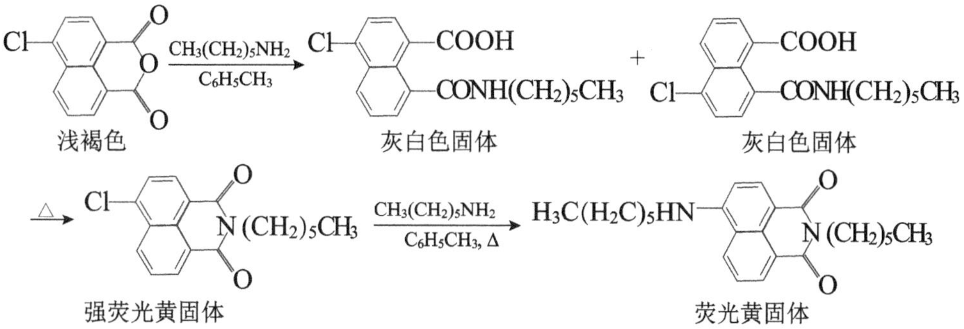

表 5.1　四个化合物的 R_f 值

溶剂	荧光的颜色	R_f
乙酸乙酯∶己烷 = 1∶5（体积比）	蓝	0.74±0.04
	黄	0.60±0.04
	蓝	0.49±0.04
	黄	0.35±0.04
甲苯	蓝	0.41±0.06
	蓝	0.27±0.06
	黄	0.20±0.05
	黄	0.14±0.04

（摘自：*Journal of Chemical Education.* 1999, Vol.76, 82～83）

5.6　微波法微量实验：2-萘酚制备乙酸-2-萘酯

【实验原理】

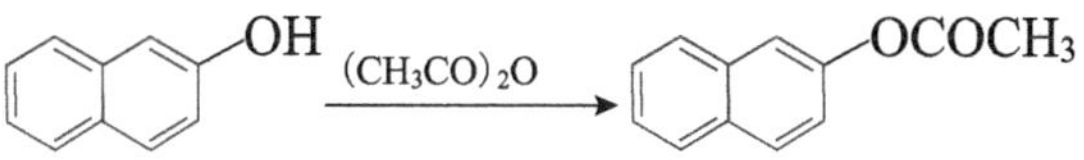

【实验步骤】

将 288mg（2mmol）2-萘酚和 1mL 乙酸酐混合在 50mL 的烧杯中，用玻璃盖盖住烧杯后放入微波炉中反应 4min（50%功率）。反应混合物取出后倒入 20mL 水中。搅拌混合物使过量的乙酸酐水解。收集固体，用 50%乙醇重结晶，干燥后测熔点和 IR 光谱。产率 60%～80%，乙酸-2-萘酯的 m.p.67～67.5℃。

（摘自：*Journal of Chemical Education.* 1966, Vol.73, A105）

第 6 章　附　　录

6.1　与化学有关的网址

6.1.1　可用于文献资料检索的网站

（1）ChIN（The Chemical Information Network）

网址：http://chin.csdl.ac.cn/

（2）中国科学院文献情报中心 （国家科学图书馆）

网址：http://www.las.ac.cn/

（3）SCI 数据库（Web of Science）

网址：http://isiknowledge.com

（4）中国科学引文数据库

网址：http://sciencechina.cn/cscd_source.jsp

（5）中国科学院科学数据库

网址：http://www.cas.cn/ky/kycc/kxsjk/

（6）Chemistry resources for Teachers and Students

网址：http://www.rsc.org/learn-chemistry

（7）美国化学会网站（American Chemistry Society）

网址：http://www.acs.org/

（8）英国皇家化学学会网站（The Royal Society of Chemistry）

网址：http://www.rsc.org/

6.1.2　与有机化学有关的部分网址

（1）Current Organic Chemistry

URL: http://benthamscience.com/journal/index.php?journalID=coc

（2）Beilstein Crossfire organic chemistry database

URL: http://www.beilstein-institut.de/en/home

（3）CCIIM: Beilstein Handbook of Organic Chemistry: printed and Database

URL: www.indian.edu/~cheminfo/cciim33.html

（4）Institute of Chemistry-Organic Chemistry

URL: www.chem.umu.se/dep/ok/thesis/index.html

（5）Organic Chemistry I：MIT open course

URL:http://ocw.mit.edu/courses/chemistry/5-12-organic-chemistry-i-spring-2005/index.htm

（6）Organic Chemistry II：MIT open course

URL: http://ocw.mit.edu/courses/chemistry/5-13-organic-chemistry-ii-fall-2006/

（7）FRESHMAN ORGANIC CHEMISTRY I :Open Yale Courses

URL: http://oyc.yale.edu/chemistry/chem-125a

or http://v.163.com/special/sp/freshmanorganicchemistry.html

（8）KryssTal: An Introduction to Organic Chemistry

URL: http://www.krysstal.com/organic.html

（9）Molecular Modelling for Organic Chemistry

URL: http://www.ch.ic.ac.uk/local/organic/mod/

（10）Organic Chemistry Resources Worldwide

URL: www.organicworldwide.net/

（11）Reaction Guide: Master Organic Chemistry

URL: http://www.masterorganicchemistry.com/reaction-guide/

6.2 有机化学实验操作考试复习题

1. 试安装用 b 型管测定熔点的实验装置，并回答以下问题：

（1）测定有机化合物的熔点的意义是什么？

（2）影响熔点测定的因素有哪些，请一一分析。

（3）为什么在接近熔点时升温的速度应放慢？若升温快了会有什么不良的影响？

2. 安装一套简单蒸馏的装置，并回答下列问题：

（1）什么是蒸馏？蒸馏的主要用途是什么？

（2）说明蒸馏装置中各部分仪器的名称及安装时的注意事项。

（3）蒸馏沸点高于 130℃的液体化合物时，应使用哪种冷凝管？

3. 安装一套简单分馏的装置，并回答以下问题：

（1）分馏和蒸馏在原理及装置上有哪些异同？

（2）在安装蒸馏和分馏装置时，温度计应放在什么位置？温度计放置过高或过低对蒸馏和分馏有什么影响？

（3）沸石在蒸馏和分馏中起什么作用？在液体沸腾时为什么不能补加沸石？

4. 安装一套水蒸气蒸馏的装置，并回答下列问题：

（1）水蒸气蒸馏的基本原理是什么？在什么情况下需使用水蒸气蒸馏？

（2）停止水蒸气蒸馏时，在操作上应注意什么？为什么？

（3）水蒸气蒸馏装置中的安全管和 T 型管各起什么作用？

5. 安装一套减压蒸馏的装置，并回答下列问题：

（1）什么是减压蒸馏，有什么实用意义？

（2）在油泵或水泵与蒸馏装置之间要安装安全瓶，为什么？

（3）当减压蒸馏完所需的化合物后，应如何结束减压蒸馏，为什么？

（4）安装减压蒸馏装置应注意什么问题？

（5）使用油泵要注意哪些事项？

6. 请测定丙酮的折光率，并回答以下问题：

（1）什么是化合物的折光率，影响折光率的因素主要有哪些？

（2）在 17.5℃时测得 2-甲基-1-丙醇 $n_D^{17.5}$=1.3968，试计算 2-甲基-1-丙醇 n_D^{20}。

（3）测定化合物的折光率对研究有机化合物有何意义？

7. 安装制备 1-溴丁烷的反应装置，并回答下列问题：

（1）本实验在回流冷凝管上为何要采用吸收装置，吸收什么气体？

（2）在回流反应中，反应液逐渐分成两层，你估计产品应处于哪一层？为什么？

（3）粗产物用浓硫酸洗涤可除去哪些杂质，为什么能除去它们？

（4）写出用正丁醇制备 1-溴丁烷的主反应和副反应的反应方程式，在本实验中，为尽量减少副反应的发生而采用了哪些措施？

8. 安装制备三苯甲醇的实验装置，并回答下列问题：

（1）为什么本实验前必须充分干燥所用的玻璃仪器和试剂，在整个反应的过程中要保持无水干燥？

（2）在制取 Grignard 试剂时，为何要加入一小粒碘？

（3）本实验中溴苯滴加太快或一次性加入，对实验有何影响？

9. 安装一套制备正丁醚的实验装置，并回答下列问题：

（1）简述在本制备中使用分水器的目的是什么？

（2）写出用正丁醇制备正丁醚的主反应和副反应式。

（3）在进行反应的后处理时，先后两次酸洗，再水洗的目的何在？

10. 试分离由 15mL 乙酸乙酯、10mL 苯胺和 1g 苯甲酸组成的混合物，并回答下列问题：

（1）简述使用分液漏斗的目的是什么？使用分液漏斗的注意事项有哪些？

（2）简述萃取和洗涤的概念，说出两者有什么主要区别。

11. 提纯粗制的乙酰苯胺，并回答以下问题：

（1）重结晶提纯固体有机物有哪些主要步骤？简单说明各步的目的。

（2）为什么重结晶时所用的溶剂不能太多，也不能太少？如何正确控制溶剂的使用量？

（3）为什么要在固体物质全溶后才能加入活性炭，而不能在溶液沸腾时加入？

12. 请安装一套从茶叶中提取咖啡因的实验装置，并回答以下问题：

（1）本实验步骤主要包括哪几步？各步操作的目的是什么？

（2）将蒸馏剩余液趁热倒入蒸发皿中后，为何要加入生石灰？

（3）什么是升华？固体有机物是否都可用升华方法提纯？升华方法有何优缺点？

（4）为什么升华操作时，加热温度一定要控制在被升华物的熔点以下？

13. 试用薄层色谱法鉴别 A、B 两瓶无标签的化合物是否为同一化合物，并回答以下问题：

（1）什么是化合物的 R_f 值？

（2）计算化合物 A 和 B 的 R_f 值。

（3）若层析缸中展开剂的高度超过薄层板点样线时，对薄层色谱有什么影响？

（4）简述薄层色谱的原理和主要应用。

14. 请安装一套从红辣椒中提取辣椒红素和 *β*-胡萝卜素的实验装置，并回答以下问题：

（1）红辣椒中主要含有哪几种色素？它们均属于哪类化合物？本实验使用什么溶剂提取这些色素？

（2）为了能充分提取红辣椒中的色素，提取操作应注意哪些问题？

15. 请用湿法安装一个分离辣椒红素和 *β*-胡萝卜素的层析柱，并回答以下问题：

（1）装柱时，若柱子中有气泡或填装不均匀，这将会给分离造成什么样的影响？应如何避免？

（2）简述用柱层析法分离辣椒红素和β-胡萝卜素的原理。

（3）简述如何用紫外光谱和红外光谱鉴定分离得到的辣椒红素和β-胡萝卜素。

16. 请安装一套制备4-硝基苯胺的实验装置，并回答以下问题：

（1）请写出由4-硝基乙酰苯胺制备4-硝基苯胺的反应方程式，是否可以从苯胺直接硝化制备4-硝基苯胺？为什么？

（2)4-硝基乙酰苯胺在酸性条件下回流后得到的透明溶液是什么？为什么加入20%氢氧化钠溶液后，4-硝基苯胺沉淀析出？又为什么要求加碱至使溶液呈碱性？

17. 请安装一套分馏蔗糖发酵液制备乙醇的实验装置，并回答以下问题：

（1）为什么用蒸馏的方法只能得到95.6%的乙醇？如何用普通乙醇来制备无水乙醇？

（2）蔗糖发酵时为什么需要使用水封装置，本实验使用的水封装置是什么？

（3）通过测定含水乙醇溶液的密度可以得到该乙醇中水的百分含量?试说明该测试的依据是什么？

18. 制备一块用于分离菠菜叶色素的薄板，并回答以下问题：

（1）本实验用什么溶液作为萃取剂提取菠菜叶色素，用什么溶液作为展开剂来分离各叶色素？

（2）用薄层色谱分离样品时，有时会出现“拖尾”现象，这是什么原因造成的，它对层析有什么影响？应如何防止该现象的出现。

（3）若增加展开剂中丙酮的比例，各色素的R_f值会发生什么变化？

（4）进行展开操作时，若将薄板上的样品点浸入展开剂液面以下，会产生什么结果？

19. 请安装一套抽滤乙酰二茂铁粗产物的实验装置，并回答以下问题：

（1）为什么反应需要使用干燥的烧瓶，并需使用氯化钙干燥管，若空气中的水进入烧瓶，对反应有什么影响？

（2）二茂铁酰化时，若有副产物二酰基二茂铁生成，试问第二个酰基应进入哪个环戊二烯负离子环？为什么？

（3）试说明如何用薄层色谱法鉴定重结晶后的乙酰二茂铁的纯度？

（4）为什么二茂铁非常稳定，具有芳香性，试从二茂铁的结构给予说明。

20. 请安装一套制备乙酸乙酯的实验装置，并回答以下问题：

（1）酯化反应有什么特点？ 本实验中采取了哪些措施来提高产品产率？

（2）蒸出的粗乙酸乙酯中主要有哪些杂质？ 如何一一除去？

21. 请安装一套制备肉桂酸的实验装置，并回答以下问题：

（1）本实验为什么能用水蒸气蒸馏纯化产品？用水蒸气蒸馏除去的是什么物质？

（2）苯甲醛和丙酸酐在无水碳酸钾的存在下相互作用后可以得到什么产物？

22. 安装一套制备乙酰乙酸乙酯的实验装置，并回答以下问题：

（1）为什么本实验所用的仪器和药品一定要干燥无水？

（2）在后处理时，加入50%的乙酸及饱和氯化钠溶液的目的分别是什么？

（3）为什么要用减压蒸馏精制产品？

（4）反应过程中，生成的黄白色沉淀是什么物质？请回答。

23. 安装一套制备乙酰苯胺的实验装置，并回答以下问题：

（1）本实验为什么不用分水器除水，而使用分馏柱？

（2）本反应在合成上有何用途？举例说明。

（3）除了冰醋酸，还可用哪些试剂作乙酰化剂？

（4）反应时为什么要控制分馏柱上端的温度保持在 105℃？

24. 请安装一套精制呋喃甲醇的实验装置，并回答以下问题：

（1）简述反应中加入 2g 聚乙二醇的目的是什么？

（2）本实验为什么要使用新鲜的呋喃甲醛？否则对本实验有什么影响？

（3）反应液为什么要用乙醚萃取，萃取的是什么产品？

（4）为什么酸化这一步是影响制备呋喃甲酸产率的关键？应如何保证完成？

25. 请安装一套制备 8-羟基喹啉的实验装置，并回答以下问题：

（1）为什么第一次水蒸气蒸馏要在酸性条件下进行？第二次却要在中性条件下进行？

（2）在 Skraup 反应中，为什么甘油的含水量必须小于 0.5%？浓硫酸和硝基酚的作用各是什么？

（3）试写出以对甲苯胺为原料，经 Skraup 反应后生成的产物是什么？硝基化合物应如何选择？

26. 请安装一套由环己醇制备己二酸的实验装置，并回答以下问题：

（1）为什么必须严格控制氧化反应的温度？

（2）能否用同一个量筒量取环己醇和硝酸？为什么？

（3）为了使制备己二酸的产量较高，在整个实验过程中要注意哪些问题？

27. 请安装一套制备环己烯的实验装置，并回答以下问题：

（1）为什么在制备过程中要控制分馏柱顶部的温度不超过 90℃？

（2）在粗制的环己烯中加入精盐使水层饱和的目的是什么？

（3）为了能提高环己烯的产量，本实验中采用了哪些措施？

（4）用 20g 环己醇为原料，用本实验的方法制备得到 12g 环己烯，试计算本反应的产率。

28. 请安装一套制备邻苯二甲酸二正丁酯的实验装置，并回答以下问题：

（1）为什么该反应需要用小火缓慢加热，若加热过快或过猛有什么不良影响？

（2）在反应的后处理过程中，中和的温度不宜超过 70℃，碱的浓度不宜过高，也不宜选用氢氧化钠，为什么？

（3）为什么要用饱和食盐水洗涤反应混合物及粗产物？